The Arabic Novel

Contemporary Issues in the Middle East

The Arabic Novel

An Historical and Critical Introduction

Second Edition

ROGER ALLEN

Syracuse University Press

Syracuse, New York 13244-5290

First Edition 1982

Second Edition 1995

11 12 13 14 15   6 5 4 3 2

This book is part of the Mohamed El-Hindi Series on Arab Culture and Islamic Civilization and is published with the assistance of a grant from the M.E.H. Foundation.

The paper used in this publication meets the minimum requirements of American National Standard for Information Sciences—Permanence of Paper for Printed Library Materials, ANSI Z39.48-1984.

ISBN-13: 978-0-8156-2641-1

Library of Congress Cataloging-in-Publication Data

Allen, Roger M. A.
The Arabic novel : an historical and critical introduction / Roger Allen. — 2nd ed.
p. cm. — (Contemporary issues in the Middle East)
Includes bibliographic references and index.
ISBN 0-8156-2641-X
1. Arabic fiction—20th century—History and criticism.
I. Title. II. Series.
PJ7577.A4 1994
892'.736—dc20   94-30685

Manufactured in the United States of America

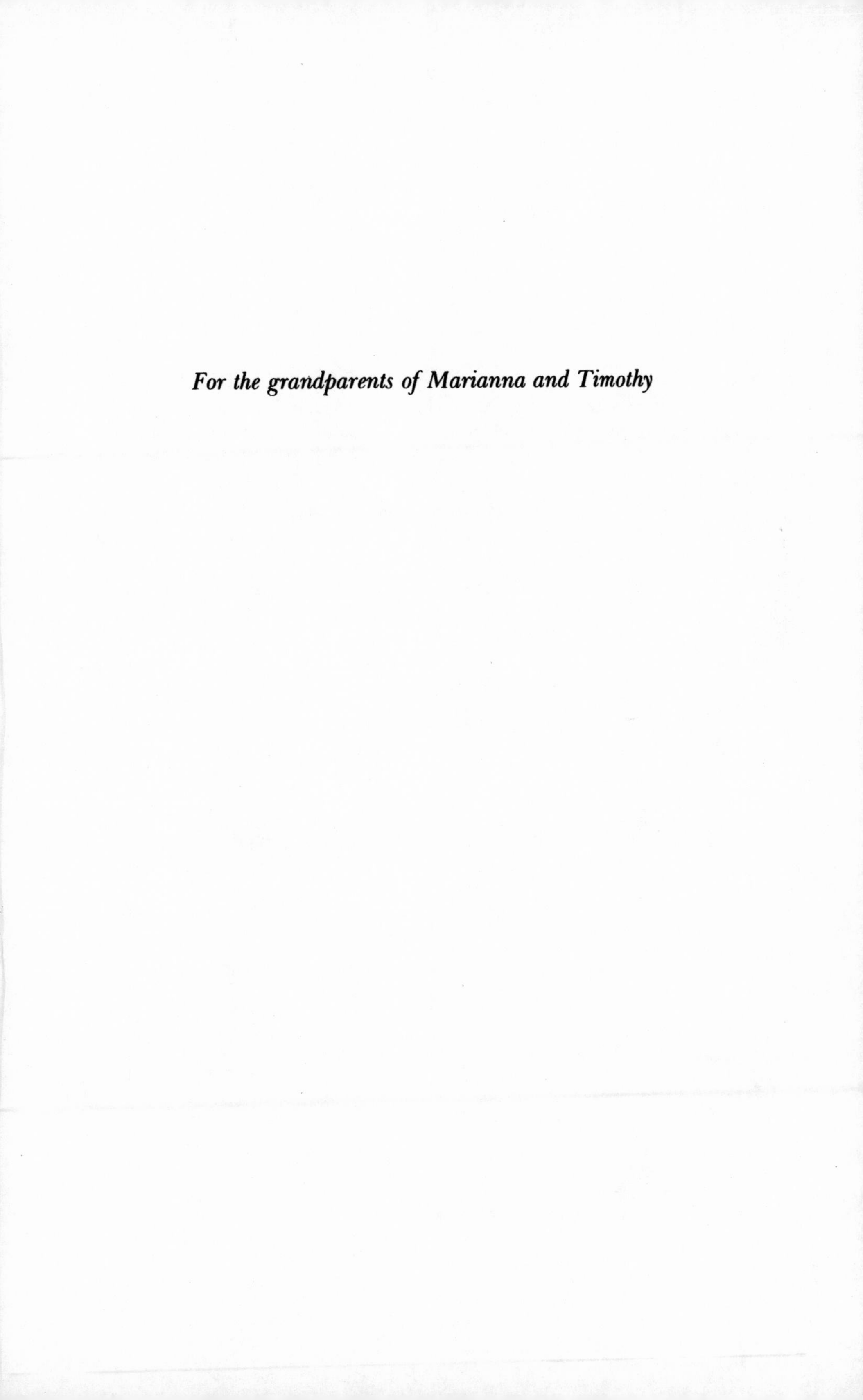

For the grandparents of Marianna and Timothy

ROGER ALLEN is the author of *A Period of Time: al-Muwaylihi's Hadith 'Isa ibn Hisham* (2d ed., 1992) and *Modern Arabic Literature* (1987). He has written and translated numerous articles on modern Arabic fiction and drama and on Arabic language pedagogy. His "Naguib Mahfouz and the Arabic Novel: The Historical Context" was included in *Naguib Mahfouz: From Regional Fame to Global Recognition,* edited by Michael Beard and Adnan Haydar, which was recently published by Syracuse University Press. Professor Allen's translations include Mahfouz's *Mirrors* and *Autumn Quail.* He teaches Arabic language and literature at the University of Pennsylvania.

Contents

Introduction

The novel is a wonderfully restless, shifting genre, each individual example of it striving with varying levels of vigor and artistic subtlety to reflect, and, in some cases, to advocate, the relentless process of change. When such a genre pursues its purpose in a context as varied and dynamic as that of the Arabic-speaking world, we are faced with a topic of ever-expanding complexity. If that wealth of material presented a problem when the first edition of the current work was being prepared in the late 1970s, how much more is that the case some fourteen years later.

In the concluding chapter of the first edition I addressed the future of the novel genre in Arabic, drawing attention to experimental trends that were in evidence in the works of certain writers and expressing the hope that "the spirit of élan and even defiance" shown by Arab novelists thus far would continue to find a fruitful outlet in novelistic production. It will be the aim of this second, revised edition to explore the extent to which those expectations have been met. The publication of novels in Arabic and critical studies of them has indeed continued and expanded throughout the Arab world. From a Western scholarly perspective, the increasing prominence given to fiction by women writers—a topic to which I referred somewhat briefly in the first edition—has been reflected in an increased focus on feminist literary criticism in general and that devoted to Arabic literature in particular.

The award of the Nobel Prize in Literature to the Egyptian novelist, Najīb Maḥfūẓ, in 1988 has, needless to say, been the most significant event in the recent history of the novel in Arabic. The first edition of this very work had the honor of being a participant in the Nobel process, being one of the books on display in the hall in Stockholm during the award ceremony itself. It has received another tribute as well, in that in 1986 an Arabic translation was published in Beirut; it thus has become one of a relatively small number of Western works that have literally been "translated" to the target culture and have thus become participants in the critical discourse of the culture to which it is addressed.

This second, revised edition has the same primary purpose as the first: it is intended as an introduction to the subject. Indeed, when we bear in mind the sheer volume of novel-writing activity that has occurred across the Arab world during the period since the first edition of this book appeared, the introductory and generalist focus of this second edition needs to be underlined with even greater emphasis. When one adds to that already large corpus the ever increasing wealth of detailed theoretical and critical studies devoted to fictional discourse in general and its Arabic examplars in particular, the scope of the task at hand becomes even more daunting. Once again, I have had to stipulate a *terminus ad quem*: in this case, approximately 1990. That is not to say that I have not alluded in the pages that follow to some more recently published novels and critical works that have been brought to my attention by my colleagues in the Arab world and the West who are novelists or critics, but merely to suggest that Arabic novel production in recent times has become sufficiently prolific and varied, making it difficult on purely practical grounds to comprehend the entire tradition of the Arabic novel as a single entity. In any case, Robert Scholes has already drawn our attention in his book, *Structuralism in Literature*, to the "reductive and highly selective" nature of writing about fiction; whereas criticisms of poetry will, more often than not, be longer than the work itself, those devoted to fiction will be considerably shorter. Bearing in mind the number of novels and novelists subsumed within the covers of this work, the selectivity becomes extreme and the task that much more difficult. The increased size of this second edition reflects an attempt to include representation of as much of this expanded creative and critical activity as possible, but I am the first to admit that the result retains all the features of a survey work. Its major purpose remains that of interesting students and general readers sufficiently in the literary-historical background of fiction in Arabic and in the themes and modes of particular examples that they may wish to embark upon a reading of some of those works in translation and thereafter, one hopes, to learn the Arabic language to the point at which they can experience the excitement of engaging the fictional world of the author in the original language.

This edition follows the same basic framework as the first. Beginning with a somewhat enlarged and reformulated chapter on ways of defining the novel, it then proceeds to analyze in turn the earlier period in the development of the genre and the more recent decades in which the genre has both matured artistically and expanded in topical and technical scope. Both these chapters reflect a broader sampling than before in terms of geographical coverage and issues discussed. For the final chapter I have selected a further four novels to add to the previous selection of eight.

I would like to conclude by expressing my warmest thanks to the staff of Syracuse University Press for the courtesy and consideration that they have shown me during the preparation of this second edition.

Philadelphia, Pennsylvania
March 1994

Roger Allen

Preface to the First Edition

The present work represents the fourth of the series of *Journal of Semitic Studies* Monographs, and as with the third one, my own *Al-Maqrizi's "Book of contention and strife concerning the relations between the Banū Umayya and the Banū Hāshim"* (1980), publication has been made possible through the funds generously supplied by the University of Kuwait for the encouragement of Arabic and Islamic Studies in the University of Manchester's Department of Near Eastern Studies. I am accordingly most grateful to the Rector of Kuwait University in thus allowing us to extend the Monograph Series.

As Professor Allen explains in his Introduction, the genesis of the present work lies in a series of lectures which he gave in the Department of Near Eastern Studies. Those of us present then heard how the novel tradition in the Arab world has grown to maturity in little more than two or three generations. The novels analysed below show many penetrating insights into aspects of contemporary Arab society: in the macrocosm, the splendours and miseries of its adjustment to the larger world, and the counter-movement of its rejection and withdrawal from it; in the microcosm, the struggle of the individual against the constrictions of society, of the village, or of the family, a struggle in which the protagonist may well appear as the *khārijī*, that archetypical figure of recent Western literature, the outsider.

It is accordingly hoped that this book will assist in making better known to the Western world these remarkable achievements of the present, vigorous generation of Arab writers.

Manchester
July 1981

C. E. Bosworth

Introduction to the First Edition

This work was first presented in the form of a series of three lectures which were given at the University of Manchester in May, 1980. The invitation to give those lectures (made possible through funds provided by the University of Kuwait) and to expand them into the present format came from Professor Edmund Bosworth, the Professor of Arabic Studies at the University of Manchester. I would like to take this opportunity of thanking him and his colleagues on the editorial staff of the *Journal of Semitic Studies* for giving me this opportunity to publish my views on the Arabic novel at such welcome length.

The novel in the Arab world has been the subject of numerous studies, but, with a few notable exceptions, they have not matched the quantity or quality of those on poetry. It may perhaps be suggested that this situation reflects the age-old love of the Arabs for poetry which extends back to the beginnings of Arabic literature as it has come down to us. In the modern period, for example, there are now available a large number of studies in European languages on modern Arabic poetry, and three complete studies in English, each of which approaches the subject from a different point of view. In the realm of the novel, studies in English tend to concentrate on a single country (especially Egypt, for reasons which will be discussed below) or a single author. Surveys of the novel as it has developed throughout the Arab world are much rarer and are in the main confined to those in the Arabic language. It is my perception of the current situation with regard to the study of the Arabic novel which has led me to attempt this introductory survey of the genre and its development. It should be made clear from the outset—and indeed it is reasonably obvious—that the novel is too complex a phenomenon and the Arab world is too large a geographical entity for this work to be anything more than an introduction to the subject. The larger study of the Arabic novel, its development and basic features, remains to be written. If others share my belief that the Arabic novel has achieved a true maturity and sense of identity since the Second World War, then they may perhaps be prepared to concede also that a slightly longer period of creativity in this genre, along with the preparation of a number of preliminary studies (of which the present volume hopes to be one), will make the writing of a much-needed longer study of the Arabic novel from the critical and historical points of view both more feasible and useful.

The format of the present work follows that of the original lectures reasonably closely. I should point out immediately that the word "Arabic" in the title of the book refers to the language; my subject is works of narrative fiction which have been written in the Arabic language. I am aware that the equivalent epithet in Arabic, namely *ʿarabī,* can refer to both people and language, but in this instance I will not be dealing, for example, with the large number of works written by the Francophone authors of the Maghrib, such as Muḥammad Dīb, al-Khaṭībī, and Kātib Yāsīn. For, while their names are unmistakably Arab, their writings are not only in the French language but show a clear affinity with the traditions of contemporary French literature, as a writer such as al-Khaṭībī readily admits. At my own university, the works of such authors are read in the French section of the Department of Romance Languages. Nor will I be dealing in detail with works which have been written by Arabs in other languages.

The first chapter begins with a discussion of the novel as a genre and surveys various attempts which have been made to define it. The origins of the genre are then investigated as a prelude to and in connection with the discussion of the narrative tradition in Arabic literature during the classical period. The second chapter traces the beginnings of the modern Arabic renaissance, and particularly those aspects most germane to the development of a tradition of prose fiction, and then the early attempts at fiction are surveyed until the outset of the Second World War. The period of maturity in the Arabic novel is the subject of the next chapter, in which the different types of novel, varied in theme, style, narrative approach, political motivation and country of origin, all written between 1939 and the present day (1980), are analyzed. The fourth chapter consists of a series of discrete analyses of a number of novels which have been selected from the vast corpus of works in this genre because I find them excellent examples of the wealth of novelistic output in the Arab world in recent decades. It is a fitting sign of that wealth that other critics have chosen and can choose an entirely different selection of their own, one which would, no doubt, reflect their own national origins, education, biases and interests, just as my own selection certainly reflects mine. My only hope is that no one will wish to claim that any of the works which I have chosen is an inferior contribution to the tradition of the Arabic novel.

I expressed above the hope that this work might serve as a contribution to further research into the vast and variegated field of Arabic fiction. It would also be a source of great satisfaction for me if this survey were also able to introduce the Arabic novelistic tradition to that much wider Western audience who have in general had little access to what it has to offer; all varieties of literature study, and particularly the comparative dimension, would seem to be liable to benefit from such access.

In writing this book I have made every effort to keep technical terminology in Arabic to a minimum, but inevitably some words have crept in. To assist and encourage this hoped-for wider audience I have appended a short glossary of Arabic terms that are found in the text.

Abbreviations

ASQ	*Arab Studies Quarterly*
EI2	*Encyclopaedia of Islam*
IC	*Islamic Culture*
JAL	*Journal of Arab Literature*
JAOS	*Journal of the American Oriental Society*
JARCE	*Journal of the American Research Center in Egypt*
MEJ	*Middle East Journal*

The Arabic Novel

1

The Novel

Parameters of Definition

> Unassisted by established critical traditions, faced with chaotic diversity among the things called novels, critics of fiction have been driven to invent an order of some kind, even at the expense of being dogmatic. "Great traditions" of innumerable shapes and sizes, based on widely divergent universal qualities, have in consequence been discovered and abandoned with appalling rapidity. The novel began, we are told, with Cervantes, with Defoe, with Fielding, with Richardson, with Jane Austen—or was it with Homer? It was killed by Joyce, by Proust, by the rise of symbolism, by the loss of respect for—or was it the excessive absorption with?—hard facts. No, no, it still lives, but only in the work of . . . . Thus, on and on.

In this passage, Wayne C. Booth shows us clearly how difficult it has been and is to provide universal definitions when dealing with the novel.[1] Some attempts at definition or description are forced into something very close to the kind of discourse to be found in the genre itself, as with E. M. Forster (himself, of course, a renowned novelist): "The novel is a formidable mass, and it is so amorphous . . . most distinctly one of the moister areas of literature—irrigated by a thousand rills and occasionally degenerating into a swamp."[2] The death of the genre has been proclaimed on many occasions and denied just as often.[3] Roland Barthes even sees a link between the

1. Wayne Booth, *The Rhetoric of Fiction* (Chicago: Univ. of Chicago Press, 1961), 36.
2. E. M. Forster, *Aspects of the Novel* (London: Penguin, 1966), 13.
3. "The Novel Is Not Dead," *The Economist,* 14 Feb. 1970: 40–41.

novel and death.[4] Compilers of glossaries of literary terms, such as M. J. Abrams, find themselves compelled to adopt a severely reductionist or even cynical mode: "The term novel is now applied to a great variety of writings that have in common only the attribute of being extended works of prose fiction. . . . A novel is a prose work of a certain length having something wrong with it."[5] In a more positive search for common ground, one may begin by observing that the genre has striven from the outset to live up to the element of "newness," "difference," implicit in the origins of the word "novel" itself. As Edward Said notes, "to be novel is to be an original, that is, a figure not repeating what most men perforce repeat."[6] From the point of view of generic purpose then, the novel may be viewed as the literary genre whose primary topic is the process of change, whether as reflection or advocate or both. As such, it is by definition subject to the very same process as is its primary topic: change. Indeed, one might suggest that those critics who have on occasion been tempted to proclaim the death of the novel may have been viewing it purely in retrospect, perhaps failing to see (or even disapproving of) the changing and changed nature of the genre with which they have been familiar. Mikhail Bakhtin captures this aspect well when he uses the term "uncanonical" to refer to the novel, continuing: "It is plasticity itself. It is eternally searching, eternally researching itself and revising all its former forms. It can only be thus for a genre which is constructed in the zone of immediate contact with generating reality."[7] Having thus identified part of the novel's essence, what might be termed its deliberate and continuing undefinability (in the sense of establishing limits), a clearer picture of the nature and role of the novel can be obtained when it is viewed in a diachronic per-

4. Roland Barthes, *Writing Degree Zero* (Boston: Beacon, 1967), 39: "The Novel is a Death; it transforms life into destiny, a memory into a useful act, duration into an orientated and meaningful time."

5. M. J. Abrams, *A Glossary of Literary Terms* (New York: Holt, 1971), 110. Much the same conclusion is reached by Frank Kermode in *The Art of Telling: Essays on Fiction* (Cambridge, Mass.: Harvard Univ. Press, 1983), 52. Also Randall Jarrell, cited in *New York Times*, Thursday, 8 July 1993, sec. C17.

6. Edward Said, "On Repetition," in *The World, the Text, and the Critic* (Cambridge, Mass.: Harvard Univ. Press, 1983), 117.

7. P. N. Medvedev and Mikhail Bakhtin, *The Formal Method in Literary Scholarship: A Cultural Introduction to Sociological Poetics* (Baltimore: Johns Hopkins Univ. Press, 1978), xxi. I have substituted *plasticity* for *moldability* in the original English translation since I glean from the footnotes that the original Russian uses the word *plastiknost*.

spective.[8] It is considerably easier to discuss the novel in its stages of development, most particularly if the context can be narrowed by type, "school," or period.

In a contemporary critical context in which similar methodologies are being applied to a number of different types of narrative, it is perhaps feasible to apply the term "novel" to a variety of works of considerable antiquity, even if the title adopted is *The Novel Before the Novel*.[9] However, from the perspective of the novel as *the* preferred modern fictional form,[10] it seems more profitable to see the most prominent strand in novelistic development as being its origins as a reaction to the tradition of the romance. One critic who does so is the Palestinian novelist, Jabrā Ibrāhīm Jabrā, in a chapter from a collection of articles entitled "Al-Riwāyah wa-al-Insāniyyah" (The novel and humanism).[11] He suggests that the novel is a fusion of various elements drawn from the Aristotelian categories: from the tradition of tragedy, it takes the major theme of the conflict of the individual with forces more powerful than himself, something which he traces from Aeschylus to Dostoevsky and Faulkner; the epic supplies such themes as the clash of the individual with society, betrayal, envy, chivalry, and so on; from the dramatic comes the concern with the portrayal of situations and emotions, and in particular, the characterization of individuals through dialogue. The beginnings of the genre are traced back to the mediaeval romance in which the knight

8. Roman Jakobson notes that "pure synchronism proves to be an illusion." "Problems in the Study of Language and Literature," in *Language in Literature*, ed. Krystyna Pomorska and Stephen Rudy, (Cambridge, Mass.: Belknap Press of Harvard Univ., 1987), 48. It is thus hardly surprising that Tzvetan Todorov should emphasize the evolutionary nature and function of literary genres, as Fedwa Malti-Douglas observes in *Structures of Avarice* (Leiden: E. J. Brill, 1985), 158.

9. See, e.g., P. G. Walsh, *The Roman Novel* (Cambridge: Cambridge Univ. Press, 1970); Roderick Beaton, ed., *The Greek Novel* (London: Croom Helm, 1988); Tomas Hagg, *The Novel in Antiquity* (Berkeley: Univ. of California Press, 1983); A. R. Heiserman, *The Novel Before the Novel: Essays and Discourses about the Beginnings of Prose Fiction in the West* (Chicago: Univ. of Chicago Press, 1977); J. Paul Hunter, *Before Novels: The Cultural Context of 18th-Century English Fiction* (New York: Norton, 1990).

10. Ian Watt, *The Rise of the Novel* (London: Penguin, 1963), 33: "The majority of readers in the last two hundred years have found in the novel the literary form which most closely satisfies their wishes for a close correspondence between life and art."

11. Jabrā Ibrāhīm Jabrā, "Al-Riwāyah wa-al-insāniyyah," in *Al-Ḥurriyyah wa-al-ṭūfān* (Beirut: Dār Majallat Shiʿr, 1960), 58 ff. These connections are explored further by Georg Lukacs, *The Theory of the Novel*, trans. Anna Bostock (Cambridge, Mass.: MIT Press, 1971), esp. chaps. 2 and 3; and by Ian Watt, *The Rise of the Novel*, esp. 9 ff.

sallies forth to combat the forces of evil. With the passage of time and the transformation of society, the venue changes from castle and forest to society and the city.[12] With the appearance of Romanticism, the novel takes up the cause of freedom of the individual and social justice. The emergence of a middle class and its aspirations for a better life, the acquisition of material goods and money, these topics give the realistic novelist a wide scope to describe in vivid detail the rise and decline of families within the social spectrum. More recently, Jabrā notes, the focus has shifted from an investigation of society and its conflicts to another kind of complex maze, that of the inner self of man, as novelists probe the secrets of his conscience using the techniques of modern psychology on the scientific plane and stream of consciousness and interior monologue on the more literary level.

The novel becomes then, in Jacques Barzun's words, the genre that "has persistently made war on two things—our culture and the heroic."[13] In the postindustrial era it has taken the rise of the modern city and the continuing social transformations of the middle class as its primary focus. Possessing such a rich variety of narrative possibilities, it has covered the range from the directly pedagogical and reformist, to the personally reflective, to the outright fantastic. In the post-Freudian era, our increasing awareness of levels of consciousness has led a number of writers into the exploration of techniques that attempt to mirror mental states as the immensely complex process that we now understand them to be, a trend that has led to notable experiments in the use of narrative voice and even a degree of intolerance for the narrator whose omniscience is not explained or justified. These represent just a few of the trends in twentieth-century fiction that have contributed to its continuing sense of "novelty" and its quest for change. Above all, the contemporary novel shares with other literary genres a quintessential characteristic of modernity in art, an unwillingness to be governed or

12. Harry Levin makes the same observation in *Contexts of Criticism* (New York: Atheneum, 1963), 71: "The medium that most completely mirrors the increasing stature of the middle class has been, of course, the major vehicle of literary realism, the novel. The Novel originated, with a characteristic gesture, by repudiating its medieval predecessor: the picaresque tale overtook the knightly romance; and Cervantes, by pitting the daily realities of the developing cities against the chivalric ideals of the declining castle, provided an archetype for all novelists and future realists."

13. Quoted in Lionel Trilling, *Sincerity and Authenticity* (Cambridge, Mass.: Harvard Univ. Press, 1971), 84.

trammeled by any preconceived notions regarding form, style, or indeed almost any other aspect of the creative act.[14] As noted above, its primary topic renders any such static attitude illogical.

Before turning to a consideration of the novel in the Arab world, we need to address, albeit briefly, a somewhat practical issue that confronts the researcher on modern Arabic fiction: an ambiguity in the use of technical terms for the various genres, an ambiguity, it must be added, that closely mirrors the analogous situation in Western languages. Whereas French and German both have three etymologically distinct terms for the three major fictional genres—thus, in French *roman, nouvelle,* and *conte,* English has adopted "novel" for the longer genre while retaining "novella" for the oldest of the three. One of the unfortunate results of this is that many writers assume the latter genre to be merely a smaller version of the former rather than a distinct genre with its own conventions. Most confusing of all perhaps is the choice of "short story" for the third, the combination of a noun describing a general type of narrative and of an adjective of length (or rather, lack thereof). Within English critical writings devoted to the short story, this has tended to result in an excessive concern with the relatively insignificant issues of length and reading time.[15]

In addressing the situation in Arabic, the first point to observe is that the language possesses no general word equivalent to the English term "fiction," as a means of describing a different way of looking at the world and its phenomena and indeed, through the play of irony, of creating worlds of its own. Arabic has, of course, produced technical terms for the identification and description of specific literary genres of fiction. The nomenclature used has in general followed the pattern of English, choosing the term *qiṣṣah qaṣīrah* for the short story and, for the most part, *riwāyah* for novel. "For the most part" is intended to reflect the fact that, for a minority of writers in

14. The most famous exponent of the concept of the modern in the contemporary Arab world is the Syro-Lebanese poet, Adūnīs (ʿAlī Aḥmad Saʿīd). He has reflected in numerous works on the nature of modernity, e.g., *Zaman al-shiʿr* (The time of poetry) (Beirut: Dār al-ʿAwdah, 1972) and also on the relationship to the past that is implied by such a posture. See, for example, *Al-Thābit wa-al-mutaḥawwil* (The static and dynamic), 3 vols. (Beirut: Dār al-ʿAwdah, 1974–79). Saʿīd Yaqṭīn's work, *Taḥlīl al-khiṭāb al-riwāʾī* (Beirut: Al-Markaz al-thaqāfī al-ʿArabī, 1989), begins with an excellent analysis of more recent trends in the critical analysis of fictional discourse.

15. I discuss these issues in detail in "Narrative Genres and Nomenclature: A Comparative Study." *JAL* 23, no. 3 (Nov. 1992): 208–14.

the Arab world, the preferred term for novel is *qiṣṣah,* the generic term for "story" or "narrative." Among publications that have opted for this latter choice is the second edition of the *Encyclopedia of Islam* (1954 et seq.), an editorial choice that has led to the unfortunate consequence that the short story has not been satisfactorily covered.[16]

The purpose in raising this issue here is not, of course, to advocate the use of one term or another; the different communities of the Arab world will presumably resolve the issue through the natural process of language development. I merely wish to note that in the various regions of the Arab world there is a certain amount of ambiguity inherent in the assignment of titles to critical works on fictional genres.[17] Indeed, one might point out further that Arabic has no established term "novella" (other than the transliteration of the European term). Bearing in mind that twentieth-century literary criticism has tended to frown on the use of generic criticism for prescriptive purposes and that a relatively large percentage of writing on the novella has been of that kind, the general reaction to this situation in Arabic might be one of relief. One of its consequences, however, is to cause a certain confusion regarding the generic features of particular works. In modern Arabic fiction there are, for sure, what may be designated as long short stories and short novels. In this particular study, the latter will be discussed but the former will not.[18] Furthermore, works which I consider to be contributions to the novella genre *per se* (as opposed to "short novels")—a grouping in which I would include such famous works as *Qindīl Umm Hāshim* by Yaḥyā Ḥaqqī and *ʿUrs al-Zayn* by Al-Ṭayyib Ṣāliḥ—will also not be discussed.[19]

Bearing in mind the generic characteristics of the novel noted above and the course of its early development in the Arab world, it clearly constitutes an imported genre in the world of Arabic. Charles

16. In the words of the Moroccan novelist Aḥmād al-Madīnī, "the modern literary *genres* in this context have not yet been clearly categorized or verified." See *Modern Literature in the Near and Middle East 1850–1970,* ed. Robin Ostle (London: Routledge, 1991), 194. I have explored this issue at some length in "Narrative Genres and Nomenclature."

17. For the record, the Arabic translation of the first edition of this work uses *riwāyah.*

18. It is my intention to write a study on the short story in modern Arabic at a later date.

19. I have discussed the status of the novella in Arabic (and the two works cited) in "The Novella in Arabic: A Study in Fictional Genres," *IJMES* 18, no. 4 (Nov. 1986): 473–84.

Vial is quite unequivocal on the matter: "The modern *kissa* owes nothing to Arab tradition. It is linked neither with the folklore of the *Thousand and One Nights* nor with tales of chivalry nor with narratives of *adab*."[20] Its assimilation into the wonderfully varied environment made up of the regions and nations of the Arab world thus constitutes a fascinating study in the transfer of literary genres from one culture to another and also in the tensions arising from the confrontation between a modern, imported genre and the great literary heritage of the past.[21] A novelist such as ʿAbd al-raḥmān Munīf can express his views on the matter quite explicitly: "The Arabic novel has no heritage. Thus, any contemporary Arab novelist has to look for a means of expression for himself, with hardly any guidance to aid him. It is thus inevitable that he will make some mistakes and display shortcomings."[22] This willingness to acknowledge a debt to the West on the matter of the novel is generally regarded as having provided a stimulus to the process of writing. The development of the novelistic craft has of necessity been an accelerated one, involving some false starts and dead ends; many writers have described the process as one of "catching up." Two highly distinguished novelists whose works we will be studying in detail have expressed the relationship in those terms in their writings: Najīb Maḥfūẓ, Nobel Laureate in Literature for 1988, and Jabrā Ibrāhīm Jabrā.[23]

The "catching up" process, and the tensions between the quest for the expression of the modern and the linkages to the past, are constant themes in the development of the modern Arabic novel

20. See the Charles Vial article "Ḳiṣṣa," in *EI*^{2} (Leiden: E. J. Brill, 1954– , in progress); also Shākir Muṣṭafā, *Al-Qiṣṣah fī Sūriyā ḥattā al-ḥarb al-ʿālamiyyah al-thāniyah* (Cairo: Maʿhad al-buḥūth wa-al-dirāsāt al-ʿArabiyyah), 1957, 44.

21. This creative tension is noted by Yūsuf ʿIzz al-dīn, *Al-Riwāyah fī al-ʿIrāq: Taṭawwuruhā wa-athar al-fikr fīhā* (Cairo: Maʿhad al-buḥūth wa-al-dirāsāt al-ʿArabiyyah, 1973), 12. With reference to the exploration of such linkages, Jacques Berque provides a timely warning that "the genealogies of creativity do not, and need not, follow a straight line. The history and variations of artistic genius presuppose discontinuity, interaction, an unexpected intersection of lineages rather than a simple linear succession." See *Cultural Expression in Arab Society Today* (Austin: Univ. of Texas Press, 1978), 200, cf. 259–60. This issue is the topic of a detailed chapter in Muḥsin Jāsim al-Mūsawī, *Al-Riwāyah al-ʿArabiyyah: al-nashʾah wa-al-taḥawwul*, (Beirut: Dār al-Ādāb, 1988), 13–39.

22. Interview with Munīf in *al-Maʿrifah* (Feb. 1979): 193.

23. For Maḥfūẓ, see *al-Marāyā* (Cairo: Maktabat Miṣr, 1972), 66, and *Mirrors*, trans. Roger Allen (Chicago: Bibliotheca Islamica, 1977), 42; for Jabrā, see "Modern Arabic Literature and the West," *JAL* 2 (1971): 76–91, and *Yanābīʿ al-ruʾyā* (Beirut: al-Muʾassasah al-ʿArabiyyah li-al-dirāsāt wa-al-nashr, 1979), 138.

that will be explored in the following two chapters. However, I believe that it is worth emphasizing at this juncture that, since the emerging tradition of Arabic fiction has assimilated ideas from a worldwide tradition that, by its very nature, is itself constantly in a process of change, the relationship between the two traditions and, in the case of the Arabic genre, between the present and past, has also been subject to change and adaptation.

At the beginning of the modern Arabic literary revival *(al-nahḍah)*, certain subgenres of the novel, the historical and the romantic for example, were readily available vehicles for the expression of pressing issues of the day: the search for historical roots as an underpinning for emerging nationalist sentiments and the exposure of societal problems—in particular, the status of women—as an expression of reformist ideals. The enormous popularity of these early works, ably fostered by the burgeoning press tradition, was to overwhelm attempts at using revived traditional prose genres to express modern concerns, and with remarkable speed (as compared, say, with the equivalent situation in poetry). However, as the novel genre in Arabic has achieved some degree of maturity (the topic of chapter 3), its development has accompanied dramatic changes within the society to which it is primarily addressed, changes that have transformed the societies' self-view, their attitudes towards other parts of the world (for example, the emerging concept of a "third world"), and their relationship with their past. The liberating sense of independence in the 1950s and the achievements and disappointments that followed were, of course, reflected in a large number of fictional works. The dreadful debacle of June 1967 led to a complete reexamination of the bases of Arab society and a profound search in its heritage for root causes and solutions.

It is precisely within such a context that some writers of fiction have found new inspiration in the texts, generic structures, and narrative modes of the past. When novelists such as Jamāl al-Ghīṭānī, ʿAbd al-raḥmān Munīf, and Najīb Maḥfūẓ make use in works penned in the 1980s of texts and techniques from the corpus of classical Arabic prose, we have in a sense come full circle. The novel genre has become a full participant in the literary life of the various nations of the Arab world, both reflecting and contributing to the ongoing processes of change. While some writers choose to imitate Western experiments in fiction or else carve out their own paths, there are others who find creativity and novelty in the invocation of names, texts, and techniques from the classical era, from precisely those genres which, within the historical context of transcultural generic transfer, are not, as Edward Said so aptly notes, "formally and dynastically prior and useful as, say, in the rather directly useful way that Fielding antedates Dickens."[24] Perhaps nothing can better illustrate this new tendency among novelists writing in Arabic, this new sense of exploration and independence, than John Updike's evident discomfort with the nature of ʿAbd al-raḥmān Munīf's narrator in *Mudun al-milḥ* (Cities of salt). It is, he notes, "unfortunate . . . that Mr. Munif . . . appears to be . . . insufficiently Westernized to produce a narrative that feels much like what we call a novel."[25] Such remarks seem to suggest an unwillingness to address the issues involved in generic transfer between cultures (and indeed other topics involving implicit notions of cultural hegemony) and to consider contemporary fiction in Arabic as a contributor to the development of world fiction as opposed to a mere imitator of Western trends.[26] While Mr. Updike may feel that Munīf is "insufficiently Westernized," I would prefer to suggest that the treatment of the narrator of popular tales *(ḥakawātī)*, of the campfire storyteller, these evocations of traditional narrative, become, at the hands of the modern novelist writing in Arabic, fresh contributions to the development of that continually innovating narrative type that is the novel.

However, whether or not a Western readership wishes to acknowledge the existence of a tradition of fiction written in Arabic and to take its innovations into account in making comparative critical judgements, it remains true that the genre of the novel has never been more alive, vigorous, and relevant in the Arab world than is the case today. Recent decades have witnessed a considerable increase in the number of novels published in Arabic and in publication venues and houses. Increases in publication opportunities are, no doubt, more than partially responsible for a concomitant increase in the number of littérateurs writing novels, and no more so that in the case of women writers, who are, needless to say, bringing entirely

24. Introduction to Halīm Barakāt, *Days of Dust*, trans. Trevor Le Gassick (Wilmette, Ill.: Medina Press International, 1974), xiii. The topic of the developing novel's relationship to the past is discussed by Muḥsin Jāsim al-Mūsawī, *Al-Riwāyah al-ʿArabiyyah*, 13–39.

25. See Updike's review in the *New Yorker*, Oct. 17, 1988, 117.

26. As Najīb Maḥfūẓ has recently observed in an interview, "We Arab writers did borrow the modern concept of the short story and the novel from the West, but by now they have been internationalized in our own literature." *Paris Review* 123 (Summer 1992): 70.

new perspectives to the tradition of fiction. The variety of the novel in Arabic has never been greater. It is in a desire to place these developments into a historical and critical context that I will use the chapters that follow to trace the course of that process as it affects the novel written in Arabic, and to offer it as a contribution to the broader topic of world fiction studies.

2

Early Developments in the Arabic Novel Tradition

Contemporary Arabic literature is the result of a long but often accelerated process which has its basis in *al-nahḍah,* the movement of cultural revival or renaissance which began in earnest during the nineteenth century, although some of its roots can be traced to an earlier period. This phenomenon varied widely in its course and impact within the different regions of the Arabic-speaking world, but in every case the particular local development was the result of a process which involved two principal forces. These are variously known as the old and the new, the traditional and the modern, the classicists and the modernists, and so on; more specifically, the encounter with the West, its science and culture, on the one hand, and on the other, the rediscovery and stimulation of the great classical heritage of Arab-Islamic culture.[1] In more literary terms, increasing contacts with Western literatures led to translations of works of European fiction into Arabic, followed by their adaptation and imitation, and culminating in the appearance of an indigenous tradition

1. It has to be admitted that there is a considerable disparity in our knowledge of the precedents of these two cultural influences. Thus, while we know a considerable amount about Arab visitors to the West and the kinds of cultural phenomena to which they were exposed, the period of Arab-Islamic culture preceding the nineteenth century—one might say, the entire period from 1300–1800—has been woefully underinvestigated. Ibrahim Abu Lughod is clearly right in naming his study of the nineteenth-century revival's principal figures *Arab Rediscovery of Europe* (Princeton: Princeton Univ. Press, 1963). Yet the few glimpses that we have of pre-nineteenth-century cultural life in the Arab world, prominent among which is Peter Gran's, *Islamic Roots of Capitalism* (Austin: Univ. of Texas Press, 1979), make clear how much basic information we are lacking when endeavoring to analyze the nature of the changes involved in the earliest stages of *al-nahḍah.*

of modern fiction in Arabic. The search into the literary heritage of the classical era was to remind scholars of the existence of earlier models for a neoclassical revival of certain prose genres. Not for the first time in Arabic literary history, the clash between the "old" and the "new" became a source of fertile tension among littérateurs.

The classical tradition of Arabic narrative comprises a number of different types of narrative: anecdotes, vignettes, moral tales, stories of miraculous escape, and so on. These had been gathered under a wide variety of titles into collections for the use and entertainment of the literate (and mostly bureaucratic) classes. Such volumes and their organizing principles were not to meet the generic needs of the early pioneers of modern fiction in Arabic. From a Western perspective, what is remarkable is that another source of possible inspiration, the world's greatest collection of narratives, *A Thousand and One Nights,* was also left out of the picture—at least, during the early stages in the development of the novel in Arabic. One may begin by noting, as the British orientalist Edward Lane does, that copies of the collection were extremely rare, at least in Egypt, at the time of the beginnings of *al-nahḍah.*[2] This rarety of written versions and lack of interest among littérateurs can be traced to a common cause: the *Thousand and One Nights* collection was intended as a set of narratives for oral performance. One might surmise that any written versions that existed were intended as mnemonics for the storytellers themselves rather than written versions for a wider readership (which, due to levels of literacy, did not exist in any case). The society at large has traditionally regarded the stories in *A Thousand and One Nights* as part of popular culture. Such attitudes, coupled to a strongly felt sense of linguistic hierarchy that assigns enormous cultural value to the language of "high" culture—and especially religious and literary texts—while virtually denying any worth to expression in the colloquial dialect (a point we shall discuss in detail below), have left this world-famous collection of tales, which has had such a profound and prolonged effect on Western literatures, in a sort of cultural netherworld in the Arabic-speaking countries of the Middle East. Only contacts with Western scholarship and, more recently, the development of a tradition of folklore studies in Middle Eastern academic institutions, have begun to stimulate a larger interest among Arab littérateurs and critics.[3]

2. Edward Lane, *An Account of the Manners and Customs of the Modern Egyptians* (London: Everyman, 1954), 420.

3. The first major study in Arabic was that of Suhayr al-Qalamāwī, *Alf Laylah*

There was, however, one narrative genre that did attract the attention of the earliest pioneers: the *maqāmah*. Apparently initiated by Badī' al-zamān al-Hamadhānī (968–1008), the basic form consisted of a picaresque narrative that exploited the antics of a narrator and "rogue" (in al-Hamadhānī's case, 'Īsā ibn Hishām and Abū al-Fatḥ al-Iskandarī respectively) to provide both social commentary and, mostly through inverse implication, moral enlightenment; the genre also invoked a kind of discourse found most notably in the text of the Qur'ān itself, namely the rhymes and cadences of *saj'* (usually translated as "rhyming prose"), the virtuoso use of which provided a long-established stylistic vehicle for displays of erudition. The cultural opportunities that this particular genre provided for rhetorical display addressed to a wide variety of possible topics help to account for the fact that it remained in vogue through the centuries preceding *al-nahḍah*. It was therefore the prose genre most readily at hand to provide early pioneers with a framework within which to revive the glories of the past heritage, most particularly in the realm of language and style, while at the same time addressing themselves to the social issues of the day.[4]

In what follows I will briefly survey the particular circumstances within which each major region of the Arab world confronted these cultural trends at the outset of *al-nahḍah*.

Syria and Lebanon

The use of two separate names for the area under consideration here is based on the exigencies of twentieth-century history (Leba-

---

wa-Laylah (Cairo: Dār al-Ma'ārif, 1966), originally written as her doctoral dissertation for Cairo University (1939) under the supervision of Ṭāhā Ḥusayn, who had encountered European interest in the collection while completing his own education in France. More recent research on the narrative aspects of the *Thousand and One Nights* collection and increased interest among modern Arab littérateurs in the narrative techniques to be found there have led both creative writers and critics to take a fresh look at this great collection. See, e.g., Jabrā, Ibrāhīm Jabrā, *Yanābī' al-ru'yā* (Beirut: al-Mu'assasah al-'Arabiyyah li-al-dirāsāt wa-al-nashr, 1979), 68–71; 'Abbās Khiḍr, "Al-Mūnūlūg al-dākhili fī *Alf Laylah wa-laylah*," *Al-'Arabī* (Aug. 1980): 120–122. Among studies in English, see Feryal Ghazoul, *The Arabian Nights: A Structural Analysis* (Cairo: Cairo Associated Institution for the Study and Presentation of Arab Cultural Values, 1980); and David Pinault, *Story-Telling Techniques in the* Arabian Nights (Leiden: E. J. Brill, 1992).

4. For the development of the *maqāmah* genre during the thirteenth–eighteenth centuries, see Muḥammad Rushdī Ḥasan, *Athar al-maqāmah fī nash'at al-qiṣṣah al-Miṣriyyah al-ḥadīthah* (Cairo: Al-Hay'ah al-Miṣriyyah al-'āmmah li-al-kitāb, 1974).

non became a separate entity as a result of a political compromise worked out in 1942). The area of the Ottoman province of Syria known as Mount Lebanon has always been geographically discrete, but was considered administratively as part of the province centered on Damascus. A distinct feature of Mount Lebanon was its Christian communities, primarily Maronite and Orthodox, and it was among such communities that the first glimmerings of *al-nahḍah* may be traced.

These communities had been in contact with the West, and especially Rome and France, for a large part of that period which has been dubbed "the period of decadence," a title of rather dubious validity, in my estimation, in view of the almost total dearth of knowledge about the literature of the period, of which the popular tales mentioned above are just one example.[5] Connections with the Roman Catholic church were firmly established and were reflected in the educational opportunities available. The name of Bishop Germanus Farḥāt (d. 1732), who wrote a wide variety of works, including books of poetry and grammar, is often cited as a precursor of a revival of interest in the Arabic language. In the nineteenth century this missionary and educational activity intensified when Protestant missionaries began to arrive, most notably from the United States. A Bible translation project was merely one manifestation of these new contacts, and in 1866 the Syrian Protestant College was founded in Beirut, an institution which, under its more familiar modern title, the American University in Beirut, has played a notable role in the fostering of education and culture in the region and the Arab world as a whole.

A whole series of families—the Bustānīs, Yāzijīs, Shidyāqs, Naqqāshs, and so on—were now to make notable contributions to the process of reviving among the Arabs an awareness of the riches of their own language and its literature. To cite just a few examples: Buṭrus al-Bustānī (1819–83) came under the influence of Cornelius Van Dyke, an American missionary, and helped in the translation of the Bible into Arabic. He also wrote a dictionary, *Muḥīṭ al-muḥīṭ,* and the larger part of an encyclopaedia, *Dā'irat al-Ma'ārif,* on which he was working at the time of his death. Nāṣīf al-Yāzijī (1800–1871) is credited as being the pioneer in the reinvestigation of the great works of Arabic literature from the past. He read the *maqāmāt* of the eleventh-century prose writer al-Ḥarīrī in the French edition of Syl-

5. See the article on the *'aṣr al-inhiṭāṭ* by Shukrī Fayṣal, in al-'Alī, Ṣāliḥ et al., *Al-Adab al-'Arabī fī āthār al-dārisīn* (Beirut: Dār al-'Ilm li-al-Malāyīn, 1971), 291–311.

vestre de Sacy and was thus inspired to write a set of his own entitled *Majmaʿ al-baḥrayn.* Aḥmad Fāris al-Shidyāq (1804–87) was also much influenced by the classical tradition and the renewed interest in the history of the Arabic language when he came to write his famous work, *al-Sāq ʿalā al-sāq fīmā huwa al-Fāryāq.* The puns and rhymes within the title and the complex language employed in certain chapters provide abundant evidence of Shidyāq's interest in, and debt to, earlier examples of elaborate prose; indeed he states in the work's introduction that his purpose is "to reveal peculiarities and rarities of language."[6] The "hero," named Al-Ḥāris ibn Hithām in a clear echo of the earlier *maqāmah* tradition, takes the narrator on a trip that demonstrates the author's acquaintance with both the Mediterranean area and Northern Europe, most specifically England. The autobiographical element, already evident in the title's use of the name "Fāryāq," a combination of the "Fār-" of Fāris and "-yāq" of Shidyāq, can also be clearly seen in the book's vigorous anti-clerical tone, a reflection of the fact that Aḥmad's own brother, Asʿad, was killed on the orders of the Maronite Patriarch after converting to Protestantism. This same tone is also encountered in the works of Jubrān Khalīl Jubrān and Faraḥ Anṭūn, to be discussed below.[7]

Among early experiments in the development of modern Arabic fiction in the Syro-Lebanese region, the works of Faransīs Marrāsh (1836–73) and Salīm al-Bustānī (1848–84) deserve mention. Born in Aleppo in 1836, Marrāsh also traveled to Paris, but ill health forced him to return to Syria where he died at an early age. In 1865 he published in Aleppo a work entitled *Ghābat al-ḥaqq* (The forest of truth), a highly idealized, philosophical work, which is essentially an allegory about freedom. The rhyming title of a later work, *Durr al-ṣadaf fi gharāʾib al-ṣudaf* (Beirut, 1872), not only prepares us for the montage of coincidences that occur within the plot, but also illustrates the author's debt to earlier narrative genres.[8] Salīm al-Bustānī, eldest son of the above-mentioned Buṭrus al-Bustānī, began the crucial process of attracting a readership for historical fiction with a series of novels published in the periodical *al-Jinān.* Part entertain-

6. Aḥmad Fāris al-Shidyāq, *Al-Sāq ʿalā al-sāq fīmā huwa al-Fāryāq* (Paris, 1855), 1. See Muḥammad Yūsuf Najm, *Al-qiṣṣah fī al-adab al-ʿArabī al-ḥadīth fī Lubnān* (Beirut: Dār al-Thaqāfah, 1966), 245–49.

7. See Khalīl Ḥāwī, *Kahlil Gibran, His Background, Character and Works* (Beirut: American Univ. of Beirut, Oriental Series no. 41, 1963), 43.

8. See Sayyid Ḥāmid al-Nassāj, *Panorama al-riwāyah al-ʿArabiyyah* (Beirut: Al-Markaz al-ʿArabī li-al-thaqāfah wa-al-ʿulūm, 1982), 112; Matti Moosa, *The Origins of Modern Arabic Fiction* (Washington, D.C.: Three Continents, 1983), 147–53.

ment, part instruction, they combined episodes from Islamic history with travel, love stories, and adventure in a manner that managed to secure an ever-widening public for this subgenre of the novel. *al-Huyām fī jinān al-Shām* (Passion in Syrian gardens, 1870), for example, is set in the period of the Arab conquest of Syria soon after the death of Muḥammad in 632.[9]

A significant proportion of the works by Syrian and Lebanese writers that we have just discussed were written and published elsewhere. The primary cause was a prolonged period of civil war that began in the 1850s and culminated in the massacre of a large number of Christians in Damascus in 1860.[10] At this, a large number of Christian families decided to leave; some went to Egypt, while others traveled still further, coming to Europe and the Americas, in the latter case forming the basis for one of the most important schools in modern Arabic literature, the *mahjar* or emigré school.

It is hardly surprising that, in the wake of this exodus, the movement of cultural revival in Syria and Lebanon should have slowed down somewhat. In any case, this tragic set of circumstances was not the only factor involved, for the area was under the strict control of the Ottoman government in Istanbul. The dissemination of written materials was made yet more difficult by the problems of censorship which are well characterized for us by Muḥammad Kurd ʿAlī in his *Memoirs:* "What pained me most was the heavy censorship and the complications involved in obtaining the permit for publication. . . . There was nothing to go on in censorship except the whim of the censor. . . . How often I suffered from the publisher's deletion of whole paragraphs of mine, and sometimes entire articles."[11]

Iraq and the Arabian Gulf

To the east of Syria lies the state of Iraq. At the outset of *al-nahḍah,* Iraq was separated from the Arabic-speaking areas that were

9. For Salīm al-Bustānī, see Najm, 41–77; Ibrāhīm al-Saʿāfīn, *Taṭawwur al-riwāyah al-ʿArabiyyah al-ḥadīthah fī bilād al-Shām 1870–1967* (Baghdad: Manshūrāt Wizārat al-thaqāfah wa-al-iʿlām, 1980), 75–80; Moosa, *Origins of Modern Arabic Fiction,* 123–46; and M. M. Badawi, "The Origins of the Arabic Novel," in *Modern Arabic Literature and the West* (London: Ithaca, 1985), esp. 131–34.

10. Albert Hourani, *Arabic Thought in the Liberal Age* (London: Oxford Univ. Press, 1962), 61–64.

11. Khalil Totah, trans. (Washington, D.C.: American Council of Learned Societies), 1954, 13.

in contact with the Mediterranean world by the effective barrier of the Syrian desert. In any case, many of Iraq's religious, cultural, and commercial connections had for a long time been primarily with the contiguous areas of Iran, the Persian or Arabian Gulf, India, and the East.[12] These geographical and cultural factors resulted, as Salma Jayyusi suggests in her work on modern Arabic poetry, in the prevalence of traditional genres and critical norms.[13] Furthermore, the region was divided up into three Ottoman provinces. Censorship was strict and rigorously enforced, as the travels of the two Iraqi poets, al-Ruṣāfī and al-Zahāwī, in search of work and/or publication opportunities, make clear. In view of these facts, it is not surprising that, while Iraq has been a major center of poetic activity and innovation throughout the modern period, Iraqi fiction developed relatively later than was the case elsewhere; as Yūsuf ʿIzz al-dīn notes, it is essentially a twentieth-century phenomenon.[14]

The desert and the nomadic way of life that its climate demands also kept the regions of the Arabian Peninsula not only tribal but extremely traditional; as was the case in classical times, this particular region has been a repository of the older genres of the classical Arabic heritage.[15] Both Iraq and the Arabian Peninsula have been radically transformed by the discovery of oil, during the first decade of this century in Iran and, the world's largest repository, on the southern side of the Arabian Gulf in the 1930s. A region steeped in a thoroughly conservative and traditional culture has thus found itself thrust with disarming rapidity into a position as an object of the world's continuing attention, an area with the largest repository of a vital contemporary resource. The effect of such a transition on local culture and, in particular, its nomadic population, is itself the topic of one of the most complex novel projects undertaken in Arabic thus far: ʿAbd al-raḥmān Munīf's monumental quintet, *Mudun al-milḥ* (Cities of salt), to be discussed in chapter 3. Along with such political and societal transformations has come a new and increasingly com-

12. It is, after all, from Baṣrah, the southern Iraqi port, that Sindbad sets sail to ply his trade in the lands of the Far East.

13. Salma Khadra' Jayyusi, *Trends and Movements in Modern Arabic Poetry* (Leiden: E. J. Brill, 1977), 1:26. The same feature is noted by ʿIzz al-dīn, *Al-Riwāyah fī al-ʿIrāq*, 13.

14. ʿIzz al-dīn, *Al-Riwāyah fī al-ʿIrāq*, 41.

15. See, for example, the works of Steven C. Caton, *Peaks of Yemen I Summon* (Berkeley: Univ. of California Press, 1990); and Saad Abdullah Sowayan, *Nabati Poetry* (Berkeley: Univ. of California Press, 1985).

prehensive educational system. Newspapers, journals, books, television, all the trappings of a contemporary society, have begun to have their effect on the society in recent decades, leading gradually but inevitably to the emergence of what is the most recent in a series of developing fictional traditions, one that almost inevitably provides an interestingly different perspective from that of other regions of the Arab world.

The Maghrib

In the heady days of the 1950s, the Egyptian president Jamāl ʿAbd al-nāṣir (Nasser) described all the peoples living in the region "from the Atlantic Ocean to the Arabian Gulf" as Arabs. The western segment of this vast area is generally referred to as "the Maghrib" (west, sunset). In the context of North African political geography the term is used both as a somewhat vague designation of the nations to the west of Egypt and more precisely as Morocco (*al-Maghrib al-aqṣā*). If Iraq was somewhat isolated from the geographical center of the Arab world, the same is even more true in the cases of Morocco, Algeria, and Tunisia. Umberto Rizzitano notes that "Il Marocco, infatti, rimasto fuori dal blocco del territori arabofoni languenti sotto l'egemonia dell'impero ottomano."[16] Here, too, traditional culture held sway, and the influence of the revival movement affecting certain regions of the "Mashriq" (the eastern part of the Arab world) was not to be felt until the twentieth-century.[17] However, another factor was to have a profound effect on the nature and development of Arabic literature in this region. In 1830 France began the process of colonizing Algeria, and the extent to which the French succeeded in penetrating deep into the cultural and societal structures of the region is amply reflected in the bloody war of revolution (the so-called "War of a Million Martyrs") fought between 1954 and 1962. As Svetozar Pantucek observes:

> Les Français ne se bornèrent pas à occuper militairement l'Algérie, ils s'efforcèrent de la dominer économiquement et culturellement,

16. Umberto Rizzitano, "Il 'racconto' (*qiṣṣah*) nella narrativa araba contemporanea del Marocco," *Atti del terzo congresso di studi arabi e islamici* (Ravello, Naples: Istituto Universitario Orientale di Napoli, 1967), 569–93.

17. See ʿAbdallāh Kannūn, *Aḥādīth ʿan al-adab al-Maghribī al-ḥadīth* (Casablanca: Dār al-Thaqāfah, 1981), 17; also Svetozar Pantucek, *La littérature algérienne moderne* (Prague: Oriental Institute in Academia, 1969), 28.

> afin que leurs positions dans ce pays fussent vraiment solides. Les écoles arabes en Algérie furent fermés, la possibilité d'acquérir un enseignement arabe était systematiquement limitée et empêchée, tandis qu'avec l'accroissement de nombre d'immigrants français, l'influence de la langue française et de l'enseignement français était sans cesse renforcé.[18]

In 1881, one year before the British occupation of Egypt, the French occupied Tunisia. The process of revival commenced somewhat earlier here, due in no small part to the ideas and actions of Khayr al-Dīn Pāshā and also the influence of Muḥammad ʿAbduh, the great Egyptian reformer.[19] Thus Islamic education was able to survive, and even live, alongside the influx of French culture and indeed produce in ʿAbd al-Qāsim al-Shābbī one of the modern period's most fiery and eloquent romantic poets. It has to be admitted, however, that figures like al-Shābbī are exceptionally rare in the development of modern literature in the Maghrib; the pervasive influence of French culture and the conservative nature of such Islamic education as did exist made such a situation almost inevitable.

This geographical separation and the vigorous enforcement of a French-based educational system on that part of the population that was to receive an education has also tended to have an effect on the study of the region's literary output in Arabic, namely that it has been overlooked by a substantial number of scholars and critics in both the Eastern region of the Arab world and, it must be admitted, in the English-speaking world. Fortunately, a considerable increase in publication opportunities in the Maghrib and, to a certain extent, changing international alignments and political trends have recently led to a greater availability of the works of Maghribi authors and critics.

Egypt

In many of the regions of the Arab world the encounter with the West was a gradual process that needs to be viewed over a lengthy period of change. In the case of Egypt, the situation is somewhat different in that the meeting of East and West was at its most brusque. When Napoleon invaded the country in 1798, Egyptians were brought face to face with European advances in technology

18. See Pantucek, 21–22.
19. See Hourani, 84–94.

and military science, and, in the wake of their defeat, with the wonders of European culture and scientific knowledge. The precise nature of this historical encounter between cultures and the almost exquisite match of dates with the turn of a century have made it a godsend for those who choose to view the narration of history as a series of conflicts between the forces of opposing authority systems and of convenient chronological sequences rather than as a more subtle and elongated process involving other segments of society. Thus, while 1798 is clearly a date of major importance in the history of Egypt and thus of the entire Middle Eastern region, the model that it provides of the process of cultural change is clearly sufficiently unique to make clear that it cannot serve for the entire Arab world region. While the forces involved in *al-nahḍah* may have been basically the same for the area as a whole, the means, the sequence, and the pace varied widely from one region to another.

With the withdrawal of French forces, Muḥammad ʿAlī, an Ottoman soldier from Albania, took over the government of the country. Impressed by the efficacy of the French army, he decided that Egypt needed to train an army along similar lines. Beginning in the 1820s, he sent missions of young Egyptians to Europe, initially to Italy but later primarily to France. Rifāʿah Rāfiʿ al-Ṭahṭāwī (1801–1873) was chosen to accompany one of these early missions to Paris as *imām*. After a stay of five years in France, he wrote his famous work, *Takhlīṣ al-ibrīz fī talkhīṣ Bārīz*, a description of life in France that included accounts of dress, food, government, laws, and many other topics.[20] It serves as one of the very first examples of a whole series of narratives in which Arab visitors to Europe have recorded their impressions. We have already mentioned al-Shidyāq's contribution. In fact, the subject has served as the framework for a series of novels which have appeared during the course of the twentieth century by Tawfīq al-Ḥakīm, Ṭāhā Ḥusayn, Yaḥyā Ḥaqqī, Suhayl Idrīs, al-Ṭayyib Ṣāliḥ, and ʿAbd al-raḥmān Munīf.[21]

20. For al-Ṭahṭāwī, see (among many others) Albert Hourani, *Arabic Thought*, 67–83; ʿAbd al-muḥsin Ṭāhā Badr, *Taṭawwur al-riwāyah al-ʿArabiyyah al-ḥadīthah fī Miṣr* (Cairo: Dār al-Maʿārif, 1963), 51–61; and Saad Elkhadem, *History of the Egyptian Novel: Its Rise and Early Beginnings* (Fredericton, N. B.: York, 1985), 6–8.

21. Jūrj Ṭarābīshī, *Sharq wa-gharb: rujūlah wa-unūthah* (Beirut: Dār al-Ṭalīʿah, 1977); Issa J. Boullata, "Encounter Between East and West: A Theme in Contemporary Arabic Novels," *MEJ* 30, no. 1 (Winter 1976): 44–62; and Nedal M. al-Mousa, "The Arabic *Bildungsroman*: A Generic Appraisal," *IJMES* 25, no. 2 (May 1993): 223–40.

While al-Ṭahṭāwī's work certainly aroused the interest of the Egyptian readership concerning European society and its bases, his importance within the early development of the novel lies more in two other areas: translation and the press. In 1836 he was placed in charge of a new School of Languages in Cairo. During the following decades he and his pupils translated numerous significant works of European thought: Voltaire, Montesquieu, and Fénélon, to name just a few.[22] To these were added, slowly but inevitably, works of literature, particularly at the hands of his famous pupil and collaborator, Muḥammad ʿUthmān Jalāl (1829–1898). Not only did he translate a large number of French literary works, such as Molière's plays and the fables of La Fontaine; he also set in motion an important facet in the development of an indigenous fictional tradition by "egyptianising" their plots and characters, thus paving the way first for attempts at imitation and later for the development of an incipient novel genre. With these translation activities underway, it is hardly surprising that by the 1870s and 1880s the adventure novels of Alexandre Dumas père and Jules Verne, early favorites for translation, were being rendered in Arabic. It is worth noting that these priorities in selection mirror very closely the parallel translation movement in Turkish where Fénélon's *Télémaque* was translated in 1859, Hugo's *Les misérables* in 1862 and Dumas' *The Count of Monte Cristo* in 1871.[23]

Al-Ṭahṭāwī's contribution to the emergence of an Egyptian press tradition was equally significant. He served as editor of the Egyptian newspaper *al-Waqāʾiʿ al-Miṣriyyah* (founded by Muḥammad ʿAlī in 1823); while it may have functioned as the official gazette, it also laid the foundations for the later emergence of a vigorous tradition of Egyptian journalism. It is here that one can make one of many links with the events in Syria in the 1850s and 1860s noted above, in that Egypt offered a haven of safety and freedom of expression to the large number of Syrian Christians who came to Egypt following the civil war in their homeland. They brought with them their research into the classical language and its literature, as well as early experiments in fiction and drama, and numerous journals and magazines of both a scientific and cultural nature.

22. Hourani, 71.

23. The translations are discussed in detail by Matti Moosa in *Origins of Modern Arabic Fiction*, chaps. 1 and 4; see also Ahmet Evin, *Origins and Development of the Turkish Novel* (Minneapolis: Bibliotheca Islamica, 1983), 41–49.

It is hard to overestimate the important role the press has played in the revival of Arab cultural awareness throughout the Arab world during the last century.[24] It came to full fruition when nationalist sentiments and opposition to foreign domination were beginning to be heard; in fact, in many cases, these causes led to the foundation of newspapers. However, in addition to providing a forum for the discussion of ideas concerning nationalism and Islamic reform, the newspapers and journals also published works of fiction; initially translations from European languages, but gradually and inevitably including early experiments composed in Arabic. There were even a few publications which were entirely devoted to the publication of such entertainment literature. The renowned Cairo newspaper, *al-Ahrām,* for example, founded in Alexandria in 1875, provided a forum for narratives and, indeed, still does. Novels were published in serial form and drew a wide readership. One of the first published novels of this type was *Dhāt al-khidr* (*Lady of the harem*) by a member of the illustrious al-Bustānī family, Saʿīd (d. 1901). Appearing in *al-Ahrām* in 1884, it displays all the complexities of plot and plethora of coincidence that were encountered in the earlier works of Marrāsh and Salīm al-Bustānī. The press in the Arab world continues to fulfill this "previewing" role until the present day. While publishing opportunities and circumstances may differ in nature and scope from one country to another, Najīb Maḥfūẓ, the Nobel Laureate from Egypt, still avails himself of the literary pages of newspapers and journals in Cairo to introduce his new works to the public. But even this should not cause any surprise, for, as R. G. Cox notes, "a great deal of Victorian literature, verse and general prose as well as novels, was first published in periodicals; they can be seen as forming a vast nursery for its production." Later he adds that "during the nineteenth century then, periodicals performed a wide variety of functions. . . . They played a large part both in creating the public and in keeping it alive, active and at once receptive and critical. . . . At a more practical level the periodicals played an important part in furnishing an interim market for literary work."[25] Novel writing is not a profession by which one can earn a living in the Arab world; even Najīb Maḥfūẓ was only able to devote himself entirely to writ-

24. Vial, "Ḳiṣṣa," sec. 2; Pantucek, *La littérature algérienne moderne,* 24; Ilyās Khūrī, *Tajribat al-baḥth ʿan ufq* (Beirut: P.L.O. Research Centre, 1974), 12.

25. R. G. Coxe in *The Pelican Guide to English Literature,* vol. 6, *From Dickens to Hardy* (London: Pelican Books, 1958, 1960, 1963), 198, 202.

ing following his retirement from a civil service job. For that reason, the Arabic press has continued to play a valuable role in the development of the Arabic novel, firstly by making the works available to a wider public through serialization, and secondly—in the case of the better known writers—by offering a variety of positions as editors in cultural journals and magazines, thus providing a regular source of income in an area not too far removed from their real sphere of interest. However, that very same opportunity brings with it a negative side. It has to be admitted that the abuse of this convenient employment opportunity has occasionally and, in some countries, habitually led to cronyism among the older generation of writers and to the virtual exclusion of younger generations from publication opportunities.

The expanding press tradition, with its need for a clear and precise prose style and the translation movement, which, like all such endeavors, fostered a good deal of thought about the nature of the target language to be used, combined to encourage the development of a completely new kind of literary discourse, one that would satisfy the tastes of the ever-growing public for popular fiction while at the same time fulfilling as far as possible the cultural expectations of more conservative critics. While several writers contributed to this process, none was more influential than Muṣṭafā Luṭfī al-Manfalūṭī (1876–1924). Using the medium of the press once again, he published a whole series of essays and vignettes on a variety of topics; they were later published in book form as *al-Naẓarāt* and *al-ʿAbārāt.* The latter title (Tears) demonstrates the excessively romantic and sentimental nature of the content of these works. From the first collection, "al-Ka's al-ūlā" (The first drink) tells the story of a man who allows himself to drink a single glass of wine, whereupon his entire life disintegrates. Another piece, "Ṣidq wa-kidhb" (Truth and falsehood) betrays through its title the way in which qualities are painted in terms of black and white, with few, if any, intermediate hues of grey. But to dwell on these faults is hardly necessary, since they were attacked with characteristic vigor by Ibrāhīm al-Māzinī in the famous critical work, *al-Dīwān,* that he published along with ʿAbbās Maḥmūd al-ʿAqqād.[26] In spite of such vigorously expressed criticism, al-Manfalūṭī's works have remained popular with adolescents for many decades. Viewed in a historical perspective, we may suggest that the

26. ʿAbbas Maḥmūd al-ʿAqqād and Ibrāhīm al-Māzinī, *Al-Dīwān* (Cairo: N.p., 1921), 1–32.

most significant feature of these essays was the manner in which al-Manfalūṭī chose to express his ideas, a curious blend of Islamic modernism, an awareness of the classical heritage, and anti-Western sentiments, a blend typical of the period at the turn of the century in which he wrote.[27] His style was straightforward, often in the form of a vignette, a letter which he had received, or an anecdote which he had heard. These "essays" introduced a new and captivating kind of literature to the Egyptian reading public, and that in a style which was immediately accessible. Thus while the content may place them firmly within the realm of early romanticism, the language in which they were expressed and the readership that they fostered were an important step in the development of the novel tradition in Egypt.

This brief survey of the circumstances surrounding *al-nahḍah* in the different parts of the Arabic-speaking world has shown that, while the basic features were the same in each area, factors involving history (the civil war in Syria of the 1850s, the policies of the colonial powers), geography, and politics (censorship, for example)—to identify just a few—combined to make the speed and chronology of the process quite different in the various countries under consideration. Within this frame of reference, the enlightened educational policies of Muḥammad ʿAlī, the influx of Syrian immigrants into Egypt, the concentration of the British occupiers on matters of finance and administration rather than on culture and education, and the geographic centrality of the country within the region, all contributed to the emergence of Egypt as a major focal point of literary activity at the end of the nineteenth century and during the first decades of the twentieth century. It is the Iraqi writer, Jamīl Saʿīd, who comments, "Iraqi writers did not produce much fiction because their colleagues in Egypt and Syria were ahead of them. Iraqi readers preferred to read books—on whatever subject—written by Egyptians rather than Iraqis; they even preferred books printed in Egypt rather than in Iraq."[28] Thus, in choosing Egypt as the focal point for the early development of the novelistic tradition in Arabic, we are talking chronologically about a tradition that in essence combined

27. H. A. R. Gibb, *Studies on the Civilization of Islam,* ed. Stanford J. Shaw and William Polk (London: Routledge, 1962), 258–68.

28. Jamīl Saʿīd, *Naẓarāt fī al-tayyārāt al-adabiyyah al-ḥadīthah fī al-ʿIrāq* (Cairo: Maʿhad al-dirāsāt al-ʿArabiyyah al-ʿāliyah, 1954), 7–8, 25.

two, those of Egypt and Syria-Lebanon. In the other regions of the Arabic-speaking world, the development of the novel tradition moved *mutatis mutandis* along similar lines. What is most important from the historical perspective of the 1990s is that, through that process of what Jabrā terms "rapid chain-explosions" and catching up on the "back-log," such early chronological differentials have, to a large extent, been replaced by a generic variety that is not only anticipatable but surely desirable, bearing in mind the enormous size of the region.[29]

Jurjī Zaydān and the Historical Novel

The novels of Jurjī Zaydān provide us with a splendid illustration of the Egyptian environment which I have just described. Zaydān (1861–1914) was a Lebanese immigrant to Egypt, where in 1892 he founded the magazine, *al-Hilāl,* which is still being published in Cairo. Like Faraḥ Anṭūn's journal, *al-Jāmiʿah,* and Yaʿqūb Ṣarrūf's *al-Muqtaṭaf,* Zaydān's was a major conduit for information on the history and science of the West. However, beyond these varieties of information, Zaydān was apparently also eager to acquaint his readership with aspects of the history of the Arabs and Islam (as a means of encouraging and fostering a new cultural awareness), while at the same time providing works of fiction which would entertain in the same way as some of the more melodramatic historical novels from Europe which had been serialized in the press. To this end, he wrote a whole series of historical novels somewhat in the mode of Walter Scott, which elevated this subgenre of fiction to new levels of sophistication and also popularity; in fact they are still in print today.[30] As Sabry Hafez notes, this resort to history was "[not] a sheer love for antiquity . . . but an endeavour to awaken the readers' sense of national pride . . . and to provide them, by recalling past glories, with an inspiration and model in their search for a national

29. Jabrā Ibrāhīm Jabrā, "Modern Arabic Literature," 81.

30. For assessments of Zaydān, see ʿAbd al-muḥsin Ṭāhā Badr, *Taṭawwur al-riwāyah,* 93–106; Thomas Philipp, *Gurgi Zaidan, His Life and Thought* (Beirut: Orient-Institut der Deutschen Morgenlandischen Gesellschaft-Franz Steiner, 1979); Najm, 176–207, & 225–26; J. Brugman, *An Introduction to the History of Modern Arabic Literature in Egypt* (Leiden: E. J. Brill, 1984), 218–24; Sasson Somekh, *The Changing Rhythm* (Leiden: E. J. Brill, 1973), 7; Matti Moosa, *Origins of Modern Arabic Fiction,* 157–69.

identity."[31] Avoiding some of the more spectacular coincidences and heroics to be found in the adventure novels of earlier years that we have mentioned briefly above, Zaydān selected a number of incidents from Islamic history as plotlines for his novels. *Armānūsah al-Miṣriyyah* (1896) is concerned with the conquest of Egypt in 640; *al-Ḥajjāj ibn Yūsuf* (1902) is about the famous governor of Iraq during the period of the Umayyad caliphs; *Shajarat al-Durr* (1914) explores the reign of the famous queen of Egypt. *Istibdād al-Mamālīk* (Mamluk tyranny, 1893) may serve as an illustration of the narrative principles used. Set in the time of ʿAlī Bey al-Kabīr and his struggle with his son-in-law, Muḥammad Abū Dhahab (1769–73), the novel swings back and forth between Egypt and Syria (which the Egyptian army has invaded). The local color is provided by the disasters which befall the family of Sayyid ʿAbd al-raḥmān, a wealthy merchant who finds himself prey to the exactions of the Mamluks and who is forced to fight in the Egyptian army in order to save his son, Ḥasan, from a similar fate. Against the backdrop of the historical events leading to ʿAlī Bey's defeat at the hands of Muḥammad Abū Dhahab, the family goes through a series of adventures, miraculous escapes from death, and disguises, in order to emerge unscathed as Abū Dhahab celebrates his victory.

For all their combination of history and contrived romantic interest, not to mention the emphasis on action, these novels were far superior to many of the translated, adapted, and original works which were being serialized during these decades, novels marked (rather like some contemporary Indian films) by a little bit of everything: murder, intrigue, love, fights, and rapid action. The availability of such works did little to advance the development of the novel genre; indeed it seems to have given it something of a social stigma. Here one can draw an analogy with the theatrical tradition at this time, noting that the Egyptian intelligentsia did not regard the writings of such works with any favor, as will become clear when we consider shortly the case of Haykal.

The Egyptian critic, ʿAbd al-muḥsin Ṭāhā Badr, chose to place these novels into a category "between education and entertainment."[32] While such works may represent period pieces within the context of a retrospective on the development of fiction in Arabic, it cannot be

31. Sabry Hafez, "The State of the Contemporary Arabic Novel: Some Reflections," *The Literary Review Supplement,* The Arab Cultural Scene (London: Namara, 1982), 17.

32. Badr, *Taṭawwur al-riwāyah,* 93 ff.

denied that they were to play an enormously important role in the fostering of a readership for works of modern Arabic fiction. Members of the transplanted Syro-Lebanese community, prominently involved in the expansion of the press in Egypt, were also primary contributors to this type of fiction, much of which appeared in serial form. Through periodicals such as *al-Riwāyāt al-shahriyyah* (Monthly novels), Nīqūlā Ḥaddād (d. 1954) published a number of extremely popular novels with such titles as *Ḥawwā' al-jadīdah* (Modern Eve, 1906), *Asīrat al-ḥubb* (Prisoner of love, n.d.) and *Fātinat al-imperator* (Enchantress of the Emperor, 1922), works which acted as a link between an increasing popular taste for entertainment fiction and the emergence of a tradition more closely focused on present reality.[33] Ya'qūb Ṣarrūf (1852–1927), the founder of the journal *al-Muqtaṭaf*, and Faraḥ Anṭūn (1874–1922), the founder of the journal *al-Jāmi'ah* and a renowned secularist, also contributed to the corpus of historical novels. Ṣarrūf's *Amīr Lubnān* (1907) deals with the history of his native land during the religious struggles of the 1850s and 1860s; Anṭūn's *Ūrishalīm al-jadīdah aw fatḥ al-'Arab bayt al-maqdis* (New Jerusalem or the conquest of the Holy City, 1904) is set during the Muslim conquest of Jerusalem in the seventh century A.D. However, in other works, both Ṣarrūf and Anṭūn focused their narratives on the present. Ṣarrūf's novels, *Fatāt Miṣr* (1905) and *Fatāt al-Fayyūm* (1908) are set in his adopted country among its Christian (Coptic) community.[34] Anṭūn's other contributions to the novel genre mirror the fictional trends of the era, from the somewhat philosophical, *al-'Ilm wa-al-dīn wa-al-māl* (Science, religion and money, 1903), which is a discussion of the conflict of science and religion, to *al-Ḥubb ḥattā al-mawt* (Love till death, 1899) and *al-Waḥsh, al-waḥsh, al-waḥsh* (1903), both of which treat the problems of Lebanese society confronted with returnees from the emigrant community in America.

The novels of Zaydān and other contributors to the historical-romantic and philosophical novel certainly fulfilled the important function of bringing fictional genres into the public awareness and

33. See Najm, 123–29, 212–16; Brugman, 228–31; and Rotraud Wieland, *Das Bild der Europaer in der modernen arabischen Erzähl-und Theaterliteratur*, Beiruter Texte und Studien 23 (Beirut: Orient-Institut der Deutschen Morgenlandischen Gesellschaft, 1980) 171–85.

34. Faraḥ Anṭūn was a relative of Nīqūlā Ḥaddād by marriage. Concerning his works, see Donald M. Reid, *The Odyssey of Farah Antun* (Minneapolis: Bibliotheca Islamica), 1975. Badr, *Taṭawwur al-riwāyah*, 863–68; Najm, 93–100, 208–11; Brugman, 224–81; Wieland, *Das Bild der Europaer*, 214–17.

at the same time using episodes from Middle Eastern history as a means of rousing and fostering an emerging Arab Nationalist consciousness. It was, as Sabry Hafez notes, "natural . . . that the historical novel and romantic fiction with their nationalistic call for recognition and passionate adoration of the country's captivating beauty (e.g. Haykal's *Zaynab*) were the two major fictional types during the early period of the Arabic novel."[35] However, that very Western source which had provided exemplars of the novel for translation and imitation did not allow fiction in Arabic the luxury of a prolonged period of development and experimentation in order to develop its interest in, and understanding of, the novel genre. The First World War and its aftermath were to present the Arab world as a whole with some new and unpleasant realities. The same cultural traditions whence the novel had come were now represented by the Mandate Powers, whose incursions had to be challenged and resisted through a series of local nationalisms. Thus, while these types of novel continued to enjoy a certain vogue, Arab writers found in the problems of the present and aspirations for a better life a fertile ground for their fictions. In moving towards that goal, a different vision of the novel's generic purpose and newly developed skills were needed.

Muḥammad al-Muwayliḥī and Societal Criticism

While Zaydān culled his subject matter from the past, other writers used the columns of the press to publish serialized works which commented on and criticized contemporary society and politics. Egypt in the 1890s provided a fertile subject for such scrutiny. Following the ʿUrābī rebellion of 1882, the British had occupied the country; Lord Cromer had been assigned the task of putting Egypt's finances in order. Opposition to the occupation was almost universal but multifaceted. One of the most famous of these opponents was Jamāl al-dīn al-Asadābādī (usually known as "al-Afghānī," 1839–97). The influence that Jamāl al-dīn and his famous Egyptian pupil, Muḥammad ʿAbduh (1849–1905), had on an entire generation of writers in Egypt was profound; among his intellectual "disciples" were some of the most famous names in the Egyptian reformist movement: Qāsim Amīn (1865–1907), who wrote in support of the

35. Sabry Hafez, "The State of the Contemporary Arabic Novel, 17.

cause of women, Ḥāfiẓ Ibrāhīm, (1872–1932) the "poet of the Nile," Muṣṭafā Kāmil (1874–1908), a famous figure in the growth of Egyptian nationalism, and Muḥammad al-Muwayliḥī (1858–1930).[36] The cultural and political tensions of this environment provided Muḥammad al-Muwayliḥī, an Egyptian journalist, with plenty of material for his sarcastic pen. The resulting episodes, initially entitled "Fatrah min al-zaman," (A period of time), were published over a four-year period (1898–1902) in the columns of the family newspaper, *Miṣbāḥ al-Sharq*.[37] They were narrated by a young Egyptian named ʿĪsā ibn Hishām, that being precisely the name used many centuries earlier by Badīʿ al-Zamān al-Hamadhānī in his *maqāmāt*. We are thus dealing with the deliberate revival of the past heritage and its application to the present, a fully conscious neoclassicism, something made abundantly clear by the style known as *sajʿ* (rhyming prose) used at the beginning of each serialized episode. In al-Muwayliḥī's work, however, this stylistic device, which during the medieval period of Arabic literature had become a highly rhetoricized vehicle for verbal display, is limited to the first columns of each episode, after which he moves into a clear and polished style reminiscent of the best classical models.[38]

Ḥadīth ʿĪsā ibn Hishām represents a major advance over its predecessors in at least one way: it focuses on Egyptian society during the author's own lifetime and criticizes its foibles in a bitingly sarcastic fashion. The narrator, ʿĪsā ibn Hishām, meets Aḥmad Pāshā al-Manīklī, a Turkish minister of war from the previous era (that of Muḥammad ʿAlī), who rises from his grave. Together they explore the many problems, inconsistencies, and ironies of life in Egypt some fifty years after the Pāshā's death, fifty years which have witnessed much modernization and Westernization and, above all, the British occupation of the country. During the initial episodes the Pāshā is

36. The intellectual environment of the period is discussed in detail in Roger Allen, "Writings of Members of 'the Nāzlī Circle'," *JARCE* 8 (1969–70): 79–85.

37. The political focus of the newspaper and the context of the articles are discussed in Roger Allen, "Some New al-Muwailiḥī Materials," *Humaniora Islamica* 2 (1974): 139–80.

38. The work is studied at length in Allen, *A Period of Time* (Reading, England: Garnet, 1993). Among other sources that deal with the work are: Werner Ende, "Europabild und kulturelles Selbstbewusstsein . . . ," D. Phil. diss. Hamburg Universitat, 1965; Henri Pérès, "Editions successives de Ḥadīth ʿĪsā ibn Hishām," *Mélanges Louis Massignon* 3 (1957): 233–58; Ibrāhīm al-Hawārī, *Naqd al-mujtamaʿ fī Ḥadīth ʿĪsā ibn Hishām* (Cairo: Dār al-Maʿārif, 1981); and Aḥmad Yūsuf Ramitch, *Usrat al-Muwayliḥī wa-atharuhā fī al-adab al-ʿArabī al-ḥadīth* (Cairo: Dār al-Maʿārif, 1980).

arrested for assaulting an importunate donkeyman; readers are thus given an introduction to the chaotic Egyptian legal system in which religious (Sharīʿah) and secular courts (based on the French model) are endeavoring to apply the law under a British governmental administration. In later episodes, the figure of the *ʿumdah* (village headman) and his two colleagues, the *khalīʿ* (playboy) and the *tājir* (merchant), are used to contrast life in the countryside with that in the "modern" city and to show up the differences between the traditional tastes and values of the *ʿumdah* and the Westernized fads espoused by the *khalīʿ*.[39] As this series of episodes evolved (and, as in some of the works of Dickens, that process can be seen as a response to the reaction of the readership), it was already being referred to as "The story of ʿĪsā ibn Hishām." Thus, when al-Muwayliḥī decided to publish his serialized episodes as a book in 1907, it is hardly surprising that one of the first monuments of modern Arabic prose should have been given the title *Ḥadīth ʿĪsā ibn Hishām*. The work was an immediate success; a second edition appeared in 1912 and a third in 1923. In 1927 it was given some form of canonization by being adopted as a school text, although, from my conversations with numerous Egyptians, that also seems to have secured the death of its popularity. This was also an unfortunate decision in that much of the more controversial (and therefore interesting) criticism of society which the first three editions had contained—pointed criticisms of al-Azhar, the Royal Family, and Muḥammad ʿAlī's Turkish ways—was omitted, and in its place were inserted a number of episodes of "Fatrah min al-zaman" describing a visit which ʿĪsā ibn Hishām (al-Muwayliḥī) made to the Great Exhibition in Paris in 1899. These episodes, now called *al- Riḥlah al-thāniyah*, may be yet another example of the "European visit" theme, but show little of the pungent sarcasm of the Egyptian episodes.

Several critics have endeavored to show that *Ḥadīth ʿĪsā ibn Hishām* is the beginning of the Egyptian novel, but there are a number

39. The *ʿumdah* figure is one of the greatest targets of social criticism through humor in modern Egyptian literature, and no more so than in the plays of Najīb al-Rīḥānī (d. 1949). He introduces the character of Kishkish Bey, who is proverbial for both his gullibility in urbane society and his venality. See L. Abou-Saif, "Najīb al-Rīḥānī: From Buffoonery to Social Comedy," *JAL* 4 (1973): 1–17. This trait has remained within the repertoire of Egyptian writers of fiction, as, e.g., in Tawfīq al-Ḥakīm's memorable *Yawmiyyāt nāʾib fī al-aryāf* (Diary of a public prosecutor in the provinces) (Cairo: Maṭbaʿat lajnat al-taʾlīf, 1937) and in the novel of Yūsuf al-Qaʿīd, *Al-Ḥarb fī barr Miṣr* (War in the land of Egypt) (Beirut: Dār Ibn Rushd, 1978).

of problems connected with such attempts. In the first place, if the work is to be considered a novel, then by any yardstick it is a thoroughly bad one. As is typical with a series of episodes written over a four-year period, the narrative thread is extremely contrived and often invisible. Only in certain chapters—the initial ones in which the Pāshā is heavily involved in the action, and the later ones involving the rustic *ʿumdah*—is any real effort made to maintain continuity. Furthermore, there is no characterization in any real sense of the word, and certainly no development of character through action. But all this is basically unfair to al-Muwayliḥī, since, in my opinion, he had no intention of writing a novel or the converting of his series of newspaper articles into one. The level of criticism implicit in the treatment of each societal group is certainly a constant, but the chapters remain discrete entities with little to link them to other chapters, apart from the presence of the narrator and his companion. In this way, the work greatly resembles the narrative emphases implicit in al-Hamadhānī's *maqāmāt,* the narrator of which provides al-Muwayliḥī's work with its title. Al-Muwayliḥī clearly had no intention of writing literature which would entertain in the same way that the adventure novels mentioned above were doing. He was not one to make concessions to any emerging audience for popular fiction. When we bear in mind his vitriolic reaction to attempts by the famous poet, Aḥmad Shawqī (1868–1932), to introduce new ideas about poetry into his collected works, we may be able to gauge his reaction to the kind of fiction which was becoming so popular.[40]

Ḥadīth ʿĪsā ibn Hishām thus serves an invaluable bridging function. The invocation of al-Hamadhānī's narrator and the brilliant use that al-Muwayliḥī made of the *sajʿ* style of the *maqāmah* certainly suggest the norms of a neoclassical prose work, one that seeks to revive an awareness of the glories of the cultural heritage of Arabic literature. But, alongside this feature, we have to acknowledge that by using contemporary Egypt and its problems as a primary focus, and analyzing both in a humorous and accurate fashion, al-Muwayliḥī's work represents a major shift in focus when contrasted with previous works, most of which were totally detached from their author's environment in either place or time or both. When we consider the novel's great, perhaps principal, role—the depiction of the

40. See Roger Allen, "Poetry and Poetic Criticism at the Turn of the Century," in *Studies in Modern Arabic Literature,* ed. R. C. Ostle (Warminster, England: Aris and Phillips, 1975), 1–17.

process of change, and most especially societal change—it is somewhat ironic that one of the most "classical" texts of all, *Ḥadīth ʿĪsā ibn Hishām,* may fulfill a particularly significant role. For it was al-Muwayliḥī's work that served as the major precedent for a work of fiction that does serve as a landmark in the development of the novel in Arabic, one that marks the transition from a first phase—one of translation, imitation, and adaptation—to a second phase of creation and experimentation, Muḥammad Ḥusayn Haykal's *Zaynab.*

The Status of Haykal's *Zaynab*

There has been a good deal of discussion concerning the status of Muḥammad Ḥusayn Haykal's novel, *Zaynab,* ever since H. A. R. Gibb and others identified it as the first "real novel" in Arabic.[41] The key phrase that has been invoked to distinguish Haykal's work from those of his predecessors is "of literary merit," or, in ʿAbd al-Muḥsin Ṭāhā Badr's words, a *riwāyah fanniyyah* (artistic novel).[42] Some critics regard *Zaynab* too as one more step on the road to the emergence of a "genuine" novel, while more recently others have found novelistic qualities in a still earlier work of Maḥmud Ṭāhir Ḥaqqī, entitled *ʿAdhrāʾ Dinshaway* (1907; *The Maiden of Dinshaway,* 1986).[43] Ḥaqqī's work situates real Egyptians in a contemporary Egyptian setting in both place and time, namely the actual events which ensued when, in vengeful reprisal for the death of a British soldier who was on a pigeon shoot near an Egyptian village, the authorities were forced by the occupying power to pass sentences of execution on a number of villagers and to carry them out in public. The savagery of this verdict has remained indelibly recorded in the collective Egyptian consciousness ever since. Ḥaqqī's work thus presents us with a contribution to fiction combining some of the elements that we have already identified: from al-Muwayliḥī's book a concern with the de-

41. The subject is taken up in Brugman, 210–11, and Matti Moosa, *Origins of Modern Arabic Fiction,* 147, 157. Gibb's opinion can be found in his series of articles on modern Arabic literature, published initially in the *Bulletin of the School of Oriental Studies* (1933) and republished in *Studies on the Civilization of Islam,* 286–303.

42. For "literary merit," see ʿAli B. Jad, *Form and Technique in the Egyptian Novel* (London: Ithaca, 1983, passim); also Badr, *Taṭawwur al-riwāyah,* 318: "Haykal's novel . . . represents the first and authentic beginning to the artistic novel."

43. See Rotraud Wieland, *Das Bild der Europaer,* 196; Elkhadem, 23–26; and, most particularly, al-Nassāj, 23–25, where he advocates regarding Ḥaqqī's work as a "genuine" contribution to the novel.

scription and analysis of present-day Egypt (to which can be added publication in a newspaper, in this case Ḥaqqī's own *al-Minbar*); and from the historical-romantic novel, a local love story. As we bear in mind these examples and other categories of fiction that were emerging in Egypt at this time, it is perhaps more accurate and useful not to burden *Zaynab* with the designation as the first example of any particular category or quality of novel, but rather as an extremely important step in a continuing process. Without in any way diminishing the place of Haykal's novel in the history of modern Arabic prose literature, we would suggest that a clearer historical perspective can be obtained by placing it in a broader generic context.[44]

Zaynab was published in Egypt in 1913 under the pseudonym *Miṣrī fallāḥ* (A peasant-Egyptian) although, as Hamdi Sakkut observes, the true identity of Haykal was known to literary critics at the time.[45] A primary feature of this work is the loving attention which is devoted to the description of the Egyptian countryside. If previous attempts at novel writing had lacked a realistic backdrop, then Haykal places his reader right in the midst of Egyptian village society as he recalls it from afar and proceeds to elaborate on natural phenomena—the fields and crops, the sunrise and sunset, and so on—at great, almost tedious, length. Not for nothing is the work subtitled *Manāẓir wa-akhlāq rīfiyyah* (Country scenes and manners). One has to admit that the overall effect is more than a little sentimental, a fact attributable, no doubt, to the nostalgia that the author, himself the son of a wealthy landowner, felt while studying abroad.

The plot of the novel is based on two focal points: Zaynab, a beautiful peasant girl who works in the fields owned by the father of the second focal point, Ḥāmid, a student in Cairo who returns to his parental home during the vacations and whose views seem very much a reflection of Haykal's own. The two foci meet briefly in that Zaynab is one of the girls with whom Ḥāmid flirts, but nothing comes of this dalliance, and their stories are essentially separate. To Ḥāmid, Zaynab serves as consolation when he learns that his cousin, ʿAzīzah, with whom he has been carrying on a sort of epistolary love affair, is to be married off to someone else. When he finally despairs

44. As Brugman suggests, 211.

45. Hamdi Sakkut, *The Egyptian Novel and Its Main Trends 1913–1952* (Cairo: American Univ. in Cairo Press, 1971), 12. Al-Nassāj even imputes marketing motives to Haykal's choice of anonymity, 34.

of the prospect of finding true love, he goes back to Cairo and sends his parents a letter full of his ideas about society and its problems, ideas that are patently those of Haykal himself:

> Since the day I began thinking about love and happened to meet my cousin, I have wanted to marry her. . . . When I saw her and began to realise how impossible it was to find any opportunity to talk to her alone, I got very annoyed and became even more intolerant of society and its customs than those who have to put up with the painful tortures which it imposes on people. The subject of marriage became for me the object of the most bitter criticism. . . . In my opinion, marriage which is not based on love and which does not endure on the basis of love is despicable.[46]

This passage provides just one of many possible illustrations of the way in which a characteristic of many early works of fiction is to be found in abundance in Haykal's work, namely homilies on social issues often addressed in the form of letters. It is all too easy to point to the problems of psychological fallacy here, as Ḥāmid, the student in Cairo acquainted with Western works on liberty and justice such as those of John Stuart Mill and Herbert Spencer, proceeds to discuss the question of marriage in Egyptian society on such a lofty plane with his parents, who have always lived deep in the Egyptian countryside.

It is, however, not Ḥāmid who lends his name to the title of this work, and we should now consider the other focus. Zaynab is also unable to marry the person whom she loves; in her case, it is Ibrāhīm, the poor fellow-worker who cannot afford the bride price. She therefore accedes to her parents' wish that she should marry Ḥasan, another villager, who can come up with the requisite amount. In spite of her love for Ibrāhīm, Zaynab does all she can to be a good wife to Ḥasan, who treats her most considerately. However, Ibrāhīm is so poor that he cannot even bribe his way out of military service as most other people seem to be able to do. He is drafted into the army and sent off to fight in the Sudan. In what may be considered a classic version of the romantic ending, Zaynab begins to pine for her true beloved and dies of tuberculosis, asking

46. Muḥammad Ḥusayn Haykal, *Zaynab* (Cairo: Maktabat Nahḍat Miṣr, 1963), 268–69. The translation used here is my own. For another translation of the complete novel, see Mohammed Hussein Haikal, *Zainab,* trans. John Mohammed Grinsted (London: Darf, 1989). The passage in question is on pp. 173–74.

with her dying breath that Ibrāhīm's handkerchief be buried with her. As we shall see in the next chapter, this is not the last time that such an ending is employed in the Arabic novel.

Thus Zaynab and Ḥāmid both emerge as victims of societal custom. Neither can marry the person whom he or she really loves. Furthermore, Ḥāmid's cousin, ʿAzīzah, seems, if anything, to have less freedom of movement than Zaynab herself; at least the latter can walk around the village and fields unveiled and even respond to Ḥāmid's advances. ʿAzīzah may have the advantage of an education, but the narrative implies that it will be of little value to her under such societal norms.[47] In this work Ḥāmid clearly serves as a mouthpiece for Haykal himself, who had already been exposed to the ideas of such reformers as Qāsim Amīn, the writer on women's rights mentioned earlier. Through the two principal characters in *Zaynab,* Zaynab herself and Ḥāmid, Haykal criticizes the customs of Egyptian society. ʿAzīzah and Zaynab, Ḥāmid and Ibrāhīm, serve as symbols of the status of marriage in Egypt and particularly of woman's role in it.

In a work that is so replete with description, not to mention communication by letter, dialogue tends to be somewhat sparse. But it was in this sphere that Haykal followed the lead of earlier pioneers such as ʿUthmān Jalāl, ʿAbdallāh Nadīm, and Yaʿqūb Ṣanūʿ by adopting the colloquial dialect as a literary medium and using it in his passages of dialogue. To digress somewhat, the term in Arabic for the written language is *al-fuṣḥā,* a comparative adjective derived from the verbal base which means "to be eloquent" and "to use Arabic correctly." The colloquial dialect is by contrast assigned the term *ʿāmmiyyah,* (plebeian). The literary establishment's general attitude towards it is well captured in the words of Ṭāhā Ḥusayn, the great Egyptian littérateur (1889–1973):

> I am now and will always remain unalterably opposed to those who regard the colloquial as a suitable instrument for mutual understanding and a method for realising the various goals of our intellectual life. . . . The colloquial lacks the qualities to make it worthy of the name of a language. I look on it as a dialect that has been corrupted in many respects. It might disappear, as it were, into the classical if we devoted the necessary effort on the one hand to elevate the cultural level of the people and on the other to

47. Charles Smith, "Love, Passion and Class in the Fiction of Muḥammad Ḥusayn Haykal," *JAOS* 99, no. 2 (1979): 251.

> simplify and reform the classical so that the two meet at a common point.[48]

Cultural attitudes on this issue have fluctuated widely during the course of this century—affected, among other things, by the pulls of local nationalisms, pan-Arabism, and resurgent Islam. Discussion of the issue has raged fiercely, providing much fire but little light. The most vigorous debates have occurred, needless to say, within the realm of the theatre. In the novel form, the writer's communication with the recipient is not via the aural medium, and yet the question of the use of the colloquial language in dialogue in the fictional genres has been fought out with great intensity. The majority of creative writers have, in fact, done exactly as they saw fit, leaving the polemics to critics. Nevertheless, as the novel has developed, each writer has had to make a conscious decision as to which language to use in his works and, if he becomes famous, to justify his choice. And, just in case it is assumed that Ṭāhā Ḥusayn's views are those of a much earlier period, here is Najīb Maḥfūẓ expressing his views on the same topic: "The colloquial is one of the diseases from which the people are suffering, and of which they are bound to rid themselves as they progress. I consider the colloquial one of the failings of our society, exactly like ignorance, poverty and disease."[49] In a context so fraught with assigned cultural and religious value, Haykal's early adoption of the colloquial dialect as a linguistic medium for the fictional expression of realistic communication is clearly of considerable historical importance.

Returning to a consideration of the status of *Zaynab* as a contribution to the development of the novel in Arabic, we may note that it is normally afforded a place of importance because it depicts Egyptian rural life peopled by Egyptian characters. However, it seems difficult to support the claim that the work presents a picture that is in any sense "realistic." The advocacy of Qāsim Amīn's views on the place of women in society is clear enough, but the discussion of such issues forms a moralizing overlay that sits awkwardly on top of an idealized and nostalgic portrait of country life conceived by an Egyptian intellectual while studying in France. The ideas advocated

48. Ṭāhā Ḥusayn, *Mustaqbal al-thaqāfah fī Miṣr* (The future of culture in Egypt), trans. Sidney Glazer (Washington, D.C: American Council of Learned Societies, 1954), 86.

49. See Fu'ād Duwārah, *'Asharah udabā' yataḥaddathūna* (Cairo: Dār al-Hilāl, 1965), quoted in Pierre Cachia, *An Overview of Modern Arabic Literature* (Edinburgh: Edinburgh Univ. Press, 1990), 71–72.

by the characters represent aspirations more than realities, thus making of the work something of a historical anomaly. While it is indeed a landmark in modern Arabic fiction, the wide temporal gap that separates it from the appearance of further exemplars of its genre serves to underline the essential disjuncture at this period between the actual historical moment within society and the generic purpose of social-realist fiction to which it aspires.

Developments in Egypt After *Zaynab:* 1913–1939

Haykal's work was noted and reviewed at the time of its appearance, but it cannot be said to have prompted an increased interest in writing works of fiction that would address themselves to the realities of the present. Indeed, apart from *Thurayyā* by ʿĪsā ʿUbayd (d. 1923), a short work heavily focused, like Haykal's, on a story of unfulfilled love,[50] one has to wait until the 1930s for the appearance of further experiments in longer fiction.

One genre that clearly thrived in this period was the short story, which was well suited to the new medium of the press, not to mention its unique ability to deal with smaller segments of life in society in intense and often allusive detail. It has been suggested by some critics that it was a desire on the part of some authors to concentrate on the short story genre that accounts for the temporal gap between the publication of *Zaynab* and the appearance of a whole host of novels in the 1930s. The view that the short story can serve in such a way as a sort of training ground for incipient novelists is, needless to say, one that short story writers vigorously reject.[51] Indeed, when we come to consider those writers who did turn their attention to the novel in the 1930s, including Ibrāhīm al-Māzinī, ʿAbbās Maḥmūd al-ʿAqqād, and Tawfīq al-Ḥakīm, it becomes clear that the reason for the paucity of novels in the 1920s is due as much to a whole cluster of other social and cultural factors as to the popularity of the short story. Not all authors, for example, had available to them the oppor-

50. For ʿĪsā ʿUbayd, see Badr, *Taṭawwur al-riwāyah* 233–58; Brugman, 246–47; ʿAli B. Jad, *Form and Technique*, 27–28 and 107–8.

51. See Suzanne Ferguson, "The Rise of the Short Story as a Highbrow, or Prestige Genre," in *Short Story Theory at a Crossroads,* ed. Susan Lohafer and Jo Ellyn Clarey (Baton Rouge: Louisiana State Univ. Press, 1989), 179. Consider also the following comment by H. E. Bates: "Because a short story is short it is not therefore easier to write than a novel, ten, twenty, or even thirty times its length—the exact reverse being in fact the truth." H. E. Bates, *The Modern Short Story 1809–1953* (London: Robert Hale, 1988), 2.

tunities that Haykal's social status afforded him: the possibility of traveling abroad; studying a foreign culture and its literary output; viewing his homeland from a fresh perspective; and, perhaps most practical of all, finding a publishing outlet for his pioneering piece of fiction. While the emerging press tradition certainly fostered, as we have just seen, the appearance of novels of a certain kind, the ephemeral nature of the newspaper and journal medium and the amount of time needed to create a work of novel length—quite apart from the writing skills and imagination required—were formidable obstacles in the face of any young writers who would aspire to write a novel and to do so essentially as a spare-time activity (that being, incidentally, the circumstances under which Maḥfūẓ wrote his major contributions to the genre until the time of his retirement). In this context it is therefore extremely important to recognize one segment of the population that clearly did have such amounts of time, both as writers and readers, namely, women. The circumstances that Haykal depicts in *Zaynab* may have reflected a social situation which prevented the general public availability of all but a tiny fraction of their output, but, as researchers begin to concentrate more on this hidden segment of the creative and receptive side of fiction, it becomes clear that a different view of the early history of fiction in Arabic will be needed.[52]

A work that was to make a major contribution to the development of prose literature was published during the 1920s; it has become one of the most beloved of all works in modern Arabic literature: *al-Ayyām,* Ṭāhā Ḥusayn's famous autobiography, originally serialized in *al-Hilāl* and then published as a book. Almost every commentator on the modern Arabic novel includes some reference to this work, and rightly so. The traditional narrative mode of autobiography is given a touch of gentle irony by the sense of detachment from his protagonist that the author achieves through the simple device of couching the narrative in the third person. When we couple with these features a limpid prose style which flows with such deceptive ease, the sum total is a work which has remained one of the most enduring masterpieces in a modern Arabic prose literature.[53]

52. A glimpse into this world and the perspectives that it offers can be obtained from *Opening the Gates: A Century of Arab Feminist Writing,* ed. Margot Badran and Miriam Cooke (Bloomington, Indiana: Indiana Univ. Press, 1990).

53. It is the subject of a most perceptive study: Fedwa Malti-Douglas, *Blindness and Autobiography:* Al-Ayyām *of Ṭāhā Ḥusayn* (Princeton: Princeton Univ. Press, 1988).

In 1929, Haykal's *Zaynab* was published in a second edition. By this time Haykal was well-known both as editor of a famous newspaper, *al-Siyāsah,* and as a cultural figure of some renown. The republication of the work and the discussion which surrounded it stimulated a tremendous interest in the genre which was to bear fruit in the next decade. In 1930 a competition in novel writing was announced; the eventual winner was *Ibrāhīm al-Kātib* (1931; *Ibrāhīm the Writer,* 1976) by Ibrāhīm al-Māzinī.[54]

It has often been suggested that the process of writing novels will always introduce elements of the personal, the autobiographical, into the resulting text; one might suggest further that the autobiographical element is particularly prevalent in many first attempts at novel writing. The title of al-Māzinī's novel thus points to a feature which seems especially prominent in the series of novels written by Egyptians in the 1930s. While al-Māzinī himself consistently denied it, most critics agree that "Ibrāhīm the author" is in many ways precisely that. The story itself provides a rather disjointed account of the love of a man for three different women: a Syrian nurse, Mary, who helps him through his convalescence from illness; his cousin, Shūshū; and Laylā, whom he meets in Luxor, where he has gone to escape from the memory of his failure to marry Shūshū. In this work, as in Haykal's, there is some implicit criticism of societal customs, in that Ibrāhīm is not allowed to marry Shūshū, whom he loves, because her elder sister remains unmarried. Even so, there is an inconsistency in al-Māzinī's treatment of this theme, in that Shūshū is eventually married to a doctor even though her elder sister still remains unmarried. However, we have suggested above that a clear narrative thread is not the major virtue of this novel; where it does represent an advance is in characterization. As is evident from al-Māzinī's contributions to the short story, he is a master at crafting vignettes of characters and types, particularly when he has the opportunity to pepper the sketch with some of his unique brand of humor. Many situations in the work—for example, the narrator's experiences with Aḥmad al-Mayyit (the dead) at his cousins' house, the strange encounter with the man who has robbed him in Alexandria—illustrate that same, almost farcical sense of fun which typifies so many of his stories. Thus if this work is not entirely successful, it makes a distinct contribution to the further develop-

54. English trans.: *Ibrahim the Writer,* trans. Magdi Wahba (Cairo: General Egyptian Book Organization, 1976).

ment of the novel genre by providing the reader with some memorable Egyptian characters and some poignant and amusing moments.

It is no accident that the first novel which succeeds in providing a totally convincing portrait of a family within a restricted environment should have been written by Tawfīq al-Ḥakīm, whose major interest was and remained the drama. In *ʿAwdat al-rūḥ* (1933; *Return of the Spirit,* 1990) we are introduced to Muḥsin, a young student living with his relatives in Cairo.[55] Through a dialogue of considerable subtlety and variety, we are introduced to the various members of the closely-knit family. The male members all find themselves fascinated by the charm of the daughter of a neighbor, Saniyyah, while in contrast, Zannūbah, the spinster of the family, spends large amounts of money on beautifying herself in an attempt to find a husband. While the potential of this mixture of characters is well exploited in the first part of the book, the atmosphere is transformed (and the liveliness of the characterization somewhat dissipated) when, in the central part of the work, Muḥsin returns to his parents' country estate for the vacation. This allows al-Ḥakīm to elaborate on the theme which provides the novel with its title: Egypt's awareness of its ancient heritage, eternal Egypt unchanging in spite of the passage of time and the succession of foreign occupiers, all this encapsulated in the so-called Pharaonism movement, which had a considerable vogue at the time when this work was written. The application of this idea to the 1919 Revolution in Egypt, in which the members of the family are finally involved, may be appropriate in itself, but the attempt to combine this heavily symbolic motif with the lively and realistic portrait which forms the first part of the work is not fused together successfully, and the work loses a sense of balance. Once again, one facet of the complex process of novel writing—the dramatic role of dialogue in contributing to character portrayal—has been convincingly demonstrated, paving the way for the emergence of the Arabic novel in its full maturity.

A second work, *ʿUṣfūr min al-sharq* (1938; *Bird from the East,* 1967) takes the same student, Muḥsin, to Paris in order to continue his studies, suggesting again an autobiographical link between character and author.[56] The work is used to suggest a rather facile contrast between the spiritual East and the material West in a way which

55. The novel is now available in translation: *Return of the Spirit,* trans. William M. Hutchins (Washington, D.C.: Three Continents, 1990).

56. English trans. R. Bayly Winder as *Bird from the East* (Beirut: Khayyat, 1966).

shows little characterization or action and which can be seen as an early precedent to the more sophisticated treatment of the same "Arab student in Europe" theme to be found in later works by Yaḥyā Ḥaqqī, Suhayl Idrīs, and al-Ṭayyib Ṣāliḥ to which we shall refer later. The same subject is to be found in Ṭāhā Ḥusayn's *Adīb* (1935), but once again the subject of European education is allowed to preponderate. That topic, together with the excessive use of the letter format, produces a rather tedious work. Ṭāhā Ḥusayn's later novels, and particularly *Shajarat al-bu's* (Tree of misery, 1944), are much more successful contributions to the genre.

In yet another novel from this decade, Tawfīq al-Ḥakīm succeeded in creating one of the most memorable works of early modern Arabic fiction, *Yawmiyyāt nā'ib fī al-aryāf* (Diary of a public prosecutor in the provinces, 1937; *The Maze of Justice,* 1947).[57] Al-Ḥakīm makes use of a first-person participant narrator to introduce us to the customs and beliefs of a small community in the Egyptian provinces. The vividness of the emerging picture suggests that he has incorporated into his narrator's tale much of his own experience when he occupied the same position following his return from study in Europe. The reader thus finds the traditional way of life of this particular segment of the Egyptian populace filtered through the vision of a prosecutor who is in the almost impossible position of applying the French legal system to situations involving Egyptian peasants during a period when the country is under British occupation. The narrative is couched in the form of a diary, and thus chronological time provides a dominant organizing principle. And yet al-Ḥakīm does not rely on this alone to give his work structural unity. Running through the course of events is the linking thread of the story of Rim, the stunning village beauty who is initially thought to be involved in a murder, but then disappears, only to be discovered, towards the end of the story, as a corpse in a canal. The narrator-prosecutor's attempts to investigate this case; the bewitching nature of the girl's beauty; the vast repertoire of shenanigans employed by the various legal authorities, both local and "visiting"; and the pathetic and ultimately useless protests of the peasants; all these are linked in a narrative that is convincingly sustained and developed. *Yawmiyyāt nā'ib* shows al-Ḥakīm's talent for constructing narrative and painting lively characters through dialogue in a remarkably de-

57. English trans. Aubrey [Abba] S. Eban as *The Maze of Justice* (London: Harvill, 1947).

veloped fashion. The result is clearly one of the finest examples of early modern Egyptian fiction.

Another contributor to this process was the poet and critic, ʿAbbās Maḥmūd al-ʿAqqād, with *Sārah* (1938).[58] Al-ʿAqqād was to a large degree self-taught, and combined interests in literature with those in the natural sciences. It is thus hardly surprising that he became involved in the application of psychological analysis literature, as, for example, in his study of the famous classical poet Ibn al-Rūmī.[59] His contribution to the novel certainly falls within this category, and, in his introduction to the second edition, he himself suggests that *Sārah* is either "a novel of psychological analysis or an analysis in a narrative form."[60] The subject of this "analysis" is the breakdown of a love affair between Hammām and Sārah. The author's technique is made clear from the titles of individual chapters, many of which take the form of questions: "Who was she?", "How did he get to know her?", "Why did he fall in love with her?". There is almost no background against which this detailed dissection is conducted, and very little action or dialogue to provide some relief from the relentless process of investigation. The psychological dimension may be explored in depth, and indeed later writers may have benefited from this example, but the overall effect is not a little tedious.

Ṭāhā Ḥusayn, al-ʿAqqād, and al-Ḥakīm are three of the most illustrious names in the history of modern Arabic literature, and it is clearly a sign of the increasing interest in the novel genre that they wrote the works which we have just described. Alongside the developing skills which are evident in these works, however, are obvious flaws in technique. With that in mind, it is both sad and ironic that a novel written during this decade which *does* show a considerable artistic consistency, Maḥmūd Ṭāhir Lāshīn's *Ḥawwā' bi-lā Ādam* (1934; *Eve without Adam,* 1986), has suffered from the same neglect which has affected the author's work as a whole and which seems to have contributed in no small way to his decision to stop writing altogether. What makes this work particularly noteworthy is not only that it seems to be a piece of complete fiction—in other words, without any autobiographical content or allusions—but also that 'the outcome

58. English trans. M. M. Badawi as *Sara* (Cairo: General Egyptian Book Organization, 1978).

59. See ʿAbbās Maḥmūd al-ʿAqqād, *Ibn al-Rūmī: ḥayātuhu min shiʿrihi* (Cairo: Maṭbaʿat Ḥijāzī, 1938); also David Semah, *Four Egyptian Literary Critics* (Leiden: E. J. Brill, 1974), 3–65.

60. See *Sara,* trans. M. M. Badawi, Introduction, 12.

appears as a natural development from the interaction of characters and their environment."[61] Through the character of Ḥawwā', an orphaned girl who has been brought up by her grandmother and who works as a teacher, Lāshīn provides his readers with an effective illustration of the incompatibility between the dicta of modern education (particularly with regard to the emancipation of women) and traditional values. Ḥawwā' herself is well educated and belongs to a feminist society, before which she gives a stirring speech on education and its goals. However, her lonely and cloistered upbringing has not provided her with any experience on emotional matters, but has rather stifled them. Thus when she falls in love with the brother of the aristocratic girl whom she is tutoring, a young man considerably younger than herself, her feelings run away with her, if only in her own mind. When the young man is engaged to another girl, Ḥawwā''s entire life collapses. After agreeing to her grandmother's suggestion that they use magic and exorcism—the very personification of the values which she has been rejecting—she commits suicide.

This novel addresses itself forcibly to some prominent societal issues, and the statements and actions of the characters contribute to the discussion in a realistic and logical fashion. It succeeds to a remarkable degree in combining several of the different facets in novel composition into a satisfactory unity, all of which makes one regret that the next generation of writers was apparently unaware of his achievement. Lāshīn himself chose to spend the rest of his working life in the Department of Public Works. In the words of Hilary Kilpatrick, "his silence was Egypt's loss."

Variations on the Scheme: to West and East

In the preceding pages, we have identified some of the most significant contributors to the development of the novel in Egypt, involving contributions from not only Egyptian writers themselves but writers from other countries as well. It needs mentioning again that Egypt was chosen to provide a model for the earliest phases in the development of a novelistic tradition in the Arabic-speaking world because historical, geographical, and cultural factors com-

61. See Hilary Kilpatrick, "*Ḥawwā' bilā Ādam*: An Egyptian Novel of the 1930s," *JAL* 4 (1973): 48–56; see also Jad, *Form and Technique,* 67–71, 121–23.

bined to make it the Arabic-speaking society most conducive to the advancement of the novel genre during the period under discussion. In other parts of the region analogous processes were occurring; the chronology and local features were, needless to say, varied, but the basic sequence was the same: first, translation and/or arabization; second, imitation or adaptation; and then indigenous creation. Before turning to a discussion of more recent developments, we need to describe briefly developments in the other parts of the Arab world that were mentioned at the beginning of this chapter.

The model that was provided by Muḥammad al-Muwayliḥī's *Ḥadīth ʿĪsā ibn Hishām,* that of a classical genre being used to reflect the intellectual tensions of the era and to serve as a bridge to future developments, was replicated in other examples in Egypt and elsewhere in the Arab world. The famous Egyptian poet, Ḥāfiẓ Ibrāhīm (d. 1932), a close friend of the al-Muwayliḥī family, published a work of his own, *Layālī Saṭīḥ* (*Nights of Saṭīḥ,* 1906).[62] Ḥāfiẓ makes use of encounters between his narrator and a variety of inhabitants of Egypt to comment on a number of pressing issues of the time, including British rule of the Sudan, the presence of Syrian emigrés in Egypt, and the need for reform in women's rights. Among authors from elsewhere in the Arab world whose works show signs of the influence of the classical or neo-classical *maqāmah* tradition, mention should be made of Sulaymān Fayḍī al-Mawṣilī in Iraq with his *al-Riwāyah al-Īqāẓiyyah* (The Story of *al-Īqāẓ*—the name of Fayḍī's newspaper, 1919), ʿAlī al-Duʿājī (1909–49) in Tunis with his *Jawlah ḥawla ḥānāt al-baḥr al-abyaḍ al-mutawassiṭ* (Trip around the pubs of the Mediterranean, 1935), and in Morocco Muḥammad ibn ʿAbdallah al-Mu'aqqit with his *al-Riḥlah al-Marākushiyyah aw mir'āt al-masā'il al-waqtiyyah* (Marrakesh journey or mirror of problems of the time, 1920s) in which a narrator uses a Shaykh ʿAbd al-Hādī to guide him on his travels to and around the Maghrib.[63] While the dates of publication serve to illustrate the different time frames for the development of modern fiction in the separate national literatures of the

62. For *Layālī Saṭīḥ,* see Badr, *Taṭawwur al-riwāyah,* 77–83; Matti Moosa, *Origins of Modern Arabic Fiction,* 107–16; and Fedwa Malti-Douglas, "Al-Waḥdah al-naṣṣiyyah fī 'Layālī Saṭīḥ'," *Fuṣūl* 3, no. 2 (Jan.–Mar. 1983): 109–17.

63. For Fayḍī, see al-Nassāj, 158; ʿIzz al-dīn, *Al-Riwāyah fī al-ʿIrāq,* 41; ʿAbd al-raḥmān Majīd al-Rubayʿī, *Al-Shāṭi' al-Jadīd: Qirā'ah fī kuttāb al-qiṣṣah al-ʿArabiyyah* (Tunis: Al-Dār al-ʿArabiyyah li-al-kitāb, 1983), 54. For al-Duʿājī, see al-Nassāj, 192; ʿAbd al-kabīr al-Khaṭībī, *Le roman maghrebin,* 2d ed. (Rabat: Société Marocaine des Editeurs Réunies, 1979), 68; Ferid Ghazi, *Le roman et la nouvelle en Tunisie* (Tunis: Maison Tunisienne de l'édition, 1970), 47. For al-Mu'aqqit, see Nassāj, 203.

Arab world, all of these works can be regarded from the perspective of the 1980s as bridges between the narrative genres of Arabic classical prose and the emergence of a new entity which was to become the modern Arabic novel.[64]

Syria, Lebanon, and Palestine

The consequences of the the civil war of the 1850s caused the literary community of Syro-Lebanon to be fractured into several pieces. The contributions of members of this community to the cultural and literary life of Egypt have already been discussed. An equally important community which was to play a major role in the history of modern Arabic literature up until the beginning of the Second World War were the members of the *mahjar* (emigré) school in the United States. The acknowledged leader of that literary community was the renowned Jubrān Khalīl Jubrān (1883–1932). His works of fiction belong to the earlier part of his career and show a lively concern with some of the pressing societal issues of his time. *Al-Ajniḥah al-mutakassirah* (1908; *Broken Wings,* 1957) and *Al-Arwāḥ al-mutamarridah (1908; Spirits Rebellious,* 1941) discuss women's rights, forced marriage and the tyranny of the clergy in a forthright manner which antedates more modern advocates of these causes by many decades. As is the case with al-Manfalūṭī, these works, while not directly relevant to the development of a novel tradition *per se,* were of considerable importance in creating a readership for narratives that would fervently advocate the process of social change, written in a style that was refreshingly different from the verbal complexities of the *maqāmah* and traditional belles-lettrist prose.[65]

Jubrān's friend and biographer, Mīkhā'īl Nuʿaymah (1889–1983), made further contributions to the development of fiction, but mostly in the form of short stories. Many of them are set in Lebanon, but in this case we are not dealing with the simplistic contrasts of Jubrān (on which Nuʿaymah himself commented negatively in his

64. It should also be noted that the parodic spirit of the *maqāmah* genre is much in evidence in so contemporary a work as Emile Ḥabībī's *Al-Waqā'iʿ al-gharībah . . . ,* to be discussed in detail below.

65. Because of Jubrān's immense popularity in the Western world, works about his life are legion. It has to be observed that the critical merit of the majority is extremely questionable. Among works which discuss his fictional output, we would single out for mention: Hawi, *Kahlil Gibran;* Najm, *Al-qiṣṣah fī al-adab al-ʿArabī al-ḥadīth fī Lubnān,* 138–49; and Nadim Naimy, "The Mind and Thought of Khalīl Gibrān," *JAL* 5 (1974): 55–71.

biography), but with brief character sketches of Lebanese people, some of the most notable of which are set in mountain villages. These stories explore details in the life of these villagers: issues such as attitudes towards their families, their neighbours, and new ideas. Titles such as "Sanatuhā al-jadīdah," (Her new year) and "Maṣraʿ Sattūt (Sattūt's demise) are accomplished portraits of entrenched attitudes of family life, children, and the like. Nuʿaymah's excursions into longer fiction are less successful. Some episodes of his first novel, *Mudhakkirāt al-arqash* (1949; *Memoirs of a Vagrant Soul, or the Pitted Face,* 1952) were published as early as 1917, but his other novels belong to the period following the Second World War. These works have been characterized as "really sermons based on the doctrine of metempsychosis and of the ultimate union of the human soul with its divine origin," and the resorts to the supernatural which are to be found in them, in the view of one critic, "exercise beyond all legitimate limits the reader's willing suspension of disbelief."[66]

The Syrian analogue of Jurjī Zaydān in contributing to the repertoire of historical novels was Maʿrūf al-Arnā'ūṭ (1892–1947) who, beginning in 1929, published a series of four novels tracing early Islamic history, including one each on ʿUmar, the second caliph, and Ṭāriq ibn Ziyād, the hero of the conquest of Spain in the eighth century.[67] His contemporary, Shakīb al-Jābirī (b. 1912) was to make use of a familiar theme for his early experiments in fiction: the Arab visitor to Europe. For many critics, his novel, *Naham* (Greed, 1937), is the first Syrian novel to address itself to contemporary time and the issues of the day, although the detachment that separated the author of *Zaynab* from his homeland is here transferred into the fiction itself, in that the story is set in Germany and, apart from its hero, peopled by the citizens of that country.[68] This work too must

66. *Mudhakkirāt al-arqash* was serialized in 1917–18 but published in book form in Beirut by Maktabat Ṣādir in 1949; it was also translated into English by the author as *Memoirs of a Vagrant Soul* . . . (New York: Philosophical Library, 1952). For these and other details on Nuʿaymah, see C. Nijland, *Mīkhā'īl Nuʿaymah: Promotor of the Arabic Literary Revival* (Istanbul: Nederlands Historisch-Archaeologisch Instituut, 1975), 29. The novels are analyzed in detail in Muḥammad Ṣiddīq, "Mikhail N'aimy as Novelist," *Al-ʿArabiyya* 15, nos. 1 and 2 (Spring and Autumn 1982): 27.

67. For al-Arnā'ūṭ, see Ibrāhīm al-Saʿāfīn, *Taṭawwur al-riwāyah al-ʿArabiyyah al-ḥadīthah fī bilād al-Shām 1870–1967* (Baghdad: Manshūrāt Wizārat al-thaqāfah wa-al-iʿlām, 1980), 161–85.

68. Al-Jābirī's works are discussed in ʿAdnān ibn Dhurayl, *Adab al-qiṣṣah fī Sūriyyā* (Damascus: Manshūrāt Dār al-Fann al-ḥadīth al-ʿālamī, n.d.) 150–71; Husām al-Khaṭīb, *Riwāyāt taḥta al-mijhar* (Damascus: Manshūrāt Ittiḥād al-Kuttāb al-ʿArab,

be regarded as an important intermediate step, leading to the emergence of a more sophisticated kind of fictional creativity, most particularly through the work of Tawfīq Yūsuf ʿAwwād which we will consider in the next chapter.

The most important figure in the early history of Palestinian fiction was Khalīl Baydas (1875–1949), whose novel, *al-Wārith* (The heir, 1920), is regarded as the first in this national tradition. An unsubtle account of a Syrian who falls into the clutches of a Jewish dancer in Egypt, it is the forerunner of a number of works by more recent Palestinian novelists that treat the manifold problems of their people in fictions of wide variety and great virtuosity. That this early example should involve a negative portrait of a relationship with a Jewish character as early as 1920 shows not a little prescience.[69]

Iraq

As Yūsuf ʿIzz al-dīn demonstrates in his study of the development of the novel in Iraq, many features present there were similar to those in Egypt. The beginnings of prose fiction were again tied closely to the emergence of a press tradition, something which Ottoman censorship kept under tighter control. Initial experiments in novel writing tend to fall into the historical and/or entertainment categories, including within the former category a translated historical novel about King Henry the Fourth of England entitled *al-ʿAdl asās al-mulk* (Justice is the basis of monarchy, 1909) and another by Sulaymān al-Dakhīl entitled *Nāẓim Pāshā,* (1911), which claims to be a literary, historical, social, and political story.[70] For much the same reasons as those mentioned above regarding Egypt, Iraqi writers during the period before 1939 tended to concentrate their efforts in the realm of the short story. The most famous prose writer of the period was Maḥmūd Aḥmad al-Sayyid. His novel, *Fi sabīl al-zawāj* (On the marriage path, 1921) is a melodramatic and highly roman-

---

1983), 38–73; and Eros Baldissera, "Shakīb al-Jābirī, pionere del romanzo siriano," *Quaderni di studi arabi* 4 (1986): 117–28. The predilection among Arab male novelists for introducing idealized, sexually liberated European women into their works is discussed by Rotraud Wieland in *Das Bild der Europaer,* 489–553.

69. For a discussion of Baydas, see Aḥmad Abū Maṭar, *Al-Riwāyah fī al-adab al-Filasṭīnī 1950–75* (Beirut: Al-Mu'assasah al-ʿArabiyyah li-al-dirāsāt wa-al-nashr, 1980), 48–50; and *An Anthology of Modern Palestinian Literature,* ed. Salma Khadra' Jayyusi (New York: Columbia Univ. Press, 1992), 11–16.

70. See ʿIzz al-dīn, *Al-Riwāyah fī al-ʿIrāq,* 18–20.

ticized tale set in India; while it contains a certain amount of implicit criticism of woman's position in society, it remains within the tradition of swashbuckling historical romances of the European tradition and, as ʿIzz al-din observes, of *A Thousand and One Nights* as well. A later work, *Jalāl Khālid* (1928), is regarded as more significant in the history of the Iraqi novel in that it is used to portray some of the events surrounding the Iraqi revolt against the British occupying forces in 1920.[71]

The Maghrib

"The development of the Arabic novel in the Maghrib," says Muḥammad ʿAfīfī in his study of the Maghribi novel and drama, "was influenced to a large degree stylistically, artistically and creatively by the development of the literary press, by Western genre definitions, and by examples of Western works which were translated in the press."[72] The combination of a society with a solidly conservative religious base on the one hand and the prevalence of the French language as the privileged medium of culture and education on the other has served to retard the development of a narrative prose tradition in Arabic until comparatively recently. Pantucek can describe the situation in Algeria by saying that "il serait difficile de qualifier cette periode de véritable expansion au sens propre des belles-lettres."[73]

In spite of such cultural factors, writers in the Maghrib were to contribute significant works not only to their own incipient national literary traditions but also to the fictional tradition in Arabic as a whole. A prominent Tunisian author, Maḥmūd al-Masʿadī (b. 1911) was to make contributions to modern Arabic narrative very different from the picaresque romp of his fellow countryman, ʿAlī al-Duʿājī. The most famous was entitled *al-Sudd* (The dam, written between 1939 and 1940 but not published until 1955) and was in the mode of the philosophical tales penned earlier by Jubrān and Nuʿaymah; its comparatively later publication date can be regarded as a reflection

71. For Maḥmūd al-Sayyid, see al-Nassāj, 156–60; ʿIzz al-dīn, *Al-Riwāyah fī al-ʿIraq*, 66–75, 151–66; and ʿAbd al-raḥmān Majīd al-Rubayʿī *Al-Shāṭiʾ al-jadīd: Qirāʾ-ah fī kuttāb al-qiṣṣah al-ʿArabiyyah* (Tunis: Al-Dār al-ʿArabiyyah li-al-kitāb, 1983), 54–60.

72. Muḥammad ʿAfīfī, *Al-Fann al-qaṣaṣī wa-al-masraḥī fī al-Maghrib al-ʿArabī 1900–1965* (N.p.: Dār al-Fikr, 1971), 85–86.

73. Pantucek, 81–82.

of differing chronological patterns of literary development in the various regions of the Arab world. The work, which was warmly welcomed by Ṭāhā Ḥusayn,[74] narrates the tale of Ghaylān and his female companion, Maymūnah, who come to a valley where the people worship a goddess named Ṣāhabbā'. Ghaylān determines to change the way of life of this community by building a dam, but no sooner is the structure completed than it is destroyed by mysterious forces. Whatever the other qualities of the work, critical opinion is virtually unanimous in its esteem for the extreme elegance of its language, a factor which seems to have insured it an enduring place in the history of modern Maghribi fiction. Another work of al-Mas'adī's, *Ḥaddathanā Abū Hurayrah Qāla* (Abū Hurayrah told us the following story, 1979), saw a similar time lapse between composition and publication, from 1944 to 1979. This work makes creative use of the discourse mode of *ḥadīth* (records of the Islamic Prophet Muḥammad's actions during his lifetime) to create a picture of ancient times in order to serve as an allegory for the present.[75]

In 1947 Aḥmad Riḍā Hūhū published what is generally regarded as the first Algerian novel in Arabic, *Ghādat umm al-qurā* (The maid of the city). As the title implies, its primary topic is love and marriage; the focus is on the death of Zakiyyah, a young girl who is forced into a marriage with a rich man when she is really in love with her cousin, Jamīl. Topic and treatment are both very reminiscent of Haykal's earlier novel.[76]

Commentators on the development of the novel genre in Morocco see its development as being intimately tied to the need to reflect on the political and societal tensions that led up to the Revolution of 1956. Indeed it is not until 1957 that what the critical establishment regard as the first Moroccan novel in Arabic is published: 'Abd al-majīd ibn Jallūn's *Fī al-ṭufūlah* (In childhood).[77] Clearly reflecting the author's own childhood experiences (including a period spent in Manchester, England), it is used to criticize the mores of the author's homeland and to advocate social and political change. In 1961 Muḥammad 'Afīfī can still express the opinion that "narrative

74. Ṭāhā Ḥusayn, *Min adabinā al-mu'aṣir* (Beirut: Dār al-Ādāb, 1958), 113 ff.

75. In discussing al-Mas'adī, Ferid Ghazi talks of "son style attachant," 45. See also Ḥusayn, *Min adabinā al-mu'āṣir,* 116; and Jean Fontaine, *20 Ans de littérature tunisienne* (Tunis: Maison Tunisienne de l'édition, 1977), 36.

76. See al-Nassāj, 220; and 'Abd al-kabīr al-Khaṭībi, 70.

77. Laḥmadānī Ḥamīd, *Al-Riwāyah al-Maghribiyyah wa-ru'yā al-wāqi' al-ijtimā'ī* (Casablanca: Dār al-Thaqāfah, 1985), 253–61.

art in Morocco is still in the formative stage; it has yet to achieve a personality of its own, and, if any well-integrated works exist, they are very few in number."[78]

The contributions of Maghribi authors that are reflected in the contents of the next chapter will show that, whatever may have been the retarding effects of these cultural factors on the development of the novel, vigorous programs of arabization (*taʿrīb*) have led to a situation where writers of Arabic expression are now not only full participants to the world of Arabic fiction, but are also among the most experimental in their adoption of new modes of expression.

One area not covered thus far in this recklessly brief survey of novelistic beginnings in the Arab world is the Arabian Peninsula. The transformation of the societies of that rugged area is intimately associated with the discovery of oil and the opportunities for development and urbanization that such enormous mineral resources have made possible. The results of such trends in the educational and cultural sphere are now becoming known not only to littérateurs in other parts of the Arab world but also to Western scholars. From the limited amount of fiction that has been published thus far, it is clear that many new voices from this region are making original contributions to the novelistic tradition in Arabic.

Hilary Kilpatrick begins an article, "The Arabic novel—a single tradition?" with an alarming, yet pertinent, question: "Does the Arabic novel exist?"[79] While acknowledging that, in comparison with Egypt, the novel was slow to develop in the other countries of the Arab world, she points out that the process of the *nahḍah,* characterized (as in any such movement) by occasional false starts and accelerations, has now done its own chronological leveling. The chiastic framework adopted in this chapter has attempted to reflect the variegated nature, timing, and pace of this process. As we have just noted, the novel in Arabic has been a relatively recent literary phenomenon in certain regions, and for particular cultural and political reasons. However, since the Second World War the novel in Arabic has developed in its awareness of both generic purpose and potential for creativity. Today it constitutes a vigorous cultural medium based on common indigenous factors of language and cultural and religious heritage, and on the continuing response to the challenge of

78. Muḥammad ʿAfīfī, *Al-Qiṣṣah al-Maghribiyyah al-ḥadīthah* (Casablanca: Maktabat al-Waḥdah al-ʿArabiyyah, 1961), 7.

79. Hilary Kilpatrick, "The Arabic Novel—a single tradition?" *JAL* 5 (1974): 93–107.

the West, expressed initially in opposition to colonial occupation and thereafter in the exploration of new political and cultural relationships with the nations of the West. Within this larger framework, it is also true—and undoubtedly desirable—that there are a number of local novelistic traditions, each one concentrating on the burning issues of the nation or region while at the same time inevitably reflecting its political, social, and cultural priorities and biases. It is this happy mixture of unity and diversity which will be studied in the next chapter.

3

The Period of Maturity

Political and Social Background

The novel, according to Philippe Sollers, is "la manière dont cette societé se parle."[1] During the last five decades the societies within the Arab world have witnessed changes on a wide scale in both their political and economic way of life. It should come as no surprise therefore that this same period has seen a tremendous expansion within the field of the Arabic novel. It is the purpose of this chapter to trace the developments and experiments which have taken place by examining themes and techniques used by novelists writing since the outset of the Second World War. However, bearing in mind the close connection noted above between novel writing and circumstances within society (however "pure" some writers and critics may wish the genre to be),[2] it seems useful to give a brief summary of some of the major events and trends in the Arab world against the background of which this outpouring of fiction will be viewed.

To the West the mention of the Arab world has traditionally invoked images of the camel and of men wearing the *kaffiyyah* and headband. To these stereotypical images has surely been added in recent decades that of the oil well. The discovery of oil in the Arab world has of course had an immense impact on the recent history of the region and has caused a radical shift in the balance of influence within the area itself and of economic power within the world as a whole. ʿAbd al-raḥmān Munīf (b. 1933), the Saudi novelist whose works will be examined in detail below, asserts in an interview that "as a sphere and topic, oil may help uncover some novelistic aspects

1. Quoted in Jonathan Culler, *Structuralist Poetics* (Ithaca, N.Y.: Cornell Univ. Press, 1975), 189.

2. See Booth, pt. 1, 89 ff.

in our contemporary life in the Arab world."[3] It should be noted that Munīf's academic training was as a petroleum economist; he may thus be not a little *parti pris.* Indeed, during the 1980s he has followed up on this somewhat coy opinion by penning the Arab world's largest novelistic project to date, the quintet of novels, *Mudun al-milḥ.* Incidentally, we will be examining later in the chapter the effect of novel writing as an avocation on the development of the genre in the Arab world. In his novel *al-Baḥth ʿan Walīd Masʿūd,* (In search of Walīd Masʿūd, 1978), Jabrā Ibrāhīm Jabrā provides us with a historical frame of reference on this point from which to view the extent of the changes which have occurred. Ibrāhīm al-Ḥājj Nawfal, one of the narrators in the novel, comments on his career as a businessman in Iraq and points out to his audience that he had been writing about economics at a time when "the demand that Iraq have a twenty-per cent share in the revenues of the British Petroleum Company was regarded as a nationalist demand which would prove enormously difficult to achieve and would require both perseverance and determination."[4] To a world that has become accustomed not only to a different approach towards the Middle East region, its various nations states and their alignments, but also to the significance of oil as a commodity and an economic weapon, the changes that have occurred in the period under consideration here are indeed striking.

These current realities are part of the larger and longer process, namely the complex web of relationships between the cultures of East and West, itself the subject of a whole series of novels. A comparison of al-Ṭayyib Ṣāliḥ's novel, *Mawsim al-hijrah ilā al-shamāl* (1967; *Season of Migration to the North,* 1969)—discussed in detail in the next chapter—with earlier works in which Arabs give their impressions of Europe and Europeans provides another illustration of the changing nature of the relationship between the cultures of the Middle East and the West (which, from a Sudanese perspective, Ṣāliḥ prefers to term North and South).

In an earlier chapter we described the process whereby the Arab world "rediscovered" Europe during the nineteenth century. The interest of Europe in the Arab world took a rather more pragmatic form as France and Britain occupied, or otherwise participated in

3. *Al-Maʿrifah* 204 (Feb. 1979): 188.

4. Jabrā Ibrāhīm Jabrā, *Al-Baḥth ʿan Walīd Masʿūd* (Beirut: Dār al-Ādāb, 1978), 311.

the governmental process of, various countries in the region. A natural reaction to this was the formation of a number of nationalist movements whose aspirations, whether purely local or pan-Arab, were dashed by the mandate agreements which followed the First World War. The apparent successes of the "Arab Revolt," even if they were often viewed by English readers through the distorting lens of T. E. Lawrence's narrative, had raised among the Arab nations considerable hopes for independence when the fighting was over. With the publication of the Balfour Declaration of 1917, declaring that a homeland for the Jewish people was a goal of the British government, the basis was created for a continuing series of misunderstandings and deceptions over the future of Palestine. Hopes for independence that had been engendered among the Arabic-speaking peoples of the Middle East were crushed as the French and British announced their agreement to divide the former Ottoman dominions into a series of "protectorates": France undertook the administration of the Maghrib, Lebanon, and Syria; the British became the mandate power in Palestine and Transjordan. These arrangements were duly ratified by the newly-established League of Nations in July 1922, along with a declaration of a strictly limited independence for Egypt and Iraq. Against such a background of foiled political aspirations, it is hardly surprising that there were wide-scale revolts aimed at the colonial power in both Egypt (1919) and Iraq (1920), but they were soon quashed. Both these events have often been used by littérateurs writing in all genres as a symbol of resistance to foreign domination in any form and of the expression of the popular will.

Within such a scenario of political expediency and broken promises, the relationship between the Arab nations and the Western powers (most especially, the two "protecting" powers, Britain and France) during the interwar period was, not unnaturally, one of suspicion and distrust. In Palestine, the British found themselves bogged down in a political quagmire largely of their own devising; what few attempts were made to reconcile the unreconcilable only succeeded in antagonizing both the indigenous Palestinians and the increasing number of Zionist immigrants. On the political front, Egypt and Syria were granted a modicum of independence; in the Arabian Peninsula the Saudi family was allowed to consolidate its control; in 1943 an agreement between Sunnis and Maronites in Lebanon led to the foundation of a Lebanese state, one that was based on a tragically fragile balance as the events of the last decade have shown all too clearly. However, for the majority of nations in the Arab world, the limited nature of the political gains during this period was abruptly underlined by the actions of the occupying powers at the outset of the Second World War. Whatever gestures of "independence" may have been granted were now abruptly swept aside as the armies of the Axis powers and the Allies fought their way across North Africa, thus involving a large segment of the Arab world directly in the conflict, and other parts through overt military occupation.

The Second World War and its consequences led to a transformation in the patterns of Western influence and hegemony in the Middle East. While the Arab nations may have shared in the international sense of relief that global conflict was at an end, their feelings were also somewhat more sanguine; the memory of the way expectations could so easily be dashed in such circumstances was too fresh. Along with renewed hopes for independence there was continuing resentment towards not only the colonial powers but also many of the *anciens régimes* with their entrenched and often corrupt power structures. This was a volatile political and social mixture, as a number of uprisings and political assassinations during the immediate postwar period can demonstrate. Jacques Berque quite rightly terms the moment "a decisive juncture in contemporary Arab history. . . . The assassination of an Egyptian prime minister bore witness to the rise of extremism, the founding of the Baʿth party and the 'free officers' conspiracy signaled the summons to new political horizons."[5]

The conduct of the Great Powers during the war had convinced even the most dogged pursuers of local national interests of the need to unite efforts and forces. The urgings of a number of advocates of Arab nationalism (such as Qusṭanṭīn Zurayq, Edmond Rabbāth, and Ṣāṭiʿ al-Ḥuṣrī) were now to bear fruit in the establishment in Cairo of the Arab League in March 1945.[6] The choice of the Egyptian capital as the site for the League's headquarters not only acknowledged Cairo's central geographical position in the Arab world but also symbolised a role for Egypt which ʿAbd al-nāṣir was to pursue with vigor in the next decade.

Hishām Sharābī is of the opinion, in retrospect, that from the outset "the League fell far short of the hopes and aspirations of most Arab Nationalists."[7] In any case, the newly-created body was presented within a year or so with a major crisis, one which again in-

5. Berque, 271.

6. See Hourani, 260–323.

7. Hisham Sharabi, *Nationalism and Revolution in the Arab World* (Princeton: Van Nostrand, 1966), 8.

volved the Western powers, namely the establishment of the state of Israel. In November 1947 a "partition plan" for Palestine was published. In April 1948 many inhabitants of the Palestinian village of Dayr Yasin were massacred by Zionists, an event which prompted many families to leave the region. In May, the State of Israel was proclaimed, marking the first of many subsequent conflicts between Arabs and Israelis. The period which we are considering in this chapter is punctuated with unfortunate regularity by conflict between the Arab nations and the Zionist state. The years 1948, 1956, 1967, 1973 (termed by Berque a "semi-success"),[8] and 1982 are important events in the history of the modern Arab world. The plight of the Palestinian people continues to be one of the major focuses of Arab novelists; in Abdallah Laroui's words, it is "the Arab problem *par excellence.*"[9]

In the decades that followed the conclusion of the Second World War, the majority of countries within the Arab world went through a period of considerable turmoil and transformation, both political and social. With the emergence of two "superpowers," the United States and the Soviet Union, alignments, both international and local, were adjusted and in many cases completely transformed. The 1950s witnessed a number of revolutions in the Arab world (1952 in Egypt, for example, and 1958 in Iraq and the Sudan). The long-sought goal of independence was granted to several nations: Sudan, Tunisia, and Morocco in 1956, Kuwait in 1961, and, after a protracted and vicious civil conflict beginning in 1954, Algeria in 1962. Elsewhere conflicts between different peoples have proved more difficult to resolve; those involving the Kurds in Iraq and the peoples of the Southern part of the Sudan continue to preoccupy the rulers of those countries. There were attempts at bringing the idea and ideal of Arab unity to fruition: one which was implemented between Egypt and Syria—the United Arab Republic, 1958–61; and another attempt to include Iraq in the Republic which was never brought to full fruition. The Egyptian Revolution and its charismatic leader, Jamāl ʿAbd al-nāṣir (Nasser), took the lead in forging new alliances which directly confronted the interests of Britain, the former occupying power. The arms deal with the Czechs in 1955, the military and political fiasco surrounding the tripartite attack on Suez in 1956

8. Berque, 93.

9. Abdallah Laroui, *The Crisis of the Arab Intellectual* (Berkeley: Univ. of California Press, 1976), 171. See also Salma Khadra'Jayyusi's comments on this period: *Modern Arabic Poetry: An Anthology* (New York: Columbia Univ. Press, 1987), 15–16.

followed by the withdrawal of British and French forces from the region and the nationalization of the Suez Canal, the beginnings of the movement of nonaligned nations; these were heady days indeed.

With all this movement and sense of dynamism, it is hardly surprising that this was also a period of intense discussion of the role of literature and the writer in society.[10] The decade of the 1950s witnessed a fierce argument over the issue of commitment. The foundation of the literary periodical *al-Ādāb* in 1953 was and has remained the most obvious symbol of the development in these decades of a movement whose bases are well summarized in the quotation from Ra'īf al-Khūrī to the effect that "the Arab writer is committed, particularly in this period of Arab national revival, to producing works with a conscious and deliberate political meaning."[11] As will be shown below, the novel, "as the model by which society conceives of itself, the discourse in and through which it articulates the world,"[12] has been one of the primary areas of such activity and of critical commentary on it.

And yet, amid all the dynamism there were also profound doubts about the direction in which the Arab world was heading and the means which were being used to get it there. Littérateurs were not slow to express their views along these lines, often at considerable cost to their own well-being. Poems were written which expressed varying degrees of dissatisfaction and disgust with the state of Arab society; one thinks of Qabbānī's "Khubz wa-ḥashīsh wa-qamar" (Bread, hashish and moonlight, 1955), Adūnīs's "Marthiyyat al-ayyām al-ḥāḍirah" (Elegy for the present days, 1958), and Khalīl Ḥāwī's "al-Aʿzar ʿām 1962" (Lazarus 1962, 1965). In the same novel from which we have already cited an extract, Jabrā Ibrāhīm Jabrā once again provides us with a clear expression of views on this subject. Parenthetically, I might point out that Jabrā's predilection for setting the action of his novels among groups of intellectuals and his use of the multinarrator technique serve to make his novels a gold mine of views on a whole variety of subjects connected with life in the modern Arab world. In the current instance, we are dealing with the main character of this novel, Walīd Masʿūd, the Palestinian who emerges from a period in an Israeli prison during which he has been

10. That the coincidence of these political and literary phenomena is in fact no accident is suggested by Berque, 271, and M. M. Badawi, *A Critical Introduction to Modern Arabic Poetry* (Cambridge: Cambridge Univ. Press, 1975), 207–8.

11. See Jayyusi, *Trends and Movements*, 557.

12. Culler, 189.

tortured. In an unforgettable passage he describes the darker side of Arab society at this time:

> I saw my homeland for which I had just been prepared to go through the very tortures of Hell itself applying those very same tortures to anyone who fell into the hands of the people in authority. From the Arab Gulf to the Atlantic Ocean I heard a cry, I heard weeping and the sound of sticks and plastic hoses. Capitals and casbas, the secret police were everywhere, on mountain tops and in the valleys below; men in neat civilian suits walking to and fro like a thousand shuttles on a thousand looms, hauling off to the centres of darkness people by the tens and hundreds.[13]

The almost sneering use of ʿAbd al-nāṣir's ringing phrase of Arab unity, "from the Arab Gulf to the Atlantic Ocean," draws attention to the grim side of the life of intellectuals in many countries of the Arab world at this time. Najīb Maḥfūẓ's novel, *al-Karnak* (1974), made into a highly exploitative film during the heyday of President Sādāt's regime, is just one of many fictional works that portray just how grim such a life could be;[14] others include Munīf's *Sharq al-Mutawassiṭ* (East of the Mediterranean, 1977; *À l'est de la Mediterranee,* 1985), Ṣunʿallāh Ibrāhīm's *Tilka al-rāʾiḥah* (1966; *The Smell of It,* 1971), and the quartet of novels by the Kuwaiti writer Ismāʿīl Fahd Ismāʿīl, set in Iraq, to be discussed in detail in the next chapter.

The 1960s emerge then as a decade when the different revolutionary regimes in the Arab world moved from the initial flush of success, which independence and its aftermath had brought, towards a process of formulating some of the ideological principles on which the revolution had been or was to be based, and of putting such principles into practice. This process almost inevitably led to a number of challenges, particularly from those whose view of revolution in general and of the particular revolution in question was different from that of the authorities. The challenges which took written form were of varying degrees of frankness. As many novelists have observed, the copious use of symbolism at this time was not merely an artistic phenomenon but a matter of strict practicality. The more explicit writers could be handled with considerable severity, as Ṣabrī

13. Jabrā, *Al-Baḥth ʿan Walīd Masʿūd,* 249.

14. See also Raymond William Baker, *Egypt's Uncertain Revolution under Nasser and Sadat* (Cambridge, Mass.: Harvard Univ. Press, 1978), 151.

Ḥāfiẓ notes.[15] The attitude of intellectuals to the governmental structure in Egypt, and their sense of alienation, is portrayed with brilliant clarity in Maḥfūẓ's novel, *Thartharah fawq al-Nīl* (Chatter on the Nile, 1966; *Adrift on the Nile,* 1993), a work which clearly antagonized the Egyptian authorities at the highest level and almost led to his incarceration.

The June War of 1967 has clearly been a defining moment in the modern history of the Arab nations. The Arabic term used to describe it is *al-naksah,* meaning, "setback" (in itself, a typically creative use of the language's own potential for verbal puns, in that the earlier 1948 war was termed *al-nakbah,* "the disaster"). But as a large number of anguished studies of the event and its implications were to point out, it was in fact a devastatingly terminal blow to the pretensions carefully nurtured by the political sector during the early years of independence and revolution; in the words of Fārūq ʿAbd al-qādir, an Egyptian critic of drama, it was "a total defeat of regimes, institutions, structures, ideas, and leaders."[16] Ḥalīm Barakāt is both a sociologist and novelist, and his novel, *ʿAwdat al-ṭāʾir ilā al-baḥr* (The return of the Flying Dutchman to the sea, 1969; *Days of Dust,* 1974) manages to identify some of the major sources of the anger and resentment that were to follow. For the Arabs this was a war with no heroes; where the battle for control of the air was concerned—and that was crucial—it was over much too quickly. What made the impact even worse and the anger more intense was that the Arab world was being told by its leaders until the very last moment that it was on its way to a glorious victory. In the view of many, these events provided an all-too-graphic illustration of the kinds of problems to which intellectuals and littérateurs had been addressing themselves, in necessarily guarded and often symbolic terms, throughout the earlier years of the decade and before. Now, however, the carefully crafted images of political leaderships and the visions of a wonderful future based on notions of equality and justice were shown to be cruel distortions of the realities of the Arab world; the extent of the disease was shown to be so great that there was no longer a question of suppressing overt discussion of its many

15. Sabry Hafez, "The Egyptian Novel in the Sixties," *JAL* 7 (1976): 77. See also Yūsuf Idrīs, as quoted in the *New York Times Review of Books,* 16 Mar. 1980: 3 ff.

16. Fārūq ʿAbd al-Qādir, *Izdihār wa-suqūṭ al-masraḥ al-Miṣrī* (Cairo: Dār al-fikr al-muʿāṣir, 1979), 164.

ramifications. What ensued has been characterised by Abdallah Laroui as a "moral crisis" which "culminated in a period of anguished self-criticism, a searching reappraisal of postwar Arab culture and political practice."[17]

The consequences of this conflict remain contributing factors to the course of strategic and political events in the region. In general, regimes survived. In Jordan, King Ḥusayn found his country overwhelmed by an influx of Palestinian refugees from the West Bank. This post-1967 period witnesses a turn by Palestinian groups towards more direct means of influencing policy, most notably in the appearance of the *fidā'iyyīn* (fedayeen, those prepared to sacrifice themselves). By 1970 the tensions between the political priorities of the Jordanian government and those of the Palestinians had reached a breaking point, and in a period of brutal fighting, termed "Black September" by the Palestinians, the freedom fighters were driven out of Jordan and into Lebanon and Syria. In the intervening period, the relationship between Jordan and the Palestinians has oscillated between enmity and cooperation, as political alliances have swung this way and that, but today (1993) ʿAmmān, Jordan's capital, teems with Palestinians; the numbers have recently been increased by a further influx resulting from the expulsion of Palestinians from Kuwait in the wake of the Gulf War of 1990. As the other nations of the Arab world face their own problems and priorities, the fate of the Palestinians—punctured with dreadful regularity by such barbaric acts as the Tell al-Zaʿtar and Sabrah-Shatilah massacres in Beirut—is to remain without a homeland, condemned to one or another kind of exile; in the words of the Palestinian poet, Tawfīq Ṣāyigh (1923–71):

> "Your passport"?
> without it there is no entry
> and you don't carry it
> therefore no entry.[18]

In Egypt, the regime of Jamāl ʿAbd al-nāṣir, for so long the admired political figurehead of the Arab world, also survived, but the crushing nature of the 1967 defeat, and his attempts at reconciling differences between groups and nations in such a situation fraught with

17. Laroui, viii. See also Muḥammad Barādī, in *al-Ādāb* (Feb.–Mar. 1980): 3.

18. Poem 24 from *Qasidat K,* trans. Issa J. Boullata in *Modern Arab Poets 1950–1975* (Washington, D.C.: Three Continents, 1976), 147.

recrimination and frustration, proved overwhelming, and he died in September 1970. His successor, Anwar al-Sādāt, was essentially an unknown quantity on the international scene. The Israeli capture (and exploitation) of Sinai served as a continuing affront to Egyptian honor, a situation that led to a lengthy confrontation and stalemate at the Suez Canal during the early 1970s. Al-Sādāt, however, gave the appearance of concentrating much of his attention on the domestic agenda. Certain civil liberties that had been generally lacking during the 1960s were restored under the most carefully controlled circumstances, including the right of speaking (and writing) "absolutely frankly," all within limits of appropriateness determined by the government. That most of the books written at the time were violently anti-Nasser (including Tawfīq al-Ḥakīm's *ʿAwdat al-Waʿy* [1972, published 1974; *Return of Consciousness,* 1984]) made it clear that a change in political priorities and alignments was underway. As if to underline that direction, al-Sādāt announced his policy of *infitāḥ,* opening up Egyptian markets to both local and international capitalism. The major result of that policy has been to widen still further the gap between the wealthy and poor of the country, a theme that has, not surprisingly, spawned a very large amount of fictional writing.

As these social transformations were in progress, the confrontation at the Suez Canal continued. The pressure for action mounted, and in October 1973 al-Sādāt responded: the "crossing" of the Suez Canal caught the Israeli forces by surprise, and, even though the Arab armies were eventually driven back, the cracking of the "Bar Lev Line" was a substantial psychological boost for al-Sādāt, even though its impact elsewhere in the region was minimal; Berque terms the event a "semi-success."[19] In 1977 al-Sādāt undertook another bold initiative when he agreed to travel to Jerusalem and addressed the Israeli Knesset. This was followed by a peace agreement between the two countries and, in March 1979, the signing of the Camp David accords in Washington. However well these events may have played on the world stage, the assassination of al-Sādāt in 1981 by members of a popular Islamic group in his own country and the almost empty streets in Cairo on the day of his funeral were potent reminders of the extent to which he had lost touch with the political realities of Egypt and the region as a whole. In 1974 Abdallah Laroui had suggested that the post-1967 period was to be charac-

19. Berque, 93.

terized by "an increasingly pronounced polarization of forces."[20] The recent history of Egypt and its relationships with other Arab states provides just one illustration of how accurate his comment was to be.

1979 witnessed another transforming event in the recent history of the Middle East: the ouster of the Shah of Iran and his replacement by a conservative Shiʿite religious leadership headed by Ayatallah Khomeini. It is obviously impossible to explore here all the ramifications of the Iranian revolution, but the impetus that it has given to Shiʿite communities and to the revival of Islam as a potent political force throughout the region is obvious enough. A brief consideration of events in Lebanon and in Iraq and the Gulf states may serve as examples. The constitution for the Lebanese state, drafted in the early 1940s, had been based on a delicate balance between the different communities—Maronite Christian, Orthodox Christian, Sunni Muslim, Shiʿite Muslim, Druse, and others. This balance, insofar that it ever existed in fact, had been completely disrupted by a number of factors: among them, differential birthrates, patterns of emigration, and the influx of Palestinian refugees. Outbreaks of communal strife had occurred previously (in 1958, for example), but in 1975 a full-scale civil-war erupted. Since the groupings of forces involved not only political but religious affiliations, the conflict was able to transform and renew itself throughout the 1980s, involving differing configurations and alliances both local and international. The emergence of the Shiʿite community in the south of Lebanon, the region that lies directly to the north of Israel, and the vigorous support that the community continues to receive from Iran, have been major factors in the course of recent Lebanese history. Ḥanān al-Shaykh's novel, *Ḥikāyat Zahrah* (1980; *The Story of Zahra,* 1986) is set among this community, both in Beirut and in the south, and it serves as just one of a whole series of works that recount the agony of a society in the process of tearing itself apart. And yet, throughout all this, Beirut has managed to remain a major center for book publication and intellectual life in general. It is such resilience that will be needed in large quantities as the various communities attempt to turn an uneasy peace into a new version of the open and prosperous nation that Lebanon previously presented to the outside world.

The complexities of the Gulf region (and the failure of many Western politicians to appreciate them) reside in no small measure

20. Laroui, viii.

in the presence of significant communities of Shiʿite Muslims in Iraq and the areas of Gulf states (including Saudi Arabia) that face the Arabian Gulf. The fact that the majority of the world's proven oil reserves lie under precisely this particular region has, of course, not been lost on the leaders of the nations of the Western world as they have become ever more dependent on such sources of supply.[21] The exact size of these Shiʿite communities constitutes the kind of information that the rulers of the countries concerned prefer not to release; Iraq certainly has a Shiʿite majority. As the proselytizing activities of the Iranian revolution expanded across the Gulf, it was clearly in the interest of Saudi Arabia and the other oil-rich states of the southern Gulf that Iraq engage in a war with Iran that would help to curb the increasing amount of political agitation that was occurring within the Shiʿite communities. The Iran-Iraq war of the 1980s was immensely costly in terms of human lives and military hardware.[22] It was when Kuwait, in what would appear to be a somewhat hubristic gesture, demanded repayment of the money that it had loaned Iraq to conduct the war, that Ṣaddām Ḥusayn, the President of Iraq, annexed Kuwait in order to achieve a number of political goals: to fulfill Iraq's long-standing claim to the territory, to punish Kuwait for its oil-pricing policies, and—a well-tried ploy—to distract attention from his own domestic difficulties. The result of Iraq's invasion was the Gulf War, involving yet another incursion by Western forces into the region, the destruction of most of Iraq's social infrastructure, and the emergence in the aftermath of the conflict of a number of potentially interesting new alignments, not the least of which is the possibility of peace agreements between Israel and its various neighbors.

While these have been some of the most prominent political events in recent decades, the Arab world has also witnessed a series of apparently never-ending conflicts in regions that are less in the limelight of publicity: in the south of the Sudan, an ongoing conflict between the Muslim ruling forces of the northern part of the country and the peoples of the south; in former Spanish Sahara, a conflict between Polisario forces supported by Algeria and the Mo-

21. The history of the development of that interest and its results on one (unnamed but easily identifiable) country in the region are the subject of ʿAbd al-raḥmān Munīf's vast quintet of novels, *Mudun al-milḥ* (Cities of salt) (Beirut: Al-mu'assasah al-ʿArabiyyah li-al-dirāsāt wa-al-nashr), to be discussed below.

22. The war memorial on the Faw Peninsula in Iraq lists some two million dead.

roccan army; in the state of Libya, a continuing involvement in the internal affairs of Chad to the south; and in Iraq (along with Iran and Turkey) the struggle of the Kurdish peoples for independence and a separate homeland.

Conflict, then, has been a continuing feature of the recent history of the Middle East region, a contemporary reflection perhaps of a reality that has scored this strategically (and now economically) important area for centuries. As will be detailed below, conflict is also a major theme of many works of modern Arabic fiction, hardly surprising in view of the impact of the events described above on the societies of the nations involved. Alongside the international, national, and communal conflicts involving weapons of destruction, there have also been conflicts of politics and ideology. As noted above, the 1967 defeat led to a complete re-examination of priorities from every point of view. Two terms occur frequently in publications of the 1970s: *turāth* (heritage) and *aṣālah* (authenticity to one's historical roots). A whole series of distinguished Arab intellectuals devoted themselves to a complete revision of ideas concerning the relationship of the Arab present to the past and the implications for the future. A brief listing of such intellectuals would include Abdallah Laroui (from whom we have already quoted), Ṣādiq al-ʿAẓm, Ḥasan Ḥanafī, Muḥammad ʿĀbid al-Jābirī, Ḥusayn Muruwwah, and Ṭayyib Tizzīnī.[23] A further significant factor in many Arab societies (and in their literary traditions) has been the emergence of the woman's voice, expressing the desire for profound changes in attitude, behavior, and opportunity, and doing so with particular effectiveness in the realm of fiction.[24]

While these intellectual currents have formed the backdrop to much debate about principles in the Arab world during the last two decades, it is clearly the revival of Islam as a popular religious phenomenon that continues to be a predominant feature of most of the countries of the region; indeed, it would appear that the process is rapidly expanding and intensifying. Adapting to different local situations, the leaders of these movements have been extremely successful in exploiting a number of societal factors to their own advantage:

23. The ideas of these and other thinkers are lucidly expounded in Issa J. Boullata, *Trends and Issues in Contemporary Arab Thought* (Albany, New York: State Univ. of New York Press, 1990).

24. Ibid., 199–37; also Miriam Cooke, *War's Other Voices* (Cambridge: Cambridge Univ. Press, 1988); and Evelyne Accad, *Sexuality and War: Literary Masks of the Middle East* (New York: New York Univ. Press, 1990).

most importantly, the availability of the Islamic heritage as a newly contemporary way of combatting the general intellectual and moral malaise of the community; the diminished role of socialism as a guiding ideology and the resulting secularist tendencies; and resentments over the influence of Western values and the crass consumerism and inflation that they engender. These are, of course, just a few of the many factors governing the emergence of a powerful force in the contemporary Arab world, one that will clearly continue to play a major role in the social and intellectual life of Arab countries.

This brief survey of events and trends in the Middle East since the Second World War cannot possibly do more than scratch the surface of an enormous topic to which colleagues in other disciplines have devoted many tomes. However, this backdrop, however sketchy, will, I hope, make it possible to turn now to an analysis of the way in which littérateurs have chosen to create fictional worlds that will comment on and reflect some of these realities and ideas. In order to cover the novelistic production of the Arab world over the last half-century in as representative a manner as possible, the organizing principle of the remainder of the chapter will be primarily thematic, with concluding segments on new experiments in novel writing and on the social dimensions of the writer, text, and reader. In the next chapter a selection of novels from this period will be analysed in greater detail.

The Decades of Realism

The political events and social transformation that have just been described form the backdrop to fictional writing in the Arab world during the course of the last fifty years. Bearing in mind the push towards independence and, from the 1950s, the development of national and pan-Arab identities and social contracts, it is hardly surprising that the majority of novelists chose to engage these political and social realities in the most obviously available fictional mode, that of realism. Before we investigate the means by which this large-scale project was implemented and the success of Arab authors in doing so, we should pause briefly to consider two other fictional modes which had previously enjoyed much popularity.

As we noted in the previous chapter, the historical novel, with its combined pedagogical and entertainment functions, had played an important role within the general process of *al-nahḍah,* involving a rediscovery of the classical heritage and a reassertion of nation identity. In Egypt, for example, the period following the 1919 revolution saw an upsurge in national pride, and the sensational discoveries in 1922 of the tomb of Tutankhamun made this sense of history even more intense. Najīb Maḥfūẓ's first published work took the form of a translation of an Egyptological work by James Baikie into Arabic. His initial contributions to longer fiction, a set of three historical novels, may perhaps be seen as part of this increasing awareness of historical roots which finds its clearest expression in the so-called "Pharaonism" movement (seen at its most obvious, perhaps, in Tawfīq al-Ḥakīm's novel, *ʿAwdat al-rūḥ*. As Yūsuf ʿIzz al-Dīn notes, the same process is evident in Iraq.[25] During the period under consideration here, writers continued to produce historical novels set in both ancient and medieval times. Al-Bashīr Khurayyif, the Tunisian writer (1917–83), uses his novel, *Barq al-layl* (Night lightning, 1961), to portray life in his native country under Ḥafṣid rule in the sixteenth century, although the inclusion of a reference to the Spanish invasion in 1535 no doubt served to remind his readers of the realities of occupation in the twentieth century.[26] In Syria, Maʿruf al-Arnāʾūṭ (d. 1947) wrote a series of works dealing with periods from early Islamic history.[27] However, while Arab novelists in a variety of countries continued to write historical fiction for informational and entertainment purposes, the forces of rapid change led Arab writers in different directions. In his novel, *al-Raghīf* (The loaf, 1939), for example, Tawfīq Yūsuf ʿAwwād (b. 1911) gives a vivid account of Arab resistance to the Turks during the First World War with "a good deal of focus and artistic acumen."[28] In still more recent times when, as we have noted above, history has been able to provide a regrettably rich repertoire of conflict in the Arab world, novelists have still found inspiration in the events of earlier decades of this century. The Syrian writer, Fāris Zarzūr, sets his novel, *Lan tasquṭ al-madīnah* (The city will not fall, 1969) during the First World War,

25. ʿIzz al-dīn, *Al-Riwāyah fī al-ʿIrāq*, 160. For examples from Egypt, see Sakkut, pp. 46–84.

26. For Khurayyif's work, see Ghazi, 62.

27. The novels are: *Sayyid Quraysh* (1929), *ʿUmar ibn al-Khaṭṭāb* (1936), *Ṭāriq ibn Ziyād* (1941) and *Fāṭimah al-Baṭūl* (1942). See al-Saʿāfīn, 161–85; and al-Nassāj, 118.

28. The evaluation is that of Suhayl Idrīs in *Al-Ādāb* (Feb. 1957): 15. For other views on the novel, see Jūrj Sālim, *Al-Mughāmarah al-riwāʾiyyah* (Damascus: Manshūrāt Ittiḥād al-kuttāb al-ʿArab, 1973), 103–7; and al-Saʿāfīn, 377–436.

while *Ḥasan Jabal* (1969) is an excessively documentary account of resistance to the French occupiers during the 1920s and 1930s.[29] In Egypt, the historical novels of authors such as ʿĀdil Kāmil (b. 1916), ʿAlī al-Jārim (1881–1949), Muḥammad Saʿīd al-ʿIryān (1905–64), and Muḥammad Farīd Abū Ḥadīd (1893–1967) retained a certain popular appeal well into the 1950s.[30] Such treatments as these, however, have assumed a diminished importance within the development of the novel genre during the last half-century. As we will note below, the *use* of history and historical texts (and pastiches of them) is very much an aspect, indeed a prominent feature, of much contemporary and modernist Arabic fiction, but the generic purpose of such works has changed considerably.

In the early stages of the development of the novel in Arabic, the historical trend was followed by the romantic, Haykal's *Zaynab* being an early example. This trend has remained extremely popular (as indeed it has in the Western world). As the Egyptian critic, ʿAbd al-Muḥsin Ṭāhā Badr trenchantly remarks, the prevalence of the realistic genre as the favored type in the tradition of the Arabic novel has done nothing to diminish the popularity of the romantic trend: "They continue to exist because of readers who do not enjoy having their consciousnesses raised; all they want is to be entertained. In every society you'll find semi-literate types who are ready to pander to the taste of this readership. Many such readers have recently been enticed away from entertainment novels towards radio plays and films, and most recently of all, to television."[31] The most popular of such authors is undoubtedly Iḥsān ʿAbd al-Quddūs, famous son of a famous mother, the actress Rose al-Yūsuf; ʿAbd al-Quddūs earned a wide reputation for himself by writing a whole series of works of romantic fiction which broached the subject of the structure of the family and the position of women in a provocative way, making him perhaps in fiction the analogue of Nizār Qabbānī in modern Arabic poetry. Examples of romantic fiction from other parts of the Arab world can serve as a useful illustration of the differing chronologies that still exist at this stage in the development of the novel genre. In

29. See al-Saʿāfīn, 397; ʿAdnān Ibn Dhurayl, *Al-Riwāyah al-ʿArabiyyah al-Sūriyyah* (Damascus: n.p., 1973), 133–37; Ibrāhīm Ḥusayn ʿAbd al-Hādī al-Fayyūmī, *Al-Wāqiʿiyyah fī al-riwāyah al-ʿArabiyyah al-ḥadīthah fī bilād al-Shām* (ʿAmmān: Dār al-Fikr, 1983), 209–99.

30. For these authors, see Sakkut, chaps. 2 and 3; and al-Nassāj, 71–76.

31. Badr, *Taṭawwur al-riwāyah,* 169.

Algeria, Aḥmad Riḍā Hūhū published *Ghādat umm al-qurā* (The maid of the city, 1947), in which the topic is love and marriage.[32] This theme has also been particularly popular with Sudanese novelists, among whom we would mention Badawī ʿAbd al-qādir Khalīl with *Hāʾim ʿalā al-arḍ aw rasāʾil al-ḥirmān* (Roaming the earth or letters of deprivation, 1954) which, as the title suggests, makes heavy use of the epistolary mode, and Shākir Muṣṭafā with *Ḥattā taʿūd* (Till she returns, 1959) where Maḥmūd and ʿAwāṭif's love story is broken when he marries a foreign woman; he only returns to his real beloved as she lies dying.[33]

Principal Themes in the Modern Arabic Novel

Those relatively few critics of the novel in Arabic who have chosen to transcend the boundaries of a single nation's output in the genre have adopted a number of organizing schemes. Shukrī ʿAyyād, for example, himself a creative writer of fiction as well as critic, uses the following categories: those works which seek for some kind of national identity; those which concern themselves with the passage of time; those which deal with the individual and his experience within society; those which adopt a critical posture; and lastly those which investigate the metaphysical.[34] Still other critics have preferred some kind of blend of the thematic approach and the broader categories which we used earlier (such as historical, romantic, and realistic) as they endeavour to sift and assess current trends.[35] However, bearing in mind the tremendous changes in the fabric of Arab societies during the period under consideration here, it is to be expected that the novel be called upon to fulfill that role which it performs better than any other literary genre, that of serving as a mirror and critic of the society within which it is conceived. It has become an active participant in the commitment (*iltizām*) of literature, reflected in the Arab-world context in the foundation of the

32. Al-Nassāj, 220; and al-Khaṭībī, 70.

33. Al-Nassāj, 233–35.

34. Shukrī ʿAyyād, "Al-Riwāyah al-ʿArabiyyah al-muʿāṣirah wa-azmat al-ḍamīr al-ʿArabī," *ʿĀlam al-fikr* 3, no. 3 (Oct.–Dec. 1972): 619–48.

35. Khālidah Saʿīd, "Al-Riwāyah al-ʿArabiyyah bayna 1920–1972," *Mawāqif* 28 (Summer 1974): 75–88; Vial, "Ḳiṣṣa"; al-Khaṭībī, 43; al-Rubayʿī, 28–29; and Halim Barakat, *Visions of Social Reality in the Contemporary Arab Novel* (Washington, D.C.: Center for Contemporary Arab Studies, Georgetown Univ., 1977), 36.

illustrious literary review, *al-Ādāb,* in Beirut in 1953. The societal imperatives reflected in this set of priorities are captured by a critic and university teacher who is also a sociologist and novelist, Ḥalīm Barakāt:

> Contemporary Arab writers have been preoccupied with themes of struggle, revolution, liberation, emancipation, rebellion, alienation. A writer could not be a part of Arab society and yet not concern himself with change. To be oblivious to tyranny, injustice, poverty, deprivation, victimization, repression, is insensitively proper. I would even say that writing about Arab society without concerning oneself with change is a sort of *engagement* in irrelevances.[36]

Bearing in mind the prevalence of conflict in the summary at the beginning of this chapter, it is hardly surprising that war has served as a predominant theme of the novel in Arabic. It is to that topic that we will turn our attention first.

Conflict and Confrontation

The plight of the Palestinians. Novelists from nations all across the Arab world have addressed themselves in their fiction to the continuing conflict with Israel over the status of the Palestinians. It is, to be sure, a multi-faceted topic: the series of confrontations and wars that have taken place in 1948, 1956, 1967, 1973 and 1982; the often violent gestures of "freedom fighters" or "terrorists" (depending on point of view); the impact of the conflict on people living in neighbouring countries such as Lebanon, Syria, and Jordan; and the lives of Palestinians, whether in Israel itself, in the occupied territories such as the West Bank, or in one of many refugee camps or prisons. All these aspects of life have been the focus of fictional works in Arabic. Some works will almost certainly prove to be of purely ephemeral merit, but there are clearly many others which are destined to endure.

It is hardly surprising that Palestinian novelists figure prominently in the listing of those writers who have addressed themselves to the many phases and aspects of the recent history of their people.

36. Halim Barakat, "Arabic Novels and Social Transformation," in *Studies in Modern Arabic Literature,* ed. R. C. Ostle (Warminster, England: Aris and Phillips, 1975), 126–27.

Ghassān Kanafānī (1936–72), political journalist and press spokesman for the Popular Front for the Liberation of Palestine, was assassinated by a car bomb in Beirut. His most famous work is undoubtedly *Rijāl fī al-shams* (1963; *Men in the Sun,* 1978). In this short and powerful work in which the symbolic functions seem often akin to allegory, three Palestinians attempt the difficult journey across the desert to Kuwait, where they hope to find employment. The desert here is a totally inhospitable environment, and the Palestinians, in their quest, are pounded mercilessly by the desert sun. To serve these travelers and others like them, a whole group of middlemen are available near the border to convey them into Kuwait illegally and to steer them clear of marauding Bedouin who will otherwise rob them of everything they own. The three individuals are picked up by Abū Khayzurān, the driver of a water tanker, who agrees to take them over the border inside the water tank. It emerges that Abū Khayzurān has been rendered impotent by a previous war wound, and, with this fact in mind, the events which ensue give an additional element of absurdity to the dire plight of the men in the tank. At the Iraqi border all goes well. But when the tanker reaches the Kuwaiti post, the driver is delayed while the customs official teases him about his girlfriend in Basrah. Fatal minutes pass, and when Abū Khayzurān eventually opens the tank, his three passengers are dead. In a desperate move of clear and devastating symbolic significance, he takes the corpses to the communal garbage dump and abandons them there after removing all their valuables. Why, he wonders, did they not beat on the side of the tank?[37]

The powerful way in which this work depicts the plight of Palestinians in their exile within the Arab world has given it a wide readership. But, while the message is important, and no more so than in the case of Kanafānī, the work is carefully constructed so as to give maximum impact to the concluding events. Each character is introduced as a separate individual representing a different aspect of Palestinian life, and it is only when they join Abū Khayzurān in their fateful journey that the experience becomes unified. Thereafter, events move swiftly, and the symbolic supersedes the individual. Indeed, one may criticise the novel as a whole for giving the reader a

37. Ghassān Kanafānī, *Rijāl fī al-shams,* in *Al-Āthār al-kāmilah* (Beirūt: Dār al-Ṭalīʿah, 1972), 1:152. For an analysis of this and other novels by Kanafani, as well as other Palestinian novelists, see Barbara Harlow, "Readings of National Identity in the Palestinian Novel," in *The Arabic Novel Since 1950, Critical Essays, Interviews, and Bibliography* [*Mundus Arabicus,* 5:89–108]). Cambridge, Mass.: Dār Mahjar, 1992).

rather two-dimensional view of the characters. That having been said, however, it must be added that the imagery used to convey the impact of the symbols, particularly the descriptions of the desert and the unbearable heat of the sun, is couched in a language which is clear and effective.

In *Mā tabaqqā la-kum,* (1966; *All that's left to you,* 1990 [to be discussed in detail in the following chapter]) there are signs of a growing sophistication in technique which lead one to suspect that, had he lived longer, Kanafānī would have continued to experiment with fictional modes and styles. At the same time, it has to be acknowledged that in some of these works the author's intense feelings of commitment result in an approach akin to reportage. But, even if some of them are less successful as works of fiction than others, they all manage to portray the agonies of deprivation and suffering in camps and the resulting frustration, anger, and violence with an unparalleled vividness. Of all modern Arab novelists, he is, in the words of the Egyptian writer Yūsuf Idrīs (1927–91), "the first Arab writer to take his experience of problems to the extent of martyrdom."[38]

Baghdad, Rome, Jerusalem, Beirut, Cambridge, all these are the scenes of events in the novels of Jabrā Ibrāhīm Jabrā (b. 1919). Critic of literature, art, and music; poet; translator of English literature; and novelist, he went into exile as a result of the fighting in 1948 and has lived since that time in Baghdad. Bearing in mind the breadth of Jabrā's education and interests (one of his novels, *Hunters on a Narrow Street,* was originally written in English [London, 1960]),[39] it is hardly surprising that his novels are full of political, literary, and philosophical discussions, raising questions regarding their potential and actual readership which will be addressed below. The characters who people these works are mostly intellectuals: writers, artists, members of the social elite, radical politicians, and the like. They live a life of alienation, and Palestinian and non-Palestinian alike, they aspire towards a newer and better existence so as to escape from the problems of life in contemporary Arab society. This applies as much to the female characters as it does to the male; in several of the

38. See Ghassān Kanafānī, *Rijāl fī al-shams,* in *Al-Āthār al-kāmilah* (Beirut: Dār al-Ṭalīʿah, 1972), 1: Introduction, 11. For a complete study in English on Kanafānī, see Muḥammad Ṣiddīq, *Man Is a Cause: Political Consciousness and the Fiction of Ghassan Kanafani* (Seattle: Univ. of Washington Press, 1984).

39. It has recently been reissued: *Hunters on a Narrow Street* (Washington, D.C.: Three Continents, 1990).

novels, the women revolt against the traditional values of society as a way of expiating their own personal frustrations. It is the *ʿashāʾiriyyah* or tribalistic attitudes of Iraqi society which stand in the way of the happiness of ʿIṣām and Lumā in *al-Safīnah* (1969; *The Ship,* 1985) Jabrā's novel which we examine in detail in the next chapter. Also given a vivid portrayal in his novels is the barbaric way in which many of these intellectuals are treated by the governing authorities. The example of Maḥmūd Rāshid in *al-Safīnah* provides one such example, but the theme is a constant in his works, and no more so than in *al-Baḥth ʿan Walīd Masʿūd* from which we have already quoted. In this latter novel Jabrā expands still further on the multi-narrator technique that he had used to good effect in *Al-Safīnah.* Now, instead of the two principal narrators in *al-Safīnah* (with Emilia Farnesi serving a clarifying role in one chapter) and a narrative sequence governed by the chronology of a voyage, we are presented with a counterpoint of different narrative voices as they confront a single situation. A group of Arab intellectuals, male and female, are brought together at a dinner party in Baghdad. They are invited by their host to listen to a cassette tape left in the car of Walīd Masʿūd, a Palestinian intellectual, who has disappeared and perhaps been killed. When confronted with the message on the tape, some of his male and female acquaintances recount in successive chapters the course of their relationship with the missing "hero." The complexity of his lifestyle and the network of linkages with the fedayeen and intellectual circles provide a vivid picture of both the recent history of the Palestinian people and the tensions implicit in the search for solutions to its problems. The resulting novel is a most accomplished exercise.[40]

During the last decade Jabrā has branched out in other directions. Apart from commencing his autobiography (with a volume entitled *al-Biʾr al-ūlā* [The first well, 1987]), he has written a disturbing novel called *al-Ghuraf al-ukhrā* (The other rooms, 1986) which takes the reader from the apparently "real" world of a city square into a nightmarish maze of dreams and the subconscious in which the nar-

40. Studies of the works of these and other Palestinian novelists will be found in several books in Arabic; among them, I would cite: Aḥmad Abū Maṭar, *Al-Riwāyah fī al-adab al-Filasṭīnī: 1950–75* (Beirut: Al-Muʾassasah al-ʿArabiyyah li-al-dirāsāt wa-al-nashr, 1980), 219–28; Najīb al-ʿAwf, *Darajat al-waʿy fī al-kitābah* (Casablanca: Dār al-nashrah al-Maghribiyyah, 1980), 341–60; Ilyās Khūrī, *Tajribat al-baḥth ʿan ufq,* 68–74. Fārūq Wādī, *Thalāth ʿallāmāt fī al-riwāyah al-Filasṭiniyyah: Ghassān Kanafānī, Emile Ḥabībī, Jabrā Ibrāhīm Jabrā* (Acre: Dār al-Aswār, 1981), 141–82.

rator finds himself accused of committing various crimes, of which he is completely unaware, and comes to doubt his own sanity. *ʿĀlam bi-lā kharāʾiṭ* (A world with no maps, 1983) is an even more interesting departure from his previous works in that it is a richly complex novel jointly written with ʿAbd al-raḥman Munīf, the Saudi-born writer whose works we will be considering below. The very title of this novel introduces the reader to a fictional world where revolutionary societies have replaced ideals and reformist goals with oppression and terror. The two novelists fuse their narrative skills—Jabrā's ability to depict the angst of the Arab intellectual and Munīf's penchant for a broader and more traditional narrative canvas—into a tale of love and intrigue set in the city of ʿAmmuriyyah. Once again the events of the story are orchestrated around the fate of a single character, Najwā al-ʿĀmirī, who has been found murdered. The novel retraces without resolution her passionate affair with ʿAlā al-dīn Najīb, a friend of her husband. The narrative is set against the backdrop of the conflicts in Palestine and Lebanon which continue to impinge on the consciousness of the citizens of this and other Arab cities.[41]

As opposed to both Kanafānī and Jabrā, Emile Ḥabībī (b. 1921) is a Palestinian novelist who has addressed himself to the issues confronting his people while remaining inside Israel. He is a founding member of the Israeli Communist Party and former member of the Knesset (1951–71), and in 1992 was awarded the Israel Literature Prize. In his works, he has succeeded in revealing the bitter ironies of daily life in Israel for the Arab citizens of that country. *Sudāsiyyat al-ayyām al-sittah* (Sextet on the six days, 1969) recounts a set of stories of meetings between the Arab community in Israel and their relatives living elsewhere, a work in which "Emile Ḥabībī manages to pull together in six integrated tableaux a large nexus of human relationships centered around the themes of the land and struggle."[42] His most famous work, however, is *al-Waqāʾiʿ al-gharībah fi-ikhtifāʾ Saʿīd Abī al-naḥs al-mutashāʾil* (1974 and 1977; *The Secret Life of Saeed, the Ill-fated Pessoptimist,* 1982). It depicts with a generous overlay of sardonic and bittersweet humor the daily life of Arabs in Israel. *Al-Waqāʾiʿ al-gharībah* is a quite unique contribution to modern Arabic

41. For a summary of these and other novels of Jabrā and Munīf, see M. M. Badawi, "Two Novelists from Iraq: Jabrā and Munīf," *JAL* 23, no. 2 (July 1992): 140–54.

42. Ilyās Khūrī, *Tajribat al-baḥth ʿan ufq* 47; quoted in *Modern Arabic Literature,* Library of Literary Criticism Series, ed. Roger Allen (New York: Ungar, 1987), 107.

fiction, not only for its sardonic wit, but also because it presents its reader with an intertextual feast. The same pattern is repeated in Ḥabībī's work *Ikhṭiyyeh* (a character's name, but also a Palestinian expletive meaning something akin to "what a shame," 1985).[43] Once again, the author is at pains to use the utterly mundane, in this case a huge traffic jam in Haifa, as a starting point for an elaborate narrative excursion that leads the reader into a maze of time frames, levels of consciousness, and allusions to earlier eras in Arabic cultural history. If the resulting work does not quite attain the heights of *al-Waqā'iʿ al-gharībah,* that is because the latter work establishes a yardstick for pointedly humorous narrative that is hard to match; we will explore its qualities further in the next chapter.

While women writers such as Fadwā Ṭūqān (b. 1917) and Salmā al-Jayyūsī (b. 1928) had been contributing to Palestinian expression in poetic form for some time, it was not until the 1970s that a major female voice entered the world of the novel. The very title of the first novel of Saḥar Khalīfah (born in Nablus in 1941), entitled *Lam naʿud jawārī la-kum* (We're no longer handmaids at your beck and call, 1974), already reveals one of the two major thematic strands in her works, a concern for the plight of women in general and Palestinian women in particular.[44] If the tone of this first novel is somewhat strident and its construction diffuse, then her next work, *Al-Ṣubbār* (1976; *Wild Thorns,* 1985), must be reckoned a major contribution to the Palestinian and Arabic novel, both for its masterly treatment of a complex collection of characters and for the style in which the novel is couched, a mixture of poetic description, feisty colloquial banter, and a wealth of cultural references. Here we move from the concerns of Palestinians in exile and inside Israel itself to

43. Palestinian colleagues inform me that "ikhṭiyyeh" is colloquial Palestinian for "Oh dear" or "What a shame!" and that such is the meaning intended here. A French translation of this work, *Péchés oubliées,* tr. Jean-Patrick Guillaume (Paris: Gallimard, 1991), appears to be working on the assumption that the form is a plural of the word for "sin, offense."

44. For Khalīfah, see Amīnah al-ʿAdwān, *Maqālāt fī al-riwāyah al-ʿArabiyyah al-muʿāṣirah* (Amman: al-Mu'assasah al-ṣuḥufiyyah al-Urdunniyyah, 1976), 47–50; Fakhrī Ṣāliḥ, *Fī al-riwāyah al-Filasṭīniyyah* (Beirut: Dār al-kitāb al-ḥadīth, 1985), 75–106; Fayṣāl Darrāj, "Dirāsah fī riwāyah Saḥar Khalīfah: Qawl al-riwāyah wa-aqwāl al-wāqiʿ," *Shu'ūn Filasṭīniyyah* 112 (1981): 108–29; Muhammad Siddiq, "The Fiction of Saḥar Khalīfah: Between Defiance and Deliverance," *ASQ* 8 no. 2 (1986): 143–60; Isabella Camera d'Afflitto, "Sulla Narrativa dei territori occupati (*al-ḍiffah wa-al-qiṭaʿ*)," *Oriente Moderno* 5, nos. 7–9 (Luglio-Settembre 1986): 145–53; and Harlow, 100–102.

the West Bank and the dilemmas facing the Palestinian community, both regarding its own traditional social structures and in the manifold daily tensions that result from a process of survival depending to a large degree on one or another kind of interaction with the reality of Israel. Through utterly authentic portraits of a whole series of Palestinian men and women Khalīfah addresses herself to the controversial topic of the exploitation of Palestinian workers by both their traditional Palestinian overlords and their new bosses at the jobs inside Israel, to which many of them travel by bus each day. Emile Ḥabībī was one of those who took Khalīfah to task for such a linkage, but she has insisted on the authenticity of her vision.[45] One of the principal characters, Usāmah, returns to Palestine on a journey that is the reverse of Kanafānī's trio in *Rijāl fī al-shams:* from a job in the Gulf back to the occupied West Bank. Commissioned by the resistance to blow up the buses which take the workers to their jobs in Israel, Usāmah discovers to his horror that his family and friends have adjusted to the practicalities of occupation. Refusing to deal with realities (as opposed to his colleague, Zuhdī), he insists on carrying out his plan. The workers who die in the resulting explosion are Arabs from his own town. Usāmah and his resistance colleagues are killed in the ensuing gunfight. Nor is that the end, for, in accordance with Israeli policy, soldiers proceed to evacuate the family home and blow it up. It is left to ʿĀdil, Usāmah's cousin, to endeavor to hold together what is left of the family, a process that carries over into a sequel, *ʿAbbād al-shams* (The sunflower, 1980). Here, the author's concern with the role and fate of Palestinian women, thrust somewhat into the background in *al-Ṣubbār,* again comes to the fore in the depiction of the lives of Saʿdiyyah, Zuhdī's widow, who doggedly pursues her quest for that most symbolic of Palestinian goals, a plot of land, and Rafīf, a female journalist, who indulges in a fluctuating relationship with ʿĀdil. This feminist aspect of the author's fictional writing has recently been pursued further in *Mudhakkirāt imraʾah ghayr wāqiʿiyyah* (Memoirs of an unrealistic woman, 1986).[46]

Another woman novelist from Palestine, Liyānah Badr (b.1950), has used her fictions to depict the constant disruptions that punctu-

45. See Ṣiddīq, "Saḥar Khalīfah," 147–48.

46. A segment of this work is translated in *An Anthology of Modern Palestinian Literature,* ed. Salma Khadra' Jayyusi (New York: Columbia Univ. Press, 1992), 589–96.

ate the lives of those Palestinians who have attempted to carry on the process of resistance from one refugee camp to the next; as a member of the Palestine Liberation Organization (PLO) who has worked in such camps, she is uniquely qualified to do so. Her most recent work, *ʿAyn al-mirʾāt* (The eye of the mirror, 1991), presents a multifaceted view of the slow buildup to the massacre of Palestinians at the Tell al-Zaʿtar camp in Beirut in 1976.[47] In an earlier work, *Būṣlah min ajl ʿabbād al-shams* (1979; *A Compass for the Sunflower,* 1989), the heroine, Jinān, recounts a life in which incidents coincide with many of the events of the post-1948 Palestinian experience: the June War, Black September, aircraft hijackings, refugee camps in ʿAmmān. In these and other works the element of autobiography seems especially strong.

While the plight of Palestinians in Israel, in the diaspora of exile, and in permanent transit, has obviously been of prime concern to Palestinian littérateurs, the international dimension of the issue has meant that novelists from across the Arab world have used it as a theme for their works.[48] Some writers, such as Nabīl Khūrī and Rashād Abū Shāwir, choose to follow the plight of the Palestinian community over a significant period of time.[49] A large number of writers focus on the conflicts of 1948 and, in particular, 1967. One of the most prominent of these is Ḥalīm Barakāt, the Lebanese novelist, sociologist, and critic. In his novel *ʿAwdat al-ṭāʾir ilā al-baḥr* (1969; *Days of Dust,* 1974), examined in detail in the next chapter, he provides us with a *cinema vérité* view of the fighting and the terrible plight of Arab refugees during the six days of the June War. An earlier work, the uncannily named *Sittat ayyām* (1961; *Six Days,* 1990), takes its temporal context from the 1948 fighting. Another six-day period forms a time frame in which Israeli forces lay siege to the seaside town of Dayr al-Baḥr. It is mainly through the eyes of Suhayl, the novel's hero, that the reader is made aware of attempts by the villagers to organize resistance to the Israeli siege, but this is not the only narrative dimension. Through a generous use of interior

47. Commemorated in Maḥmūd Darwīsh's famous poem, "Aḥmad al-Zaʿtar." See *Aḥmad al-Zaʿtar,* trans. Rana Kabbani (Washington, D.C.: Free Palestine, 1976).

48. The Moroccan critic, Laḥmadānī Ḥamīd notes that physical and psychological distance from Palestine and the Palestinians leads to a wide variety of approaches to the topic among Arab novelists. See *Fī al-tanẓīr wa-al-mumārasah: dirāsāt fī al-riwāyah al-Maghribiyyah* (Casablanca: Manshūrāt ʿUyūn, 1986), 132.

49. Nabīl Khūrī, *Al-Raḥīl* (1969), discussed in Abū Maṭar, 125–29; and Rashād Abū Shāwir, *Al-ʿUshshāq* (n.d.), discussed in al-Rubayʿī, 181–83.

monologue, the thoughts of several of the major characters are revealed: in particular Suhayl himself, the two women with whom he consorts—the worldly-wise Lamyā and the initially cloistered, but later liberated, Nāhidah—and Farīd, the local resistance leader. The author's concern with societal issues leads him to indulge in sometimes lengthy digressions on the general backwardness of the country, the problems of intermarriage, and a sense of alienation among the younger generation.[50] As a result, some characters seem more akin to stereotypes than to real people.

We have noted in the historical introduction to this chapter that the aftermath of the June War was a period of self-doubt, reflection, and recrimination. In ʿAbd al-Raḥmān Munīf's novel, *al-Ashjār wa-ightiyāl Marzūq* (The trees and Marzuq's assassination, 1973), Manṣūr, a history teacher, considers the implications of this destructive and potentially reconstructive process, only to learn that the powers-that-be still find the use of historical interpretation for political and social opposition a danger to their survival.[51] Among the more obvious and lasting manifestations of this continuing search for alternatives was the appearance of the "fedayeen" (*fidāʾiyyīn),* those willing to sacrifice themselves. The various narrators who tell their stories in Jabrā's novel, *al-Baḥth ʿan Walīd Masʿūd,* depict both Walīd himself and his son, Marwān, as being heavily involved in a guerilla cell. Tawfīq Fayyāḍ's novel, *Majmūʿah 778* (778 Group, 1974) carries its action into Israel itself. A resistance group based in ʿAkkah is goaded into initiating guerrilla activities by the results of the 1967 debacle, and by contacts with colleagues on the West Bank. A lack of good information leads initially to failure, and the implications of their comments on poor organization among the leadership on the West Bank are very similar to those of Saḥar Khalīfah's novel, *al-Ṣubbār,* discussed above. The *fidāʾī* also figures prominently in Laylā ʿUsayrān's (b. 1936) novel, *ʿAṣāfīr al-fajr* (*Dawn birds,* 1968). A son of a family living in Beirut disappears while supposedly studying in Germany. He joins a *fidāʾī* cell in Jerusalem, but is wounded in action, and asks to return to his family in Beirut. Maryam, his sister, is delighted by his decision to abandon his studies in Europe. In a

50. Ḥalim Barakāt, *Sittat ayyām* (Beirut: Dār Majallat Shiʿr, 1961) 25, 36–37, 90–96.

51. For Munīf's novel, see al-ʿAdwān, 12–20; Samar al-Fayṣal, *Malāmiḥ fī al-riwāyah al-Sūriyyah* (Damascus: Manshūrāt ittiḥād al-kuttāb al-ʿArab) 1979, 279–94; Muḥammad Kāmil al-Khaṭīb, *Al-Mughāmarah al-muʿaqqadah* (Damascus: Manshūrāt wizārat al-thaqāfah, 1976), 133–38; Ilyās Khūrī, *Tajribat al-baḥth ʿan ufq,* 106–8.

gesture typical of the rather obvious symbolism of many novels of this subgenre, she decides not to marry a Lebanese man who has refused to become involved in the continuing struggle.[52]

Revolution and independence. Abdallah Laroui notes in his discussion of the Arab intellectual that the Palestine question is "the Arab problem par excellence," a view to which Jabrā also subscribes.[53] The fact that in the preceding pages we have been able to mention works by novelists from Morocco, Saudi Arabia, Lebanon, and Iraq, as well as Palestine itself, gives ample proof of the widespread concern over the fate of the Palestinians and the manifold ramifications of the issue throughout the Arab world. On the literary plane as well as the political, it is an obvious, perhaps the most obvious, focus of commitment among the Arab intelligentsia. For that reason, we have considered it first and in some detail. The confrontation with Israel is, of course, one aspect, albeit a conspicuous one, of a larger issue, the confluence and clash of the cultures of East and West, which in turn leads on the political level to such topics as opposition to European imperial domination, nationalist movements and the struggle for independence, and, on the social plane, to an examination of the processes of revolution and the impact of societal change. The modern Arabic novel, that genre which can show, in Trilling's words, "the extent of human variety and the value of this variety," has addressed itself to these issues as they have affected the different countries of the Arab world, each one with its particular set of local circumstances. The result is a tradition of realist fiction of considerable diversity. We will now examine some of its principal themes in more detail.

The social and political processes that led up to independence and sometimes revolution were extremely varied, and this is reflected in the fiction that attempts to describe the complex of issues involved in each country's struggle for self-determination. In the case of Egypt, for example, the revolution of 1952 was essentially a bloodless affair, one that has been the subject of few novels; Najīb Maḥfūẓ's *al-Summān wa-al-kharīf* (1962; *Autumn Quail,* 1985) gives a graphic depiction of the events leading up to the takeover by the

52. Fayyād's novel is discussed in ʿAbd al-Karīm al-Ashtar, *Dirāsāt fī adab al-nakbah* (n.p.: Dār al-Fikr), 1975, 105–38; for Laylā ʿUsayrān, see al-Ashtar, ibid., 59–73, and ʿAlī Najīb ʿAṭwī, *Taṭawwur fann al-qiṣṣah al-Lubnāniyyah al-ʿArabiyyah baʿd al-ḥarb al-ʿālamiyyah al-thāniyah* (Beirut: Dār al-Āfāq al-jadīdah, 1982), 245–47.

53. Laroui, 171; Jabrā, *Al-Riḥlah al-thāminah* (Sidon: Al-Maktabah al-ʿāṣriyyah, 1967), 103.

Free Officers, but the work is more concerned with the issues of bureaucratic corruption and attempts at reconciling the old and the new. The same however cannot be said for the period preceding the revolution, a period fraught with political and social conflict. Here too, our principal chronicler is Najīb Maḥfūẓ, the Nobel Laureate in Literature for 1988 to whose career we devote a special section below. His famous trilogy of novels, *Bayn al-qaṣrayn* (1956; *Palace Walk,* 1990), *Qaṣr al-shawq* (1957; *Palace of Desire,* 1991), and *al-Sukkariyyah* (1957; *Sugar Street,* 1992), provide a vivid account of the many political, social, and intellectual conflicts of the interwar years. *The Trilogy* and Maḥfūẓ's earlier novels, including *Khān al-Khalīlī* (1945[?]), *Al-Qāhirah al-jadīdah* (1946[?]), and *Zuqāq al-midaqq* (1947; *Midaq Alley,* 1966) were carefully crafted portraits of Egyptian society that explored in precise detail the turbulent processes the Egyptian people had gone through in order to reach political independence, with its new privileges and responsibilities. The sheer bulk and sophistication of Maḥfūẓ's contribution to Arabic fiction in Egypt, and the Arab world as a whole, has tended to push other contributors somewhat into the shadows. In the context of this albeit brief discussion of Egypt's drive towards independence, mention should be made of *Mallīm al-Akbar* (Mallim the great, 1944) by ʿĀdil Kāmil, a study of class differences and social unrest during the 1940s, and of *Rāmah wa-al-tinnīn* (Rāmah and the dragon, 1979) by Edwār al-Kharrāṭ (b. 1926), a complex experimental work that reflects within its own narrative framework its author's personal experience of imprisonment for political causes in the late 1940s.[54]

The theme of the struggle for independence is particularly prevalent in fictional works written by Maghribi novelists. In Tunisia, Muḥammad al-Mukhtār Jannat (b. 1930) in his *Nawāfidh al-zamān* (Windows of time, 1974) and Muḥammad al-Ṣāliḥ al-Jābirī (b. 1940) in *Yawm min ayyām Zamrā* (One day in Zamrā, 1968), paint vivid portraits of popular uprisings against French colonial rule, laying particular stress not only on the heroism of those fighting for national freedom but on the treachery of local collaborators as well. In *Dafannā al-māḍī* (We have buried the past, 1966), by the Moroccan novelist ʿAbd al-karīm Ghallāb (b. 1917), the scene is set in Fez, that most traditional of Moroccan cities. The family of al-Ḥājj Muḥam-

54. For Kāmil's *Mallīm al-Akbar,* see Sakkut, 108–11; and Jad, *Form and Technique,* 153–57. For al-Kharrāṭ's *Rāmah wa-al-tinnīn,* see Jean Fontaine, *Romans arabes modernes* (Tunis: Institut des belles lettres arabes, 1992), 12–53.

mad is portrayed as a microcosm of the larger society, revealing all the latent tensions of a nation under foreign domination, as reflected in the different personalities of the children of the family. While ʿAbd al-ghanī, the eldest son, opens a shop in the market, ʿAbd al-raḥmān goes to the *madrasah* (secular school) and becomes involved in nationalist activities, which lead inevitably to his imprisonment for long periods and to a sense of shame and resignation in his traditionalist father. Maḥmūd, the son who results from al-Ḥājj Muḥammad's purchase of the slavegirl Yasmīn, becomes a member of the judiciary responsible for sentencing nationalist troublemakers such as his own half-brother, ʿAbd al-raḥmān. If this brief description of the characters and their functions within the plot seems somewhat trite, then that indeed reflects the overall impact of the novel. In a rather pretentious introduction, the author informs us that this work is a "committed novel," and indeed it displays many of the faults which can often be attributed to an excessively close involvement on the author's part in the action of the work itself. Many chapters are filled with sermonettes of varying length in which the characters discuss current societal issues: the education of women, modernism versus traditionalism, loyalty to the homeland, and so on. This close involvement of the author in his work of fiction is carried even further in *Sabʿat abwāb* (Seven doors, 1965) which, in Muḥammad Mandūr's words, is a graphic description of the author's incarceration without trial for a period of six months for engaging in nationalist activities.[55]

The Algerian novelist al-Ṭāhir Waṭṭār (b. 1936), has taken the Algerian struggle for liberation from French rule, the most protracted of such conflicts (the "war of a million martyrs," 1954–62) as the subject for his fiction. In *al-Lāz* (the name of the hero, 1974), he broaches a problem which was typical of many postrevolutionary situations in the Arab world. Al-Lāz is the illegitimate son of Zaydān, a communist who operates a guerrilla cell in the mountains. Al-Lāz, who does not initially know who his father is, has been serving as an agent for the guerrillas in a French camp. He is betrayed, and flees to his father's hideout, but discovers that, since his father has re-

55. Muḥammad al-Mukhtār Jannat, *Nawāfidh al-zamān* (Windows of time) (Tunis: Al-Sharikah al-Tūnisiyyah li-al-tawzīʿ, 1974); Muḥammad al-Ṣāliḥ al-Jābirī, *Yawm min ayyām Zamrā* (One day in Zamra) (Tunis: Al-Dār al-Tūnisiyyah li-al-nashr, 1968); ʿAbd al-karīm Ghallāb, *Sabʿat abwāb* (Seven doors) (Cairo: Dār al-Maʿārif, 1965), 5. Ghallāb has expressed his personal approach to novel writing in Muḥammad Barrādah, ed., *Al-Riwāyah al-ʿArabiyyah* (Beirut: Dār ibn Rushd, 1981), 331–49.

fused the demand of the Muslim members of the Nationalist Front (FLN) that he recant his Communist beliefs, he is about to die. Even after such a lengthy and bloody struggle for independence, there are still other scores to settle. Waṭṭār brings his hero back in a more recent work *al-Lāz, al-ʿishq wa-al-mawt fī al-zaman al-ḥarāshī* (*Al-Lāz: love and death in the Ḥarāshī times,* 1982) in which the focus has moved from the revolutionary war itself to its no less problematic aftermath.[56]

In the case of Iraq, while there was no actual fighting on the scale of the Algerian conflict, the decade which preceded the bloody overthrow of the Iraqi monarchy in 1958 was one of political instability and social unrest. Several prominent Iraqi writers choose to focus on the "bad old days," and particularly corruption. Dhū al-nūn Ayyūb (1908–88) made it a primary focus of his novels. *Al-Duktūr Ibrāhīm* (Doctor Ibrāhīm, 1939) shows the impact of Western culture on those Arabs who go to Europe to study and then return to their homeland. The work paints a sordid picture of opportunism, as a young Iraqi with a Persian father is sent to England for his university education, totally assimilates British values, marries an English girl, and acquires a doctorate. He then returns home, and by peddling influence and prejudice manages to secure himself a position in the Ministry of Agriculture. He joins all the right societies and organizations in order to gain the attention of his Minister and of the British, and then proceeds to acquire as much prestige and money as he can, mostly at the expense of his colleagues. When their enmity towards him and his own awareness of his political vulnerability reaches a certain point, he transfers his funds out of the country and takes out American citizenship. Once again, the sociocritical purpose of this work is not handled with the subtlety of some later works, but we are led to believe that Ayyub himself was made to suffer internal exile in Iraq as a result of departmental intrigue.[57] This fact, together with the historical circumstances in which the novel was con-

56. For al-Waṭṭār's works, see Muḥammad Maṣāyif, *Al-Riwāyah al-ʿArabiyyah al-Jazāʾiriyyah al-ḥadīthah bayna al-wāqiʿiyyah wa-al-iltizām* (Algiers: Al-Dār al-ʿArabiyyah lī-al-kitāb, 1963) 25–53; Muḥammad Ṣiddīq, "The Contemporary Arabic Novel in Perspective," *World Literature Today* 60 no. 2 (Spring 1986): 206–11; and Aida Bamia, "The North African Novel: Achievements and Prospects," in *The Arabic Novel Since 1950* 5:61–88.

57. For Ayyūb's novels, see ʿIzz al-dīn, *Al-Riwāyah fī al-ʿIrāq,* 210 ff.; ʿUmar al-Ṭālib, *Al-Fann al-qaṣaṣī fī al-adab al-ʿIrāqī al-ḥadīth* (Najaf, Iraq: Matbaʿat Nuʿmān, 1971), 281–309; al-Nassāj, 168–70; and Jamīl Saʿīd, 33–38.

ceived, no doubt contributed to the somewhat excessive fervor with which the author portrays the evil qualities of his hero. The same tendency is to be found in *Ḍajjāh fī al-zuqāq* (Din in the alley, 1975) by Ghānim al-Dabbāgh (b. 1923), in which al-Dabbāgh makes use of his main character, Khalīl, to portray corruption in the petty bureaucracy in the provincial city of Mawṣil, the author's birthplace, during the tyrannical regime of Nūrī Saʿīd in the 1950s. More accomplished than either of these two works is *Khamsat aṣwāt* (Five voices, 1967) by Ghā'ib Ṭuʿmah Farmān (1927–1990). The novel provides a realistic picture of the prerevolutionary period seen through the eyes of five characters drawn from the intellectual, bourgeois class. The author assigns a number from one to five to each character and then introduces them in turn. The first is Saʿīd, a young man in his twenties who works on the complaints column of the newspaper *al-Nās*. The second is Ibrāhīm, the editor-in-chief to the newspaper. Through these two characters and their profession the reader is introduced to a wide variety of social and political issues; indeed, their livelihood is frequently threatened by "suggestions," "recommendations," and even orders from the censors. At the conclusion of the work the newspaper is closed down altogether.[58] The other three "voices" are, in turn, ʿAbd al-khāliq, Sharīf, a would-be poet and philanderer, and lastly Ḥāmid, a senior bank official. The frequent meetings between these five characters in bars, restaurants, buses and so on, allow for discussions of a wide variety of topics of local and international interest: Palestine, the Arab League, Guatemala, the alienation of intellectuals, the virtues of city and provincial living, and the rights of women. However, the action of the narrative revolves around Saʿīd's receipt of an anonymous letter concerning the plight of a housewife who is being maltreated by her husband. Research reveals that the husband is none other than Ḥāmid himself, something which causes considerable embarrassment to the entire group. Eventually Ḥalīmah, Ḥāmid's wife (or Najāt, as she called herself in the initial letter to Saʿīd), returns to her home town of Karbalā'. With the closing of the newspaper, Saʿīd makes the decision adopted by so many young Arab intellectuals who find themselves at odds with the authorities, namely to leave the country. The work ends with him saying farewell to his father.

58. Ghā'ib Ṭuʿmah Farmān, *Khamsat aṣwāt* (Five voices) (Beirut: Dār al-Ādāb, 1967), 22, 49, 63, 287. Farmān spent much of his later life in exile in Moscow, where he died, but the focus of his fiction remained on life in Iraq. For further details, see "Gha'ib Ṭuʿmah Farmān" in *Encyclopedia of 20th Century World Literature*, vol. 5 (New York: Ungar, 1993).

A particularly interesting aspect of this novel is its narrative technique. The majority of chapters deal with one of the five characters, but on two occasions the canvas expands to incorporate all five at once. The narrative throughout is told in the third person, so that the portrait of each individual remains more external than is the case in, for example, Maḥfūẓ's *Mīrāmār* (1967; *Miramar,* 1978) or Jabrā's *al-Safīnah* (1970; *The Ship,* 1982), other examples of what Ḍiyā' al-Sharqāwī termed "*riwāyāt ṣawtiyyah.*"[59] However, even though Farmān does not manage to exploit the potentialities of the "novel of voices" to the full, his novel is a convincing portrait of Iraqi society at a crucial period in its modern history, and the final chapter in which the five voices are merged depicts well that tantalizing mixture of despair and hope which characterized the period immediately prior to the revolution of 1958.

Accounts of political and social conditions in Iraq after the 1958 revolution suggest that one tyranny was replaced by another, in the form of the regime of ʿAbd al-karīm Qāsim, who was to be overthrown in 1963 by yet another bloody revolution. The atmosphere of those early days of the Iraqi Revolution is well captured by Ismāʿīl Fahd Ismāʿīl in his quartet of novels which will be discussed in detail in the next chapter. For one of the characters in that work, the very name Qāsim is one which haunts his entire life. Having written a poem against the country's ruler, he is first imprisoned without trial or charge, then found to have no links with any of the banned political organizations, and finally prevented from obtaining any kind of employment because he is now forever labeled as "a dangerous political extremist."

It will be recalled that Tawfīq Yūsuf ʿAwwād's novel, *al-Raghīf* (discussed above), took as its theme the nationalist struggle in Syria during the First World War. In *al-Maṣābīḥ al-zurq* (Blue lamps, 1954), an early work by Syria's most prominent novelist, Ḥannā Mīnah (b. 1924), the same struggle is in progress, although the time frame is now the Second World War and the enemy is the French. This novel appeared during a decade when the notion of commitment was very much to the fore, and it suffers a good deal because the political message is allowed to predominate over the presentation of characters and events. In fact, the ending of the novel follows the tradition of the romantic novel, with the heroine Randah dying of tuberculosis, while her beloved, Fāris, the freedom fighter who has

59. Ḍiyā' al-Sharqāwī, "Al-Miʿmār al-fannī fī riwāyat *al-Safīnah,*" *Al-Maʿrifah* 193–94 (Mar.–Apr. 1978): 7–57.

joined the army in order to earn enough money to get married, is killed while fighting in Libya. The echo of Haykal's *Zaynab* of many decades earlier seems particularly strong. Mīnah's second novel, *al-Shirāʿ wa-al-ʿāṣifah* (The sail and the storm, 1966) is a more accomplished work. We are here dealing with the call of the sea; in this case, literally so, as opposed to the sea's more figurative function in Barakāt's *ʿAwdat al-ṭāʾir ilā al-baḥr*. In Mīnah's novel, it is not condemnation to a continuing exile that is involved, but rather an aspiration on the hero's part to rejoin the element in which he feels most at home, a theme which several critics have connected with Hemingway's *The Old Man and the Sea*.[60] Al-Ṭurūsī, the main character of this work, has lost his ship at sea and opened a café in the Syrian town of Lādhiqiyyah (Lattakia), a community wracked by civil unrest and nationalist activity. For him, this period on land is a time of alienation, but it is also a time during which he becomes aware of the injustices suffered by his fellow men, the porters and dockers in the harbor who have to carry prodigious loads under the merciless scrutiny of the local racketeers and their thugs. In a brutal fight, al-Ṭurūsī defeats one of these thugs and thus symbolically confronts the social injustices of his homeland. The café now becomes an even greater focus for the activity of the local nationalist groups. Al-Ṭurūsī even goes into the business of smuggling arms to resistance groups. But the event which acts as the catalyst for his exile on land is a violent storm in which he rescues another sailor, al-Raḥūmī, from his sinking boat. After many years of alienation, the hero is now given the opportunity to return to his natural environment, the sea, where the turbulence and unpredictability reflect the societal conditions on land which he has worked so hard to combat and defeat.

In these early novels the narrative sequence is uncomplicated and the impact is often similar to the heroic saga, something to which even more emphasis is given in *al-Shirāʿ wa-al-ʿāṣifah* by the way in which the major character is presented. Mīnah states his views

60. See Ghālī Shukrī, *Al-Riwāyah al-ʿArabiyyah fī riḥlat ʿadhāb* (Cairo: ʿĀlam al-Kutub, 1971), 235; Sālim, *Al-Mughāmarah al-riwāʾiyyah*, 94. For a treatment of this novel as well as a survey of the earlier tradition of the Syrian novel, see ʿAdnān Ibn Dhurayl, *Al-Riwāyah al-ʿArabiyyah al-Sūriyyah*, esp. 162–69; and Ḥusām al-Khaṭīb, *Al-Riwāyah al-Sūriyyah fī marḥalat al-nuhūḍ*, (Cairo: al-Munaẓẓamah al-ʿArabiyyah li-al-tarbiyah wa-al-thaqāfah wa-al-ʿulum, 1975). Mīnah's novels are also discussed in al-Saʿāfīn, 288–91, 394–97; Muḥsin Jāsim al-Mūsawī, *Al-Mawqif al-thawrī fī al-riwāyah al-ʿArabiyyah al-muʿāṣirah* (Baghdad: Manshūrāt Wizārat al-Iʿlām, 1975), 75–80; and "Wajhan li-wajh," *Al-ʿArabī* (Oct. 1987): 97–104.

on this subject clearly: "I must acknowledge that, as far as I am concerned, realism should neither avoid romanticism nor totally adopt it. Rather it should use romanticism along with all the other literary schools for the purpose of its own particular creative vision. Realism is broad enough to encompass a palate of numerous hues, yet it remains the vehicle whereby they are all blended together."[61]

From such direct concern with the quest for freedom from external domination and exploitation and the narrative modes needed to express such sentiments, Mīnah turns in later works to analysis of class differences and later to the autobiographical novel. In the former category we can place *al-Shams fī yawm ghā'im* (Sun on a cloudy day, 1973) in which he again makes creative use of the period of the French occupation to illustrate the need for societal change. In this case, the son of an aristocratic family living on its past glories falls in love with a poor girl from whom he learns a particular folkloric dance. With the stage thus set, using a rather obvious symbolism, the story proceeds with the hero rebelling against his own class background and the way in which poorer people are exploited.[62] To the autobiographical category Mīnah has contributed *Baqāyā ṣuwar* (Picture fragments, 1974; *Fragments of Memory,* 1993), in which the struggles of Syrian society in the interwar period are effectively related through a child's eyes.

Another Syrian writer, Ṣidqī Ismāʿīl (1924–72), used his novel, *al-ʿUṣāt* (The rebels, 1964) to produce a study of political corruption in Syria across three generations of a prominent family in Aleppo. From a first generation that is in the service of the Turkish regime, we move into the second phase, that of the Nationalist cause against the French. However, the burden of the novel's message regarding both present and future resides in the depiction of the third generation which finds itself combating corruption and disillusion among fellow Syrians.[63]

Civil war in Lebanon. As was noted at the beginning of this chapter, an independent Lebanese state was formed in 1943 from the

61. See *Al-Mawqif al-adabī* 5 no. 3 (July 1975): 122.

62. For analyses of *Shams fi yawm ghā'im,* see Ibn Dhurayl, *Al-Riwāyah al-ʿArabiyyah al-Sūriyyah,* 174–81; Ilyās Khūrī, *Tajribat al-baḥth ʿan ufq,* 87; Shukrī ʿAzīz Māḍī, *Inʿikās hazīmat Ḥuzayrān ʿalā al-riwāyah al-ʿArabiyyah* (Beirut: Al-Mu'assasah al-ʿarabiyyah li-al-dirāsāt wa-al-nashr, 1978), 137–44; and al-Mūsawī, *Al-Mawqif al-thawrī,* 185–97.

63. For analyses of *Al-ʿUṣāt,* see Ibn Dhurayl, *Al-Riwāyah al-ʿArabiyyah al-Suriyyah,* 115–26; al-Fayyūmī, 101–206; al-Saʿāfīn, 340–45.

territory of the Ottoman province of Syria. The region of Mount Lebanon had always had an identity of its own, and the political system upon which the intended operation of the new state was based was an attempt to reconcile the interests of the many religious communities contained within its borders. The arrangement showed deep flaws from the outset, and yet the maintenance of a fragile balance allowed the country to become a booming market for trade and banking. However, pressures that began to build up during the 1950s, 1960s, and 1970s—the influx of Palestinian refugees and the rapid growth of the Shiʿite community based in the south of the country (much stimulated in recent times by the example and support of the Iranian Revolution)—combined with a host of other factors, both local and international, to shatter the fragile political and social structure of the country, leading to a civil conflict of horrifying barbarity. The agony of the country and its different communities has been a subject of a large number of works of fiction.[64]

The city of Beirut, a center of finance, culture, and—in our context, most significant—book publication, became a divided and shell-pocked city. Tawfīq Yūsuf ʿAwwād (1911–88), the author of *al-Raghīf* (1939) described above, includes the name of the city in the title of his *Ṭawāḥīn Bayrūt* (The mills of Beirut, 1972; *Death in Beirut,* 1976). The arrival in the city of Tamīmah Naṣūr, a Shiʿite woman from the south, is used to depict the problems of Lebanon, and especially its youth, in the wake of the June War of 1967.[65] Israeli raids on fedayeen camps in southern Lebanon make for continual disruptions in the lives of the Shiʿites who live there and serve as one of several factors in the process of rousing the community to a more vigorous assertion of their rights within the society, a premonition of things to come. In the capital city, the seeds of future civil conflict are clearly visible, as Tamīmah's loss of provincial innocence becomes a narrative vehicle for the revelation of the widening cracks in the societal fabric; she participates in student demonstrations, is seduced by Ramzī Raʿd, a prominent revolutionary journalist, and finds herself falling in love with Hānī Rāʿī, a Maronite. In this picture of Lebanese society on the verge of disaster, ʿAwwād's narrator orchestrates the patchwork of intercommunity relationships in a

64. The role of women authors in depicting the dimensions of this conflict and shaping their own identities is explored in two studies: Accad, *Sexuality and War,* and Cooke, *War's Other Voices.*

65. For ʿAwwād's novel, see Ilyās Khūrī, *Tajribat al-baḥth ʿan ufq,* 82–86; al-Mūsawī, *Al-Mawqif al-thawrī,* 125–36; and Māḍī, 82–85.

rather obvious way. However, his novel's role as a *cri de coeur* from a fervent believer in the Lebanon that was in the past is made infinitely more poignant by the the fact that the author himself was killed in the very civil conflict that it so clearly predicts.

For Ghādah al-Sammān (b. 1942), Beirut is a place of "nightmares." Her novel *Kawābīs Bayrūt* (Beirut nightmares) describes the fighting around the hotels of the city in November 1975. The protagonist, trapped along with her cousin and uncle, narrates the tale as a mixture of reality and nightmarish fantasy.[66] Equally nightmarish are the descriptions provided by the narrator in the second part of Ḥanān al-Shaykh's *Ḥikāyat Zahrah* (Zahrah's tale, 1980; *The Story of Zahra,* 1986), a novel that will be discussed in detail in the next chapter. Here the behavior brought about by conflicts in the mind and emotions of another young Shiʿite woman serves as a brilliant psychological foil to the total collapse of humanitarian norms that engulfs the Lebanese people during the civil war.

An accomplished critic who has used this tragic conflict as a theme for his works is Ilyās Khūrī. In *al-Jabal al-ṣaghīr* (1977; *Little Mountain,* 1989) the scene is set amidst the chaos of warfare between differing communities within the same city. The title is the name traditionally given to the Christian east sector of Beirut, where Khūrī himself grew up, but the narrative switches rapidly from one venue and group to another. The repetition of phrases as a means of marking a return to a previously mentioned venue serves to underline the instability of the situation and the narrative describing it; for this is a community where churches are being used as armed camps for fighters. In a final chapter set in Paris, the narrator contemplates the fate of his homeland and realizes that, while it has been substantially destroyed, the job had not been completed. Khūrī's next novel, *Abwāb al-madīnah* (1981; *Gates of the City,* 1992) is even more symbolic. A nameless figure known simply as "the Man" is admitted to an anonymous city and wanders around it in a daze. His observations are interrupted by hallucinations and thwarted by amnesia; his inability to comprehend what is going on around him serves as an apt symbol for the increasingly complex web of local and international enmities that Lebanon had become. Khūrī's concern with the fate of Lebanon is continued in its most creative expression yet with *Riḥlat Ghāndī al-ṣaghīr* (1989; *The Journey of Little*

66. Ghādah al-Sammān, *Kawābīs Bayrūt* (Beirut nightmares) (Beirut: Dār al-Ādāb, 1976).

Ghandi, 1994). The setting of the novel is the Israeli invasion of Lebanon in 1982 and its aftermath, but, apart from that temporal contextualization, there is little about this narrative that suggests an organizing principle based on chronology or any other criterion. Alice, a prostitute, informs the author (who himself participates in the narrative) that Ghandi is dead; his journey through life as a shoeshine is recounted in the novel, but it is his death that provides the motto theme. The author candidly explains that the entire story is a matter of coincidence: "Had Kamāl the soldier not died, Alice would never have encountered Ghandi. If she hadn't, he would never have told her his story. If he hadn't died, Alice would never have told me the tale. And, if Alice hadn't vanished or even died, I would not have written what I'm writing now."[67] Even names are not fixed here. Ghandi is a nickname for someone called ʿAbd al-karīm; no one knows how he came to be called Ghandi. But as the author—the one inside the narrative—explains at the conclusion of this remarkable work, "Ghandi knew why he died. The bullets weren't aimed at him, but rather at the heart of a city that had destroyed itself. Like Ghandi it was trying to make a story out of its name."[68]

Changing Relationships Between the Middle East and the West

As the colonizing powers who had occupied and administered the territories of the Middle Eastern region withdrew or were forced out as a result of war, revolution, or negotiation, the freshly independent Arab states found themselves not only confronting the realities of two superpowers, who duly proceeded to manipulate the politics of the region to their own ends as their predecessors had done, but also needing to develop entirely new relationships with their former colonizers.

It will be recalled that the relationship with the West had provided one of the principal themes of early attempts at narrative writing in Arabic: from al-Ṭahṭāwī and al-Muwayliḥī in the nineteenth century to Tawfīq al-Ḥakīm, Shakīb al-Jābirī, and Dhū al-nūn Ayyūb in the 1930s. As East and West sought new modes of contact and understanding in the post–World War II period, novelists continued this long tradition of utilizing travel to the West as a means of ex-

67. Ilyās Khūrī, *Riḥlat Ghāndī al-ṣaghīr* (Little Ghandi's journey) (Beirut: Dār al-Ādāb, 1989), 18.

68. Ibid., 207.

ploring their own sense of identity and that of their nation, society, and culture.[69] In 1953 Suhayl Idrīs (b. 1923), founder of the Arab world's most influential literary magazine, *al-Ādāb,* published his novel, *al-Ḥayy al-Lātīnī* (The Latin Quarter). The theme of cultures in contact is now examined through a relationship between an Arab man and a French woman, carrying to a more symbolic level the many points of cultural difference. The "hero" of Idrīs's novel treats Jeanine Montreux in a manner that reflects not only the existentialist angst which is one of the author's favorite themes but also, on a broader scale, the apparently inexorable need to misunderstand that was symptomatic of the attitude of both cultures towards each other during these decades of uneasy adjustment to new realities.[70]

The process of communication and interchange during the post-colonial era, and the tensions that cultural influences bring about, is the topic of one of the most outstanding contributions to modern Arabic fiction thus far, *Mawsim al-hijrah ilā al-shamāl* (1966; *Season of Migration to the North,* 1969) by the Sudanese writer, al-Ṭayyib Ṣāliḥ (b. 1929), which will be analyzed in detail in the next chapter. In this novel, the direction in the conflict of values is shifted to one of north-south, as a brilliant Sudanese student takes all the tensions of his own cultural ambiguity to England, where his relationships with women become a veritable battlefield of deliberately orchestrated misunderstandings. In *al-Mar'ah wa-al-wardah* (The woman and the rose, 1971) another African novelist, the Moroccan Muḥammad Zifzāf (b. 1945), may be seen as bringing the theme back to its point of origin. Muḥammad, the novel's hero, goes to France to find confirmation of his own sense of identity with European culture. Attaching himself to the French underworld, he finds his impressions somewhat transformed. This development, however, is really subordinate to the narrative's principal motivation, that of offering some telling comments on the lack of freedoms in his own society.[71]

69. The theme of East-West contacts is the subject of studies by, among others, Ṭarabīshī, *Sharq wa-gharb*; and Issa J. Boullata, "Encounter Between East and West," 44–62.

70. Idrīs takes up the same basic theme in his third novel, *Aṣābiʿunā allatī taḥtariq* (Our burning fingers) (Beirut: Dār al-Ādāb, 1963). His novels have been analyzed by a large number of critics from among whom we would single out, in addition to those noted in the above note: Shujāʿ Muslim al-ʿĀnī, *Al-Riwāyah al-ʿArabiyyah wa-al-ḥaḍārah al-Ūrūbiyyah* (Baghdad: Manshūrāt Wizārat al-thaqāfah wa-al-funūn, 1979), 60–71; al-Khaṭīb, 115–20; al-Saʿāfīn, 444–69.

71. Ḥamīd notes that several critics have mistakenly assumed this work to be an

The theme of freedom for writers leads directly into discussion of a newer role that the West has come to fulfill with regard to writers of Arabic fiction who address the realities of life in their homeland, namely exile. The cities of Europe are havens to a large number of Arab-world intellectuals, and it is therefore to be anticipated that novelists will turn their attention to the topic. One such is ʿAbd al-raḥmān Munīf, himself long since condemned to exile from his native Saudi Arabia for the finely detailed societal commentary in his fictional works. Exile and political oppression form the themes of both *al-Ashjār wa-ightiyāl Marzūq* (Trees and Marzuq's assassination, 1973) and *Sharq al-Mutawassiṭ* (East of the Mediterranean, 1977), one of the most graphic portraits in Arabic fiction of the methods and effects of imprisonment and torture, not merely on the political prisoners involved but their families and friends as well. When Rajab Ismāʿīl, the principal character of the latter work, goes to France, it is to seek a cure for the tuberculosis that he has contracted during his truly barbaric imprisonment in that anonymous country "east of the Mediterranean." His address to the people of France has a new message:

> You people of Paris, if you brought your books to the Eastern shores of the Mediterranean, you'd spend your entire life in prisons. You'd rue the day you ever wrote, you'd disavow everything. Above all, make sure you never even think about political parties; the slightest allusion to them would be assumed to be a conspiracy, subversion. Your words would cost you your entire life, to be spent in desert jails, where you'd catch tuberculosis or typhoid; and then you'd die.[72]

Societal Transformations after Independence

The impact of oil. While the nation-states of the Arab world had achieved a degree of political independence following the Second World War, the demands of a world economy and their own aspirations for a more modern way of life meant that their interests were still connected to the West in a direct way, and no more so than in the domain of the Arab world's richest resource, oil. It was to com-

---

advocacy of the West: see *Al-Riwāyah al-Maghribiyyah,* 291–317, and *Fī al-tanẓīr wa-al-mumārasah,* 109–26. One such critic is al-Nassāj, 217.

72. ʿAbd al-raḥmān Munīf, *Sharq al-Mutawassiṭ* (East of the Mediterranean) (Beirut: Dār al-Ṭalīʿah, 1975), 130. A similar passage is addressed to the Achilleus, the ship on which Rajab is traveling; see 82.

bat the continuing influence of Western oil companies on the economies of the oil-producing states that OPEC (the Organization of Petroleum Exporting Countries) was founded in 1960. The spheres of politics and economics were kept somewhat removed from each other during uneasy negotiations over oil prices during the 1960s, but in October 1973 the Western world received an abrupt reminder of just how much international configurations had changed in the postindependence era of the Arab-world states.

Ever since oil had been discovered, it had come to be regarded as a cheap form of energy. As a result, the industrialized nations of the West had come to rely on it to a substantial degree in satisfying their needs. But in 1973 the Arab-world members of OPEC for the first time asserted their sovereignty over their own natural resources by using oil as an economic weapon. The effect on the world economy and that of the Arab states themselves was enormous. The occasion was yet another confrontation between Israel and its Arab neighbors, the October War of 1973. At the root of the conflict was, of course, the continuing saga of the dispossessed Palestinian people, the fictional depictions of which we have explored above. However, the military fronts involved in 1973 were those of Egypt and Syria. When the United States began flying emergency arms supplies to Israel, the oil-producing Arab states met in Kuwait and announced price increases of up to 50 percent; an oil embargo was imposed against the United States and Holland (the primary point of entry for the commodity into the European market). The effect on the industrialized world was immediate and profound. At certain points the price of oil rose to six times its previous levels before settling down to about half that amount.

Western economies were deeply effected by these rapid developments, but so too were those of the oil-producing states themselves who found themselves catapulted into the ranks of the wealthiest nations in the world, with huge amounts of capital at their disposal and the world's largest reserve of oil beneath their soil. That part of the Arab world that had always been viewed as the most traditional and culturally undeveloped now began to move into the forefront of modernization efforts in the region, a process made considerably easier by the huge budgets they were able to devote to initiatives in industrialization, transport, education, and the influx of Western expertise to carry them out. Nor was it from the West alone that these Gulf states began to import labor and management expertise. As the consequences of the Gulf War of 1991 have shown, Kuwait imported huge numbers of Palestinian professionals to work in almost every sector of the economy, and Egypt, the Arab world's largest repository of labor, sent large numbers of its men to Iraq and the Gulf. Egypt, already the site of the Arab world's most severe population (and therefore housing) problem, has now found itself facing the issues of families that are fatherless for extended periods of time, of a grotesque rise in consumerism (urged on by Anwar al-Sādāt's policy of economic opening-up [*infitāḥ*]), and, in the view of several writers on the subject, an increasingly assertive role for the Egyptian mother, now left on her own to handle the entire business of the family. Najīb Maḥfūẓ in particular has followed these trends in Egypt in his fictional works with a scarcely concealed disgust; from *al-Ḥubb taḥta al-maṭar* (Love in the rain, 1973) about the "phony war" at the Suez Canal in the early 1970s, to *al-Ḥubb fawq hadbat al-haram* (Love on the pyramid plateau, 1979) and *Yawm qutila al-zaʿīm* (1985; *The Day the Leader was Killed,* 1989), both of which are concerned with the problems of young people and, in particular, the housing crisis.

These economic transformations have thus had a significant impact on societies throughout the Arab world and particularly on societal, familial, and individual values and attitudes. The discovery of oil itself and its impact on the local societies involved is yet another narrative, and in ʿAbd al-raḥmān Munīf it has found its most illustrious storyteller. A petroleum economist by training, he turned to novel writing relatively late in life, but since the mid-1970s his output has been both varied and prolific. In *al-Nihāyāt* (1977; *Endings,* 1988), analyzed in detail in the next chapter, he introduced the Arabic novel to the savage world of the desert in a narrative that shows a highly personal concern for its fragile environment. *Sibāq al-masāfāt al-ṭawīlah* (Long-distance race, 1979) has the issues of oil as a backdrop; the topic of the novel is the machinations of the West, in the form of an Englishman, Peter MacDonald, in the circumstances leading up to the removal of the Iranian Prime Minister, Mosaddeg, in 1953 and the return to power of the Shah. In 1979 Munīf was asked about the linkage between his expertise in oil and the novel genre to which he was contributing. In retrospect, his response, already cited above but worth repeating, is a substantial tease: "Oil as a world and a topic may help us uncover some novelistic aspects in our contemporary life in the Arab world."[73]

73. ʿAbd al-raḥmān Munīf interviewed in *al-Maʿrifah* 204 (Feb. 1979): 188.

Munif has since proved the validity of his proposition beyond doubt by writing the longest novelistic project in Arabic to date, a huge quintet under the general title of *Mudun al-milḥ*: *al-Tīh* (The wilderness, 1984; *Cities of Salt,* 1987); *al-Ukhdūd* (1985; *The Trench,* 1991); *Taqāsīm al-layl wa-al-nahār* (1988; *Variations on Night and Day,* 1993); *Al-Munbatt* (Stranded, 1988), and *Bādiyat al-ẓulumāt* (Desert of darkness, 1988). In the first volume we are given a loving portrait of the traditional Bedouin society of the Gulf region of Saudi Arabia (which, however, remains unnamed) before the discovery of oil. The local inhabitants are perplexed when foreigners start digging up the ground, buying up land, and building a whole new town. The almost mythical figure, Mutʿib al-Hadhdhāl, warns that these developments bode ill for the community; his disappearance and the intermittent reported sightings of him from the community become symbolic of the disappearance of an old way of life and of suspicions regarding the motivations of the foreign visitors.[74] News of these developments travels far and wide, and among those who arrive to exploit the situation is the Syrian doctor, Ṣubḥī al-Maḥmaljī, who, by providing medical care and opening a hospital, is able to gain the attention and confidence of the ruler. The second volume moves from Ḥarrān on the Gulf (a fictional representation of Dhahran) to Mūrān, the capital (Riyadh). Here the indolent and lascivious Sultan Khazʿal indulges in his own fantasies as Dr. Maḥmaljī caters to his every whim while joining others in exploiting to the full the rapid expansion of the capital city and all the opportunities for investment and bribery that it offers. The picture drawn is savagely critical in its detailing of venality and moral corruption, but the reader is constrained to accept not only such attention to detail but also the storyteller's determination to narrate his tale at a leisurely pace appropriate to the concept of time prevalent in the culture itself. At the end of this devastating fictional exposé of an era in modern Saudi history, Dr. Maḥmaljī's influence collapses with the deposition of his patron and the installation of the Sultan's brother, Sultan Fīnār, as ruler.

The third and fifth volumes in the quintet are taken up with the early career of Sultan Fīnār (a fictional King Fayṣal) and his own reign until his assassination at the hands of one of his own relatives. In the fourth volume, *al-Munbatt,* Dr. Maḥmaljī, exiled in Germany with his patron, the former Sultan, finds that his machinations come

74. For analyses of this work, see Ṣiddīq, "The Contemporary Arabic Novel in Perspective," 206–11; and Badawi, "Two Novelists from Iraq," 140–54.

home to roost within his own family. The Sultan is advised by his confidants to divorce Dr. Maḥmaljī's daughter, whom he has added to his collection of wives. The doctor moves to Switzerland, his daughter commits suicide, and his wife abandons him to join their son who has chosen to side with Sultan Fīnār and returned to Mūrān.

With *Mudun al-milḥ* Munīf has made a major contribution to modern Arabic narrative, quite apart from providing a major fictional exploration of one of the major topics in the political, economic, and social life of the contemporary Arab world. In its sweep it needs to be placed alongside Maḥfūẓ's *Trilogy*, which will be analyzed below. But, as noted briefly above, the two works differ in one significant way: the mode of narration. For, while Maḥfūẓ was clearly concerned with the replication in the Egyptian historical context of the great social-reformist fiction of the European literary tradition, Munīf uses his previous experiences in novel writing to explore a variety of modes. We have noted above that the particular subject matter of each volume elicits a variety of narrative moods, but in commenting in an apparently negative way on this very topic, John Updike does not perhaps realize how close to the mark he actually is in referring to a "campfire narrator" who has all the time in the world to recount his story to his listeners. Particularly in *al-Tīh*, the act of narration itself is intended to be a loving portrait of an aspect of society that the discovery of oil and the cultural upheavals it has wrought has forever destroyed.[75]

The relationship of country and city. Modernization, industrialization, oil production, these concepts belong very much to the conversations among the inhabitants of the city. As has just been noted with reference to the works of Munīf, the twentieth century has seen not merely the growth of cities in almost every region of the Arab world, but in some cases the creation of entirely new ones from scratch. While the city and its middle-class people have served as the primary topic of the novel genre in the West, the largest proportion of the populace in the Middle East has traditionally resided outside the city. Rising aspirations and consumerism resulting from increased wealth in certain countries and modernization have led to a considerable rise in urban populations; Cairo staggers under the weight of a quarter of the entire population of Egypt, some sixteen million

75. Updike's review of *Cities of Salt* was published in the *New Yorker*, 17 Oct. 1988. The comment cited here is on 117.

people. From the very beginnings of modern Arabic fiction, the relationship between the city and its provinces has served as a prominent theme, exemplified by the *ʿumdah* figure in al-Muwayliḥī's *Ḥadīth ʿĪsā ibn Hishām,* and the changing relationship between the two continues to be a prominent topic of contemporary Arabic fiction.[76]

As novelists in the postindependence period sought for materials with which to illustrate the need for social change, the status of peasants in the countryside and their exploitation under the traditional feudal system presented a clear and ready topic. Some novelists prepared the way for much needed agricultural reform by providing graphic illustration of the way things had been. The title of Dhū al-nūn Ayyūb's novel, *al-Yad wa-al-arḍ wa-al-mā'* (Hand, earth, and water, 1948) reflects the rather unsubtle way in which he deals with the topic of corruption and exploitation in the countryside of Iraq during the monarchy and anticipates the process of change that began in several Arab countries during the 1950s. Al-Bashīr Khurayyif's novel, *al-Daqlah fī ʿarājīninā* (Dates in the palm trees, 1969) is a similarly suggestive title for a work that depicts the struggles of an oasis community, the remoteness of which is emphasized by the author's resort to the use of a very local form of colloquial dialogue.

In Egypt the agricultural reform laws that were passed soon after the revolution were an attempt to address many of the injustices vividly illustrated in the renowned novel by ʿAbd al-raḥmān al-Sharqāwī, *al-Arḍ* (1954; *Egyptian Earth,* 1962). The work is set during the tyrannical regime of Ismāʿīl Ṣidqī, prime minister of Egypt in the 1930s, but the contemporary import of the novel was not lost on anyone; indeed, one of the criticisms of the work may be that the message is too obtrusive at times. While the narrative concerns itself with the exploitation that the peasants suffer in tilling the soil, the focus of the village's opposition is a new road, which the authorities plan to build through the peasants' land to the house of the local Pāshā. Within that structure the reader is introduced to a whole series of authentic and vivid Egyptian peasant characters, from Waṣīfah, the earthy and sharp-tongued village beauty, to ʿAlwānī, the wily and feckless Bedouin; from Shaykh Shinnāwī, the village teacher and *muftī,* to ʿAbd al-hādī, the industrious farmer and one of several men who are in love with Waṣīfah. In conveying the daily life, squabbles, loves, and intrigues of this set of characters, al-Shar-

76. See ʿAbd al-muḥsin Ṭāhā Badr, *Al-Riwā'ī wa-al-arḍ* (Cairo: al-Hay'ah al-Miṣriyyah al-ʿāmmah li-al-kitāb, 1971).

qāwī makes excellent use of the colloquial dialect to reflect the earthy humour of these peasants as they struggle against the combined vicissitudes of nature and corruption.[77]

It is the passage of the Agricultural Reform Laws that provides an unfortunately artificial ending to what is otherwise a fine contribution to the repertoire of novels about the countryside, *al-Ḥarām* (1959; *The Sinners,* 1984) by Yūsuf Idrīs (1927–90), in which the discovery of a dead baby causes a village community initially to search for the suspect among the migrant workers living outside their community before discovering that the tragedy belongs to one of their own.

Another son of the Nile delta, Yūsuf al-Qaʿīd (b. 1944), has made village life a particular focus of his works. *Akhbār ʿizbat al-Minaysī* (1971; *News from the Meneisi Farm,* 1987) is set in the fishbowl atmosphere of a country estate, where the night watchman's daughter has been killed by her brother in a traditional crime of honor. The seducer turns out to be the owner's son, but within the traditional code it is the women of the household who are required to be the preservers of the family honor. The novel succeeds notably in creating a picture of an essentially closed community in which the inexorable logic of legitimated murder can prevail. In a more recent work, *al-Ḥarb fī barr Miṣr* (1978; *War in the Land of Egypt,* 1986) the venue is still the village, but a potentially tragic mistake acquires a tone close to the farcical. A series of narrators, all very aware of the act of narration in which they are involved, tell their own segments of the tale that results when an *ʿumdah's* son is drafted into the Egyptian army at the time of the October War of 1973. The *ʿumdah* persuades a poor villager to send his son as a substitute, but the plan go awry when the young draftee is killed in action and returned to the village as a hero. Corruption and bungling bureaucracy have long been favorite butts of Egyptian fictional humor, and here they are woven into a tragicomic narrative of considerable skill.[78]

The lands of upper Egypt have also provided Egyptian novelists with themes and venues for their works. Yaḥyā al-Ṭāhir ʿAbdallāh (1942–81) was in fact born in al-Karnak, the village just to the north

77. Ibid., 113–53; Hilary Kilpatrick, *The Modern Egyptian Novel* (London: Ithaca, 1974), 116–33; and ʿAli B. Jad, "ʿAbd al-raḥmān al-Sharqāwī's *Al-Arḍ,*" *JAL* 7 (1976): 88–100.

78. For Yūsuf al-Qaʿīd, see Paul Starkey, "From the City of the Dead to Liberation Square: The Novels of Yūsuf al-Qaʿīd," *JAL* 24, no. 1 (Mar. 1993): 62–74.

of Luxor, and many of his short stories are set in the upper Egyptian milieu with which he is so familiar. His tragically early death deprived Arabic fiction of one of its most experimental voices. His novel, *al-Ṭawq wa-al-aswirah* (The necklet and bracelets, 1975), a starkly grim tale of upper Egyptian family life, draws on characters and themes explored in earlier short stories; its characteristically taut, image-laden style belongs to one of the most poetically inclined of Egyptian writers of fiction. ʿAbdallāh was still alive to witness the way in which his beloved upper Egypt was affected by the construction of the High Dam at Aswān and the initiation of village reconstruction projects to house those Nubians whose homes were inundated.[79] Ṣunʿallāh Ibrāhīm explores the clear symbolic importance of this project for ʿAbd al-nāṣir's Egypt in his novel, *Najmat Aghusṭus* (August star, 1974), but the potential consequences of such attempts at societal engineering had already been explored by another Egyptian novelist, Fatḥī Ghānim in *al-Jabal* (The mountain, 1957). The setting is the west bank of the Nile opposite Luxor. The government has decided to build a model village for the people of Gurna in the hope of preventing the continued pillaging of the Pharaonic tombs and the manufacture of fakes through which the villagers earn their livelihood.[80] For this purpose, an architect has designed and built a modern village with all the most modern conveniences, but the villagers steadfastly refuse to move from their cave dwellings on "the mountain." Threats to move them by force are of no avail in the face of the stalwart opposition of the village *ʿumdah* and his community. Ghānim creates a realistic environment for this clash of interests, but many of the characters remain as stereotypes, and especially those whose names are not revealed—the architect, the princess and the French woman. Beyond this, the reader observes that there is very little narrative distance between the author of this work and the narrator of the story; the young investigator who comes from Cairo to write a report on the situation is himself named Fatḥī Ghānim.[81] The strategies of metafiction may encourage such authorial interpolations into the fabric of the text, but when the narrator's contemplative moments turn into lectures as happens in this work, the general effect is more to remind us of the

79. See Robert Fernea, *Nubians in Egypt* (Austin: Univ. of Texas Press, 1973), 36–47.

80. This is also the subject of a very famous Egyptian film entitled *al-Mūmiyāʾ* (The mummy).

81. Fatḥī Ghānim, *Al-Jabal* (The mountain) (Cairo: Dār al-Hilāl, 1959), 57.

homiletic purposes of earlier fiction.[82] More recently, in his novel *Sharq al-nakhīl* (East of the palm trees, 1985) Bahā' Ṭāhir makes effective use of a disagreement over land in upper Egypt and the family feud that it engenders as a focus for the flashbacks, dreams, and even hallucinations of a dissipated and disillusioned upper Egyptian student in Cairo. The dispute over land in upper Egypt is echoed by the concern of the demonstrating students in Cairo, protesting another matter of land: the loss of the Sinai Peninsula. It is through the vision of the sickly and uncommitted narrator that the reader sees this juxtaposition of violence to individuals and groups, both within the highly tradition-bound society of upper Egypt and the turbulent political atmosphere of the capital city.

In a book about the Maghrib, the Egyptian writer Samīr Amīn notes that, while there has always been a relationship of dependency between city and provinces in Egypt, the same is not true of either the Maghrib or Syria.[83] Attempts to institute agricultural reform measures in such different circumstances met with mixed success, as is clearly shown in al-Ṭāhir Waṭṭār's novel devoted to the topic, *al-Zilzāl* (The earthquake, 1974). The author manages to convey postrevolutionary attitudes with great clarity and force by using the figure of Shaykh ʿAbd al-majīd Bū-Arwāḥ, a landowner and teacher who returns to his home city of Constantine, which had given its name to the land reform plan instituted by the French between 1959 and 1964.[84] He is anxious to transfer as much of his land as possible to his heirs before the reform law takes effect. The "earthquake" of the title refers both to the physical transformation of the earth's crust (Constantine lies on a fault line), but also refers to a quotation from the Qur'ān (Sūrah XXII,1) which is repeated by the Shaykh throughout the novel. As he makes his disgruntled way around the city, his bitter musings include quotations from the text of the Qur'ān, curses invoked against Ibn Khaldūn for his theories of civilization, and hopes for a physical or societal earthquake which will eradicate all the revolutionary changes which have so completely altered his lifestyle and surroundings. This novel represents a most successful manipulation of narrative point of view, in that the achievements of the Algerian revolution attained after a great deal

82. E.g., ibid., 11, 156.

83. Samīr Amīn, *The Maghreb in the Modern World* (London: Penguin, 1970), 77.

84. Ibid., 125–26.

of social upheaval and bloodshed are seen through the eyes of a character whose attitude is totally antagonistic.

In Syria, a number of writers of social-realist novels have dealt with the problems of the country's peasantry, although it has to be admitted that, more often than not, the results bring to mind the cautionary words of Laḥmadānī Hamid on this type of fictional writing, "Writing a work of literature about oppressed groups within society is not always a cue for a positive critical response or a sign of success as a work of art, particularly if the writing in question confines itself to social description alone."[85] Thus, in *al-Ḥufāt* (Without shoes, 1971) Fāris Zarzūr (b. 1930) deals with the exploitation of migrant workers, while in *al-Mudhnibūn* (Sinners, 1974) the topic is drought and extortion. With *al-Sindyānah* (The oak tree, 1971) ʿAbd al-nabī Ḥijāzī crafts a more subtle and carefully crafted piece of fiction about a village in the Syrian provinces in which the impact of crushing poverty is exploited by the *Mukhtār* to his own benefit.

In contemporary fiction, as in poetry, the city, and particularly the capital city, emerges as "the center of exploitation and misery, of social injustice and political intrigue."[86] In the Maghrib the transfer of the farming community to the city created social problems for each community, aptly summarized in the words of Ahmed Boukous:

> Ainsi le paysan qui fuit les aléas d'une economie marquée par la precarité, pour s'installer en ville, doit commencer par désapprendre son idiome maternel et par modifier son comportement social et culturel afin de s'integrer à la masse des deracinés-salariés. Celui qui, à force de privation, parvient à s'imposer dans la domaine du commerce, doit également se "dépaysanner" pour s'embourgeoiser.[87]

This tension between city and village is a prominent theme of several Maghribi novelists. In *Fi bayt al-ʿankabūt* (In the spider's house, 1976) by the Tunisian writer Muḥammad al-Hādī ibn Ṣāliḥ (b. 1948), the entire life of the rural hero, Ṣāliḥ, is ruined when, upon discovering

85. See Ḥamīd, *Al-Riwāyah al-Maghribiyyah,* 239.

86. al-Jayyusi, *Modern Arabic Poetry,* 32. For further comments on the city, see Mustafa Badawi, "The City in Egyptian Literature," in *Modern Arabic Literature,* 26–43.

87. Ahmed Boukous, "La situation linguistique au Maroc," *Europe* (June–July 1979): 18.

that his wife is a prostitute, he takes his infant son with him to the city. In ʿAbd al-ḥamīd ibn Hadūqah's (b. 1925) early Algerian novel *Rīḥ al-janūb* (South wind, 1971), Nafīsah, an eighteen-year-old girl, is determined to go to the city to receive an education, and refuses to return to her village, where her father wishes to force upon her a compulsory marriage to an older man. Her unequivocal statement to her mother illustrates not only the changing position of women (at least, as portrayed in fiction) but also an ever-widening gap in values and expectations between two discrete communities: "Tell my father that I will not get married; I won't stop my studies. I'm going back to Algiers, no matter what. I'm not going to put up with the humiliation you have to endure. You can be mother to someone else if you like, and he can be father to whomever he wishes. I won't allow this curse to get as far with me as it has with others. I am not a woman. Do you understand? I am not a woman."[88]

Family roles and the status of women. The impact of the discovery of oil on the economies of the Arab world nations, the migration of male workers, the problems of housing, all these factors discussed in previous sections of this chapter have had a direct impact on the institution of the family, and most especially on women, who in the majority of countries continue to fulfill their traditional role of nurturer of family life and also guardian of the family honor. As we noted in a previous chapter, Arabic fiction has been concerned from the outset with the status of women. Titles such as Sarrūf's *Dhāt al-khidr,* Haykal's *Zaynab,* ʿĪsā ʿUbayd's *Thurayyā,* al-ʿAqqād's *Sārah,* Lāshīn's *Ḥawwāʾ* . . . , and Maḥmūd Taymūr's *Salwā* . . . parallel Henry Fielding's *Amelia* and Samuel Richardson's *Pamela* and *Clarissa.* This progression from the 1890s to the 1930s does reflect some modest changes in the portrayal of women's status; from Ṣarrūf's boudoir and al-Muwayliḥī's grim picture of a Cairene dancehall, the novel reflects the views of Qāsim Amīn (1865–1908), the great Egyptian advocate of women's rights, by at least placing female characters in genuine family contexts. That is where the reader finds Amīnah in *Bayn al-qaṣrayn* (1956), the first volume of Maḥfūẓ's *Trilogy,* taking care of her family, waiting patiently for the return of her debauching husband, and submitting meekly when he throws

88. Muḥammad al-Hādī ibn Ṣāliḥ, *Fī bayt al-ʿankabūt* (Tūnis: Al-Dār al-ʿArabiyyah li-al-kitāb, 1976); ʿAbd al-ḥamīd ibn Hadūqah, *Rīḥ al-janūb* (Algiers, 1971), 88–89. For ibn Hadūqah's novel, see Maṣāyif, 179–209; al-Nassāj, 222ff.; and Šalim, *Al-Mughāmarah al-riwāʾiyyah,* 67–72.

her out of house and home for going to the mosque without his permission.[89] In *Thumma azhara al-ḥuzn* (Then sadness bloomed, 1963), Fāḍil al-Sibāʿī (b. 1929) provides a picture of a struggling family in Aleppo. Following the death of her husband, Kawthar, the mother, has to struggle in order to maintain her household, which consists of five daughters and a baby son. The period involved, 1958–61, is that of the United Arab Republic when Egypt and Syria were politically united, and emotional relationships and educational contacts involving members of the family reflect the complexities of the era. The mother meanwhile has to resist the advances of the polygamous Al-Ḥājj Hilāl as she strives to maintain the educational progress and moral rectitude of her daughters.[90] The status of daughters and the continuing need to preserve their honorable status is discussed in withering terms by Laṭīfah al-Zayyāt in *al-Bāb al-maftūḥ* (The open door, 1960). While the novel is clearly a product of the idealism that marked the post-1956 period in Egypt, the heroine of the work, Laylā, defies her family's wishes regarding marriage. It is however not merely her voice that is reflected in her forthright statements:

> When a girl is born, they all give a smile of resignation. When she grows up, they put her in a prison and train her in the art of living, to smile, to curtsy, to put on perfume and look delicate, to dissimulate, to wear a corset, and to get married. To whom, you ask? Any man. All you have to worry about is his money. The woman had better be greedy for love, very greedy . . . but there should be no feelings, sentiment, thought or love shown in public or else they'll kill her.[91]

One Maghribi author who has taken the dysfunctional family as a primary topic is the Algerian Rashīd Abū Jadrah (Rachid Boujedra, b. 1941), a fascinating figure in his own right in that, having achieved an illustrious career as a novelist writing in French, he ful-

89. Najīb Maḥfūz, *Bayn al-qaṣrayn* (Cairo: Maktabat Miṣr, 1956), 187–272; English trans.: *Palace Walk,* trans. William M. Hutchins and Olive Kenny (New York: Doubleday, 1990), 164–235.

90. For al-Sibāʿī's novel, see al-Fayyūmī, 41ff.; al-Khaṭīb, 219–52; and al-Saʿāfīn, 285–89.

91. Quoted by Fu'ād Duwārah in *Fī al-riwāyah al-Miṣriyyah* (Cairo: Dār al-Kātib al-ʿArabī, 1968), 152. For Laṭīfah al-Zayyāt, see also Hilary Kilpatrick, "The Egyptian Novel from *Zaynab* to 1980," in *Modern Arabic Literature,* The Cambridge History of Arabic Literature Series (Cambridge: Cambridge Univ. Press, 1992), 250–52.

filled an earlier promise by beginning to write in Arabic, starting in 1981. His novel in French, *La répudiation* (1969), caused a sensation in both France and the Maghrib when it was published.[92] It presents a portrait of a family life with no enduring values apart from the total domination of the father-figure, one where violence and debauchery prevail as the father feels able to divorce his wife of fifteen years in order to marry a fifteen-year old girl. This situation also provides the context for Abū Jadrah's second novel in Arabic, *al-Marth* (Soaking, 1984), in which the young hero, named Rashīd, takes his young stepmother as a mistress. Abū Jadrah's first novel in Arabic, *al-Tafakkuk* (Dissipation, 1981), tells two stories that reflect the city-countryside dichotomy noted above with reference to Algeria and some of its fictional works. The female character, Salmā, has, like ibn Hadūqah's Nafīsah, received an education and feels no concern for the likes of Ṭahar al-Ghumrī, a freedom fighter during the protracted revolution, whose problems in the rural part of the country represent "the Algeria of a disillusioned generation."[93] From these and other works, Rashīd Abū Jadrah emerges as a major new voice in Arabic fiction, a writer who both through his use of many layers of consciousness and his different Arabic style (which some critics have seen as simply the inability of a French-educated Algerian to write "idiomatically") is bringing an outspoken and technically accomplished vision to the analysis of Arab societies in the process of change.

As the female characters in several novels already discussed have shown, one of the principal means by which women were to become aware of the nature of their status and the possibilties of change was through the medium of education. Here, too, Maḥfūẓ fulfills his role as fictional historian through the series of vignettes published as *al-Marāyā* (1972), with a passage that captures not only the nature of the change taking place but also the awkwardness of public contact between the sexes:

> The girl students in 1930 were very few in number, no more than ten altogether. They all had the stamp of the harem about them. They dressed modestly, wore no earrings or bracelets, and sat together in the front row of the lecture hall, as though they were in the women's section of a tramcar. At first we neither greeted them

92. See Farida Abū-Haidar, "The Bipolarity of Rachid Boujedra," *JAL* 20, no. 1 (1989): 40–56.

93. Ibid., 51.

> nor talked to them. If we absolutely had to ask a question or borrow a notebook, then the whole thing was done with a cautious shyness. However, this did not continue peaceably for long. They soon started to attract attention.[94]

And with increases in educational opportunity for young people of both sexes come, almost automatically, some notable clashes between generations and sexes. We have already seen this in ibn Hadūqah's *Rīḥ al-janūb,* but the pattern is replicated elsewhere. In the significantly titled *Ghurabā' fī awṭāninā* (Strangers in our own domains, 1972) Walīd Midfā'ī depicts a family where the sons rebel against their domineering father, and the daughter, Widād, refuses to contemplate an arranged marriage. The title of Suhayl Idrīs's (b. 1923) novel *al-Khandaq al-ghamīq* (The deep trench, 1958) is the name of a district of Beirut, but it is also symbolic of a situation in which older, more traditional values based on a surface adherence to religion—represented in the novel by the character of Fawzī, the father of the family—clash directly with the more secular values of Lebanese society as seen in the children. The differences are seen at their most vivid through the utter scorn with which the children's values acquired at home are greeted by their peers.[95]

Within a societal context such as this, the process whereby women have claimed the right to leave the home and its family ties, to enter the work force and public life, and to control their own destinies has been neither short nor easy. The pressures and temptations that were to confront professional women as they entered the workforce are shown in a somewhat unsubtle way by Yūsuf Idrīs in his novel *al-'Ayb* (The shame, 1962), and with much greater artistry by Bahā' Ṭāhir (b. 1935) in *Qālat Duḥā* (Duḥā said, 1985). This latter novel follows the civil service career of Duḥā through the eyes of a male narrator who is in love with her, but in the process it also manages to craft—through language that displays all the subtlety of a short-story writer—an authentic picture of Egyptian society seen through the eyes of the members of the younger generation in its often vain struggle to achieve even the most basic of middle-class aspirations. While these works provide portraits of women charac-

94. Najīb Maḥfūẓ, *Al-Marāyā* (Cairo: Maktabat Miṣr, 1972), 160; English trans.: *Mirrors,* trans. Roger Allen (Chicago: Bibliotheca Islamica, 1977), 106.

95. For Midfa'ī, see Ibn Dhurayl, *Al-Riwāyah al-'Arabiyyah al-Sūriyyah,* 157–58; and al-Sa'āfīn, 319ff. For Suhayl Idrīs's work, see *Al-Ādāb* (Dec. 1958): 12; (Feb. 1959): 13.

ters carving out their own space in a predominantly male world, Marilyn Booth notes that any additional rights that may have been won have not implied a diminution of traditional expectations; their reality has still tended to be "shaped and usually constrained by the rigid social expectations surrounding home management and child-bearing in marriage as women's prescribed roles."[96]

From a historical perspective, the appearance of *Anā aḥyā* (I am alive, 1958), the novel by Laylā Baʿalbakkī (b. 1936?), is clearly a significant landmark. The very title presents a forceful statement, a challenge. The account of family relationships and feelings is no longer given within the framework of a distanced, omniscient third-person narrative, but shifts to a direct first-person experiential montage. As a commentator in French notes, "Ce qui a surtout choqué certains lecteurs de langue arabe, c'est la franchise avec laquelle cette jeune fille aborde les problèmes des rapports familiaux et des rélations sexuelles."[97] *Anā aḥyā* takes as its primary focus the position of the girl within the family and her view of herself. Līnah, the heroine, underlines her views on the subject in the novel's final paragraph: "So home I went again. It's as though I was forced to do it. I always have to go home; to eat at home, to sleep, to bathe. My entire destiny seems to be tied up in this home."[98] To Khālidah Saʿīd this novel was "a *cri de coeur* protesting against not only the enslavement of women but also the female syndrome, daughter-wife-mother, which restricted her entire existence to the level of biological functions."[99] And yet, while there can be no doubt about the writer's commitment to change, the overall effect is not a little narcissistic. As Ḥalīm Barakāt notes, "The defiant mood of Lina . . . is deeply rooted in her egotistic assertion of her individual freedom. Her strong feelings and ideas spring from a point of view which focuses on her ego to the almost total exclusion of social reality. What is at issue for her is her personal problems."[100] This predominance of the personal is underlined by the extreme prolixity of the work. Baʿalbakkī's second

96. *My Grandmother's Cactus,* selected and trans. by Marilyn Booth (London: Quartet, 1991), Introduction, 6. Virginia Woolf's views on the same subject are cited by Accad, 39.

97. *Anthologie de la littérature arabe contemporaine: le roman et la nouvelle,* ed. Raoul et Laura Makarious (Paris; Editions du Seuil, 1964), 330.

98. Laylā Baʿalbakkī, *Anā aḥyā* (I am alive) (Beirut: Dār Majallat Shiʿr, 1963), 317.

99. Khālidah Saʿīd, 82.

100. Barakāt, *Visions* 23–24.

novel, *al-Ālihah al-mamsūkhah* (Deformed deities, 1960), shows a greater control of the narrative structure, but the characters in both works remain somewhat two-dimensional.

The Syrian novelist, Colette Khūrī (b. 1937), continues the challenge to entrenched values by publishing the provocatively titled *Ayyām maʿahu* (Days with him, 1959) and *Laylah wāḥidah* (A single night, 1961). The former was an instant *cause célèbre* because of its frank description of a love affair between a young girl and an older man whom she eventually rejects.[101] Another Syrian writer, Ghādah al-Sammān (b. 1942), used her earlier works of fiction—mostly in the short story form—to assert the role and rights of women as independent individuals, but, as noted above, the Lebanese civil war led her and many other women writers to use the novel genre to concentrate on less individualistic aspects of her society.[102] Such writers would definitely include Ḥanān al-Shaykh (b. 1945) who has addressed herself in direct fashion to the position of women in a world dominated by the values of men. Her finest work to date is certainly *Ḥikāyat Zahrah* (1980; *The Story of Zahra,* 1986), a study of the daughter of a dysfunctional Lebanese Shiʿite family living through the horrors of civil war, a novel that will be analyzed in the next chapter.

The works of these writers were by women and about women, a mixture already explosive enough for conservative circles, but the impact was made even stronger by the fact that use was often made of the first-person narrative mode. This has led some critics to suggest that these works of fiction are personal confessions or reminiscences rather than works of creative fiction.[103] However, while these writings do indeed deliberately confront prevailing societal attitudes and norms, there can be no justification within a *critical* context for denying them the ironic privileges accorded to fiction. Laylā Baʿalbakkī, Colette Khūrī, and Ghādah al-Sammān have the same right to authorial detachment from the statements and reflections of their fictional protagonists as any other writers. Whatever one's verdict may be about the literary merits of their fiction, it seems reason-

101. For a discussion of Colette Khūrī's works, see Fontaine, *Romans arabes modernes,* 93–97.

102. See the study of Ḥanān ʿAwwād, *Arab Causes in the Fiction of Ghādah al-Sammān 1961–1975* (Sherbrooke, Canada: Editions Naaman, 1983); and Cooke, *War's Other Voices,* passim.

103. See, e.g., the comments of Yūsuf al-Shārūnī in *Al-Laylah al-thāniyyah baʿd al-alf,* ed. Yūsuf al-Shārūnī (Cairo: Al-Hay'ah al-Miṣriyyah al-ʿammah li-al-kitāb, 1975), 14–15.

able in retrospect to note that they have considerably expanded the creative space within which contemporary writers of both sexes may portray their worlds. In other words, the fictions that they create and the narrative strategies that they employ to bring them into existence are to be regarded as contributions to the technical repertoire of Arabic fiction, quite apart from whatever kind of adjustment of balance or advocacy of change they may be effecting in the broader societal frame.[104]

A more wistful and less strident tone is established in the fiction of the Lebanese writer, Emily Naṣrallāh (b. 1938). While she shares with Baʿalbakkī, Khūrī, and others a concern for the status of women, her choice of themes and moods is completely different. Her well-known novel, *Ṭuyūr Aylūl* (September birds, 1962) manages to combine several of the themes that have been mentioned above: the life of women within the traditional societal system, the contrast between the city and the village, and contact with the West and in particular emigration. The very title of the work, with its romantic associations with nature, recalls the fictional works of Jubrān. As in his *al-Arwāḥ al-mutamarridah* (Spirits rebellious) of many years earlier, the countryside of Lebanon and its natural phenomena are used as the backdrop for a work of social criticism, although, in Naṣrallāh's case, the homiletic element so obtrusive in Jubrān's works is entirely absent and the message is allowed to emerge from the events themselves. The narrator, a village girl who has moved to the city, looks back on her childhood and adolescence in the traditional society of her native village. Along with the narrator's sense of alienation from and longing for this microcosm, there emerge the tragedies of a number of young people brought up in the village who feel imprisoned within the web of idle chatter and arranged marriages concocted for them by their elders. Some of them manage to escape the inevitable by emigrating to the United States. Others find refuge in death, and still others resign themselves to the inevitable dictates of tradition. The condemnation implicit in the events of the narrative is made even more forceful by contrast with the description of the village itself and its environs, something which is achieved in a language of extreme poetic sensitivity.

The Lebanese village and its confining customs provides the venue for two further novels by Naṣrallāh, *Shajarat al-diflah* (The

104. With regard to Laylā Baʿalbakkī's role, this view is shared by Muḥyī al-dīn Ṣubḥī, *Al-Baṭal fī maʾziq* (Damascus: Manshūrāt ittiḥād al-Kuttāb al-ʿArab, 1979), 206.

oleander tree, 1968) and *al-Rahīnah* (The pawn, 1973). However, with the beginning of the civil war in April 1975 issues of emigration cease to be a matter of adherence to traditional values and become an agonizing decision between personal safety and loyalty to one's homeland. Mahā, the heroine of *Tilka al-dhikrayāt* (Those memories, 1980), has made her decision: "the staying is now in Lebanon whereas it had originally been in the village."[105] With *Iqlāʿ ʿaks al-zamān* (1981; *Flight Against Time,* 1987) Naṣrallāh combines her themes by depicting the journey of an older couple during the civil war to visit their children who have emigrated to Canada. After a while, the old man decides that he has to return to his homeland. One evening he is murdered by three unknown men.

We have left till last consideration of the Arab world's most famous woman writer, Nawāl al-Saʿdāwī (b. 1930). She has been a fearless advocate of women's rights both inside and outside her native Egypt, and her outspokenness has frequently brought her into conflict with the authorities. This led in 1981 to her arrest and imprisonment during the regime of President Anwar al-Sādāt, and she was only released upon his assassination; in a typical gesture, she responded by writing a much publicized account of her imprisonment.[106] In addition to a large number of works on public health (she is a medical doctor by training) and feminist issues, she has written a good deal of fiction. Of her novels the most famous are *Imraʾah ʿinda nuqtat ṣifr* (1975; *Woman at Point Zero,* 1983) concerning a prostitute named Firdaws who refuses to conform with the exploitative game that society foists upon her and is executed for murder, and *Suqūṭ al-Imām* (1988; *Fall of the Imam,* 1988) which concerns itself with the depiction of a nightmare society in which women are subservient to a religious leader. As the themes of these works makes clear, fiction at the hands of Nawāl al-Saʿdāwī becomes an alternative and powerful means of forwarding her opinions concerning the rights of women in Middle Eastern society. The voice of her narrators is stri-

105. Cooke, *War's Other Voices,* 154. See also Miriam Cooke, "Women Write War: The Feminization of Lebanese Society in the War Literature of Emily Naṣrallāh," *Bulletin of the British Society for Middle Eastern Studies* 14 no. 1 (1988): 52–67; and Fontaine, *Romans arabes modernes,* 97–103.

106. Nawāl al-Saʿdāwī, *Mudhakkirātī fī sijn al-nisāʾ* (Cairo: Dār al-Mustaqbal al-ʿArabī, 1984); English trans.: *Memoirs from the Women's Prison,* trans. Marilyn Booth (London: Women's, 1986). She discusses many aspects of her life and career during the course of an interview with Fedwa Malti-Douglas and Allen Douglas, in *Opening the Gates* 394–404.

dent, and the message unequivocal. It remains to be seen what position her works will retain in the history of modern Arabic fiction, but there can be little doubt that she will be numbered among the most prominent fighters for her cause in the latter half of the twentieth century.

The individual and freedom. From the most general level of contacts between cultures and political and economic blocs, via the more localized concerns of national identity and the establishment of societal priorities and directions, we come to the level of the individual. With the oeuvre of an author such as Najīb Maḥfūẓ, the transition from a concentration on the more general picture of society as clusters of people in family and other groupings to a portrait of the individual trying to cope with the labyrinth of modern man's existence is clearly marked by the difference of the novels of the 1960s from those that preceded. The characters who people works such as *al-Liṣṣ wa-al-kilāb* (1962; *The Thief and the Dogs,* 1984), *al-Shaḥḥādh* (1965; *The Beggar,* 1986), and *Thartharah fawq al-Nīl* (1966; *Adrift on the Nile,* 1993) are revealed through a more symbolically charged language to be living in a world, a society, in which they can feel little sense of purpose or belonging. They are, in a word, completely alienated. The stimuli for the emergence of such portraits in Egypt and elsewhere during this particular period are not hard to trace.

In the period following the Second World War, the newly independent Arab nations set about the process of establishing within their own borders the set of parameters that would govern individual freedoms and the rights of public expression. Newly installed leaders and governments who were often quick to announce reforms of various kinds, particularly (as we have seen) in the area of agriculture, were just as swift to create an elaborate secret police apparatus. More often than not, opposition groups that had assisted in the overthrow of the old system, especially communists and members of Islamic groups, soon found themselves behind bars. The suppression of opposition to governmental policy and the maintenance of "public order" was, more often than not, achieved through the creation of an atmosphere of fear and suspicion. If the process of confronting the problems of the modern world has led intellectuals in many different cultures to declare themselves alienated from their environment and society, how much more was this the case for Arab writers in the roller-coaster atmosphere of official optimism, cynicism, and suspicion that pervaded so many Arab countries during this period. When one becomes sufficiently inured to such an intellectual environment, there is a variety of possible reactions: resistance—often leading to imprisonment or worse—a resort to symbolism or dark humor, exile, or silence.

Perhaps nothing demonstrates the sheer courage of the Arab novelist so much as the fact that there is a disarmingly large repertoire of works of fiction on the subject of prisons in their various aspects: the circumstances of arrest, the conditions inside—including the most barbaric kinds of torture—and the sense of alienation following release.[107] While works such as Nabīl Sulaymān's *Al-Sijn* (Prison, 1972) and Sharīf Ḥatātah's *al-ʿAyn dhāt al-jifn al-maʿdanī* (1981; *The Eye with an Iron Lid,* 1982) describe the tedium and barbarity of prison itself, other writers concern themselves with the broader implications of such modes of political suppression for the society as a whole.[108] Both Karīm al-Nāṣirī in *al-Washm* (The tattoo, 1972) by ʿAbd al-raḥmān Majīd al-Rubayʿī (b. 1939) and Rajab Ismāʿīl in Munīf's *Sharq al-Mutawassiṭ* have to deal with the fact that they have been released from jail, but that, in signing "confessions," they have placed the lives of their still incarcerated colleagues in the greatest jeopardy. The hero of Ṣunʿallāh Ibrāhīm's (b. 1937) pioneering work in this genre, *Tilka al-rāʾiḥah* (1966/1986; *The Smell of It,* 1971), written following his release from political prison in 1964, partially published in 1966, banned, and only published complete in Arabic in 1986, is a masterful portrait of the impact that such imprisonment has not only on the imprisoned person, but on everyone around him. All motivation vanishes, and minutiae assume an extreme importance; the entire day seems taken up with mere survival. Precisely the same atmosphere of oppressive surveillance and hopelessness, one whereby the oppositional views or actions of a single member will engulf the entire family group in a continuing nightmare, pervades the quartet of novels by Ismāʿīl Fahd Ismāʿīl analyzed in the next chapter.

It is, of course, the particular function of the novel genre to

107. There are at least two studies devoted to this subgenre of the Arabic novel: Samar Rūḥī Fayṣal, *Al-Sijn al-siyāsī fī al-riwāyah al-ʿArabiyyah* (Damascus: Manshūrāt ittiḥād al-Kuttāb al-ʿArab, 1983); and Nazīh Abū Niḍāl, *Adab al-sujūn* (Beirut: Dār al-Ḥadāthah, 1981). See also Nabīl Sulaymān, "Naḥwa adab al-sujūn," *Al-Mawqif al-adabī* 3, nos. 1 and 2 (May–June 1973): 137–41. These works provide analyses of a large number of novels, of which only a few can be mentioned here.

108. Nawāl al-Saʿdāwī may perhaps claim some pioneer status in this sphere, too, in that her writings on public health and her fearless expression of her views on the lack of women's rights in her homeland led to her imprisonment during the regime of Anwar al-Sādāt in 1981. She was released following his assassination to write an account of her experience, *Mudhakkirātī fī sijn al-nisāʾ* (1983; *Memoirs from the Women's Prison,* 1986).

reflect and criticize such societal phenomena as these, and novelists writing in Arabic have shown both ingenuity and artistry in addressing themselves to their various aspects. In *al-Thalj ya'tī min al-nāfidhah* (Snow comes in through the window, 1969), Ḥannā Mīnah shows a gradual shift away from his earlier attempts at realism towards a more subtly symbolic mode. The work portrays a Syrian political activitist, Fayyāḍ, living in Beirut and struggling to earn a living while endeavoring to resolve his own sense of political priorities in an atmosphere of literal and psychological exile.[109] In *al-Zaynī Barakāt* (1971; *Zayni Barakat,* 1988) Jamal al-Ghīṭānī creates an elaborate stylistic pastiche of the chronicles of the Mamlūk historian, Ibn Iyās (1448–c.1522) in order to present a picture of the activities of the secret police in Egypt during the 1960s. His fellow countryman, ʿAbd al-ḥakīm Qāsim, whose *Ayyām al-insān al-sabʿah* is also analyzed in the next chapter, paints a portrait of an entirely different kind in *Qadar al-ghuraf al-muqbiḍah* (Fate of the oppressive rooms, 1982). Using the various rooms in which the principal character (called ʿAbḍ al-ʿazīz as in *Ayyām al-insān al-sabʿah*) has lived—houses in small Delta villages, Alexandria, Cairo, prison cells, and West Berlin—as a physical environment, Qāsim, too, gives his reader a view of society quite as depressing as the title implies.

Two Arab novelists who are also critics carry the sense of alienation to the kind of philosophical level that links their works with the Western tradition of this type of writing. The most disturbing vision may be that of Jūrj Sālim in his novel, *Fī al-manfā* (In exile, 1962). Using the devices of anonymity with skill, he creates an oppressively detached atmosphere very redolent of Kafka, not least via the use of an inquisitor.[110] The historiographer ʿAbdallāh al-ʿArwī (Laroui) has written two novels. The first, *al-Ghurbah* (Exile, 1971), is a work of considerable complexity, full of allusion, internal monologue, and time switching. Al-ʿArwī uses it to show the nature of cultural fragmentation in postindependence Moroccan society. Shuʿayb, an ardent nationalist who has spent time in prison, is completely disillusioned about the current state of his country. Idrīs, another Moroccan, falls in love with Maria while in Paris; they discuss the impact of colonialism at length, but in the end Idrīs returns to Morocco and Maria remains in France. There are to be no happy endings here; in

109. For Mīnah's novel, see ʿAdnān ibn Dhurayl, *Al-Riwāyah al-ʿArabiyyah al-Sūriyyah,* 133–37; and Ilyās Khūrī, *Tajribat al-baḥth ʿan ufq,* 87–92.

110. For Jūrj Sālim, see al-Saʿāfīn, 523–30.

fact, no endings at all. The present is all alienation, and, at the societal and individual levels alike, the future is one of complete uncertainty.[111]

Najīb Maḥfūẓ: Egyptian Novelist and Nobel Laureate

Such is the variety of themes and the sheer bulk of novels that make up Najīb Maḥfūẓ's total output that it is hardly surprising that his name has already been cited at several points in our discussions. In the first edition of this work, he was accorded a central position in this lengthy survey of the themes in modern Arabic fiction, in that his career marks the establishment of the genre as a centrally important player in the cultural life of the Arab world. With the award of the Nobel Prize in Literature to him in 1988 it clearly becomes necessary to consider his role in the development of the novel genre in Arabic in detail.[112]

Maḥfūẓ's first novel, *ʿAbath al-aqdār* (Fates' mockery), appeared in 1939. It is the first of three which depict incidents from periods of ancient Egyptian history, a subject on which Maḥfūẓ had translated an English work by James Baikie from English into Arabic in the early 1930s. It may be considered a fortunate event in the history of the genre that in the early 1940s, under the combined inspiration of the social and political pressures of the period and his copious and systematic reading of European fiction, he changed his mind and applied himself to the issues of the contemporary period on a

111. For *al-Ghurbah*, see Ḥamīd, *Al-Riwāyah al-Maghribiyyah*, 264–88. In the second novel, *Al-Yatīm* (The orphan, 1978), the story of Idrīs and Maria is continued; see Ḥamīd, ibid., 321–60, and al-ʿAwf, 375–95.

112. Particularly in the wake of the award of the Nobel Prize, the literature on Maḥfūẓ has assumed enormous proportions. Among the most notable (in book form) are: Ghālī Shukrī, *al-Muntamī, dirāsah fī adab Najīb Mahfūẓ* (Cairo: Dār al-Maʿārif, 1969); Maḥmūd Amīn al-ʿĀlim, *Taʾammulāt fī ʿālam Najīb Mahfūẓ* (Cairo: al-Hayʾah al-Miṣriyyah al-ʿāmmah li-al-kitāb, 1970); Maḥmūd al-Rabīʿī, *Qirāʾat al-riwāyah* (Cairo: Dār al-Maʿārif, 1974); Nabīl Rāghib, *Qaḍiyyat al-shakl al-fannī ʿinda Najīb Mahfūẓ* (Cairo: al-Hayʾah al-Miṣriyyah al-ʿammah li-al-kitāb, 1975); Hāshim al-Naḥḥās, *Najīb Mahfūẓ ʿalā al-shāshah* (Cairo: al-Hayʾah al-Miṣriyyah al-ʿāmmah li-al-kitāb, 1975); ʿAbd al-Muḥsin Ṭāhā Badr, *Najīb Mahfūẓ: al-Ruʾyā wa-al-adāt* (Cairo: Dār al-Thaqāfah li-al-ṭibāʿah wa-al-nashr, 1978). In English, Somekh, *The Changing Rhythm*; and Mattityahu Peled, *Religion My Own: The Literary Works of Najīb Mahfūẓ* (New Brunswick, N.J.: Transaction, 1984). Excellent collections of essays are Trevor Le Gassick, ed., *Critical Perspectives on Naguib Mahfouz* (Washington, D.C.: Three Continents, 1991); and Michael Beard and Adnan Haydar, eds., *Naguib Mahfouz: From Regional Fame to Global Recognition* (Syracuse: Syracuse Univ. Press, 1993).

broader canvas, that of the realistic novel. In a series of works, the first of which was published in 1945 and the last, *The Trilogy,* in 1956–57, Maḥfūẓ depicts with loving attention to detail the lives of Egyptians in various quarters of the city of Cairo.[113] Quite simply stated, these novels moved the genre in Arabic to a completely new plateau of achievement, and it is hard to overestimate the impact that they have on the development of the novel genre, not merely in Egypt but throughout the Arab world. Maḥfūẓ's accomplishment combines elements of both quantity and quality. From the point of view of sheer industry and dedication, he may even have set an unfortunate precedent regarding the status of creative writers in the Arab world by producing eleven novels (counting, legitimately I believe, *The Trilogy* as three) in thirteen years, essentially in his spare time. The research for *The Trilogy* alone, he once told me, took him more than five years to assemble. But what also needs to be emphasized here is the palpable development in technique that is so evident in this series of novels (which, incidentally, were not published without some difficulty or with instant acclaim). The milestone that is *The Trilogy,* with its amazing attention to detail, its profound insight into character, and its complete authenticity to time and place, can be seen as a culmination of the series of works that precede it, with *al-Qāhirah al-jadīdah* (Modern Cairo, 1946) and *Zuqāq al-midaqq* (1947; *Midaq Alley,* 1966) providing microcosms of Egyptian characters trapped in historical circumstance and *Bidāyah wa-nihāyah* (1951; *The Beginning and the End,* 1985) offering a portrait of the tragedy of a single family.[114] *The Trilogy* is a huge work of over fifteen hundred pages, tracing the life, beliefs, tragedies, and loves of the ʿAbd al-jawwād family in the period between the two world wars and into the Second World War. Like the great novelistic sagas of Tolstoy, Galsworthy, Trollope, Hugo, and others, it operates on numerous levels. The setting of each volume in a different part of the city illustrates well the transformations within society, of which the fate

113. Najīb Maḥfūẓ, *Bayn al-qaṣrayn* (Cairo: Maktabat Miṣr, 1956); English trans.: *Palace Walk,* trans. William M. Hutchins and Olive E. Kenny (New York: Doubleday, 1990); Najīb Maḥfūẓ, *Qaṣr al-shawq* (Cairo: Maktabat Miṣr, 1957); English trans.: *Palace of Desire,* trans. William M. Hutchins, Lorne Kenny, and Olive Kenny (New York: Doubleday, 1991); and Najīb Maḥfūẓ, *Al-Sukkariyyah* (Cairo: Maktabat Miṣr, 1957); English trans.: *Sugar Street,* trans. William M. Hutchins and Angele Botros Samaan (New York: Doubleday, 1992).

114. The problems of dating the publication of these works exactly is explored by Somekh, 198–99.

of this family is an example. From the first volume, in which the father exerts a tyrannical hold over his family while employing a double standard with regard to his own behavior, we proceed to the second, in which the second son confronts his father's traditional beliefs with the evolutionary theories which he is studying in Teachers' College. In the third volume, men and women are studying together at university. Two of the grandsons of the first generation finish up in jail, one as a Communist, the other as a member of the Muslim Brethren. There could hardly be a better example of the feuds and divisions in Egyptian society and the sense of alienation among intellectuals which marked the period before the 1952 Revolution.[115] And yet, the main protagonist of this work is surely Time itself. The manner in which Maḥfūẓ holds together this vast historical survey of Egyptian society in the process of change recalls Georg Lukacs' remarks on Flaubert's *L'éducation sentimentale:*

> The unrestricted, uninterrupted flow of time is the unifying principle of the homogeneity that rubs the sharp edges off each heterogeneous fragment and establishes a relationship—albeit an irrational and inexpressible one—between them. Time brings order into the chaos of men's lives and gives it the semblance of a spontaneously flowering, organic entity; characters having no apparent meaning appear, establish relations with one another, break them off; disappear again without any meaning having been revealed.[116]

When *The Trilogy* was published in 1956 and 1957, the historical moment cannot have been more apt. Requiring four years to move from completion to publication, the work emerged into a new, post-revolution Egypt, one that had just witnessed a spectacular failure of the old pattern of international hegemony, the tripartite Suez Invasion of 1956, that firmly established Jamāl ʿAbd al-nāṣir as a leader of world stature. Maḥfūẓ's monumental work recorded in tremendous detail the course of the long struggle that had brought the Egyptian people to this point. In this context, one is inevitably reminded of Lionel Trilling's remark regarding the purpose of the novel as "an especially useful agent of the moral imagination . . . the literary form which most directly reveals to us the complexity, the difficulty, and the interest of life in society, and best instructs us in

115. A point duly noted by Laroui, 120.
116. Lukacs, 125.

our human variety and contradiction.[117] Maḥfūẓ's reputation as a novelist was now firmly established; his works were reprinted and reviewed throughout the Arab world. The novel now became a medium to be reckoned with, one that showed the ability of a genre to reflect the aspirations and struggles of a people and to advocate change. In the decades of the 1950s and 1960s, that potential was to be tested in a variety of ways, often to the personal detriment of the novelists who wrote such works. Nevertheless, I believe that it is possible to say that the fact that the social-realist novel in Arabic, with all its creative and reformist potential, was placed at the disposal of so many writers throughout the Arab world at this crucial moment in its modern history is due primarily to the genius and industry of Najīb Maḥfūẓ.

The manuscript of *The Trilogy*, Maḥfūẓ tells us, was completed in April 1952 before the revolution. Quite apart from the problems of publishing such a voluminous work, there was also the reality of a new political order, a revolution the precise impact and course of which were far from clear at the outset. During the initial years of the revolution Maḥfūẓ turned his attention to another love of his, the cinema.[118]

His next fictional work, *Awlād ḥāratinā* (1959; *Children of Gebelawi*, 1981) signaled a significant change in topic. It is an allegorical work in five sections. Jabalāwī/Gebelawi is a beneficent authority figure who selects his son, Adham, to supervise the religious endowment (*waqf*) of which he has the charge. This decision is violently opposed by another son, Idrīs, who is therefore expelled from the house. Later, the outcast Idrīs goes to see his brother and ask him to look in "the Book" to see what Gebelawi has written in it about him. For his brother's sake, Adham agrees to do so, but he is caught by his father, Gebelawi; as punishment he, too, is thrown out of the house.

It did not require a great deal of interpretation by readers of the newspaper *al-Ahrām*, where the work was first published in serial form, to realize what the import of this new narrative was: that Adham, a name close in sound to that of Adam, and Idrīs, close to Iblīs (the devil) represented the opening of what was to be an ambitious and controversial undertaking by Maḥfūẓ, one which was to make

117. Lionel Trilling, *The Liberal Imagination* (New York: Scribners, 1940 and 1950), vii.

118. His activities during this period are discussed in detail in al-Naḥḥās.

use of the context of violence in human societies as a framework within which to consider a topic which had been a concern of his for some time, the role of religion in modern society.

From a first section entitled "Adham," we move through "Jabal" ("mountain," implying Moses), "Rifāʿah" ("resurrection," implying Jesus), "Qāsim" ("apportioner," implying Muḥammad), and lastly the magician "ʿArafah" (implying "knowledge in general," but more specifically "scientia, science"). At the end of the work ʿArafah goes to Jabalāwī's (Gebelawi's) house and kills him. "God's will be done," he says, "after his long life Jabalāwī is now dead!"[119]

This series of articles brought down on the author the wrath of the al-Azhar authorities. It was determined to be sacriligious. A formal ban on publication in Egypt was issued, but at the time no further action was taken against Maḥfūẓ himself. Indeed, if we take into consideration the political situation in Egypt in the 1960s under President ʿAbd al-nāṣir, the relative influence of religion within the political and social life of the country at that time, and the status of Maḥfūẓ himself, it is difficult to see what further action might have been taken. The work was published in book form in Lebanon in 1967, and copies made their way on a regular, if informal, basis to Cairo as well as to other Arab cities. It could in any case be consulted in its original form in the archives of the *al-Ahrām* newspaper. In what may be seen as a typical compromise, the religious establishment in Egypt apparently considered themselves to have defended an important principle and saw no further need to interfere. Thus the situation remained until the Nobel year of 1988–89, when the coincidence of Maḥfūẓ's award with the issuing of a death sentence by Imam Khomeini against Salman Rushdie for his book, *Satanic Verses,* once again brought *Awlād ḥāratinā* into the limelight. As a newly prominent Muslim writer of world renown, Maḥfūẓ was asked to comment on the death sentence decreed against Rushdie. His response was an unequivocal condemnation of the decree and a confirmation of writers' freedom. Later he was to supplement his comments by saying that he found the contents of the book distasteful in the extreme, but that was not before his earlier defense of Rushdie's rights as an author brought down upon him a death sentence from ʿUmar ʿAbd al-raḥmān, a popular Islamic preacher in Egypt. Duly

119. Najīb Maḥfūẓ, *Awlād ḥāratinā* (Beirut: Dār Al-Adāb, 1967), 498; English trans.: *Children of Gebelawi,* trans. Philip Stewart (Washington, D.C.: Three Continents, 1981) 320.

supplied by this international furor over Rushdie's novel and Maḥfūẓ's reaction to it with a totally new context, a variety of religious commentators now went back to *Awlād ḥāratinā* and read it in a completely new (and achronological) light. It was suggested that Maḥfūẓ should have been condemned to death when the work was first published and indeed that, had Maḥfūẓ not written *Awlād ḥāratinā,* Rushdie's work would not have appeared. Maḥfūẓ himself is alleged to have termed his earlier work "my illegitimate son."[120]

Following the original publication of *Awlād ḥāratinā* in 1959, Maḥfūẓ's novelistic writing took a new turn, concerning itself, as we noted above, with the depiction of the alienated individual in a society in which ideals and reality seemed rarely to blend. This phase in Maḥfūẓ's career is marked most obviously by a more economical treatment of the description of place, but also evident are an increased awareness of the psychological dimensions of character through the use of internal monologue and stream of consciousness and a subtle and effective use of symbols. The characters who people these works find themselves for one reason or another out of place in Egyptian society. In *al-Liṣṣ wa-al-kilāb* (1961; *The Thief and the Dogs,* 1984) Saʿīd Mahrān is the thief who feels betrayed not only by his wife, who has deserted him while he was in prison, but also by Ra'ūf ʿIlwān, a journalist who has abandoned his former radical positions towards society and the rights of the poor in favor of a new life of prosperity. Mahrān's attempts to kill those who have betrayed him fail, and he is hounded down by the police with their dogs. The novel ends, tellingly, in a cemetery. *Al-Summān wa-al-kharīf* (1962; *Autumn Quail,* 1985) tells the story of ʿĪsā al-Dabbāgh, a senior government official under the old royal regime, whose life collapses around him in the wake of the Revolution, the purges of corrupt civil servants, and his own unwillingness to face up to the realities of the situation. The novel narrates not only his personal withdrawal to Alexandria after his fall but also the many ways in which life is carrying on without him. This series of novels written in the 1960s can been seen as a rising crescendo of unease and disillusion at the course of the Egyptian revolution. The volume of criticism is already high in *Thartharah fawq al-Nīl,* analyzed in the next chapter, but it reaches a peak in *Mīrāmār* (1967; *Miramar,* 1978). While the heroine of this novel, the peasant girl Zahrah—an obvious symbol of the

120. The events are discussed in detail by Milton Viorst, "Man of Gamaliya," *New Yorker,* 2 July, 1990, 34–35.

ideal of Egyptian society—can be seen as stepping with determination into the future, the character most associated with the actual course of the revolution, Sirḥān al-Buhayrī, is involved in a scheme to swindle his company out of some of its property, and commits suicide.

Many littérateurs in Egypt and elsewhere in the Arab world reacted to the June War of 1967 (the so-called *naksah* or setback) in a variety of ways: anger, silence, self-imposed exile. Few responded immediately, but Maḥfūẓ was one who did. He chose to express his reflections on the disaster in a series of extremely symbolic and often cyclical short stories which made their way into collections published in 1969 and 1971. They all reflect the sense of questioning, challenge, and recrimination which were so characteristic of this period. When he turned his attention to the longer genre again, it was in *al-Marāyā* (1972; *Mirrors,* 1977), a series of alphabetized vignettes through which, in a retrospect on his own life and career, the narrator surveys the recent history of Egypt and its people in all walks of life. Needless to say, many of the subjects of these vignettes comment with extreme frankness about politics, including the Egyptian revolution itself, international relations, and the continuing dilemma regarding the fate of the Palestinian people in their struggle with Israel. I personally now regard *al-Marāyā* as symbolic of an important transition in Maḥfūẓ's career, one which leads into what I would call a "retrospective" phase. The period of the early 1970s marked the beginning of the Sādāt era, a time which involved the so-called *thawrat al-taṣḥīḥ* or correctional revolution. It also witnessed some sensational revelations about the Nasser era and particularly the grim days of the early 1960s. It was at this stage that Tawfīq al-Ḥakīm wrote and circulated privately his famous retrospective, *ʿAwdat al-waʿy* (return of consciousness). That work infuriated a large segment of the intellectual elite of Egypt, as can be gauged from the selection included in the late Bayly Winder's translation.[121] It was into this scenario that *al-Marāyā* appeared as a book in 1972, designated as a *riwāyah* (although not by the author). This particular phase in Egypt's history was certainly one of "looking back in anger." In *al-Karnak* (Karnak cafe, 1974) Maḥfūẓ paints a particularly gruesome portrait of the lives of young people during the 1960s, including descriptions of torture and rape in prison. His works of fiction

121. Tawfīq al-Ḥakīm, *The Return of Consciousness,* trans. R. Bayly Winder, (New York: New York Univ. Press, 1985).

published during the late 1970s and into the 1980s make it abundantly clear that the values of Egyptian society and its leadership have given Maḥfūẓ much to be angry about; one quote from one of the characters in *Yawm qutila al-zaʿīm* (1985; *The Day the Leader Was Killed,* 1989), itself a significant title in view of Sādāt's assassination, should suffice as illustration. "He's just a lousy actor, that's all. . . . He goes around saying My friend Begin, my friend Kissinger. Let me tell you, the uniform belongs to Hitler; the routine is sheer Charlie Chaplin."[122]

The policy of opening up Egyptian markets (*infitāḥ*), and the way in which the already-glaring inequities between classes and between city and provinces were aggravated and emphasized by it, became a constant theme of his fiction. To be fair, given the extreme circumstances of Egyptian society at the time and Maḥfūẓ's own sense of priorities, it is hard to see what else might have preoccupied his attention. Coupled to all this is the fact that Maḥfūẓ retired from his Ministry of Culture job and began to supplement his pension—yet another reference to the status of littérateurs in the Arab world today—by writing a weekly news column for *al-Ahrām,* thus forging a link that was guaranteed to maintain his preoccupation with the particular problems of his own society. However, certain of Maḥfūẓ's more recent novels clearly transcend this pattern. For example, Maḥfūẓ has turned to the classical literary tradition, following perhaps the example of his young colleague and admirer, Jamāl al-Ghīṭānī, invoking the "characters" of *A Thousand and One Nights* in *Layālī Alf laylah* (Nights at A Thousand Nights, 1982), and, in a notable further contribution to his continuing discussion of religion, *Riḥlat ibn Faṭūmah* (1983; *The Journey of Ibn Fattouma,* 1992). As I write these words, Maḥfūẓ's diminishing eyesight and hearing have brought his lengthy writing career to a halt. It would thus appear that, in an appropriate gesture, *Qushtumur* (n.d. [1988?]), an affectionate portrait of childhood haunts and colleagues in Abbasiyyah where the author himself grew up, may be his final contribution to the novel genre.

The primary topic of Maḥfūẓ's enormous output in novel form has thus been an apt reflection of the earlier development of the Western fictional tradition, in that he has chosen to focus on the life and problems of Egypt's urban middle class and in particular the

122. Najīb Maḥfūẓ, *Yawm qutila al-zaʿīm* (Cairo: Maktabat Miṣr, 1985), 47; The translation is my own. The work is also translated as *The Day the Leader Was Killed,* trans. Malak Hashem (Cairo: General Egyptian Book Organization, 1989).

subset of that social grouping with which he himself is intimately acquainted, intellectuals and civil servants. This is not, of course, to suggest that his concerns or readership were restricted to Egypt alone or to a single group within that society. His pre-1967 works in particular addressed themselves to the larger issues facing modern man with a sweep which reflects his own broad reading in the literary traditions of the world. However, whereas other modern Arab novelists have been motivated by political and literary concerns to venture outside the environs of the modern metropolis in order to portray the harsh realities of the life among the rural peasantry, Maḥfūẓ has consistently set his works in the city and among the class he knows best.

The characters who people his novels and the plots that are constructed to contain them are crafted with extreme care. In both these areas he demonstrates the skill of a meticulous planner and craftsman. The views of Scholes and Kellogg seem appropriate in assessing his skills in this area: "Of the giants of the age of the novel can we not say that the principal thing which unites them is the special care for characterization which is inextricably bound up with the creation of character from the facets of the artist's own psyche?"[123]

In using his novels to portray this class and to reflect the values of his generation, he has honed a writing instrument of great symbolic power and nuance. During the course of his long career he has clearly taken great pains to develop a prose style which, in its clarity and directness, can both describe and suggest. An important stylistic issue of debate regarding the development of the Arabic novel has revolved around the question of the language of dialogue. While other writers have sought to lend an element of authenticity by introducing conversation in the colloquial dialect of their region, Maḥfūẓ has preferred to remain within the syntactic structures of the standard language, occasionally peppering his character's comments with individual words and phrases which evoke colloquial discourse. This rich stylistic medium has served as a vehicle not only for the wide variety of atmospheres and scenarios to be found in his works but also for the often sardonic witticisms which his Egyptian characters, reflecting a well-known national trait, hurl at each other. The fictional world into which the reader is thus drawn is created in a style which describes and characterizes with great subtlety.

Najīb Maḥfūẓ is, simply and directly stated, the founder of the

123. Robert Scholes and Robert Kellogg, *The Nature of Narrative* (London: Oxford Univ. Press, 1966), 192.

mature tradition of the novel in Arabic and indeed the forger of new paths in two separate phases in that developmental process—in terms of publication, 1945–52 and 1959–67. That such has been achievable in the lifetime of a single author and under the circumstances, personal, professional, and political, within which Maḥfūẓ has had to work is truly remarkable. The award of the Nobel Prize is a thoroughly apt recognition of that role. In his hands the historical moment (or rather, bearing in mind the length of his career and the bulk of his contribution, "moments" seems more appropriate) and the novel genre were ideally linked. The novel in Arabic is the continuing beneficiary of that fact.

Transformations in Fictional Perspective

The thematic approach adopted thus far in this chapter has allowed us to survey a large number of authors and works that may be regarded as an apt reflection of the wealth of the contemporary novel in Arabic in the process of fulfilling its traditional role as reflector and even advocate of social and political change. A large number of novels have been written within what may be termed a "realist" vision, creating worlds that attempt to provide some kind of structured logic for the lives of the characters who people them. Some novelists clearly found the confines of officially sanctioned fictional scenarios constricting at an earlier stage than others, but, with the debacle of June 1967, and accompanying revelations about the false bases on which so much optimism had been cynically orchestrated, reality itself was so completely shattered that, for many authors, attempts at imposing an external and authorized organizing vision on their fictional imaginings became an impossibility. Expressed, as it must be, in a more positive way, alternative approaches became not just available but, in fact, in the view of many writers, the only feasible means of expression in fictional form. If the circumstances in the case of the novel in Arabic were particularly pressing, this trend also needs to be placed into a broader context conveniently summarized by Frank Kermode:

> Certain old habits have been discontinued; for example the old assumption that a novel must be concerned with the authentic representation of character and milieu, and with social and ethical systems that transcend it—what may be called the kerygmatic assumption—is strongly questioned. The consequence is a recognisable estrangement from what used to be known as reality; and a

> further consequence, which can be equally defended as having beneficent possibilities, is that the use of fiction as an instrument of research into the nature of fiction, though certainly not new, is much more widely recognized.[124]

In the Arab world the result of tendencies such as these has been the appearance of a wealth of new approaches to fiction.

Kermode's mention here of the use of fiction to conduct research into itself leads us into the realm of metafiction, an approach which, in the wake of a recoil from the perceived inability of realism to reflect the needs and aspirations of fictional writing, has been a focus of much attention among Arabic novelists in recent times. Bearing in mind the political and societal circumstances in which the majority of these writers have found themselves, it is hardly surprising that metafiction, which, to cite Patricia Waugh, involves "fiction writing which self-consciously and systematically draws attention to its status as an artefact in order to pose questions about the relationship between fiction and reality," should have appealed to their imaginations.[125] Ilyās Khūrī's already-mentioned novel, *Riḥlat Ghāndī al-ṣaghīr,* is clearly an excellent example of this trend, but other innovative contributions to this aspect of the recent development of the Arabic novel can be cited.

When two novelists decide to write a novel together, as Jabrā Ibrāhīm Jabrā and ʿAbd al-raḥmān Munīf have done in *ʿĀlam bi-lā kharāʾiṭ,* the reader's interest in the techniques of the text will already have been aroused. But Jabrā and Munīf move beyond this more obvious aspect of composition into the realm of metafiction by crafting a narrative in which one of the characters in the novel, ʿAlāʾ, is himself a novelist in the process of writing a work of fiction, a novel to be entitled *Shajarat al-nār* (The Fire-tree). While ʿAlāʾ's technique as a writer is criticized on the outside by the character of Najwā, a woman with whom he is in love, the character of Riyāḍ within the inner novel haunts him to the extent of arguing about the way in which he has been created.[126] The reader thus encounters a text cre-

124. Kermode, *The Art of Telling,* 53. The particular circumstances in the Arab world are explored by Edwār al-Kharrāṭ in Ostle, 185–88; Fontaine, *Romans arabes modernes,* 10–11; and Mūsawī, *Al-Riwāyah al-ʿArabiyyah,* 107–8.

125. Patricia Waugh, *Metafiction: The Theory and Practice of Self-conscious Fiction* (London: Methuen, 1984), 2. Cited in Muḥsin Jāsim al-Mūsawī, "Metafiction as a Theoretic Discourse in Contemporary Arabic Writing," *Gilgamesh* 2 (1988): 51–59.

126. Jabrā Ibrāhīm Jabrā and ʿAbd al-raḥmān Munīf, *ʿĀlam bi-lā kharāʾit* (Beirut: Al-Muʾassasah al-ʿArabiyyah li-al-dirāsāt wa-al-nashr, 1983), 214–30. Rajab, the pro-

ated by two authors in which the narrative is concerned with the attempts of a single author to create a text that will satisfy the demands of both characters in his own world—that of Jabrā and Munīf's novel—and of the fictional world he is trying to create. The Egyptian novelist Yūsuf al-Qaʿīd (b. 1944), makes use of the Nile Delta region with which he is so familiar as a backdrop to a series of works that show an increasing tendency to draw the reader into the processes of challenging the traditional contracts of fiction and of forging new ones. In *Yaḥduth fī Miṣr al-ān* (It's happening in Egypt now, 1977), an authorial figure named Yūsuf keeps intruding into the narrative to point out the strategies that are being employed, constantly subverting the effects of traditional fictional techniques and producing a kind of elaborated reportage within which the reader has to work out the real story of the exploitation of land and peasants. The technique is continued and even expanded in the three parts of *Shakāwā al-Miṣrī al-faṣīḥ* (Gripes of the eloquent Egyptian, 1981–85) which begins with the frank admission that "writing's a curse."[127] The Moroccan novelist and critic, Muḥammad Barrādah (b. 1938) adopts a style very different from that of al-Qaʿīd in his novel, *Laʿbat al-nisyān* (The forgetting game, 1987), but readers find themselves similarly challenged to make their way through a text that is much concerned with time and memory but at the same time reveals yet again a narrator at odds with his "author." As the former observes, "We had a long discussion but failed to agree. More than once the author repeated in my hearing what he had written in his manuscript: the dilemma with novels is that you're supposed to write about a finite time within a process that is by definition infinite."[128]

Bearing in mind that one of the primary features of the period immediately following the 1967 June War was a search into the past for both explanation and confirmation, it is hardly surprising that in the realm of the novel, earlier genres of writing, culled from both the elite and popular cultural heritage, were to provide a fruitful

---

tagonist in Munīf's earlier novel, *Sharq al-Mutawassiṭ* (1977), had discussed the relative merits of fiction and factual accounts as a means of recording his experiences in prison. I discuss aspects of the prison novel in "The Arabic Novel and the Quest for Freedom," *JAL*, forthcoming.

127. See Fontaine, *Romans arabes modernes*, 40–42; Starkey, 62–74.

128. Muḥammad Barrādah, *Laʿbat al-nisyān* (The forgetting game) (Rabat: Dār al-Amān, 1987), 135. The "narrator of narrators" in this work also explores his relationship with the author earlier in the text: 53–57. It is interesting to note that the author terms his work a "naṣṣ riwāʾī" (novelistic text).

source of models for expression and experiment, while at the same time drawing attention in a different way to the nature of fiction as artefact. The narrator of Emile Ḥabībī's famous work, *al-Waqāʾiʿ al-gharībah . . .* , is well aware of the "anxieties of influence" that impinge upon his narrative, but triumphantly transcends the presence of such a wealth of intertext by the very sardonic mode whereby he draws attention to it, at one point noting specifically that certain readers have drawn attention to similarities between his work and Voltaire's *Candide.*[129] As we noted in the opening chapter above, ʿAbd al-raḥmān Munīf can be "accused" by a Western writer of a failure to understand the nature of novelistic narration when he chooses to replicate the priorities of a traditional storyteller and thus permits the investigation of some interesting new relationships between Gerard Genette's different categorizations of narrative time.[130] Munīf introduces into his novel, *al-Nihāyāt* (1977; *Endings*, 1988) a series of animal fables, two of which are taken from *Kitāb al-ḥayawān* (The book of animals) by the famous ninth century polymath, al-Jāḥiẓ. However, the modern Arab novelist who has taken the potential of transtextuality to its limits is undoubtedly Jamāl al-Ghīṭānī. From *al-Zaynī Barakāt* (1971) with its pastiches of different types of historical text—annals, proclamations, travel narratives, and so on, we move to *Khiṭaṭ al-Ghīṭānī* (Al-Ghīṭānī's city guide, 1980) in which al-Ghīṭānī invokes the *khiṭaṭ* genre, made famous in the earlier works of al-Maqrīzī (1346–1442) and ʿAlī Mubārak (1824–93) which described in great detail the streets and monuments of Cairo, to describe an unnamed city in which the relentless push to modernize is riding roughshod over the treasures of the past.[131] Al-Ghīṭānī's stylistic virtuosity reaches its peak however in the huge three-part novel, *Kitāb al-Tajalliyyāt* (Book of illuminations, 1983–87), a work which explores the societal tensions of Egypt in the 1970s through a brilliant evocation of the multilayered mystical writings of the Andalusian writer Ibn ʿArabī (1165–1240).

Such is the quality and quantity of experimentation in the realm of the Arabic novel in recent decades that it is clearly impossible to include here discussion of the multifarious ways in which novelists

129. Ḥabībī, *Al-Waqāʾiʿ al-gharībah* bk. 2, Bāqiyah, 94–99; *The secret life of Saeed*, 72–75.

130. "Récit," "histoire," and "narration." See Gérard Genette, *Narrative Discourse: An Essay in Method*, trans. Jane E. Lewin (Ithaca, N.Y.: Cornell Univ. Press, 1980).

131. For an excellent study of this work, see Samia Mehrez, "Re-writing the City: The Case of *Khiṭaṭ al-Ghīṭānī*," in *The Arabic Novel Since 1950*, 143–67.

are making use of contradictions, fractured or cancelled time, and textual pastiche and subversion, to express in fiction a vision of contemporary society and their sense of alienation towards it. Kermode notes that "the urgency of technical innovation as a means to modern truth is felt by novelists rather than their readers."[132] While we will explore the practical ramifications of this situation in the section on readership below, it is quite clear that the fictional works of contemporary novelists such as Ilyās Khūrī, Edwār al-Kharrāṭ, ʿIzz al-dīn al-Madanī (b. 1938) in a work such as *al-ʿUdwān* (The assault, 1969), and Walīd Ikhlāṣī (b. 1935), in addition to those just mentioned, turn the act of reading into a process of discovery that is often complex. Some readers clearly find this process unpalatable, as in this assessment of a work by Ikhlāṣī: "The chief problem with Walīd Ikhlāṣī's novels is that they indulge in symbolism and imaginative fantasies to such an extent that some of them are impossible for the critic to analyse, let alone the ordinary reader!"[133] Ikhlāṣī's first novel, *Shitāʾ al-bahr al-yābis* (*Winter of the dry sea,* 1964), is a sequence of five synchronous stories whereby "events metamorphose into a hazy atmosphere through which characters are seen as phantoms and incidents as dreams."[134] These same tendencies are evident in *Zaman bayna al-wilādah wa-al-ḥulm* (Time between birth and dream, 1976) by the Moroccan novelist, Aḥmad al-Madīnī. Critical reaction to this work has ranged from the question of Sayyid Ḥāmid al-Nassāj, the Egyptian critic, as to how it is possible to depict the reality of things through a chaos of writing, to the comment of the Iraqi novelist, ʿAbd al-raḥmān Majīd al-Rubayʿī, that the novel lacks the basic underpinnings required by the genre.[135] In *Barārī al-ḥummā* (1985; *Prairies of Fever,* 1993), the poet Ibrāhīm Naṣrallāh writes a

132. Kermode, *The Art of Telling,* 37–38.

133. Mu'ayyad al-Ṭalāl in *Al-Thawrah,* 15 June 1976. This attitude needs to be contrasted with the views of Frank Kermode. "Good novelists claim as a traditional entitlement that their readers should make a substantial contribution to their enterprises. If what they are doing calls from them a large exercise of imagination, displaying the full powers of their minds in a happy delineation of the varieties of human nature—then we must accept that the demand their performances make on us is one of the criteria by which we distinguish the real thing from the easy substitute." Frank Kermode, *London Review of Books* 14, no. 19 (8 Oct. 1992): 14.

134. See Admer Gouryh, "The Fictional World of Walīd Ikhlāṣī," *World Literature Today* (Winter 1984): 25. For further discussion of Ikhlāṣī's novels, see al-Fayṣal, *Malāmiḥ fī al-riwāyah al-Sūriyyah,* 35–54.

135. See Ḥamīd, *Al-Riwāyah al-Maghribiyyah,* 409–26; al-Nassāj, 218; al-Rubayʿī, 176.

novel in which reality and fantasy are blended within a language environment where metaphorical language is intermingled with the tersest of dialogue and several poems. The heat implicit in the title may refer to the remote village in the Empty Quarter region of Saudi Arabia where the novel is set, but equally symbolizes the mental fever which possesses Muḥammad Ḥammād, the main character in the work, as his alienation from his surroundings intensifies, a process for which, via stream of consciousness, the author invokes a nightmarish combination of hallucinations, visions, images, and dreams.

The Writer, the Reader, and the Text

In order to conclude this lengthy, yet almost recklessly selective, survey of recent novel writing in the Arab world, I would like to move the discussion away from the interior of the text and into the public domain, considering in turn the current status of the writer, the reader, and the novelistic text itself.

The Writer

The freedom of writers of fiction in the Arab world to write and publish their creative output is restricted in varying degrees and by a number of methods, of which banishment, imprisonment, and censorship are merely the most overt. In societies in which the power of the word is well understood and carefully monitored, novel writing becomes an act of adventure and courage. As Salmā al-Jayyūsī notes concerning Arab littérateurs, "Because they live in oppressive times and suffer from reactionary social and political conditions, they cannot always resort to direct statement; they often employ ambiguity, various kinds of obliquity, and complex systems of imagery to express their vision."[136] Farīdah al-Naqqāsh gives a gruesome picture of a society that regularly involves "prisons and torture, police chases and a constricting surveillance, exile, tunnels and deserts, death by martyrdom and death instead of others, emigration away from the homeland and into the realm of the self, thousands of masks—false names and hideaways—and compulsory banishment from the real source, the masses at large."[137] Such a gloomy view of reality, one

136. Jayyusi, ed., *Modern Arabic Poetry*, 28.

137. Farīdah al-Naqqāsh, *Al-Ādāb* (Feb.–Mar. 1980): 33.

that we have seen portrayed in many works discussed in this chapter—a world, to cite Lukacs, "abandoned by God,"[138] has in many cases also been the living reality of the novelists themselves. Of the fourteen novelists that Jean Fontaine interviewed for a recent study on the Egyptian novel, no less than ten had spent time in prison for political reasons; among them are several whose works we have already described: Edwār al-Kharrāṭ, Ṣunʿallāh Ibrāhīm, Nawāl al-Saʿdāwī, Yūsuf Idrīs, ʿAbd al-ḥakīm Qāsim, and Jamāl al-Ghīṭānī.[139] Novelists from other Arab nations have shared the same fate, and for many writers the alternatives have often been exile or silence, or both. Other measures adopted by the authorities may be perhaps less extreme, and yet their impact is none the less discouraging: Ḥalīm Barakāt was dismissed from his teaching position at a Lebanese university, and Laylā Baʿalbakkī was subjected to arrest and trial on an accusation of obscenity.[140] Dhū al-nūn Ayyūb and Ghā'ib Ṭuʿmah Farmān spent long periods in exile, and ʿAbd al-raḥmān Munīf currently resides in Damascus, having previously migrated from Saudi Arabia to Yugoslavia, Iraq, and France.

The Moroccan writer, Khanāthah Banūnah, poses what is for all Arab novelists a crucially important question, and then proceeds to answer it on her own terms:

> In our current situation in the Arab World, is writing for pleasure or necessity? My own connection with writing was fundamentally a need to justify existence on a personal level and to participate in the process of change on the objective plane. Even so, widespread illiteracy on the one hand and our preoccupation with an endless stream of defeats involved smaller and greater Palestine (the latter being the entire Arab World) on the other, has failed to fulfil the conviction I felt when I first started writing so enthusiastically. I am no longer convinced that writing stories, novels and poetry is by itself a weapon for change. There has to be a dialectical link between word and action.[141]

The Lebanese novelist and critic, Suhayl Idrīs, who through his lengthy editorship of *al-Ādāb* has done an enormous amount to fos-

138. Lukacs, 88.

139. Fontaine, *Romans arabes modernes*, 12.

140. For Laylā Baʿalbakkī's trial, see *Middle Eastern Muslim Women Speak*, ed. Elizabeth Warnock Fernea and Basima Qattan Bezirgan (Austin: Univ. of Texas Press, 1977), 273–90.

141. Khanāthah Banūnah, in Barrādah, *Al-Riwāyah*, 358.

ter the development of modern Arabic literature, allows himself to finish a statement on his personal career as a novelist with a *cri de coeur,* one that aptly summarizes the unfortunate realities just outlined; it is thus worth quoting *in extenso*:

> The crisis is one of freedom of expression. Can the Arab writer always stand up and challenge it? Doesn't such a challenge often subject him to pressures, constraints on his livelihood, and a variety of kinds of oppression and terror? . . . What is he supposed to say about other people in the dreadful atmosphere of decline in which the Arab nation finds itself today? Shouldn't he condemn the prevailing authority structures and foundations, and impute to them all the causes of this decline? Is he not to be allowed to say what he wants? Where can he find the sphere in which to express this challenge if all the modes of information are in the hands of the official organizations and financed by them? Even if there were to be independent information agencies, would they not be permanently threatened with closure if the official organizations were able to deprive their readership of what they read?[142]

The mention in Idrīs's remarks of publication permits us to move from some of the more unsubtle realities faced by novelists in the Arab world to more subtle ones. For the Syrian novelist and critic, ʿAbd al-nabī Ḥijāzī, novel writing is a confrontation with "the self, society and the authorities," and no more so than in the area of publication; for "the novel is a book, and books are a commodity exposed to a continuous chain of censorship, printing, and marketing operations. It is these factors which force the novelist to back down sometimes, albeit bitterly and regretfully."[143]

Nor do these constraints mark the only ways through which novelists find themselves frustratingly beholden to the authorities in their countries. Writing fiction is not and never has been a profession by which even the most famous writers such as Maḥfūẓ can earn a living. Ḥannā Mīnah, the prominent Syrian novelist, has held a bewildering array of jobs, from barber to stevedore. The rights of authors are still only minimally protected by whatever concept of copyright law, if any, exists, and the sums that are paid to writers upon receipt of their manuscripts have been extremely small by Western standards. As noted above, the cinema has often provided a fatally attractive alternative. As one kind of solution to this situation,

142. Suhayl Idrīs in *Al-Ādāb* (Feb.–Mar. 1980): 99.
143. Ibid., 53.

many writers have found employment within the information network itself, thus becoming a part of the very cultural bureaucracy which surveys fictional production. Indeed, editorships and other posts in literary magazines and other kinds of cultural periodical have allowed a number of writers a certain amount of time to devote their attentions to creative writing, certainly more time than they would otherwise have had if their employment had been in some other sector. This process of co-optation and its consequences are well described by ʿAbd al-kabīr al-Khatībī: "Les régimes autoritaires se fabriquent un code culturel, un autopanégyrique pour masquer leur destin d'oppresseur. L'écrivain qui est payé pour jouer un rôle est un véritable fabricant de l'alienation."[144]

Returning then to the terminology with which we began this section, we may say that creators of novels in the Arab world—as a process of communication between the writer and the reader—often find themselves regarded as controversial members of society, a posture that may have significant effects on their livelihood and even personal freedom. The descriptions on the previous pages illustrate the considerable differences between the life styles of novelists in the Arab world and those in most Western countries. And yet, the basic posture of challenge, of confrontation, and of experimentation with "the novel," are, as we have suggested before, intrinsic features of the genre. In Lukacs's words, "The novel tells of the adventure of interiority; the content of the novel is the story of the soul that goes to find itself, that seeks adventures in order to be proved and tested by them, and, by proving itself, to find its own essence."[145]

The Reader

In the Arab world, an initial question regarding the reader concerns the nature of the reading public for fictional works, and, more specifically, the level of literacy within the different societies. While little, if any, statistically valid data exist on this subject, it seems reasonable to suggest that the percentage of literate, potential readers of fiction in several countries where Arabic novels are published is substantially lower (as a percentage of the total population) than is the case in Western countries. At the same time, it needs to be recalled that the percentage of readers in the West who regularly read

144. al-Khatībī, 35.
145. Lukacs, 89.

novels is also small. As Q. D. Leavis has noted in her pioneering study of the readership of fiction, novels demand of the reader time, motivation, and intelligence, and contemporary life offers a large number of temptations in the form of less demanding and more accessible art forms.[146] Within the context of the Arab world, we are dealing then with a relatively small percentage of the literate public. Thus, when ʿAbd al-karīm Ghallāb sets forth his goals in this regard, "When I write, I am trying to speak to the public at large, all literate people, and not just the elite,"[147] his societal distinctions seem more a matter of political wishful thinking than of reality with regard to his potential audience. ʿAbd al-ḥakīm Qāsim seems to be closer to the mark when he comments that "with regard to the question of literacy, I think the problem is that we're writing for the public at large (*shaʿb*), but that particular public is not one that reads."[148]

In discussing the more innovative trends in recent novel writing, we have already made mention of the ways in which, through the process of interpreting the text, novelists have been involving their readers in the creation of their fictional worlds. That this process has always potentially been part of the reading process is, of course, a principal tenet of reception theory, as the works of Iser and Fish have explored with reference to Western fiction.[149] Beyond these theoretical aspects of the reading process, some of the more accomplished Arab novelists are demanding involvements of a more practical kind. ʿAbd al-raḥmān Munīf, Jamāl al-Ghīṭānī, and, most recently, Ibrāhīm al-Kawnī (b. 1948), the Libyan novelist and author of *al-Majūs* (The Magi, 1991), require that their readers devote a good deal of time to the exploration of their often lengthy and diffuse narratives. Indeed, one can even suggest that, just as time ceases to be the primary organizing principle of the fiction itself and as the real time required in the process of reading is restricted by the pressures and demands of modern life, so does compartmentalized and self-referential fiction not only reflect these realities but also, as the product of an increasingly technological era, encourage a nonlinear approach to the reading process itself.

146. Q. D. Leavis, *Fiction and the Reading Public* (London: Chatto and Windus, 1932), 205, 214–15, 224.

147. Ghallāb in *Al-Ādāb* (Feb.–Mar. 1980): 116.

148. Qāsim in *Al-Ādāb,* ibid.: 108.

149. See Wolfgang Iser, *The Implied Reader: Patterns of Communication in Prose Fiction from Bunyan to Beckett* (Baltimore: Johns Hopkins Univ. Press, 1974); Stanley Fish, *Is There a Text in This Class?* (Cambridge, Mass.: Harvard Univ. Press, 1980).

Kermode's comment noted above suggests that the majority of novel readers tend to prefer the more traditional fictional modes to the more innovative. Such is the complexity of some recent experiments in fiction writing in Arabic that one is often reminded of Michel Riffaterre's call for the category of "superreader."[150] Such readers clearly exist among the community of critics and writers in the Arab world, although, as some of the above comments confirm, there are adherents to less complex modes of expression in those circles as well. ʿAbd al-ḥakīm Qāsim's remark, on the other hand, suggests that few of these novelists can command a large popular following; in Q. D. Leavis's terms, they tend to be "highbrow" rather than "lowbrow." Fiction of a more popular kind has, as we noted in the earlier chapters of this book, existed from the very beginning, and certain novelists who adhere doggedly to well-tried plots and structures have continued to command a large share of the market for fiction. Iḥsān ʿAbd al-quddūs (1919–90), for example, was generally regarded as the Arab world's most popular writer of fiction, in that more copies of his works have been sold than of any other Arab novelist. The reasons for such popularity, albeit local, are not hard to find. The female protagonist of *Anā ḥurrah* (n.d., [1950s]; *I am Free,* n.d.) proclaims a defiant message that is typical of a number of works which have appealed to successive generations of adolescents and young adults faced with the task of reconciling traditional mores with the forces of change in the postrevolutionary Arab societies. More recently, Egypt has witnessed what al-Nassāj, with unconcealed disgust, terms "the Ismāʿīl Walī al-dīn phenomenon," referring to a mass producer of provocative fiction that is transferred almost instantaneously to the cinema screen.[151]

One novelist who clearly has managed to transcend these boundaries of reception and appeal to a broad readership is Najīb Maḥfūẓ. Without expanding the purview of his fictional works beyond the urban middle class of Cairo, he has still been able, through his novels written during the 1940s and 1950s, to touch a sensitive nerve in several generations of educated Arabs throughout the region, generations which witnessed a common struggle against foreign occupation, the achievement of independence, and the search for new roles and values within the societies that emerged. And, just as his

150. The concept and its implications are explored in detail in Robert Scholes, *Structuralism in Literature* (New Haven: Yale Univ. Press, 1974), 33–40.

151. See al-Nassāj, 78.

novels up to and including *The Trilogy* are vivid justifications for change, so those of the 1960s reflect the concerns of that troubled decade when the course of postrevolutionary Egyptian society, as viewed through the lens of Maḥfūẓ's novels, becomes emblematic of issues facing the entire Arab world. By using reflections on both the past and present to suggest a vision of a better future, Maḥfūẓ succeeded over a period of some two decades in fulfilling the novelist's role in a way that met with broad approval from both a community of fiction critics and a broad spectrum of the emerging and ever-shifting middle-class throughout the Arab world. Just as various revolutionary movements had put an end to the kind of world depicted in Maḥfūẓ's novels of the 1940s and early 1950s, so did the June War of 1967 bring about a transforming experience which has proved to be a watershed in modern Arabic fiction. I have described the most recent phase of Maḥfūẓ's career above as being "retrospective." His works show a distinct move from the more general concerns of societies in the process of adaptation and change to more local and specific concerns with the problems of his own country. In this context it needs to be emphasized that such a move can be seen as a natural reflection of larger political trends in the region, but equally significant in this shift of focus is his often expressed antipathy to many of the policies and cultural attitudes of President Anwar al-Sādāt. In the context of this discussion of readership, what is of interest is that, at the time of the award of the Nobel Prize in Literature to Maḥfūẓ in 1988, the popularity of his post-1967 works in the Arab world—apart from Egypt itself—was considerably less than those written in the 1940s, 1950s and 1960s. That award, and the ensuing publication of his works in numerous world languages, has radically expanded the readership for his works, with effects that are still far from clear. Whether the availability of his novels in Western languages will lead to an expansion of interest in the Arabic novel remains to be seen.

We have left till last the consideration of one particular kind of reader, namely the critic. Wellek and Warren term him "an important middle-man,"[152] and yet in 1980 the Egyptian novelist, Ṣunʿallāh Ibrāhīm has the following to say: "The author looks to the critic for a clearer focus on—I won't say, solutions to—the problems he faces when writing. He expects a penetrating opinion, one which

152. René Wellek and Austin Warren, *Theory of Literature* (New York: Harcourt, 1956), 100.

relies on a more comprehensive, analytical, comparative and experienced vision, something to which he can turn for guidance. However, except for rare instances, all Arab critics provide is something which is addressed solely to the reader."[153] Perhaps the first thing to observe in this context is that the development of more theoretical approaches to the analysis of fictional works within the Western tradition, what one might term the noninevitability of the diachronic approach, is of relatively short vintage. The emphasis that continues to be given in Arabic critical writings on fiction to studies that are predominantly historical, national, and thematic in focus thus sits firmly within the developmental pattern of its analogue in Western criticism. Certain countries, and especially Egypt, Lebanon, and Iraq, have been well served by studies of the links in those areas between political and social trends and the development of fictional genres. In recent times, a large number of studies of other parts of the Arab world have been added to this corpus.[154] Furthermore, an increasing number of critics are treating the Arabic novel within a broader perspective than the purely national or regional: works of Shukrī ʿAyyād, Ṣabrī Ḥāfiẓ, Ilyās Khūrī, ʿIṣām Maḥfūẓ, Sayyid Ḥāmid al-Nassāj, Muḥsin al-Mūsawī, and Khālidah Saʿīd exemplify this trend. During recent years it is hardly surprising that studies on Najīb Maḥfūẓ, and especially those published in Egypt, have become a growth industry, but several book-length studies of other authors—Ghassān Kanafānī, al-Ṭayyib Ṣāliḥ, Yaḥyā Ḥaqqī, and Yūsuf Idrīs, to cite just a few of the more prominent names—have also been published. Works with a thematic focus have also continued to appear in large numbers; the fate of the Palestinian people has, of course, been the primary topic, but the roles of land and sexuality within the fictional worlds of modern Arab novelists have also been topics of investigation. As closer links are developed between Western feminist critics and writers and writing in the Middle East, the study of gender in Arabic fiction will clearly continue to be a major topic of interest.

Alongside these types of analysis, other kinds of critical study have begun to appear in recent decades which suggest that Ṣunʿallāh Ibrāhīm's complaint of over a decade ago may no longer be entirely valid. One must begin by pointing to the important role that is being played by several literary journals that devote issues to synchronic,

153. Ṣunʿallāh Ibrāhīm, in *Al-Ādāb* (Feb.–Mar. 1980): 103.

154. A selection of these studies will be found in the Bibliography.

theoretical aspects of novelistic criticism: we would single out for mention here *al-Ādāb*, *Alif*, *al-Nāqid*, and *Fuṣūl*. In these publications and in an increasing number of books appearing across the Arab world region, a new generation of critics is producing a series of distinguished studies of the inner workings of the novel. In the study of narration, recent years have seen the appearance of excellent studies by Yumnā al-ʿĪd, Samia Mehrez, and Saʿīd Yaqṭīn; point of view is the focus of a lengthy section in a recent study by Injīl Buṭrus Samʿān. Works by Ḥasan Bahrāwī and Ceza Qāsim (Draz) focus on form and structure; Qāsim and Mehrez are also the authors of excellent studies of irony.[155] As a means of rounding off this briefest of surveys of an ever-expanding field, we can point to the appearance of at least two studies on the development of fictional criticism itself: those of Nabīlah Ibrāhīm (Sālim) and Ṭāhā Wādī.

Another feature of recent decades has been increasing contact between littérateurs and critics in the Arab world and their counterparts in the West. The process of translation provides a continuing means for creative contacts; the Project for the Translation of Arabic (PROTA, directed in Boston by Salmā Khadra Jayyūsī) has played an especially prominent role in this process. Scholarly exchanges have been initiated and fostered by conferences in different venues in the Middle East and the West, and a few Western works on Arabic fiction (including the first edition of this book itself) have appeared in Arabic. The listing of works in a variety of Western languages to be found in the bibliography, and the variety of approaches that they adopt, give evidence of developments in Arabic literature studies in the West and, in particular, of continuing efforts to incorporate the Arabic novel into the realm of a heavily Eurocentric Western tradition of comparative literature studies.

The Text

The primary medium whereby the readers of Arabic novels are linked with the writer through the text is, of course, the Arabic language itself. Before discussing the situation of the novelistic text within the various societies of the Arab world, I will consider briefly two linguistic aspects that have a major impact on patterns of reception.

155. An excellent bibliography of recent studies on Arabic fiction is to be found in *The Arabic Novel Since 1950*, 237–54.

The first concerns the status of Arabic in the Maghrib. While the patterns of colonization in territories controlled by the British tended to concentrate on issues of strategic and economic importance, the French colonizers of the North African region succeeded to a large degree in completely gallicizing the educational system. Attempts at "arabizing" (*taʿrīb*) the society and its cultural apparatus have been underway in the countries of the region ever since independence, with varying degrees of emphasis and success. Feelings on the issues involved can be caustically expressed, as in the following comment published in *al-Ādāb*: "For the Algerians the Arabs should be regarded as raiders into North Africa. They should treat Arab culture just as they would that of any other enemy. . . . Because of Algeria's "empathy" with the Mediterranean region, it makes more sense to deal with the countries of the region—France, Italy and Spain—rather than the Arabs of the Arabian Peninsula whose culture and technological progress is still backward."[156] These views are, needless to say, somewhat extreme, but they serve to illustrate the complex web of cultural attitudes and the specific problems of language usage which face writers in the countries of the Maghrib. The number of authors who continue to write fiction in French remains large, but the repertoire of novels in Arabic is steadily increasing. In such a context, the decision of a prominent Algerian French novelist such as Rashīd Abū Jadrah (discussed above) to change his language of fictional expression from French to Arabic becomes extremely significant. A younger generation of Maghribī novelists is now emerging to take over from earlier pioneers in the genre whose works, measured by the yardstick of the Arabic novel as a whole, seem rather conservative in both theme and technique.[157]

The question of language use in the Maghrib is a complex one, particularly if the additional factor of Berber is introduced into the situation. However, while the presence of French and the nature of its continuing impact is an interesting process of cultural assimilation to which many researchers have devoted their attention, writers of fiction in the Maghrib join their colleagues in other regions of the Arab world in confronting another particularly complex issue of language, namely cultural attitudes to the different varieties of Arabic used in each region. The extremely rich and complex situation within which the novelist writing in Arabic operates is often re-

156. ʿAbd al-ʿAlī Razzāqī, "Al-Taʿrīb fī al-Jazāʾir," *Al-Ādāb* (June 1980): 73.
157. See Muḥammad ʿIzz al-dīn al-Tāzī, *Al-Ādāb* (Feb.–Mar. 1980): 78.

duced—with little linguistic justification—to a facile dichotomy between the standard language of writing and the colloquial dialect, whereas native speakers of any region—and thus the novelist who would reflect their patterns of language—make use of a wide spectrum of levels and registers of language, governed by sets of sociolinguistic norms that are only now being studied by linguists. It is the decision as to how to reflect "authentic" dialogue, the dramatic aspect of fiction, which has provoked much vehement discussion during the developmental stages in modern Arabic fiction. Many Egyptian novelists, for example, choose to write their dialogue in the colloquial dialect of Cairo or even other areas of Egypt (see, for example, Fatḥī Ghānim's *al-Jabal*), believing, no doubt, that both television and films have helped to make these colloquials widely understood throughout the Arab world; this is a trend that goes all the way back to Haykal's *Zaynab* written in 1911. On the other hand, Najīb Maḥfūẓ does not use the colloquial dialect in the dialogues of his works, although he will occasionally slip in a dialect word or even use colloquial word order, consciously or unconsciously. His views on the colloquial language (already cited in an earlier chapter) are surprisingly conservative and forthright. "The colloquial is one of the diseases from which people are suffering and of which they are bound to rid themselves as they progress. I consider the colloquial one of the failings of our society, exactly like ignorance, poverty, and disease."[158] Cultural perspectives such as this (reflected in the earlier and equally forceful opinions of Ṭāhā Ḥusayn) are clearly a powerful factor in the decision-making process for some novelists, but there are other, more practical factors as well. Many novelists from other regions of the Arab world compose their novels entirely in the written language, the only standard language of communication, basing their decision as much on their hope for a wide readership throughout the Arab world as on such issues as perceived cultural value. Vial endeavors to summarize the situation: "The tendency to use the spoken "popular" language is more wide-spread in countries where the literary public is greatest and which believe, rightly or wrongly, that they have a better established "Arab" character—thus in Egypt, rather than Algeria."[159] Assuming that this scenario is a

158. Najīb Maḥfūẓ, quoted in Fu'ād Duwārah, *'Asharah udabā' yataḥaddathūna* (Cairo: Dār al-Hilāl, 1965), 39–43; cited in Cachia, *An Overview of Modern Arabic Literature,* 71–72.

159. Vial, "Ḳiṣṣa."

reasonable reflection of linguistic realities (and it needs to be emphasized that there is a pressing need for more research on precisely this topic), one might suggest that, when writers from what might be termed the "non-central" regions of the Arab world such as Fu'ād al-Tikirlī (b. 1927), the Iraqi novelist and author of *al-Raj' al-ba'īd* (Distant return, 1980), and a Maghribī author such as al-Bashīr Khurayyif (in *al-Daqlah fī 'arājīninā*), decide to make heavy use of local dialects in their fictional works, they are effectively restricting their public to a more local readership. As one possible, yet cumbersome solution to the dilemma, 'Alyā' al-Tābi'ī (b. 1961) makes copious use of Tunisian colloquial in the dialogue of her first novel, *Zahrat al-ṣubbar* (Cactus flower, 1991), and provides footnotes which "convert" the language into a standard Arabic version (chapter 4 has seventy-five such references).[160]

Turning now to more practical issues associated with the availability of novelistic texts, we broach first the topic of book publication and distribution. We have already alluded to the direct connection of this subject to the internal politics of the various Arab countries. The censorship of works of literature is the norm in the Arab world; for many years Beirut has been acknowledged as the only haven of unfettered publication in the region. Beyond sheer censorship—the actual banning of publication or alteration of texts—the cultural establishment possesses a bewildering array of methods through which the novelistic text can be delayed, withdrawn, or sequestered; in such cases, the expenses involved are usually borne by the publisher or author or both. The disincentives involved are too obvious to need elaboration. However, in addition to these impediments to rapid publication and continuing availability, it needs to be noted that such connections that exist between the major book publishing houses in the capitals of the Arab world are somewhat *ad hoc*. In happier times, international book fairs (such as the enormous event in Cairo each January) tend to assist in the process of circulating the works of authors in one country to a larger readership throughout the Arab world and beyond. However, such events and the distribution they make possible are among the first institutions to feel and reflect fluctuations in the political climate within the region. Major novelists will generally benefit from better distribution and indeed from more critical attention in the literary periodicals, but problems of physical and political distance will often

160. 'Alyā' al-Tābi'ī, *Zahrat al-ṣubbar* (Tūnis: Dār al-janūb li-al-nashr, 1991).

mean that the newer and lesser-known novelists have a purely local readership, and—what may, ultimately be a worse problem—their works may be only available in bookstores for a short while after publication.

The sheer quantity and variety of novelistic creativity reflected in this lengthy chapter is a sign of the courageous ways in which Arab writers are confronting and overcoming the difficulties outlined here and others, challenges and obstacles placed in their way by both the complexity of the genre itself and the concerns of those who realize full well the extent of its power to advocate change. Novels and critical writings on them continue to appear in great numbers, and increasing patterns of publication in the Gulf region, the Maghrib, and Iraq, mean that the increase in both creativity and critical comment has been exponential. The survey that we have just attempted and the analysis of twelve selected novels that now follows cannot hope to do more than serve as an introduction to the vast wealth which now confronts the student of the novel in Arabic.

4

Twelve Arabic Novels

In the previous chapter, we attempted to show the various ways in which the tradition of the Arabic novel has expanded and developed during the period following the Second World War, a process which has relied and built upon earlier experiments in the genre (the topic of our second chapter). As was pointed out, such is the breadth of the Arabic-speaking world and the continuing productivity of novelists in the region that even such a lengthy investigation of generic development as has just been essayed not only excluded, of necessity, a good deal of accomplished fictional writing, but also employed the convenient methodology of a thematic and descriptive survey. Even within the confines of a work such as this, which is intended to be an introduction to a much broader topic, it seems necessary at this point to offer some more detailed analyses of particular examples of the Arabic novel. In that way, the general traits and qualities that in the previous chapters have been identified and discussed within an investigation of the Arabic novel as a whole may be seen in the closer context of a single work by an individual author.

For this purpose, I have selected twelve novels for analysis. They are united by common features, but also separated by significant differences. On the basis of this collection of works, it is possible to suggest as an initial point of similarity that, as in other fictional traditions, the Arabic novel continues to be a genre which, in Lionel Trilling's words, "most directly reveals to us the complexity, the difficulty, and the interest of life in society, and best instructs us in our human variety and contradiction."[1] These novels have all been published within the last three decades, a period that has already been shown to be one of vast and rapid change in the Arab world

1. Lionel Trilling, *The Liberal Imagination,* vii.

coupled with a considerable amount of political and social upheaval. The aftermath of the June 1967 War has stimulated a great deal of thought and discussion about the very bases of Arab society and its values, leading many intellectuals to a profound reevaluation of their cultural heritage. With these factors in mind, it should come as no surprise that many of these novelists share with their colleagues within other literary traditions an intense preoccupation with the concerns of intellectuals in society and particularly with their sense of alienation in the face of the individual and collective tensions of life in the modern world. Such considerations have often led novelists writing in Arabic to an investigation of the values found in other cultures through a reading of their fictional and intellectual heritages. This, coupled with readings in the literary genres of the great classical tradition of Arabic narrative, produces a contemporary Arabic fictional tradition that involves the reader in a rich and often complex process of interpreting transtextual and intertextual references.

The differences in the works to be analyzed reflect the complexity and variety of the novel genre itself. Of these, style is clearly one of the most obvious, although in the sections that follow it will have to be described rather than illustrated, since translation into English (or, for that matter, any other language) is rarely, if ever, a satisfactory mirror of the stylistic qualities of the source text. Another particular feature of these works is the variegated way in which the authors treat and manipulate time and place their narrators within it. This often involves operating in a narrative present, with its opportunities for interior monologue and stream of consciousness, and relying on flashbacks to fill in details from the past. A further element of difference is that of place, and here the variety in these novels is as broad as the Arab world itself: the settings in which characters are placed vary from boats at sea, to the scorching heat of the desert, or to the rainy cold of British universities; from the village with its entrenched traditional attitudes to the manifold complexities of the modern urban agglomeration.

I should underline the fact that this assemblage of novels is not in any way an attempt on my part to assemble a canonical listing of "great Arabic novels." I hope that the previous chapter has given sufficient illustration of the variety and wealth of the contemporary tradition of fiction in Arabic to show any such attempt to be folly. These twelve novels are analyzed here purely as illustrations of trends which seem to me to be characteristic of the contemporary novel in Arabic. Each section presents one among many possible readings, from a particular perspective chosen in order to illustrate one reader's vision of the work's generic purpose and techniques. Other critics would almost certainly select a different list and different modes of analysis; indeed some of the works discussed here have been discussed by other critics in very different ways. I trust that that may be seen as a reflection of the wealth which the tradition has to offer as well as being a matter of difference of critical approach.

In the previous chapter, we devoted a particular section to the career of Najīb Maḥfūẓ, the Nobel Laureate of 1988. Bearing in mind the central role that he played in bringing the Arabic novel to a higher artistic level, it is perhaps fitting that the first novel to be analyzed should be by him.

Thartharah fawq al-Nīl, Najīb Maḥfūẓ

Those critics who have discussed the group of novels which Najīb Maḥfūẓ published during the 1960s have generally tended to regard the first of the group, *al-Liṣṣ wa-al-kilāb* (1961; *The Thief and the Dogs,* 1984) as the best. Indeed, there is little doubt that this study of oppression and betrayal provides a most convincing fusion of symbol and reality in order to make some telling comments about socialist values. The fact that this work ends on such a negative note and that Maḥfūẓ's next novel, *al-Summān wa-al-kharīf* (1962; *Autumn Quail, 1985*), has such an optimistic conclusion may even suggest that there was some official concern about Maḥfūẓ's views as expressed in the first novel.

In any case, I have always regarded *Thartharah fawq al-Nīl*[2] (Chatter on the Nile, 1966) as a work of equal distinction. In fact, in view of the extremely difficult task which Maḥfūẓ sets himself in this later work, I find the results, if anything, even more impressive. In the first place, the spatial dimension in this novel is extremely restricted: the setting is an *ʿawwāmah,* a houseboat on the Nile in Cairo. Within such an environment the action is, needless to say, confined, and one of the major features of the novel is an almost total lack of movement or change of scene.[3] The narrative opens with a sarcastic de-

2. The novel is now available in English, *Adrift on the Nile,* trans. Frances Liardet (New York: Doubleday, 1993).

3. Shawkat Toorawa dwells on this issue of movement in his study of the

scription of the ministry office in which the novel's pivotal character, Anīs Zakī, works as a civil servant. He has finished a report and submitted it to his superior. He is summoned into the latter's office to explain how it is that the last pages of the report are completely blank; Anīs Zakī's pen has run dry in the process of writing the report and he has not even noticed.[4] Apart from this introduction to one of the situations in Anīs Zakī's life, the only other occasion on which the scene shifts from the houseboat is when the characters in the novel pile into a car and go on a crazy ride down the Pyramids Road to Saqqārah, knock down and kill a peasant on the road, and drive away without stopping to face the consequences.

The opening of the novel does more than depict the tedious environment of life in the civil service. In fact, that goal may be considered as ancillary to another literary task of some difficulty which Maḥfūẓ set himself in this work, namely of portraying Anīs Zakī in an almost permanently drugged stupor, taciturn and inward-looking, hardly ever contributing to the "chatter," but reacting to the comments of his superior in the ministry or of his evening companions on the houseboat with streams of consciousness which resurrect episodes from past history and illustrate his own griefs and failures. The picture that Maḥfūẓ provides of Anīs Zakī's life and activities on the houseboat has obvious symbolic significance in that, to quote one of the other characters, he is "in charge of our houseboat,"[5] a phrase which has more than merely surface import within the atmosphere created in this narrative. Further details and descriptions are provided at different stages of the work by other characters; in this work Maḥfūẓ makes use of a limited multinarrator technique which he exploits to a fuller extent in his next work, *Mīrāmār*.[6] Less obviously than in *Mīrāmār* and other novels which Ḍiyā' al-Sharqāwī terms *riwāyāt ṣawtiyyah*,[7] Maḥfūẓ, in the present work, uses the various narrative points of view to support or challenge the impressions—and that is all they are or are meant to be—which the reader has gained from the ramblings of Anīs Zakī's consciousness.

This, then, is not a novel of action; its main focus is indeed the

novel: "Movement in Maḥfūẓ's *Tharthara Fawq al-Nīl*," *JAL* 22, no. 1 (Mar. 1991): 53–65.

4. Najīb Maḥfūẓ, *Thartharah fawq al-Nīl* (Cairo: Maktabat Miṣr, 1966), 7–8; trans., 3–4.

5. Ibid., 34; trans., 26.

6. Najīb Maḥfūẓ, *Mīrāmār* (Cairo: Maktabat Miṣr, 1967).

7. Ḍiyā' al-Sharqāwī, "Al-Mi'mār al-fannī," 7–57.

group that comes to the boat to indulge in "chatter on the Nile." The houseboat itself can, of course, be regarded as a means of detachment from the world of the city, from society and its problems, a means of retreat from the alienation of modern life itself. It is moored to the land, which in this case constitutes the venue of a crushing and disillusioning reality. The symbol of water, the river on which the boat floats, allows for a lulling sense of detachment from the unpleasant aspects of life that Anīs Zakī is forced to confront every day in his office. It is from this environment that he escapes to his houseboat, wafted by the cool evening breezes, and to the circle of companions who join him in the evening for encounters with drugs and sex. The symbolism implicit in this escape from land and reality is further underlined by the presence on the boat of ʿAmm ʿAbduh, the houseboat's general factotum, a huge man who, in addition to arranging all the necessary equipment for the evening's gathering and, when asked, procuring girls for Anīs Zakī and the company, also serves as Imām for a local group of Muslims. Throughout the work, ʿAmm ʿAbduh has little to say; more often than not, his response is a cryptic "Ah." In such a context, his forthright statement near the beginning of the narrative assumes a special importance: "I am the houseboat, because I am the ropes and lanterns. If for a single moment I did not do what I was supposed to do, the boat would sink and be carried away by the tide."[8] ʿAmm ʿAbduh thus serves as the guardian of the houseboat and provider of all the needs and comforts for the group of individuals who come to share in the atmosphere of detached irreality which Anīs Zakī has created for himself.

The group who come to the houseboat are from a variety of professions: there is Muṣṭafā Rāshid, the lawyer; Khālid ʿAzūz, a short story writer; Laylā Zaydān, a graduate of the American University in Cairo who has espoused feminist causes; Aḥmad Naṣr, a civil servant and bookkeeper who is devoted to his wife and is described as "in sum a completely ordinary person";[9] ʿAlī al-Sayyid, an art critic and companion to Saniyyah Kāmil, who, "at times of marital trouble comes back to her old friends, a woman of experience who learned all about womanhood while still a virgin, a wife and mother, who is a veritable treasure-house of experience for the

8. Maḥfūẓ, *Thartharah,* 15; trans., 11.

9. Ibid., 110; trans., 95.

young girls who come to our houseboat."[10] Much of the above description about these characters is given to the reader by Rajab al-Qāḍī, a celebrated film actor, who brings a new girl friend, Sanā' al-Rashīdī, to the group for the first time and introduces them to her one by one at the beginning of the fourth chapter. She is amazed at the blatant way in which the company indulges in illegalities, and this affords the characters—and, no doubt, the author—the opportunity to supply just one of a series of political comments which are scattered throughout the novel:

> "Aren't you scared of the police?" she asked.
>
> "We're scared of the police," replied ʿAlī al-Sayyid, "not to mention the army, the English, the Americans, the overt and the covert. By now it's gone so far that nothing can scare us."
>
> "But the door's wide open!"
>
> "ʿAmm ʿAbduh's outside. He can keep intruders out."
>
> "Don't worry, gorgeous," Rajab said with a smile, "the government's so preoccupied with building things, it doesn't have any time to bother us."
>
> "Why don't you give this brand of fortitude a try?" asked Muṣṭafā Rāshid, offering her the hashish pipe.[11]

The group's collective cynicism, their reliance on ʿAmm ʿAbduh, and the desire to cancel reality and to persuade others to do so, all these features are evident in this short extract. Into this situation comes the figure of Samārah Bahjat. We first hear of her at the beginning of the fifth chapter when ʿAlī al-Sayyid announces that his journalistic colleague is eager to pay them a visit; her curiosity has been aroused both by his conversations with her about the group and also by the publications of members of the group that have appeared in a variety of media.[12] It is this same Samārah Bahjat who provides another level of insight into the characters on the houseboat when, in the tenth chapter, Anīs Zakī reads from her diary the outline of a play which she has written, one in which all the personae are taken from the group on the houseboat.[13] She has provided a cameo sketch of each of the "characters" in her play that reflects her own opinion of the person concerned. She has, in fact, told them

10. Ibid., 34; trans., 25.
11. Ibid., 36–37; trans., 28–29.
12. Ibid., 46; trans., 36.
13. Ibid., 107ff; trans., 95ff.

earlier of her extreme interest in the theatre as something which "has focus and where every word has to have its own particular meaning."[14] She ignores Muṣṭafā Rāshid's retort to this comment, to the effect that the theatre is thus the complete opposite of what happens on the houseboat, and instead asks the stupefied Anīs Zakī why he is not saying anything. This sends Anīs off on one of his journeys into history and his own consciousness, and yet typically he makes no response.

As Samārah begins to attend the group regularly, they begin to worry about the fact that she is too serious; she seems to pose a direct threat to their escapism. As Muṣṭafā Rāshid asks, "Do you think she has plans to make us all serious some time?"[15] to which Khālid ʿAzūz responds that Rajab al-Qāḍī seems to have his own plans with regard to Samārah. As if to confirm this possibility, Sanā' no longer appears with Rajab at the group's gatherings.

After Anīs Zakī has read Samārah's diary which, unknown to the group, contains her impressions based on these conversations, an amusing chapter follows in which he argues with the group about their priorities in life, quoting throughout from Samārah's diary. Even though he does not reveal the source of his comments and the group seems only moderately disturbed by his unusual loquaciousness, Samārah herself feels most uneasy and eventually succeeds in getting the diary back after refusing to sleep with him.[16] The fact that Anīs Zakī serves as a mouthpiece for Samārah's views about the group may perhaps be seen as a premonition of what is to come. When the grossly overcrowded car in which they are speeding along the Pyramid Road kills the peasant, Samārah insists that they stop, true to her role within the group and confirming their worst fears about her. That night, Anīs Zakī is unable to fall to sleep; he only manages to do so at his desk the next day, whereupon he is arrested for assaulting the Director General, who has reprimanded him for his conduct.[17] When the group meets that night, the atmosphere is tense. Samārah insists that they go to the police, whereas everyone else is afraid of being exposed. Their efforts to point out to her that her own reputation will also be soiled are of no avail. Rajab al-Qāḍī, the driver of the car and would-be lover of Samārah, becomes in-

14. Ibid., 61; trans., 49.
15. Ibid., 80; trans., 67.
16. Ibid., 133; trans., 112–13.
17. Ibid., 173; trans., 145–46.

creasingly furious at Anīs Zakī's comments, and a terrible fight ensues, during which the figure of ʿAmm ʿAbduh appears, only to be sent away again by Aḥmad Naṣr.[18] However, the group is not ready for the consequence of this fracas. When Anīs Zakī recovers, it is to tell his colleagues that murder is one thing which cannot be taken lightly, and he makes it clear that he is referring to the death of the peasant on the road.[19] He says unequivocally that he is fully cognizant of what he is saying and that he will go to the police himself. Rajab tries to attack again, but the group takes him away. ʿAmm ʿAbduh now reappears with a cup of coffee which, he hints, will make Anīs feel better. Anīs is now left alone with Samārah, and she only has time for a short conversation about the implications of their position before the laced coffee sends Anīs Zakī off into a final reverie concerning the tragedy of man's evolution "from the paradise of apes in trees to the ground in the forest."[20]

From this brief, yet somewhat complex description, it will, I hope, be clear that we are dealing with one of Maḥfūẓ's richest essays in the use of symbolism. We have already made several suggestions on this topic, but the store is by no means exhausted. It should, for example, be pointed out that all the members of the group which meets on the houseboat belong to the intellectual class and, more specifically, to those in the sphere of culture.[21] That Maḥfūẓ should have addressed himself to the issues evoked by the problems, life style, and expectations of this group during the period of the early 1960s is in itself of extreme significance. For, as many commentators on this period have since shown, and as Maḥfūẓ himself was to record in later fictional works such as *al-Marāyā* (1972) and *al-Karnak* (1974),[22] these years may have witnessed some of the most oppressive political constraints on the artist during the entire revolutionary period. But, to remain on a more literary plane, one may observe at the very least that the characters who join Anīs Zakī in the evening are escaping into a world where they can forget or ignore aspects of their own reality. No doubt the socio-political conditions to which we have just alluded play a part in this desire to escape, but each charac-

18. Ibid., 186; trans., 156.

19. Ibid., 187; trans., 158.

20. Ibid., 199; trans., 167.

21. Compare Jabrā, *The Ship* (discussed below), in which a boat is used as a refuge in which a group of Arab intellectuals discuss their problems.

22. See Roger Allen, "Some Recent Works of Najīb Maḥfūẓ," *JARCE* 14 (1977): 101–10.

ter has his or her own reasons for doing so, some of them rooted in the past, others impinging from the present. In the case of Anīs Zakī, these include his failure to complete a degree program at a number of colleges, his loss of both his wife and daughter, and the continuing tedium and frustration of his job. Perhaps the most remarkable example of all is Aḥmad Naṣr, an apparently successful civil servant and loyal husband. And yet he too feels the need to resort to this group of individuals; Samārah Bahjat is of the opinion that it is the very security of Naṣr's business and family life that leaves him with a sense of futility deep down, in that nothing in life seems to change pace.[23] The various roads to escape which the group follows by coming to the houseboat are first challenged and then dashed by the inquiries and convictions of Samārah Bahjat. Rajab al-Qāḍī, the great lover, is unable to win Samārah's love or to persuade her not to go to the police. When she seems on the point of relenting, it is Anīs Zakī, the taciturn, somber master of ceremonies, who finally, in his own words, "wanted to try saying the things which need to be said!"[24]

A final word needs to be said about Maḥfūẓ's use of language in this novel. It has been my impression from reading Maḥfūẓ's novels for a number of years that the fictional lexicon that he employs in his works is not particularly large and that, as his technique as a novelist has developed, he has honed a style whose terse and suggestive quality is an ideal instrument for his often sardonic commentaries on the society he knows so well, a style that is quite different from the more poetic qualities of some other Arab novelists, including Jabrā Ibrāhīm Jabrā and ʿAbd al-raḥmān Munīf, whose works are discussed below. Maḥfūẓ's style tends to reflect the skills of a careful craftsman who spent much of his life as a civil servant and who has written very much on a regular, almost routine, basis. In this aspect, I would contrast his style with that of his fellow countryman, Yūsuf Idrīs, whose style had a more spontaneous and impulsive quality, one that on occasion verged almost on irregularity.[25] I should make it clear that my comments here are intended to be more a description of differences in style than a criticism of the writer whose name personifies the Arabic novel's achievement of

23. Maḥfūẓ, *Thartharah,* 110; trans., 95.

24. Ibid., 195; trans., 163.

25. For similar opinions, see Sulaymān Fayyaḍ in *Kutub ʿArabiyyah,* no. 1 (Jan. 1977): 2; and Yūsuf Sāmī al-Yūsuf, "Najīb Maḥfūẓ wa-jā'izat Nobel," *Al-Ḥurriyyah* 23 (Oct., 1988): 38.

genuine maturity. What I am suggesting with particular reference to *Thartharah fawq al-Nīl* is that Maḥfūẓ used his lexicon with consummate artistry to fuse together in a single, cryptic atmosphere the various elements of the overt and covert, the conscious and unconscious, the present and the past, all of which provide us with a rich store of symbols to depict the role and fate of the Egyptian cultural intelligentsia during the 1960s.

Mā tabaqqā la-kum, Ghassān Kanafānī

No modern Arab novelist has been able to project the tragedy of the Palestinian people in fiction with greater impact than Ghassān Kanafānī. That is hardly surprising in view of the fact that he devoted his life to the illustration in both fact and fiction of the circumstances of the Palestinians and to an investigation of the complexities of Arab attitudes to them. Into a short life of thirty-six years he managed to fit a career as an increasingly experimental writer of fiction and as spokesman for the Popular Front for the Liberation of Palestine.

Of all his works of fiction, *Rijāl fī al-shams* (1963; *Men in the Sun*, 1978) is undoubtedly the most famous, and its message concerning the inability of Palestinians to find a place or role for themselves in the glare of harsh reality and their exploitation by Arabs of other nationalities is conveyed with tremendous clarity and force. In fact, in spite of the excellent use of imagery in work and the careful way in which the plot is constructed, the impact of the symbolism is, in my opinion, too clear and forceful. It is for that reason that I have chosen another novel which broaches the same theme, the plight of the Palestinians, in a more subtle fashion, namely *Mā tabaqqā la-kum* (1966; *All That's Left to You*, 1990).[26] Furthermore, from the point of view of technique, the latter novel shows a number of interesting experimental features which demonstrates the writer's continuing interest in developing his artistry as a novelist.

In a "clarification" at the beginning of this novel, Kanafānī makes it clear that, in writing this novel, he has been particularly concerned about matters of technique:

26. The designation of this work by the Univ. of Texas Press as a "novella" (see *All That's Left to You*, 1990) would appear to be one of many examples of the confusion of the term "novella" with "short novel."

> The five heroes of this novel, Ḥāmid, Maryam, Zakariyyā, Time and the Desert, do not move in parallel or conflicting directions; that much should be obvious from the very start. Rather they intersect in a manner that is so compact that they all seem to consist of just two separate threads and no more. This fusion also affects both time and place, to such an extent that there is no specific dividing line between places that are far apart or between different time frames, and occasionally between time and place at one and the same time.[27]

This statement raises a number of interesting points regarding the novelist's technique, but one of the most striking is the almost nonchalant juxtaposition of the elements of time and place—in this case the desert—with the three main characters of the work as being "heroes" *(abṭāl),* a usage which recalls the partial ancestry of the novel genre in the older epic tradition, as was noted in our introductory chapter. In this novel, time does indeed play a pivotal role. The events take place over an interval of some eighteen hours, most of them at night. Here the background is filled in, as in so many of these novels that we are surveying, through the generous use of flashback. But time is also a more obtrusive protagonist in this work, and its role is symbolized in two instruments which tell time: a wall clock whose ticking punctuates the life of those who live in the Palestinian home which is the major focus of the action, and a watch which the hero, Ḥāmid, discards as useless on his journey across the desert.

It will be recalled that, in *Rijāl fī al-shams,* the desert represented not only a barrier to be traversed but also a place of scorching heat, a heat which led to the deaths of the Palestinians inside the water tank. In *Mā tabaqqā la-kum,* the desert is once again a barrier; in fact it is now a barrier which has to be crossed in a short time in order to avoid Israeli border patrols, but for that same reason it has to be crossed at night. Our hero is therefore not concerned with the problems of heat (except for a short time on the second day). His major concern is with cold and the loneliness of the dark desert wastes

27. Kanafānī, *Mā tabaqqā la-kum* 1:159; trans., xxi. For other studies of this work, see Maḥmūd Ghanāyim, *Tayyār al-waʿy fī al-riwāyah al-ʿArabiyyah al-ḥadīthah: Dirāsah uslūbiyyah* (Beirut: Dār al-Jīl, 1992), 258–82; Ṭalāl Ḥarb, "Fusḥat al-ikhtiyār: dirāsah bunyawiyyah," *Al-Ādāb* (July–Aug., 1980): 24–31; Hilary Kilpatrick, "Tradition and Innovation in the Fiction of Ghassān Kanafānī," *JAL* 7 (1976): 53–64; and Ṣiddīq, *Man Is a Cause,* 22–38.

when every light and every sound seems magnified a thousand times, even the ticking of his watch. And, just as *Rijāl fī al-shams* opens with Abu Qays lying on the ground feeling the heartbeat of the earth beneath him,[28] in *Mā tabaqqā la-kum* Ḥāmid throws himself to the ground "and felt it like a virgin trembling beneath him, as a beam of light silently and softly swept across the folds of sand. Just at that moment he riveted himself to the ground and felt it soft and warm."[29] In another telling juxtaposition, the beats of the earth beneath Ḥāmid's prostrate body find themselves associated with the fetus inside his sister's womb. In this way, the decisions of brother and sister, which form the focus of this novel, are, as the author noted in his "clarification," brought together in spite of a distance in time and space.

But what of the characters themselves? Ḥāmid and Maryam are brother and sister who, in the rush to leave in 1948, were separated from their mother; she now lives in Jordan, while they are quartered in a refugee camp in the Gaza Strip. The two children have been cared for by an aunt; significantly, her death is marked, as are so many episodes in this novel, by reference to the chiming of the wall clock.[30] Ḥāmid is almost twenty years younger than his sister, Maryam, but in spite of this, his aunt has repeatedly urged him, as the man of the family, to get his sister married. Maryam is thirty-five years old now and in all that time has managed to maintain her chastity. But, as if to confirm her aunt's worst fears, her one "slip" (as she explains it to her brother) is a costly one for the family as a whole.[31] She becomes pregnant and persuades the father of the child to marry her. Normally this might be considered a happy solution to the problem, but not in this case. For the father is none other than Zakariyyā, a married man with five children.[32] In the context of the fate of Palestine and its people, even that is not the major problem. In a telling flashback, Ḥāmid records how a few years earlier a young man named Sālim had been involved in underground activities against the Israeli armed forces. All the boys of the camp had been lined up, and Sālim had been told to step forward. No one had moved, but at the first sign of threat from the soldiers, Zakariyyā

28. Kanafānī, *Rijāl fī al-shams,* 1:37; trans., 7.
29. Kanafānī, *Mā tabaqqā la-kum,* 1:169; trans., 6; 1:161; trans., 1.
30. Ibid., 1:174; trans., 9.
31. Ibid., 1:180; trans., 14.
32. Ibid., 1:188; trans., 18.

had been the one to give way. Sālim duly stepped forward, and was taken away and shot in their hearing.[33]

Thus, as far as Ḥāmid and most of his contemporaries are concerned, Maryam's enforced and all-too-obliging husband is a symbol of all that is despicable and loathsome, a personification of betrayal of the Palestinian cause from within. To make matters worse, Zakariyyā begins to treat the house of his new wife as his own, using it as a kind of way station between the place where he works and his other home, where Fatḥiyya, his wife, and their children live. All this proves too much for Ḥāmid to bear. He decides to leave for Jordan in search of his mother, in spite of all the risks involved. The stage is thus set for the action of the novel itself: Maryam remains in what is left of the family home in Gaza trying to resolve the conflict between the fact that she is married to Zakariyyā and carrying his child, while her own brother is attempting to cross at night a desert full of natural and human obstacles and dangers. Ḥāmid meanwhile has abandoned his intolerable reality in Gaza and gone in search of his mother, a symbol of the security and honor that the family has lost.

It is within this framework, so rich in potential, that the technique of Ghassān Kanafānī, outlined in the above quotation, emerges as such an interesting and, in my opinion, successful portrayal of the complexities of the situation, even though, as the author himself admits, the need to distinguish speakers and time frames through the use of differing typefaces tends to complicate the process somewhat. Throughout the long night of Ḥāmid's traversal of the frontier, Maryam is unable to sleep. She feels inside herself the pulsating beat of his footsteps, which are mingled with the ticking of the clock and the movements of the baby which she is carrying. Initially, Ḥāmid is linked to her too by the ticking of his watch, but when he discards it, the sound is replaced by the pulsating of the earth beneath him. Maryam's wakefulness disturbs Zakariyyā. He tries to persuade his new bride to forget about her immature and impetuous brother who has embarked on such a foolhardy expedition. She tells him that the fetus of their child is keeping her awake, and to the sound of the chiming clock—once again—he tells her what a scandal will be created by the birth of the child so soon after their marriage and suggests that she have an abortion.[34] Maryam now comes to realize what a fateful decision she has made

33. Ibid., 1:200, 212–15; trans., 28, 38–39.
34. Ibid., 1:222–23; trans., 44.

in marrying Zakariyyā and what an opportunist and coward he really is. The horror of this realization is accompanied by the beat of Ḥāmid's footsteps as he moves ever further away across the desert.[35]

As the novel draws to its climax, brother and sister are both face-to-face with the enemy, without or within. Ḥāmid surprises an Israeli border guard and subdues him. The realization gradually dawns on him that, if he is to reach Jordan, he will have to kill his captive. Zakariyyā meanwhile threatens his wife with divorce if she does not have an abortion. When he starts to beat her, she grabs a knife. In both the desert and house scenarios, the eerie sound of howling dogs is to be heard. Maryam stabs her husband to death in a gesture which is made to suffice for both situations. The enemy which has brought this family so low on both the general and particular planes has been eradicated.

The above analysis of the plot of this novel illustrates Kanafānī's rich and skillful use of symbols, and they are accompanied and embellished by an attractive imagery. We have already mentioned the description of the earth as a breathing, pulsating creature. Equally forceful is the way in which Kanafānī portrays the crucial moment when Ḥāmid realizes that his sister is pregnant: "Sitting down she wrapped her arms round her waist. My eye fell on them, and suddenly I realised. I was overcome by panic, and beads of perspiration started trickling down from my forehead into my eyes. I felt as though a cry was emerging from beneath her hands wrapped round her waist, a wounded cry which seemed to come from between her thighs where she had put her hands as though to hide something. And then suddenly she started to cry."[36] Imagery and symbols such as these are used with great effect in most, if not all, of Kanafānī's fictional writings. What is different and consciously experimental about *Mā tabaqqā la-kum* is the narrative technique. The two protagonists, Ḥāmid and Maryam, also serve as the principal narrators; for this purpose both first and third person, narrative past and present, are used. Changes in mode or person are marked by a change of typeface; in the following examples, the heavy typeface will be represented by italics:

> *He was relying entirely on his senses, a single impulse enveloped in a certain amount of fear. But even that had a sense of excitement about it. A*

35. Ibid., 1:225; trans., 45.
36. Ibid., 1:175; trans., 10.

> *whole gamut of feelings, filling the clenched fists of a plucky adventurer as they pound on some unknown portal.* I was quivering with heat and excited at one and the same time when I saw him at the door. Ḥāmid had left just five minutes before, and now here was Zakariyyā standing by the door, full of self-confidence and asking whether he was still here.[37]

In this instance, Arabic can convey what English cannot: the adjectives which qualify the "I" following the italicized section are in the feminine and thus make it clear to the reader that the "he" of the italicized section is Ḥāmid in the course of his desert journey, while the "I" of the second segment is Maryam recounting the fateful occasion when Zakariyyā seduced her. In addition to the fact that these two episodes are joined to each other directly, it is worth noticing that, in spite of the vastly different situations involved, brother and sister are shown here to share the same combination of fear and excitement.

Occasionally this switching of time and place can be very rapid:

> *Here I am once again, faced with a fresh moment in time that I don't know how to handle. At first I started to smile, then suddenly I burst into fits of laughter.* Zakariyyā rolled over on to his side and looked at me, then rolled back again and went to sleep, as though he too were deeply involved in some insane dream. *You may know Hebrew and nothing else but that doesn't matter. Just listen. Isn't it really infuriating that we should meet face to face in this wilderness the way we did, and yet be unable to talk to each other? He continued to stare at me, enigmatic, hesitant, somewhat doubtful, but certainly scared.* For my part, I had gone beyond being scared; the feeling I had now was strange and inexplicable.[38]

Here in the space of a few lines, the situation moves twice from Ḥāmid confronted with the problem of the Israeli guard to Maryam lying in bed with her husband thinking about her brother. Also noteworthy in this passage is the way in which the person is changed in each of the four segments.

In one final example of this technique there is a switch of persons while a single narrator, in this case Ḥāmid, is recounting his situation:

37. Ibid., 1:178; trans., 12–13. This feature of the novel's style is explored in detail by Ḥarb, 25–31.

38. Ibid., 1:208; trans., 35.

He got up and stood on his feet. He started looking around him, probing into the darkness with his eyes for a sign of anything. Then he came back. He began to search the Israeli's pockets. My fingers felt his soft wallet, so I took it out and began to look through it. It was hard to know what value any of the papers had because it was so dark, and so I put them all into my shirt pocket.[39]

The effect here is almost cinematic, as the change from third to first person almost palpably brings the narrative lens closer to the scene of the action. The tremendous closeness of Ḥāmid to his anonymous Israeli foe is made even more striking by the fact that, immediately after the extract just quoted, Ḥāmid records the inevitable realization by the Israeli soldier that the only possible end to this episode is his—the Israeli's—death.

Kanafānī's life was one of commitment to the cause of the Palestinian people. His fictional writings, however, do not show that concern with the magnified realism that marks or even disfigures the works of less artistic commentators on the Palestinian cause. His literary career is marked by a constant concern with form, style and imagery. While *Mā tabaqqā la-kum* has not emerged as his most popular work of fiction, it remains a subtle and innovative treatment of this most popular of topics for modern Arab authors, and an interesting contribution to the development of narrative modes in Arabic fiction.

ʿAwdat al-ṭāʾir ilā al-baḥr, Ḥalīm Barakāt

"The Flying Dutchman has now returned to the sea. But he still feels an intense longing for the land. He cannot remain in exile and without roots for ever."[40] In this novel, *The Flying Dutchman's Return to the Sea* (translated by Trevor Le Gassick as *Days of Dust*),[41] the Syrian-born writer Ḥalīm Barakāt (now a professor in Washington, D.C.) gives us one of the most cogent and realistic pictures of the events of 1967 and of the way in which they reflect on Arab society in general. Since Barakāt is himself a sociologist by training, this latter aspect is one of the most prominent features of the work, affect-

39. Ibid., 1:212; trans., 38.

40. Ḥalīm Barakāt, *ʿAwdat al-ṭaʾir ilā al-baḥr* (The Flying Dutchman's return to the sea) (Beirut: Dār al-Nahār, 1969, 161; English trans.: *Days of Dust*, trans. Trevor Le Gassick (Wilmette, Ill.: Medina, 1974).

41. Barakāt, *Days of Dust*.

ing the portrayal of character and narrative point of view in no small way. Indeed, the name of the character through whose consciousness the story of the Flying Dutchman—the sailor condemned to roam the seas until he is redeemed by the discovery of true love—is filtered is Ramzī Ṣafadī, and he is a professor at the American University in Beirut. It is Barakāt himself who reminds us that *ramzī* is the Arabic for "my symbol" or even "the symbol of me."[42] Through Ramzī Ṣafadī, the Palestinian, Western-trained professor living in exile in Beirut, the Flying Dutchman becomes a symbol of the continuing agony of the Palestinian people; like the sailor who is forever roaming the seas, they too continue to encounter devastating failure in their attempts to regain their land. To Ramzī, as to most other Palestinians, this exile goes back to the fighting in 1948, an event captured in an earlier novel by Barakāt, which he called *Sittat ayyām* (1961; *Six Days,* 1990; discussed in the previous chapter), in an almost ill-starred prediction of the course of events in the 1967 conflict and therefore of the present work itself.

As Ramzī has this final thought about the Flying Dutchman, he is standing on a hill overlooking ʿAmmān, where he has come with a group of his colleagues and students to investigate the real extent of the disaster. In order to give his impressions a particular force, Barakāt again resorts to an extraneous source, in this case the Bible and more specifically the Book of Genesis. The final chapter of the novel, "Ayyām ʿadīdah min al-ghubār" (Many days of dust), begins:

> On the seventh day, he did not rest. Sadly his seventh day is not a single day. He has no idea how long into the future it will last. . . . Everything that the Arab created in the first six days was dust. . . . Darkness returns to cover the earth . . . the earth becomes desolate and void, and darkness is on the face of the deep. It is the beginning of creation. But the spirit of God does not move on the face of the waters. The Arab says, "Let there be light," but there is none. He cannot distinguish light from darkness. . . . The Arab saw everything that he had made, and behold, it was very bad. For that reason he did not rest on the seventh day. He is trying to erase the traces of the dominion of fishes, birds and other creatures from his body. The future is all that he has.[43]

42. See Barakāt, *Visions of Social Reality,* 37. Khālidah Saʿīd points out that Barakāt himself went on a mission to Jordan after the June War of 1967, 176n. 1.

43. Barakāt, *ʿAwdat al-ṭāʾir,* 147. The structural importance of these subdivisions of the text are discussed in Saʿīd Yaqṭīn, *Infitāḥ al-naṣṣ al-riwāʾī* (Beirut: Al-Markaz al-thaqāfī al-ʿArabī, 1989), 71–72.

With these evocative, yet damning thoughts, Ramzī brings the reader back to the beginning of the work; for the first chapter, "al-ʿAtabah" (The threshold) is set in the same location and uses the beginning of Genesis with the same telling effect. These two chapters are indeed a frame within which the narrative of the fateful "six days" of June 1967 is set. Characters, symbols, and images from the central chapters find their way into these two outlying chapters, but the moral for the Arabs of the future is laid out with brutal clarity in these two chapters. The central narrative, with its almost cinematic realism, has its own impact, needless to say; but the first and last chapters, with their use of the narrative present (even in the rewriting of Genesis), show us that, after such a total defeat, the future is all the Arab has left.

Apart from these first and last chapters when Ramzī is in ʿAmmān, the rest of the novel finds him and his colleagues in Beirut. The choice of this location serves the author's purpose admirably. It permits the portrayal in a very forceful manner of an entire people being led by their leaders to believe that they are at last on the way to total victory over the Israelis; news broadcasts from throughout the Arab world talk about crushing defeats of the enemy, enemy planes being downed, and tremendous heroism by the Arab fighting forces. The enthusiasm and sense of resurgence among some of Ramzī's students is almost palpable. And then comes the shattering news of total defeat, a defeat almost from the very start. Shock is followed by bitterness, by attacks on the American and British embassies in Beirut (on the basis of yet another news report), by Nasser's speech of resignation and the swirling violence of a huge demonstration in support of the Egyptian leader. The steady rise and abrupt crash of this corporate emotion during these six days is callously manipulated by the news media, a point which Barakāt underlines with unconcealed anger and which another Syrian writer of fiction, Zakariyyā Tāmir, carries even further in his short story "Al-Aʿdāʾ" (The enemies), in which the Arabic language is given an award for heroism for downing so many planes and immobilizing so many tanks during the war.[44] Ramzī's description of or participation in the events in Beirut mentioned above provides us with a most effective picture of the way in which the impact of this defeat was

44. Zakariyyā Tāmir, "Al-Aʿdāʾ" in *Numūr fī al-yawm al-ʿāshir* (Beirut: Dār al-Ādāb, 1978), 3ff.; trans. Roger Allen, "The enemies," *Nimrod* 24 no. 2 (Spring–Summer 1981): 61–70.

felt by the Arabs. It was not merely a total defeat, but one which was inflicted on a people who were being led by their governments to believe right up to the very last moment that they were scoring a resounding victory. Worst of all, the instantaneous loss of the air battle and complete superiority of the Israeli air force made the June War for the Arabs a defeat without heroism.

It is precisely Beirut's distance from the actual fighting which permits the impact of these vicious lessons to strike home. Many of them are discussed by Ramzī with Pamela, a beautiful American artist separated from her husband. Their torrid relationship serves to divert Ramzī's attention temporarily from what is going on in the fighting; there are some telling juxtapositions of scenes of the two of them making love, and the scene as planes rain destruction on the West Bank.[45] Pamela herself, footloose, unsure of her relationships with both her husband and Ramzī, and not a little selfish, may serve, as Ilyās Khūrī suggests, as a symbol of "the approaching breakdown of Western capitalism" within Barakāt's revolutionary intentions for Arab society.[46] But it would appear that her most valuable function within Barakāt's larger narrative scheme is to serve as a sounding board for Ramzī's views on Arab society, its traditions, and its values. The availability of Pamela, the beautiful American tourist with Wanderlust, to discuss issues which burn in the mind of "my symbol" (Ramzī) is most convenient to the didactic purpose of the novel.

In this novel, Beirut is far from the fighting, and yet to Ramzī, the exiled Palestinian, it is tantalizingly near; so much so that it arouses his guilt feelings for not being there, feelings which become particularly evident when he is making love to Pamela. Part of his mind is always in Palestine, and never more so than during these climactic days. Ramzī joins all the other Palestinians in a single experience, and Barakāt's narrative technique is a major element in the attempt to portray such a feeling of unity. In the six central chapters, each one devoted to a day in the conflict, Beirut (with Ramzī and Pamela) is just one of a number of locations. Prominent attention is also given to Ṭāhā Kanʿān in Jericho, Khālid ʿAbd al-Ḥalīm in Sabastiyah, and ʿAzmī ʿAbd al-Qādir in Jerusalem. We are also given flashes of information about other figures in numerous villages and towns on the West Bank. Even here, the activities and discussions of Ramzī and Pamela remain the central thread in the narrative, but at

45. Barakāt, *ʿAwdat al-ṭāʾir*, 90–91, 108.

46. Ilyās Khūrī, *Tajribat al-baḥth ʿan ufq*, 67; Barakāt, *Visions of Social Reality*, 36.

the same time there is a continuous sweeping of Barakāt's verbal camera from one battleground to another. These brief and realistic depictions of the futile attempts at organizing resistance on the West Bank, followed rapidly by the shattering realization of impotence and headlong flight towards the River Jordan, are rarely more than one or two pages in length; the speed at which the reader is transferred from one to the next helps to emphasize within the narrative the alarming rapidity with which the events themselves happened. At times, this pace reaches prestissimo: "Ramzī scrutinises this country, eager to find out if it's full of grain. ʿAzmī ʿAbd al-Qādir encircled in Jerusalem. Ṭāhā weeping in hospital. Khālid looking askance at his flute. Māhir searching. Abū Dahhām longing to have a ruined house of his own in Qalqīliyah. Ramzī checking the ears in search of grain."[47] Khālid's family is a tissue of fractious relationships, and the decision to abandon their home, though hard, is not as difficult as it is for Ṭāhā, who tries to organize the local resistance and is still trying to reach the authorities by telephone when events overtake him and he too decides to leave. Khālid's family reaches ʿAmmān safely,[48] whereas Ṭāhā's family pays heavily for the delay in leaving. In the narrative of the third day, aptly entitled "al-Mawt ḥaql" (Death is a field), they are bombed with napalm just after crossing the River Jordan. In a passage of gruesome realism Barakāt describes the futile attempts of the father to put out the flames which are engulfing his children.[49] While Ṭāhā continues to ʿAmmān with his two remaining children (one of whom will also die), ʿAzmī stays resolutely behind in Jerusalem. He has been waiting for the opportunity to fight again ever since 1948, and, even when his house and entire family are destroyed in the fighting and it becomes abundantly clear that this round is going to end in complete defeat for the Arabs, he still refuses to leave. The sister at a local hospital helps him to load his family on to a cart, but at this moment Israeli soldiers arrive and search the hospital. ʿAzmī escapes through a window and is last heard of "encircled in Jerusalem."[50]

This fusion of the spatial dimension into a single experience through time serves the author's purpose well. We do indeed come to feel that those who find themselves faced with the reality of the

47. Barakāt, *ʿAwdat al-ṭāʾir,* 143. For a similar narrative technique, albeit less hectic, see 35–36, 41–44, and 64–67.

48. Ibid., 83.

49. Ibid., 87.

50. Ibid., 143.

military might of Israel and the weaknesses of the Arabs—whether from close-up or from a distance—are united in their attempts to cope with the situation and in their failure to find satisfactory explanations or solutions. However, the technique also involves sacrifices in certain aspects of novelistic technique, and no more so than in characterization. The rapidity with which the scene is transferred from one battle scene to another does not afford much opportunity, needless to say, for characterization of the various figures in the different towns and villages in which the fighting occurs. However, it is perhaps more surprising that we learn relatively little about Ramzī and Pamela. Part of the reason for this may refer to an earlier comment about Ramzī as meaning "my symbol." If we also suggest that Pamela is a symbol of a decadent West, then the relationship between the two may be seen as essentially a game of symbols rather than a profound investigation into two individual characters. This impression is emphasized by the fact that Barakāt uses—one might almost say, manipulates—these characters in order to indulge in the kind of social commentary which used to characterize novels of a much earlier period (although, admittedly here, without the heavy overlay of moral judgment). Certain issues which are discussed by these two characters may indeed be fused into the general interchange of ideas and emotions of two people of different cultures thrown together during an international crisis: American attitudes towards the Arabs and the somewhat ivory-tower attitude of students in universities in the Arab world are two examples.[51] But in other cases the inclusion of certain issues into the conversation between Ramzī and Pamela or into the thoughts of Ramzī himself seems contrived in the extreme: consider, for example, the discussions of Arab "anti-Semitism" and the fate of the Palestinian refugees on the one hand, and Ramzī's ideas and hopes about the future of the Arab world on the other.[52] All these issues are entirely germane to the subject of the Palestinian tragedy and the 1967 defeat as they reflect on the Arab world in general. However, the point to be made here is that, in his desire to use certain techniques of realism in portraying both the background and the events of this traumatic episode in the history of the Arab world, Barakāt has deemphasized characterization and overemphasized the documentary aspect to a degree which diminishes the artistic merit of the work as a whole.[53]

51. Ibid., 75–76 and 45 respectively.
52. Ibid., 96 and 123; 23 and 157.
53. Compare the verdict of Jūrj Sālim regarding this novel: "In my view, the

There are times in this work when the reader almost gets the impression that Barakāt is addressing his ideas and comments to a Western audience. Within this chapter, we note in connection with other modern Arabic novels (such as Jabrā's *al-Safīnah*) that they presuppose a relatively profound knowledge of Western culture. Barakāt's work includes references to Wagner, Toynbee, T. S. Eliot, Rachmaninov, and Camus.[54] The impact of these and analogous references in works by other Arab novelists has been considered in our previous chapter, but within the context of this particular novel we should point out that references to particular universities in the United States and remarks on the anti-Arab feelings of American periodicals seem to be addressed more to an American audience than an Arab one. Typically, Barakāt expresses the dilemma of himself and others on this matter in the words of one of his characters: "What concerns me is that we're a people which has lost its sense of identity and manhood. Each one of us suffers from a split personality, particularly in Lebanon. We're Arabs, and yet our education may be French, Anglo-Saxon or Eastern-mystic. What an odd mixture! We need to go back to our roots. We're all schizophrenic."[55]

If this novel has faults in particular aspects of construction, the overall impression is undeniably powerful; the impact of the synchronic treatment of events during this fatal six-day period is considerable. Barakāt's work stands out as one of the most effective commentaries on the 1967 debacle and its implications, and, one may say, almost *ipso facto,* it will thereby remain a reference point for Arabic fiction written during this century.

Mawsim al-hijrah ilā al-shamāl, al-Ṭayyib Ṣāliḥ

Al-Ṭayyib Ṣāliḥ's novel, *Mawsim al-hijrah ilā al-shamāl* (1967; *Season of Migration to the North,* 1969) is the most accomplished among several works in modern Arabic literature that deal with cultures in contact, and particularly with the confrontation between traditional and modern values when Middle Eastern characters spend some time in the West as part of their education—a novel of upbringing or *Bildungsroman,* to use the German term, and then return to their homeland to face and cope with the differences that inevitably im-

---

value of this work lies in its reliance on a new artistic style. But for that, it would lose all its value." See Sālim, *Al-Mughāmarah al-riwā'iyyah,* 179.

54. Barakāt, *'Awdat al-ṭā'ir,* 28, 32, 68, 75, 120.

55. Ibid., 55.

pinge upon their life thereafter.[56] In this case, one of the two major characters is Muṣṭafā Saʿīd, a young Sudanese student whose brilliant career at school in the Sudan and Cairo is capped by a period spent studying and then teaching in England. The means by which this meeting or confrontation between East and West (or between North and South, as the novel expresses it) is that of Muṣṭafā's relationships with a number of English women. However, whereas the character of Mary in Yaḥyā Ḥaqqī's *Qindīl Umm Hāshim* succeeds in totally demolishing the traditional values of Ismāʿīl, the Egyptian, before building up some new ones and then abandoning him to his own devices,[57] Muṣṭafā Saʿīd in Ṣāliḥ's novel comes "as a conqueror," and "the invader who had come from the South, and this was the icy battlefield from which I would not make a safe return."[58]

A major device that the author uses to convey these misunderstandings at the broadest cultural level is that of place, and specifically, two rooms. In the Sudan, Muṣṭafā Saʿīd sets up an English scholar's study, filled with books and memorabilia, perfect in every pedantic detail—but a place of isolation; in London on the other hand he establishes a room which serves as a grotesque parody of the worst excesses of European notions (or fantasies) concerning the exotic Oriental—a place of fatal couplings, steeped in deception. The author himself has commented on this dimension when he notes: "I had in mind the idea that the relationship between the Arab world and west European civilization . . . was based on illusions both on our part and theirs." It is in the room in London that Muṣṭafā Saʿīd conducts his love affairs with three English women: Ann Hammond, an Oxford undergraduate, Sheila Greenwood, a Soho waitress, and Isabella Seymour, an older married woman who, we discover later, is dying of cancer.[59] They are all bittersweet episodes

56. Al-Ṭayyib Ṣāliḥ, *Mawsim al-hijrah ilā al-shamāl* (Beirut: Dār al-ʿAwdah, 1967 [first published in the journal, Ḥiwār in 1966]); English trans.: *Season of Migration to the North,* trans. Denys Johnson-Davies (London: Heinemann, 1969). Ṣāliḥ was born in the Sudan in 1929 and studied at the Univ. of Kharṭūm before traveling to England, where he studied at the Univ. of London. He has worked for the BBC and for UNESCO. He now resides in London.

57. See the perceptive study by Susan A. Gohlman, "Women as Cultural Symbols in Yaḥyā Ḥaqqī's *The Saint's Lamp,*" *JAL* 10 (1979): 117–27.

58. Ṣāliḥ, *Mawsim al-hijrah,* 63, 162; trans., 60, 160.

59. For Ṣāliḥ's quotation, see *Al-Mawqif al-adabī* 3, nos. 4–5 (July–Sept. 1973): 50. The lengthy description of the room in the Sudan can be found in Ṣāliḥ, *Mawsim al-hijrah,* beginning on 136; trans., 135; and of the room in London, 34–35; trans., 30–31. The reference to Isabella Seymour is on 142; trans., 141.

which end in the suicide of the woman concerned. Indeed Muṣṭafā Saʿīd's relationships with all the female participants in this narrative are nothing less than complex: from his unbelievably detached relationship with his own widowed mother, via the clearly Oedipal feelings he has for Mrs. Robinson (the wife of the British schoolteacher in Cairo), to Husnah bint Maḥmūd, his Sudanese wife and "mother of his children" as she disarmingly describes herself in responding to a question concerning her love for her husband. However, it is the relationship that he establishes with a fourth English woman, Jean Morris, which symbolizes the absolute clash of these two cultures within a Western context. She steadfastly refuses to succumb to the mysterious and vicious allures that Muṣṭafā has so craftily set up to dangle in front of his "victims," but instead succeeds in dragging him into a fatal relationship through her own outrageous conduct, taunting him to such a degree that he marries her. As Muṣṭafā Saʿīd says later, "I was the pirate sailor and Jean Morris the shore of destruction."[60] Their love-hate relationship reaches the point where, in a moment of almost ritual (and indeed sexual) violence, he murders her. Even as he listens at his trial to the words of one of his former teachers describing his brilliant career, Muṣṭafā Saʿīd displays some of the internal complexities of his stance. "'It was I who killed them. I am a desert of thirst. I am no Othello. I am a lie. Why don't you sentence me to be hanged and so kill the lie?' But Professor Foster-Keen turned the trial into a conflict between two worlds, a struggle of which I was one of the victims."[61] However, these remarks which Muṣṭafā Saʿīd finds so unpalatable and hypocritical[62] manage to secure him a relatively light prison sentence of seven years for his wife's murder. Thereafter, he returns, after some travels, to his native Sudan, and settles in a village on the Nile.

The preceding description may give the impression that this novel has an obvious hero and focal point, Muṣṭafā Saʿīd, the brilliant Sudanese student with "a mind like a knife,"[63] who goes to England, the very source of that society which had dominated his homeland for so long.[64] This impression is both deceptive and at the same time a mark of the brilliant way in which this novel is constructed. In fact, Muṣṭafā Saʿīd's narrative occupies a relatively small

60. Ṣāliḥ, *Mawsim al-hijrah,* 162; trans., 160.
61. Ibid., 37; trans., 33.
62. Ibid., 96–97; trans., 93.
63. Ibid., 26; trans., 22.
64. Ibid., 56–57; trans., 53.

portion of the work.[65] Surrounding this section is the frame of yet another story, that of the Narrator, another Sudanese student who also goes to England for seven years to earn a degree in English literature and then returns to become at first a teacher of Arabic literature and then an Inspector of Education. At the very outset of the narrative, the Narrator apparently pushes his own narrative to one side, something to be told some other time; this however is clearly just one of the creative deceptions in which this novel is steeped. Muṣṭafā Saʿīd has taken up residence in the Narrator's village during his absence. The part of the novel before Muṣṭafā's own narrative is therefore taken up with the Narrator's gradual introduction to the new member of the village society. To the Narrator's astonishment, he hears Muṣṭafā reciting English poetry one night and eventually succeeds in persuading the reluctant Muṣṭafā to tell him his story. Immediately following Muṣṭafā's narrative, the Narrator returns to his narrative function: from al-Kharṭūm, where he is carrying out his educational duties, he learns that Muṣṭafā Saʿīd has been drowned in the river. The Narrator hurries back to the village to discover that Muṣṭafā had made elaborate preparations for what appears to be his suicide and that he has made the Narrator the guardian of his wife and two children.

This situation places the Narrator in a complex position within the closely-knit structure of the village. Muṣṭafā Saʿīd's relationships with women have clearly been carried on at an unusually frenzied level of intensity, but now it is the Narrator's turn to have his mettle tested regarding his relationships with women, this time within the context of Sudanese society and its mores. Within such a context the fact that he is already married and has a daughter is not any kind of impediment when such an obvious social obligation presents itself. But the matter clearly goes beyond obligations, since, while exploring Muṣṭafā Saʿīd's study, the Narrator confides to the reader that Husnah is "the only woman he has ever loved"; and, when Maḥjūb, a village friend of the Narrator, makes disparaging remarks about Husnah, the Narrator tries to strangle him until he is knocked unconscious. The Narrator's emotions clearly run deep on this matter, but all these details are only revealed later, in fact too late. At the time, the Narrator is the recipient of many subtle and unsubtle hints from members of the village community on the subject, but he is

65. Ibid., 23–48; trans., 19–44.

unable to make the final step in spite of his true feelings. Meanwhile, Wād Rayyis, the village's most prominent womanizer, who is firmly of the belief that women's role on earth is solely to please men,[66] sets his heart on marrying the widow. Even though she tells the Narrator that she will kill herself if the marriage takes place, things are allowed to proceed. Yet again, the Narrator is called back to the village to hear the grisly tale of the death of both Wād Rayyis and his new wife, Muṣṭafā's widow. For a long time she had refused to consort with him, and Wād Rayyis finally decided to take her. After a gruesome struggle she killed him and then herself. Only Bint Majdhūb, an earthy widow of the village, can summon the necessary courage to tell the Narrator of this event, the shame of which is shared by the entire community. This event finally spurs the Narrator into investigating Muṣṭafā's room, which no one else has entered since his death. Here the Narrator encounters echoes from Muṣṭafā's past life in England, letters from his girlfriends, a huge library of European books and other memorabilia. These echoes are able to fill in many details left hanging in Muṣṭafā's narrative earlier in the novel, while the existence of such a perfect replica of the English scholar-gentleman's study in a remote village on the banks of the Nile in the Sudan points up the many tensions reflected in the life of Muṣṭafā Saʿīd. It is, in a word, a perfect symbol of his alienation from the native land whose identity he had sought to assert during his time in London.

This section finishes with the graphic description of Jean Morris's murder, as the Narrator reads from diaries of Muṣṭafā regarding his tortured existence with her.[67] On the most symbolic level of this narrative, the reader is thus presented with two murders—those of Jean Morris and Husnah bint Maḥmūd—to parallel the two rooms. In the page following the description of Jean's murder, the text takes us back to the Narrator, and in a stunning contrast we are moved from a bed in London at some point in the past to the Nile at the close of the events in the novel: the Narrator, apparently overwhelmed by the horrifying death of the widow whose guardian he was, and by the situation in the village, follows Muṣṭafā's footsteps into the Nile. However, there is a crucial difference, as the Narrator tells us. "All my life I had not chosen, had not decided. Now I am making a decision. I choose life. I shall live because there are a few

66. Ibid., 87ff.; trans., 83ff.
67. Ibid., 157ff.; trans., 155ff.

people I want to stay with for the longest possible time and because I have duties to discharge."[68] The novel ends with his calls for help as the river swirls around him.

This brief account of this work already shows the superb way in which the theme of contact between East and West is handled and how rich is the depiction of the clash of characters and cultures. The author not only succeeds in handling the complex time frame of the narrative with great skill, but also manages to sprinkle into the various sections a number of clues which call into question the separation which can be made on a purely realistic level between the characters of Muṣṭafā Saʿīd and the Narrator. We have already been told that the Narrator tries to distance his own story from this particular narrative on the very first page of the novel, but in that same context he clearly asserts his storytelling role by addressing his audience, a group of men ("gentlemen"). This narrative touch not only provides a story-performance context, which serves to underline the difference in gender roles within the society (further emphasized by the attitudes of Wād Rayyis and the genuinely unusual traits of Bint Majdhūb), but also allows him to give the appearance of establishing a narrative distance from the life and career of Muṣṭafā Saʿīd by using the framing device so characteristic of traditional storytelling as a means of incorporating the latter's own narration as a separate unit within the larger narrative structure. In spite of these ruses, however, clues concerning the connections between Muṣṭafā Saʿīd and the Narrator assert themselves throughout the work: we have already cited Muṣṭafā's thoughts about himself as he listens to the evidence at his own trial; to this can be added a comment of the Narrator's, "A disturbing thought occurs to me, that Muṣṭafā Saʿīd never happened, that he was in fact a lie, a phantom, a dream or a nightmare; that he had come to the people of that village one suffocatingly dark night, and when they opened their eyes to the sunlight, he was nowhere to be seen."[69] The link between the two characters is suggested in early parts of the novel,[70] but the reader finds himself confronted by it when the Narrator finally enters Muṣṭafā's study. "My adversary is within," he says at first, "and I needs

68. Ibid., 170; trans., 168.

69. Ibid., 50; trans., 46.

70. E.g., "Was it likely that what has happened to Muṣṭafā Saʿīd could have happened to me? He had said that he was a lie, so was I also a lie?" *Mawsim al-hijrah,* 52; trans., 49.

must confront him." But, once in the room, the link is firmly established:

> Out of the darkness there emerged a frowning face with pursed lips that I knew but could not place. I moved towards it with hate in my heart. It was Muṣṭafā Saʿīd. The face grew a neck, the neck two shoulders and a chest, then a trunk and two legs, and I found myself standing face-to-face with myself. This is not Muṣṭafā Saʿīd—it's a picture of me frowning at my face from a mirror. Suddenly the picture disappeared, and I sat in the darkness for I know not how long listening intently, and hearing nothing.[71]

These passages serve to make it quite clear that beneath the surface level of description in this work there lies a psychological stratum which is sometimes visible and always implicit. Al-Ṭayyib Ṣāliḥ has stated that at the time of writing this work he was much influenced by the writings of Freud,[72] and the whole subject is explored most convincingly by Muḥammad Ṣiddīq.[73] Whether we interpret this kind of analysis as suggesting that Muṣṭafā Saʿīd is a representative of the Narrator's subconscious or whether we choose to treat them as separate individuals, the fact remains that the final pages of the novel show clearly that Muṣṭafā Saʿīd and his story have had a profound effect on the Narrator. The tensions involved in Muṣṭafā's adoption of Western culture and in his vicious confrontation with those who live within it have led to his eventual demise. The responsibilities thrust on the Narrator by that demise and the consequences thereof lead him to a new resolution, one which may involve a compromise between extremes, something which is clearly not of Muṣṭafā's psychological profile: "It is not my concern whether or not life has meaning. If I am unable to forgive, then I shall try to forget. I shall live by force and cunning."[74] It is at this point that the Narrator starts struggling in the Nile water and calling for help. The novel ends, therefore, with the Narrator in that symbolic element—the river—that flows from south to north. Moreover, the village of Wād

71. Ṣāliḥ, *Mawsim al-hijrah,* 135–36; trans., 134–35.

72. *Al-Ṭayyib Ṣāliḥ: ʿAbqarī al-riwāyah al-ʿArabiyyah,* ed. Aḥmad Saʿid Muḥammadiyyah et al. (Beirut: Dār al-ʿAwdah, 1976), 215.

73. Muḥammad Ṣiddīq, "The Process of Individuation in al-Ṭayyib Ṣāliḥ's Novel *Season of Migration to the North,*" *JAL* 9 (1978): 67–104, esp. 70ff. The linkage between Muṣṭafā Saʿīd and the Narrator is also explored by Yumnā al-ʿĪd, *Al-Rāwī: Al-mawqiʿ wa-al-shakl* (Beirut: Muʾassasat al-abḥāth al-ʿArabiyyah, 1986), 107–13.

74. Ṣāliḥ, *Mawsim al-hijrah,* 171; trans., 168–69.

Ḥāmid which al-Ṭayyib Ṣāliḥ chooses as the location for most of his fiction lies at a point on the Nile where it bends to flow for several miles from east to west. In making his decision to live, the Narrator is indeed betwixt and between from both real and symbolic perspectives.

The above discussion of the narrative structure of this work has inevitably included some reference to the treatment of time, particularly on the larger scale, through the fragmentation of chronological sequence and the use of flashback. On a more detailed stylistic level, we should draw attention to the constant shifting between past, present, and occasionally future, which is to be found throughout the work; the following is just one example: "I had loafed around the streets of Cairo, visited the opera, gone to the theatre, and once I had swum across the Nile. Nothing whatsoever had happened except that the waterskin had distended further, the bowstring had become more taut. The arrow will shoot forth towards other unknown horizons."[75] This process of switching between the different time frames, not to mention the levels of narrative and symbol, is most effective in showing the way in which the tension implicit in the memories of the past constantly impinges upon the present in the consciousness of Muṣṭafā Saʿīd and the Narrator, whom he has chosen as guardian of his family and heritage.

The above quotation also illustrates another feature of al-Ṭayyib Ṣāliḥ's novelistic technique, namely his use of imagery in order to heighten the impact of the many confrontations to be found in this novel. Murders, infatuations, loveless sex, these symbolic enactments of cultural tensions are portrayed through images of violence and penetration. The bow and arrow, the climbing of the mountain peak, the driving of the tent-peg into the soil, all these are used to describe Muṣṭafā's callous and defiant posture; as a young man he is said to have a mind like a knife.[76] To these are added more specifically Middle Eastern associations, and particularly those that invoke the West's uneasy historical relationship with and penetration of the region: the entry of Lord Carnarvon into the tomb of Tutankhamun, Shahrayār and Shahrazād, and the wonderful, complicated personage of Othello. It is also of the greatest significance that, when the Narrator returns to al-Kharṭūm following the circumcision ceremony for Muṣṭafā Saʿīd's two young sons, he travels through the

75. Ibid., 32; trans., 28. See also 60, 108; trans., 57, 105.

76. Ibid., 31, 37, and 26, 33, 35; trans., 27, 33, and 22, 29, 31.

desert. The scenes that the Narrator describes during this journey engender a genuine nostalgia, as landscape and company provide the context for depictions of poetry and ritual that revive precisely those images, values, and ideals of the cultural heritage of the Arabs which find themselves in confrontation with the incursions of the twentieth century within the framework of this novel.

North and South, East and West, the imbalances and misapprehensions as cultural values collide and interweave, all these provide the context for this immensely rich novel in which two Sudanese students, two rooms, and two murders come to symbolize so much. When *Mawsim al-hijrah ilā al-shamāl* first appeared in 1966, it was greeted with wonderment by a number of distinguished literary critics, including Rajā' al-Naqqāsh and ʿAlī al-Rāʿī. A book containing a selection of critical articles on the work describes Ṣāliḥ as "the genius of the modern Arabic novel" in its title. These few pages have only been able to draw attention to some of the major features of this work, which has become a classic of Arabic fiction.

Ayyām al-insān al-sabʿah, ʿAbd al-ḥakīm Qāsim

We noted above the almost cruel irony that Ḥalīm Barakāt gave to his first novel about the 1948 conflict in Palestine with the title *Sittat ayyām.* The bitter lessons of the Six Day War of June 1967 imposed upon his second novel, *ʿAwdat al-ṭā'ir ilā al-baḥr,* an identical chronological framework, although as we noted above, Barakāt succeeds very well in manipulating the dictates of time to his own literary ends. Both these works are, needless to say, directly concerned with crucial political events which have had a profound effect on the entire Middle East.

The "seven days" of ʿAbd al-ḥakīm Qāsim's novel *Ayyām al-insān al-sabʿah* (1969; *The Seven Days of Man,* 1989) could scarcely provide a greater contrast.[77] International politics barely enter the narrative at all, and then only as an intruding entity brought in by the radio and its news broadcasts. The setting here is the Egyptian countryside, and that environment provides a link with a whole series of earlier

77. ʿAbd al-ḥakīm Qāsim, *Ayyām al-insān al-sabʿah* (Cairo: Dār al-Kātib al-ʿArabī li-al-ṭibāʿah, n.d. [1969?]). I regret that I have not been able to acquire a copy of the published version of Joseph N. Bell's translation of this work, *The Seven Days of Man* (Cairo: General Egyptian Book Organization, 1989), and thus cannot provide equivalent pagination in the notes that follow.

works, although, in my opinion, the present novel is the best.[78] The "seven days" represent seven stages followed by a group of dervishes in the Delta of Egypt who are in the process of preparing for the annual pilgrimage to the Delta city of Ṭanṭā to visit the shrine of al-Sayyid al-Badawī, one of the great "saints" of popular Islam in Egypt. The series of events is narrated for us through the eyes of ʿAbd al-ʿazīz, the son of al-Ḥājj Karīm, the acknowledged leader of the group. Each of the principal rituals and activities involved in the pilgrimage process is treated in one of the "seven days": the evening meeting of the group in the village, the preparation of the baked food for the festival, the journey to Ṭanṭā, the hostelry where they stay, the big night of the festival itself, the farewell, and lastly the way, a term steeped in the lore of Islamic mysticism but here used to assess the impact of time and change on such traditional practices.

However, while this work provides one of the most authentic, unsentimental and undoctrinaire accounts of an Egyptian village yet written in modern Arabic fiction, it also has other virtues of equal, if not more, significance, for the time period over which the descriptions of these seven stages are spread is at least fifteen years, and during that time ʿAbd al-ʿazīz grows up. As his education proceeds, his attitude to the village and, in particular, to his father and the group of dervishes, alters radically. Through this technique we are presented not only with vivid descriptions of life in both village and provincial city, but also with a telling contrast between ʿAbd al-ʿazīz's present and past impressions of the annual events of the pilgrimage. Flashbacks at each stage record his feelings during younger days, and the entire sequence reveals an ever-increasing distaste for the entire underpinning of tradition upon which the rituals and ceremonies are built. Through the narrator's account of the changing attitudes of the boy to his village, his father, and the traditional values which are personified in the dervishes, we are given, in a mirror, as it were, a kind of *Bildungsroman* in which the modern notions which ʿAbd al-ʿazīz acquires through his secondary schooling in Ṭanṭā and his university days in Alexandria are pitted against his love for his father and for the village where he grew up. Within this context, a touch of irony is provided by the fact that, whereas the city of Ṭanṭā represents the goal of the dervishes' aspirations during their pil-

78. For a discussion of several of these works, see ʿAbd al-muḥsin Ṭāhā Badr, *Al-Riwāʾī wa-al-arḍ* (Cairo: Al-Hayʾah al-Miṣriyyah al-ʿāmmah li-al-kitāb, 1971); and Ghanāyim, 145–254.

grimage to the shrine, for ʿAbd al-ʿazīz the very same city is the place to which he has gone for his secondary education. While he is there, he not only notices the significant differences between life in the city and in his own village, but learns—as a part of the modern educational process—certain things which call into question in his own mind the traditional attitudes and beliefs of his father and the dervish group. The entire novel may thus be seen as a view from within of a long and often difficult process of change, of the confrontation between popular religion and superstition prevalent within the village structure and aspects of the changing world outside presented by city life and modern education.

The novel opens at sunset, and in its roseate hues we are immediately introduced to ʿAbd al-ʿazīz and his father. To the group of dervishes, al-Ḥājj Karīm is "their leader, while they love him, obey him and revere him." As a father, he is "good, beloved and awe-inspiring," and the little boy "snuggles up to his father like a tiny kitten, small and full of love."[79] The choice of sunset also provides a contrast with the heat and rigors of the day. As the group gathers in the evening at al-Ḥājj Karīm's house we are introduced to them one by one through the eyes and ears of the boy: Aḥmad Badawī; Muḥammad Kāmil; Muḥammad "the dandy" (the local womanizer who is famous not only for his wife, Rawā'iḥ, who steals from everyone in the village, but also for his girlfriend, al-Gāziyah); ʿAlī Khalīl, the owner of the general store; al-ʿIrāqī, the deaf-mute; ʿUmar Farḥūd, the camel driver; and Salīm al-Sharkasī, the carpenter. During the daytime, each of them pursues his own livelihood, facing challenges and adversities of different kinds and yelling at his women and children. But in the evening the whole atmosphere changes as the group gathers to listen to readings of texts such as the famous *Burdah* poem of al-Buṣīrī and to perform the ritual of the *dhikr*. Through a variety of flashbacks and inserts, we learn a variety of details concerning the nature of the beliefs of this group, particularly through the visit of the *shaykh* of their order to the village; in this case, the visit is described as a joyous and momentous occasion, in marked contrast to Ṭāhā Ḥusayn's description of a similar event in *al-Ayyām*.[80] The entire group goes to meet the *shaykh* at the railway

79. Qāsim, *Ayyām*, 7.

80. Ibid., 36. See also Ṭāhā Ḥusayn, *Al-Ayyām* (Cairo: Dār al-Maʿarif, 1944), 88ff; English trans.: *An Egyptian Childhood*, trans. E. H. Paxton (London: Routledge, 1932), 95ff.

station, a large gathering is held at ʿAlī Khalīl's house, an animal is slaughtered, and there is much ceremony. By now, too, the news has come for which the group waits eagerly each year: the date for the annual pilgrimage to the shrine of al-Sayyid al-Badawī in Ṭanṭā has been set, and preparations must begin. To meet the expenses of those preparations, al-Ḥājj Karīm has to sell off a little more of his land to al-Mitwallī Ṣārūkh. Even the young ʿAbd al-ʿazīz is alarmed by this continuing process whereby Ṣārūkh's land holdings become a little larger each year at the expense of his father, but he is comforted by the soothing words of his father, "We ourselves own nothing. We're merely guardians."[81] This first chapter succeeds brilliantly in setting the stage for the rest of the novel. It establishes the feelings of awe and delight which the young boy has for his father and the group which he leads. At the same time, it introduces in an as yet uncritical fashion some of the problems which are to beset ʿAbd al-ʿazīz later in the work. Moreover, it gives the reader a marvelously vivid picture of the village and its participation in the activities and rituals of the group.

The second chapter deals with the preparations for departure. By focusing on "the baking" (the chapter's actual title), the narrator provides the reader with an entirely different outlook on the village, that of its womenfolk.[82] All the women of the village wish to be part of the preparation of the food for such a blessed purpose, and their conversations and gossiping in the kitchens of al-Ḥājj Karīm's house give us a further valuable dimension on the village as a whole and on the men whom we have met in the first chapter in particular. From ʿAbd al-ʿazīz's viewpoint, the situation of this chapter is also used to advantage. That he is now older is shown convincingly by his awakening sexuality and by the way in which the young girls are described. They seem relatively unaware of his presence, but he is certainly aware of them, as the nubile Sabāḥ finds out in a dark storeroom.[83] This proximity to the women of the village also implies—at least within the time frame of this chapter—a distance from his father. It is therefore significant that from the very beginning there are signs, albeit muted, of an emerging critical eye. This chapter opens with a description vastly different in impact from that

81. Qāsim, *Ayyām*, 36.

82. In the first chapter, the women remain very much in the background. See, e.g., Qāsim, *Ayyām*, 37.

83. Ibid., 76.

of the first: ʿAbd al-ʿazīz wakes up in the night in an overcrowded, stuffy room. As the chapter proceeds, we learn that al-Ḥājj Karīm has two wives; the young boy's description of the second wife makes it clear that her status in the house is not a happy one. But above all, there is a none too flattering picture of the relationship of al-Ḥājj Karīm with ʿAbd al-ʿazīz's mother: "Long years went by without the two worlds ever coming together: that of al-Ḥājj Karīm which soared on wings of divine miracles and blessings . . . and that of his own mother which was limited to pots and pans and grain stores."[84] While the young boy retains earlier memories of bitter fights between his father and mother inside him "like the vestiges of a festering wound," it is characteristic of this phase of the novel that the boy's chief regret is that his father is losing his fierce demeanor towards her.

By the third chapter, the preparations are over and the day of departure has arrived. And, if there were signs of unease in ʿAbd al-ʿazīz's thoughts in the second chapter, they have now become considerably more explicit. In a move which is considerably more than a token gesture, he now sleeps on the roof. The stuffy room which he described at the beginning of the second chapter is now a nightmarish vision, where "children lie in heaps on the floor, a pile of nakedness, sweat and vile stench."[85] In this room of his is another cause of his increasing sense of separation, his books; they were "his illness and cure, the words of which led him into weird mazes. There was nothing fixed in his life any more. The fearsome cudgels of knowledge were smashing all his illusions, one after another. They made him feel brazen and bitter; he was addicted to the sharp pain of it all."[86] As the group of dervishes makes ready to depart, we are made to feel the contradictory emotions pulling ʿAbd al-ʿazīz in different directions. He wants to go with them to Ṭanṭā, and yet he feels that "his head is weighed down with a host of uncontrollable question marks, while his heart is beset by unrelenting anxiety."[87] As if to confirm these doubts, there is a most unflattering portrait of the *shaykh* from Sharqiyyah province who had abandoned his studies at al-Azhar "without acquiring any knowledge at all."[88] By way of contrast, the arrival of ʿUmar Farḥūd with his camel to load provisions

84. Ibid., 53.
85. Ibid., 83.
86. Ibid., 83.
87. Ibid., 91.
88. Ibid., 92.

for the journey leads ʿAbd al-ʿazīz into a reminiscence of earlier trips that is full of affection for the village people and admiration for his father's important position, all expressed in a tone that recalls the opening chapter. As the train departs for Ṭanṭā, ʿAbd al-ʿazīz returns to the village; his thoughts are a mixture of a desire to travel and a feeling of intense affection for his father and the dervishes.[89]

The action of the fourth and fifth chapters is set in Ṭanṭā itself. Once again the author uses the possibilities of his approach to the changing nature of the narrator's age and therefore point of view to best advantage. ʿAbd al-ʿazīz is now going to school in Ṭanṭā. The beginning of the fourth chapter, "The hostelry," finds him proceeding through the city towards the railway station in order to meet his father and the dervish group. This procedure affords ample opportunity for description of and comment on city life, not to mention remarks about the numbers of country peasants who are, like his father and the dervishes, flocking to the city for the festival. The occasion is not wasted, and the comparisons start at once. The village is said to be like a graveyard day and night, whereas the city is full of movement, orderly and clean.[90] As ʿAbd al-ʿazīz makes his way to the station, he makes a point of describing those elements which illustrate the modernity of city life, the speeding cars and buses, the cinemas, and the shops with all their wares on display. This detailed picture of the noisy, bustling city serves to make the boy's meeting with the dervishes at the station all the more awkward: "These men in their tatty clothes and red skull-caps, their faces tanned by the sun and pock-marked by malnutrition . . . they were his relatives, his heart and eyes. . . . How he wished they looked cleaner and bolder, not so poor, stupid and scared! In school he boasted about being a peasant in front of the city kids, but inside he felt angry and resentful. If only they weren't like this."[91] This feeling obviously communicates itself to his father and his followers; the sense of strain and distance between ʿAbd al-ʿazīz and the men is almost palpable. When he declines to join them in their annual visit to the cinema, the extent of the gap separating the boy from his village origins becomes obvious to everyone.

The fifth chapter describes the events of "the big night." That designation describes the role of this particular night in the sequence

89. Ibid., 111.
90. Ibid., 114.
91. Ibid., 126.

of the pilgrimage of the dervishes to Ṭanṭā, but it fulfills the same function within the framework of the relationship between ʿAbd al-ʿazīz and his father. It opens with the same kind of repulsive impression of the surroundings as occurs at the start of the third chapter. In the hostelry where they are staying, a greasy stew is being prepared for the large assembled company. In addition to the smell of oil and grease, there is the overpowering stench of the lavatory. ʿAbd al-ʿazīz almost vomits in sheer revulsion.[92] As the tensions begin to mount inside him, he sits there "watching this human floor mat gnawing on its food . . . pouncing on it with grotesque bestiality."[93] When his father asks him to eat too, we have a forewarning of what is to come when the boy refuses point blank. Unable to tolerate the atmosphere, both physical and psychological, any longer, ʿAbd al-ʿazīz goes for a walk round the city. He visits the fairground and is then drawn inexorably towards the mosque, wondering all the while if it is some deep-rooted influence of his father which even now draws him towards the shrine. When he returns to the hostelry, it is to find things exactly as they were when he left. In a devastating comparison, he compares the figure of his father standing in the middle of the assembly with the dying body of ʿAntar, the hero of one of the medieval Arabic romances.[94] The stage is now set for the climax. With little or no warning, al-Ḥājj Karīm's son launches into a tirade against his father and his companions: "You're people with no sense, no brains. You meander about like animals, not knowing where you're golng or where you've come from. . . . What are you doing? Where are you going? Where have you come from? You stupid pagans!"[95] Everyone is stunned. It is almost as though the boy's father has been expecting something like this. He issues a stinging rebuke to his son, tells him to leave, and calls him an unbeliever. Fortunately, at this point, some of the men intervene with excuses and in any case the need for sleep draws a veil over the entire sorry scene. ʿAbd al-ʿazīz goes to the children's room and tries to sleep, even finding time to appreciate the body of Samīrah, the girl whom he is supposed to marry. But his thoughts will not allow him any rest, and he goes out into the streets.

The function of this climax within the total structure of the nar-

92. Ibid., 152.
93. Ibid., 157.
94. Ibid., 170.
95. Ibid., 171–72.

rative plays a role very similar to that of the destruction of the lamp in the mosque of Sayyidah Zaynab about which we read in Yaḥyā Ḥaqqī's famous work, *Qindīl Umm Hāshim* (1944; *The Saint's Lamp,* 1973).[96] In that work too, Ismāʿīl's destructive act is symbolic of an attack on Islam and, more particularly, popular religious beliefs within Islam. But, whereas in Ḥaqqī's work the events which follow the challenge are intended to illustrate the possibilities of compromise and reconciliation, in Qāsim's work the relentless process of change allows for no such developments. Like its two predecessors, the sixth chapter is also set in Ṭanṭā, thus forming a neat symmetry with the first three which are set in the village. Called "The Farewell," this chapter is not merely an end to one particular pilgrimage year, but the final occasion on which the group will come to the city to perform the ceremonies. Muḥammad the Dandy's girlfriend, al-Gāziyah, has died, and he himself is going blind. Both Muḥammad Kāmil and Salīm al-Sharkasī leave before all the ceremonies are over. All this leads al-Ḥājj Karīm to acknowledge that the men in his group have changed and that his own hold on them is weakening.[97] This same force of change is also having its effects on the young girls of Ṭanṭā and on the very streets of the city itself.[98] With these circumstances in mind, it is a forlorn group which makes the final visit to the mosque. ʿAbd al-ʿazīz goes with them, but his motivations are those of pity and concern for his aging and ailing father. His emotions are succinctly expressed. "He felt baffled and alone. Even though he was there with them, nothing could change his heart. Cold and lifeless. He kept looking round him in embarrassment. . . . He smiled sadly, bidding farewell to the joys, the profound joys of childhood."[99] The chapter ends as they watch the demolition of the fairground, the very place that ʿAbd al-ʿazīz had visited the "day" before.

The beginning of the seventh chapter finds ʿAbd al-ʿazīz hurrying home from Alexandria, where he is at university. He has received an unspecific message that his father is very ill. In fact, al-Ḥājj Karīm has had a severe heart attack while endeavoring to raise money and now needs medical attention and drugs, which the family cannot afford. ʿAbd al-ʿazīz's return to his village also serves to show

96. Yaḥyā Ḥaqqī, *Qindil Umm Hashim* (Cairo: Dār al-Maʿārif, 1944), 46; English trans.: *The Saint's Lamp,* trans. M. M. Badawi (Leiden: E. J. Brill, 1973), 29–30.

97. Qāsim, *Ayyām,* 183.

98. Ibid., 179, 194.

99. Ibid., 189, 191.

that the changes which in previous chapters have been illustrated through life in the city are now affecting village life as well. ʿAlī Khalīl, the owner of the general store, has died, and Muḥammad the Dandy is now completely blind. ʿAbd al-ʿazīz takes the family's water buffalo out to turn the waterwheel and irrigate their vastly diminished land. When the animal collapses and has to be disposed of, he comments on a further aspect of this change. "These were not his father's men. They had a severe look about them and laughed loudly. When they sat together in the afternoon, it wasn't for pleasant conversation; they listened to the news on the radio and kept making vigorous remarks. They all seemed bitter, headstrong, and uncouth."[100] When the decision is made to cut the animal up with minimal compensation to al-Ḥājj Karīm's family, ʿAbd al-ʿazīz reflects ruefully on the reticence of al-Sharkasī, the carpenter, and Aḥmad Badawī, two of his father's erstwhile companions, who watch the entire process from the sidelines. But he comes to realise that they, like his father, belong to a past generation; that their former modes of business transaction have gone for ever, along with their entire system of values and beliefs. As ʿAbd al-ʿazīz contemplates the state of affairs of his family and the village, it is Samīrah, the girl whom he was supposed to marry but who is now married to someone else, the same Samīrah who gave him a few moments' comfort after his blazing row with his father in Ṭanṭā, who lightens his depression.[101] When he leaves her, it is to go to the local café where he finds himself drawn with a strange naturalness into the intense discussions of politics fueled by the news broadcasts on the radio. "Deep down he felt like one of them. There was the same bitterness, anger and pain. The sweat poured from his forehead as he kept shouting out words and phrases."[102]

In the above analytical description of *Ayyām al-insān al-sabʿah,* we have followed the chapter sequence and thus the chronology of the novel itself, an aspect of the compositional technique that has already been shown to operate on a number of levels. However, illustrations from the text and comments on other aspects of technique make it clear that Qāsim's novel is conceived and executed with a great deal of skill. The first area in which this skill is apparent is in the description of the environment. The phrase "local color" is per-

100. Ibid., 220.
101. Ibid., 230–33.
102. Ibid., 235.

haps an overworked one, but that is precisely what Qāsim manages to convey in this novel to a degree beyond that of any other Egyptian novel devoted to life in the countryside. This is achieved in a number of ways. In the first place, the surroundings are allowed to emerge from within the framework of the narrative about the dervish group in a manner which is entirely deceptive in its spontaneity; as any writer of fiction knows, such spontaneity is only achieved as the result of a great deal of narrative craft. Furthermore, the author does not appear to force upon the environment or the structure of the narrative any personal or political agenda. It is obvious that Qāsim is intimately familiar with the surroundings which he describes, something which can be easily documented,[103] but the peasants and the village in which they live are not turned into overt symbols of larger political or social theories. A further feature, which undoubtedly lends realism to the environment, is the author's use of language. We refer here not only to the generous use of the colloquial dialect of the Delta,[104] but the way in which interior monologues and even the more narrative passages very much reflect the spontaneous language of speech: the short phrases, the conspicuous lack of connection between different utterances, and the adventurous use of tenses to heighten the impact of the narrative.

These last comments have brought us to the question of style, about which a further comment needs to be made, specifically, the author's use of the most picturesque phrases to describe people and objects. A few examples will have to suffice. In the description of the city of Ṭanṭā, the vendors are pictured as "working with both hands and mouths, a bundle of nerves obsessed with movement and noise." A peasant from the village who now lives in the city is said to have "eyes, two reddened cavities which looked like pigeons' anuses." Again in Ṭanṭā, the room is described in part in the following fashion: "The lanterns were hot moons, stretching out flaming antennae like gleaming cockroaches, and scorching people's faces. The pictures hanging by nails on the walls looked like faded eyeballs staring down on the proceedings with a questioning gaze, silent and vacuous."[105]

At the beginning of the discussion of this novel we noted the way

103. See *Al-Ṭalīʿah* (Sept. 1970): 21–22.

104. I acknowledge here the help of Professor Joseph N. Bell of the Univ. of Bergen, Norway, who allowed me to peruse his translation of this work, now published in Cairo, a version that greatly benefited from the opportunity to consult with the author on a number of matters relating to the text of the novel.

105. Qāsim, *Ayyām*, 117, 134, 156.

in which the succession of chapters was used not only to show the events of the pilgrimage to Ṭanṭā but also to reflect the upbringing and education of ʿAbd al-ʿazīz, the narrative lens through which the reader sees the characters and events of the story. When we realize that Qāsim himself was born in a village, went to school in Ṭanṭā and to university in Alexandria, the close association of author and narrator should come as no surprise.[106] While this close identification produces positive results in the main, there does appear to be one aspect from which the use of ʿAbd al-ʿazīz as "narrative lens" leads to an unsatisfactory result. The picture of the village which we receive in the early chapters of the novel is, as we have noted, that of the young son of al-Ḥājj Karīm. It gains its authenticity from the perspective which he provides but, by the same token, it is restricted to those aspects which concern him both as a boy of his particular age and as the son of his particular family. Other aspects of village life are not discussed. Thus, when we are presented in the final chapters with a different picture of the village, still seen through the eyes of ʿAbd al-ʿazīz but this time as an "outsider" returning from the University of Alexandria, we wonder whether the changes which have occurred can really have happened so fast. This impression is further emphasised by the careful way in which changes in city life have been portrayed in the previous chapters set in Ṭanṭā. The reader is left to ponder at the end of the work whether the changes that confront ʿAbd al-ʿazīz in the final chapter have not been taking place throughout the narrative, but he has been either too young or preoccupied to notice them.

However, even if we acknowledge the possibility of this inconsistency, *Ayyām al-insān al-sabʿah* presents the reader with a memorable portrait of Egyptian village society and some of the characters who populate it, and at the same time poses to us in a spontaneous and totally attractive fashion some of the larger issues of change, the impact of which is not confined to the countryside of Egypt. It thus fulfills in the most successful way the classic generic purpose of the novel.

Al-Safīnah, Jabrā Ibrāhīm Jabrā

"The sea is the bridge to salvation." That is the way in which the Palestinian novelist, poet, critic, and artist, Jabrā Ibrāhīm Jabrā, begins his famous novel, *al-Safīnah* (1969; *The Ship,* 1985). It is surely

106. See *al-Ṭalīʿah* (Sept. 1970): 21–22.

one of the intentional ironies of this work that, while present time is set during a cruise on the Mediterranean, the real theme of this work has nothing to do with the sea but rather with land, land as responsibility, land as both the heritage of the past and aspiration for the future. This aspect is seen most clearly in the two principal narrators of the work: ʿIṣām Salmān and Wadīʿ ʿAssāf.

ʿIṣām Salmān, an architect from Baghdād, is running away from land, the land which his family owns in Iraq, the land for which his father had killed another man, thus condemning himself to a lifelong exile away from his homeland and family and condemning ʿIṣām to a childhood and adolescence under the control of a determined mother. But above all, ʿIṣām is trying to run away from Lumā, the beautiful and intelligent girl whom he has met while studying in England and who, fatefully, turns out to be related to the man whom his father has killed.[107] Thus, although they are in love, the so-called "tribalism" of Iraqi society has ruled out any prospect of marriage. Somewhat in desperation, Luma has embarked on a marriage of societal convenience with Fāliḥ ʿAbd al-Ḥasīb, a brilliant surgeon, moody, morose, and always looking for specific answers to every question without finding them. The other narrator is Wadīʿ ʿAssāf, a Palestinian businessman living out his exile from his homeland in Kuwait. He is running towards the land, his own property in Jerusalem for which he and his martyred friend, Fāyiz, fought in vain in 1948. This quest of Wadīʿ's remains, of course, an aspiration (as it does for many other Palestinians), but that does not diminish the ardor with which he pursues it or with which he tries to persuade his girlfriend, Mahā al-Ḥājj, to join him, thus abandoning her home and medical career in Beirut.

When these and other characters board the *Hercules,* the Greek cruise ship, in Beirut, their meeting seems to be purely coincidental. ʿIṣām's reaction, for example, on seeing Lumā with her husband can be imagined, and the agony of being so near and yet so far from the woman he loves is only made worse by the fact that his cabin is next to theirs; through the thin dividing wall he even hears them making love on the bed in their cabin.[108] It emerges, however, that chance has nothing to do with this encounter. ʿIṣām has unwittingly set the process in motion by deciding to travel to Europe by boat. Lumā, eager

107. Jabrā Ibrāhīm Jabrā, *Al-Safīnah* (Beirut: Dār al-Nahār, 1970), 229; English trans.: *The Ship* (Washington, D.C.: Three Continents, 1985), 189.

108. Ibid., 14; trans., 15.

to renew her affair with him, has discovered this fact and booked a passage on the same voyage for herself and her husband. Little does she realize that, while she is arranging things to suit her convenience, her husband Fāliḥ proceeds to do exactly the same. During the course of a medical conference in Beirut, he has met Mahā al-Ḥājj, Wadīʿ ʿAssāf's girlfriend, and her friend, the Italian Emilia Farnesi. Fāliḥ and Emilia have fallen in love. Thus, when Fāliḥ suggests to Emilia that she join the cruise, she books a passage for herself and encourages Mahā to come along with Wadīʿ. Just before the cruise, Mahā and Wadīʿ have one of their periodic quarrels and she refuses to come on the cruise. Wadīʿ therefore boards the boat alone.

This, then, is the complex and explosive web of characters and relationships that confronts the reader as the novel begins. The narrative present which forms one time frame for the novel consists of the week-long cruise on the ship, during which it sails from Beirut to Athens, through the Corinth Canal, around the south coast of Italy, through the Straits of Messina, to Naples.[109] The period is marked by a few events. A Dutch traveler attempts to commit suicide by throwing himself off the boat in the Gulf of Corinth; he is unsuccessful, but the event itself serves in retrospect as a premonition, particularly in view of comments made by several of the characters at the time.[110] Later that same evening, Lumā dances on the deck to the music of Umm Kulthūm's singing, and the eyes of everyone are riveted on the gorgeous Iraqi beauty. It is this event which triggers her husband's fateful decision; in his own words, "Your dance last night was my death sentence. It helped me reach my final decision. I could have killed you yesterday. I don't know how I put up with it, how I listened to my better judgment and decided not to do it.[111] A third drama unfolds when Maḥmūd al-Rāshid, a teacher of political science on his way to teach at Lille University, goes berserk at the sight of one of the seamen on the boat and claims that it is the man who tortured him in jail. To prove his point, he strips off his shirt and reveals that his back is indeed covered with the most gruesome scars. This episode shakes even the artificial tranquility of the group, but the captain of the vessel brushes the whole thing off as a minor

109. For a treatment of time in *Al-Safīnah,* see al-Sharqāwī, "Al-Miʿmār al-fannī," 7 ff.

110. Jabrā, *Al-Safīnah,* 96 ff; trans., 83.

111. Ibid., 222; trans., 184.

problem. He is faced by something more pressing, the onset of a major storm which rocks the boat for a whole day. This serves to bring Fāliḥ and Emilia together as the only passengers (along with Wadīʿ) who are not seasick, the fate which unites ʿIṣām and Lumā in misery. It is during this episode that Wadīʿ comes to realise that Emilia and Fāliḥ are lovers.[112]

When the boat reaches Naples, a trip to Capri is suggested. Although elaborate arrangements are made, neither Fāliḥ, Lumā, Emilia, nor ʿIṣām actually go; they have all decided to make use of the involvement of the others in the trip to Capri to spend a few precious hours with their real beloved in Naples. Lumā and ʿIṣām spend a blissful day in the city, during the course of which they are spotted by Emilia and Fāliḥ, who have booked into a hotel. Emilia is hard put to arouse the interest of Fāliḥ, who has become more and more morose, and the scene in the hotel bedroom when she tries every ruse she knows to get him to make love to her is almost gothic in its sinister undertones of utter despair and frenzy. In something akin to a comedy of errors, everyone thinks that they have to get back to the boat before the Capri trippers return, and so the day is short. Feeling disconsolate after saying farewell to their lovers, ʿIṣām and Emilia turn around and go back to Naples for the evening. When they return late that night, Lumā is waiting for ʿIṣām, furious that he could go out with Emilia so soon after leaving her. They make passionate love in his cabin while Fāliḥ sleeps soundly next door. When she finally returns to her own cabin, it is only to return in a panic a few moments later; the somnolent Fāliḥ is, in fact, dead, and has been for a while in a suicide executed with all the care and finesse of a surgeon. On the table where the empty bottle of pills lies is also a set of instructions and a will which has obviously been in preparation for some time. This is a dénouement indeed, and in its wake reality intrudes into the make-believe world of the cruise with all its ruthless clarity. It is this horrific situation that confronts Mahā al-Ḥājj, Wadīʿ's girlfriend, as she comes to join the group, having decided that her love for him is her overriding priority.

We mentioned earlier that present time—as just summarized—is not in and of itself the most significant feature of the narrative element in this novel. Throughout the work, the events and surroundings trigger a whole series of flashbacks that allow the past to impinge on the present. Thus the use of two narrators (and Emilia Farnesi, who recounts the episode with Fāliḥ in Naples) not only

112. Ibid., 151; trans., 127.

allows for the unfolding of the events of the cruise in chronological sequence and for the portrayal of the various characters from different points of view, but also enables the past to interpret and affect the present almost till the end of the novel. When Wadīʿ is told of the way in which Lumā originally booked the passage, thus setting off the entire train of events, he is still unable to believe that it actually happened that way.[113]

These flashbacks serve to fill in many necessary details concerning the upbringing, education, and attitudes of the characters. ʿIṣām's first sight of Lumā in the opening chapter sets off a memory of their earlier times together in Baghdād, while the passage of the boat through the Corinth Canal to the music of Bach sends Wadīʿ back on a long journey into his past, to the feast of Christmas in Palestine, and to his boyhood friend, Fāyiz ʿAtaʾallāh (Atallah). This is followed by a long and vivid account of the fighting for Jerusalem in 1948 and the death of Fāyiz. At this point, it is worth observing that the description of Fāyiz's house in *al-Safīnah* is almost identical to Jabrā's description of his own home in Jerusalem to be found in his collection of articles, *al-Riḥlah al-thāminah.*[114] The additional fact that he also lost a friend named ʿAtāʾallāh in the 1948 fighting and that in the novel both Fāyiz and Wadīʿ share Jabrā's own passion for painting lend even further emphasis to the loving detail and intensity with which the author's hometown and the tragedy which has beset it in modern times are described in Wadīʿ's long flashback.

Other incidents recalled by the characters provide the reader with insights into their personality and, in some cases, premonitions of what is to come. Maḥmūd, for example, describes an incident as a boy at school when one of his school friends does not reveal Maḥmūd as the real culprit and takes his punishment for him, saying afterwards that he hopes Maḥmūd will do the same for him one day. As Maḥmūd observes to the company, in a manner which seems almost casual in the light of his crisis later on, he has been tortured many times since but has never implicated anybody, a revelation which, incidentally, introduces the theme of political oppression in the modern Arab world into an environment where cultural alienation seems to occupy the center of the stage.[115]

When Lumā and ʿIṣām are finally alone together in Naples, they

113. Ibid., 230–31; trans., 190–91.

114. Ibid., 58; trans., 50. See also Jabrā, "Al-Quds: al-zaman al-mujassad," in *Al-Riḥlah al-thāminah,* 107–8, and *Journal of Palestine Studies* 8, no. 2 (Winter 1979): 84.

115. Jabrā, *Al-Safīnah,* 115–16; trans., 100

discuss the hopelessness of their situation, and the whole process brings the history of their love back into the consciousness of ʿIṣām: its blossoming and fruition in England where they were both studying, and its strangulation at the hands of "tribalism" in Iraq. All of which leads to the most important flashback of all, that of Fāliḥ in his death note, although in this case the impact is on the living who remain behind and not on Fāliḥ himself. As ʿIṣām the narrator notes, it is a carefully prepared document and has been edited by its writer. To the background of Hamlet's question, "To be or not to be," Fāliḥ expresses his frustrations at being unable to find answers to questions: why did he fail to save the life of a seventeen-year-old girl, while a seventy-year-old man lived? How appropriate, too, that the author whose descriptive technique he cites should be Kafka.[116] He tells Lumā of his love for Emilia and forgives her for her own conduct; in conclusion, he discusses his own depression: "I spent my entire life searching for crises and revolutions such as these. Yet my humanity was always rejectionist, because it was maimed, disfigured, crushed from within and without. I reject the age of murder, the age of frustration. I reject despair. And now at last I reject hope. I wanted to rise above human beings, their concerns, their wretchedness and their cruelty, but I have failed."[117] And, with Fāliḥ gone, many things are clarified. For Emilia, of course, all is lost. ʿIṣām is determined to accompany Lumā back to Baghdād where they will, of course, still face the same societal problems which have kept them apart before. Wadīʿ and Mahā are now happily united, but the return to Jerusalem and the land of Palestine is still a long way off. At the conclusion of the novel, therefore, the numerous problems which had been facing the characters can hardly be said to be resolved. As the two couples leave the ship, Wadīʿ is comforted to notice Maḥmūd standing a short distance behind Emilia; and when they have taken rooms in a hotel for the night, ʿIṣām observes in a concluding comment that, since it is midnight, they must have just finished dancing on board the ship.[118]

With this immensely rich blend of the past and present and the means by which both are presented, Jabrā has fashioned a most accomplished contribution to modern Arabic fiction. To the mastery of narrative point of view and the use of fractured time which have,

116. Ibid., 217; trans., 180.
117. Ibid., 224; trans., 186.
118. Ibid., 243; trans., 200.

I hope, been amply demonstrated in the preceding analysis, should be added a copious use of symbols. The sea and the ship are, of course, two of these; the ship provides a microcosm within which this collection of Arab intellectuals rehearse many of the issues affecting themselves, their people, and humanity in general, while the sea may, as in the Gulf of Corinth, provide a serene backdrop to this activity, or else, as in the day of the storm, set the scene in an atmosphere of disruption and nausea. In the case of Wadīʿ, a number of evocative images are formed through the use of Christian symbols, the church, the cave of Christ's birth, the candles, the chanting, and so on; in the particular case of Fāyiz, the association with John the Baptist is particularly effective.[119] These symbols and other allusions illustrate another aspect of Jabrā's artistry, namely his own immense knowledge of Western culture. *Al-Safīnah* is full of discussions of works of literature (including Anatole France, Goethe, Dostoevsky, Camus and Kafka), works of music, painting, and architecture, and references to myths and legends. The entire creation is couched in a style that rises above mere descriptive prose and often achieves the status of prose poetry. In fact, the work does contain poetry by Jabrā as well as quotations from other Arab poets, but it is not to these passages that I am referring in commenting on Jabrā's style in this way. Consider, for example, the opening paragraph of the novel, which is so beautiful and appropriate that it is worth quoting in full:

> The sea is a bridge to salvation—the soft, the hoary, the compassionate sea. Today it has regained its vitality. The crash of its waves is a violent rhythm for the sap that sprays the face of heaven with flowers, large lips, and arms reaching out like alluring snares. Yes, the sea is a new salvation. Off to the West! To the agate isles! To the shore where the goddess of love emerged from the foam of the waves and the exhalations of the breeze.[120]

This is a remarkable passage, one that not only illustrates the use of language, but also the way in which the sea is treated as a symbol.

Escape, exile, loneliness, suicide, alienation, Palestine, the angst of the modern intellectual and particularly the Arab intellectual, these are the major themes which Jabrā explores with such artistry in this remarkable novel.

119. Ibid., 56; trans., 49.
120. Ibid., 9; trans., 11.

"Quartet" (*Kānat al-samā' zarqā'* [The sky was blue, n.d.], *al-Mustanqaʿāt al-ḍaw'iyyah* [The light-swamps, 1971], *al-Ḥabl* [The rope, n.d.], *al-Ḍifāf al-ukhrā* [Other shores, 1973]), Ismāʿīl Fahd Ismāʿīl

"This poet novelist," says the Egyptian colloquial poet, ʿAbd al-raḥmān al-Abnūdī, "sorrowful, forceful and well-versed in our problems, has succeeded in blending his own public and private experiences in a way which is incredibly simple and spontaneous."[121] Behind any such simplicity and spontaneity there is always the work of a literary craftsman, and that is certainly the case here. Ismāʿīl's four novels represent a complex and ambitious fictional project, and it must be admitted at the outset that the result is only partially successful. However, that should in no way be allowed to detract from the considerable merits of individual novels in the group, most particularly in specific aspects of technique; of those we would single out the treatment of time, together with the investigation of the different levels of consciousness in the major character who is the focus of attention in each of the first three novels.

This last comment reveals a feature of the overall structuring of the work as a whole. The author himself describes the process with that same deceptive simplicity which was noted above: "*Kānat al-samā' zarqā'*, *al-Mustanqaʿāt al-ḍaw'iyyah,* and *al-Ḥabl* are three short novels. *Al-Ḍifāf al-ukhrā* is an attempt to follow up on some of the characters in the previous three works within a single developing sequence of time."[122]

The particular time frame within which this series of novels is set is that of Iraq in the 1960s. The author tells us as much in a published comment on the work, and while that should not be our only guide, there are sufficient historical references in the text to confirm his setting; no doubt, Iraqi readers can find even more specific allusions within the sequence of events and statements of the characters. In any case, this period emerges as a gruesome one for many elements of Iraqi society. Regarding the atmosphere of this era few writers have spoken with such eloquence and emotion as Badr Shākir al-Sayyāb in his poem "Madīnat al-Sindbād" (City of Sindbad):

121. See the back cover of *Kānat al-samā' zarqā'* (The sky was blue) (Beirut: Dār al-ʿAwdah, n.d).

122. Ismāʿīl Fahd Ismāʿīl, "Kalimah," *Al-Ḍifāf al-ukhrā* (Other shores) (Beirut: Dār al-ʿAwdah, 1973), 7.

There is death in the streets,
and barrenness in the fields,
and all that we love is dying.
They have bound up the water in the houses
And brooks are panting in the drought.
Behold, the Tatars have advanced,
Their knives are bleeding,
And our sun is blood, our food
is blood upon the platter.[123]

Within the world of Ismāʿīl's quartet of novels, the societal conditions to which al-Sayyāb alludes above with such obvious passion are—almost horrifyingly—implicit. Each character is revealed in the attempt to cope with them, telling us in the process a great deal about his own attitudes towards society and change. The final novel attempts to gather up some of the unresolved questions from the other three and to provide resolutions for them.

Kānat al-samāʾ zarqāʾ was written, the author tells us, in 1965 "after the forces of good had been wiped out."[124] And, if we need any further indication that this novel, and indeed the entire series, is to place politics very much in the foreground, we are immediately introduced to the major character who is attempting to escape to Iran. The escape party has been discovered, and one of them, a former police officer, has been shot in the back. The narrative present of the entire novel consists of conversations between the major character and the immobile police officer. It is worthy of mention at this point that the lack of names for many of the important characters in the first three novels serves at least two functions. In the first place, it allows the author to deprive the character of a specific identity as a person and to turn him into something akin to a type, almost a case study within the many possible classes and attitudes of the society as a whole. Secondly, it forces the narrative to proceed on an impersonal and anonymous level which contributes in no small way to the generally sinister and oppressive atmosphere. The police officer's wound gradually putrefies, and he comes to realize that he is going to die. He asks the major character to bury him when he dies, and that permits the latter to remind the officer in forceful

123. Al-Sayyāb, *Dīwān* (Beirut: Dār al-ʿAwdah, 1971), 467; English trans.: "City of Sindbad," in *An Anthology of Modern Arabic Poetry*, trans. Mounah A. Khouri and Hamid Algar (Berkeley: Univ. of California Press, 1974), 97.

124. Ismāʿīl, *Kānat al-samāʾ zarqāʾ*, 4.

terms of his past crimes against humanity. This process not only reveals the tension between the two men hiding from the outside world in a tiny hut, but also allows Ismāʿīl to vent his authorial spleen "after the forces of good had been wiped out."

However, these conversations have another, more important function within the framework of the novel as a whole: they serve to trigger memories of the past in the mind of the major character that are our chief source of insight into his motivations. This trigger mechanism, the switching from present to past and vice versa, is a prominent feature of all four novels, and is handled with considerable skill. Through the use of different typefaces in the Arabic, Ismāʿīl is able to operate on a number of levels simultaneously: the narrative present, memories of the past (both narrative and dialogue), interior monologue, and stream of consciousness. The transition between the different levels is also handled with great care, as in the following example:

> "So you're going to abandon me here when I die?"
> "You'll do that to yourself before I do."
> "I'll go to hell," said the officer with a certain resignation, "isn't that the way it is?"
> "I don't think so."
> "But I'm a murderer!"
> "Murdered too."
> "Do you believe in the Day of Judgment?"
> "The way it's happened to you?"
> A laugh from the corner of the hut.
> "Is that all?"
> "I want you to die a believer . . ."
> "Why?"
> "Because you're human."
> "What about you?"
> The words "I'm not human," almost escaped from his lips. *The blue sledge-hammer started working inside his head. "You're not human," she had said. He could still hear that voice which was now sullied by display of affection, You're not human. . . . Those words of yours aren't a sufficient excuse for having emotions of stone when faced with a situation like this."*[125]

This passage not only serves to illustrate the way in which the author transfers the reader from one time to another (which we have duplicated in English type by the use of italics for the retro-

125. Ibid., 78–79.

spect), but also introduces us to the primary focus of these memories, the relationship of the major character with two women. One of them is his wife, whom his father forced him to marry in order to put an end to an adolescent dalliance with another girl. The marriage is a failure, but his wife is pregnant; he has decided not to divorce her until the children are older. This is the "situation" referred to in the above quotation. The speaker is the second woman who, it emerges much later in the work, is distantly related to him and whose love for him stirs up a crisis in his consciousness and illustrates his vacillation. She is "the girl in the blue dress," continuing the color image of blue found both in the title and the quotation above. The development of the affair between the two characters and the breakup of his marriage are narrated and analyzed against the background of a Charlie Chaplin film which the major character is watching in a cinema with "the girl in the blue dress." The juxtaposition of the absurd antics of Chaplin and the irrational vacillations of the major character makes its point with great clarity; to it is added the insistent questioning by the girl who becomes personified as "the blue dress" at the climax of his recollection of the breakup of his marriage, when his wife throws herself down in the middle of the street.[126]

In a desperate attempt to prevent him from going to Iran, the girl gives herself to him, after which, in another cutting comparison, he likens her walk to that of Charlie Chaplin. Switching back to the hut, even the dying officer finds his lack of humanity repulsive. Changing his mind yet again, the major character decides that he will go back to the girl:

> There was a smile on the officer's face. "Really?!" he asked joyfully.
>
> "When?"
>
> "Not till you die!"
>
> A feeble cackle emerged from the officer's mouth.[127]

We are to learn the sequel to these events in the fourth novel.

Ismāʿīl's commitment to illustrating some of the social tensions and conflicts of the 1960s is made apparent in a comment which prefaces the second of these novels, *al-Mustanqaʿāt al-ḍawʾiyyah.* The work is dedicated to "the humanity of two people who lived through

126. Ibid., 94.
127. Ibid., 142.

my death and participated in my birth, Jaʿfar Mūsā ʿAlī and Jamīl Jāsim al-Shabībī."[128] The "light-swamps" of the title are prison cells in which shafts of light will periodically penetrate the vile, fetid atmosphere. Using the same techniques as we have described with reference to the first novel, Ismāʿīl introduces the reader to a narrative present in which the major character (who has a name this time: Ḥumaydah) is a prisoner serving a life sentence with hard labor. He has befriended the chief warder and other prison guards, and is thereby accorded a number of privileges. We are also made aware at the outset of the novel that his wife has married his closest friend, somewhat replicating the situation of Manṣūr Bāhī in Najīb Maḥfūẓ's novel, *Mīrāmār*.[129] Once again, we learn the reasons for his imprisonment in retrospect. Emerging from a cinema with his wife a few years earlier (the film had been by Alfred Hitchcock), he had witnessed the brutal murder by two men of their sister who had become a prostitute. This is a *crime d'honneur* which inevitably calls to mind the eloquent poem by the Iraqi poetess, Nāzik al-Malā'ikah, "Ghaslan li-al-ʿār," (Washing away dishonour):

> A last gasp through her teeth and tears.
> The vociferous moan of the night.
> Blood gushed.
> Her body staggered.
> The waves of her hair
> Swayed with crimson mud.[130]

While his wife watches in horror, Ḥumaydah wades into the fray and kills both brothers in self-defence when they come at him with their knives. Public sympathy at his trial is with the brothers, who were preserving the honor of their family. After the press vilifies him as a public menace, he is sent to prison for life. The recollection of this incident is set against another like it in prison. Ḥumaydah, the friend of the warder and prison guards, intercedes in a fight between two guards over cheating in a game. In contrast to the major character in *Kānat al-samā' zarqā'*, he is unable to prevent himself

128. Ismāʿīl Fahd Ismāʿīl, *Al-Mustanqaʿāt al-ḍaw'iyyah* (The light-swamps) (Beirut: Dār al-ʿAwdah, 1971), 5.

129. Maḥfūẓ, *Mīrāmār,* 139ff. Ismāʿīl appears to be a great admirer of Maḥfūẓ in that he mentions his name twice in *Kānat al-samā' zarqā'*, 132, 140.

130. Nāzik al-Malā'ikah, *Qarārat al-mawj* (Beirut 1957), 157; English trans.: *Women of the Fertile Crescent,* trans. and ed. Kamal Boullata (Washington, D.C.: Three Continents, 1978), 20.

from making rapid decisions in a crisis, even at his own expense. The reader has now been introduced to two such cases: the result in one is life imprisonment, and in the other, solitary confinement.

This novel takes us full cycle; the final chapter begins with precisely the same description as the second: Ḥumaydah cracking stones in the heat of the midday sun. There has, however, been a change. The old prison governor who admired his political writings (and encouraged him to continue them in prison under the pseudonym of Jāsim Ṣāliḥ) has been replaced by a much less sympathetic person, whose hatred of Ḥumaydah as Jāsim Ṣāliḥ is so intense that he almost strikes him. But Ḥumaydah's friend, the chief warder, intervenes.

The unnamed hero of the third novel, *al-Ḥabl,* is a leftist, although he has never joined the party. The narrative present in the work takes place entirely within the space of a single night, as he proceeds to burgle the house of a police officer. Within this fabric, we learn through the consciousness of the protagonist what is the sequence of events that has brought him to his current position:

> A single poem, that's your entire life, just one poem. And with every succeeding burglary your poem loses another line. I wonder if the supply has run out. How many times have you challenged yourself to write another poem?! But now the only person you can find to lampoon is your own wife because she refuses to participate or even empathize with your stealing. Poetry . . . revolution . . . the left wing. . . . If only the revolution, the left . . . In the old days thieves used to have their right hand cut off. Now it's the political left which has been severed.[131]

The significance of this "poem" is that it was against ʿAbd alkarīm Qāsim who, until his bloody assassination, ruled Iraq with an iron hand in the 1960s. After spending six months in jail during which all attempts to link him with the party fail, the novel's protagonist emerges allegedly a free (and innocent) man. He soon discovers, however, that he has lost his job and furthermore cannot leave the country because he is regarded as "a dangerous political extremist." In desperation, he makes his way to Kuwait on foot in order to earn a living for his wife and himself. After making some money and buying gifts for his wife, he is returned to Iraq by the Kuwaiti authorities because he has no passport. At the border post,

131. Ismāʿīl, *Al-Ḥabl* (The rope) (Beirut: Dār al-ʿAwdah, 1972), 25.

everything he has earned and bought is taken from him. It is at this point that he decides to begin a career of burglary, stealing only from police officers' houses. All of this, spread over twelve chapters, explains the situation of the major character in the present, which he narrates to the reader.

A number of other elements impinge upon the major character's thoughts as he makes his way painstakingly towards his target house for the night, avoiding policemen and guards of various kinds on the way. In the first place, there is his father, who beats him black and blue with a saucepan as a child and forces him to run away from home at the age of ten. Then there is his wife, who strives to make ends meet by doing sewing work but who, with regard to her husband, emerges as frustrated and not a little uninterested in his activities. Quite the opposite is the maid in one of the houses which he proposes to rob. She serves him in two ways: by providing him with useful information about the house and its owners (his original intention in getting to know her), and by gratifying his sexual urges with a remarkable lack of restraint, thereby triggering a certain amount of guilt feeling towards his wife.[132] The robbery itself proceeds according to plan in that he finds jewels and perfumes. However, in leaving he disturbs the child of the family. The process of lulling her back to sleep triggers yet another host of childhood memories of his own. Leaving everything that he has taken on the child's pillow, he makes his way home with a token twenty dinars, precisely the amount removed from him by the border guards when he returned from Kuwait.

Of all the three novels that we have discussed thus far, it is *al-Ḥabl* which shows the greatest mastery of the process of integrating the different layers of time and consciousness into a single artistic whole. The novel takes us from its narrative present back to the major character's childhood, to his time in prison, to his married life in general, and to his investigation of the particular house where the maid lives, all these memories triggered by thoughts and occurrences during a single night of theft. While the local carpenter's horseshoe becomes a symbol of what is unattainable by a poor child during his youth (unless, that is, he resorts to stealing), the rope of the title is not only the means by which the burglar gains entry to the houses from which he wishes to steal but is also a symbol of the desire of his wife and himself for a normal life unaffected by "the

132. Ibid., 73.

single poem" which he wrote, a life in which they could afford to have a clothesline of their own on the roof. Their quest is merely for "work and dignity."[133] At the conclusion of the novel, it is suggested that the wife may be getting her way in that he will give up burglary, but, as in the other two novels, the outcome is left hanging.

We quoted above Ismāʿīl's own words concerning the overall structure of this quartet of novels, in which he said that *al-Ḍifāf al-ukhrā,* the last in the series, is an attempt to follow up on *some* of the characters in the other three works (my emphasis). Bearing in mind our opinion, stated above, that the major character in *al-Ḥabl* is the most fully rounded and developed character in the first three works, it is perhaps significant that he alone of the three major characters finds his way into the fourth novel as a protagonist. Indeed he is now named as Kāẓim ʿAbīd. From the other two novels, Ismāʿīl takes the figures of Fāṭimah, the girlfriend (and now wife) of the hero of *Kānat al-samāʾ zarqāʾ*, who, after abandoning his decision to flee to Iran for a short period, has fled once again, leaving her with his child by his first marriage; and of "the Visitor," none other than the chief warder in the prison where Ḥumaydah was serving his life sentence in *al-Mustanqaʿāt al-ḍawʾiyyah.* To this trio is added a "guest character" (to use the author's terminology), Karīm al-Baṣrī, whose role is derived "to some extent from the character Karīm al-Nāṣirī, the hero of *al-Washm,* a novel by the Iraqi writer ʿAbd al-raḥmān Majīd al-Rubayʿī."[134]

The setting in which the author's "single developing sequence of time" is to take place is described for us immediately in a series of staccato phrases: "Work, workers, the factory, the outskirts of the city, the fence, machines, noise, 1,200 workers, work hours, work conditions, pay."[135] This terse accumulation of phrases serves as a sufficient prelude for the planning of a workers' strike which forms the background to this novel, while the reaction of the various characters to the situation tells us a great deal about their social and political attitudes. The circumstances are laid out for the reader first by Fāṭimah, who is employed as the factory director's secretary, and she is followed by Kāẓim ʿAbīd who, having now given up a life of burglary, has found a job as a worker in the factory. The "newcomer," Karīm al-Baṣrī, is next; like Kāẓim he has served time in

133. See Ilyās Khūrī, *Tajribat al-baḥth ʿan ufq,* 95.

134. See Ismāʿīl, *Al-Ḍifāf al-ukhrā,* 7.

135. Ibid., 9.

prison, but has secured himself a somewhat more senior position as store superintendent. Lastly, we hear the version of "the Visitor," the chief warder who, after losing his job in the prison, is appointed *farrāsh* (a general factotum cleaner and messenger) in the director's office.

Each of these four characters reveals through his narrative the atmosphere of suspicion and fear that prevails. This is aided and abetted by the actions of the director. Not only does he arouse the suspicions of the workers and his staff by appointing the ex-prison warder as his *farrāsh,* but, once it is known that a strike is being planned, he dangles the possibility of a promotion in front of Karīm al-Baṣrī in order to get him to spy on the workers and find out their plans. Furthermore, the director triggers the main events of the novel by dictating a letter to Fāṭimah, which is to go to the authorities; in it he reports that a strike is being planned and that three workers, Aḥmad ʿAbdallāh, Jaʿfar ʿAlī, and Kāẓim ʿAbīd, should be arrested immediately. Fāṭimah and Karīm react to this in different ways. Fāṭimah is constrained by the fact that she must stay at her desk until it is time to go home, added to which is the problem that, as a woman, her social mobility is somewhat restricted. Karīm heads for "a cheap bar with lousy *ʿaraq* to consider his dilemma: to cooperate with the director and gain a promotion, or to be true to his ideals and help his fellow workers.[136] After getting well and truly drunk, he rushes off to Kāẓim's house and arrives just in time to notify him before the police arrive. Kāẓim escapes over the roof. The other two workers are not so fortunate and are arrested. Fāṭimah meanwhile rushes away from work to inform the other workers, but arrives too late.

The place to which Kāẓim escapes is none other than Fāṭimah's house. There he hides from the police and also witnesses (from a hiding place on the roof) Karīm's futile attempts to express his admiration for her. Fāṭimah has in fact remained devoted to her husband, even though he has abandoned her for some unknown destination four years earlier.[137] While Karīm's advances disgust her, the presence of Kāẓim in the house arouses hidden feminine instincts inside her, but even in moments of desperation she compares him with her real husband.[138] Kāẓim has proposed to the workers'

136. Ibid., 125, 224.
137. Ibid., 16, 23, 39.
138. Ibid., 244.

strike council that he resume his career as a burglar in order to get some money for a strike fund; and what more appropriate place to start than the house of the director himself? The workers firmly reject the idea. In fact, they are deeply suspicious of the offers of support and help from Karīm and Kāẓim, both of whom are extremely annoyed by this implicit questioning of their commitment to the cause. Kāẓim discusses his idea with Fāṭimah, and she too rejects it. In spite of all the opposition, he goes ahead with the plan and robs the director's house. He not only finds valuable jewels, but also manages to avoid arousing "the Visitor" (now also serving as the director's bodyguard), who continues to sleep soundly through the burglary.

At the end of the novel, Karīm al-Baṣrī has not only failed to gain the promotion for which he has acted with such fervent duplicity, but has been fired by the director. He resorts yet again to his cheap bar and, after getting totally drunk, is arrested for accosting passers-by. Kāẓim resolves to go to Kuwait once again; he has had to endure the full force of Fāṭimah's anger because his robbery has led to the arrest and torture of "the Visitor." In a parting gesture, he decides to take twenty dinars from the proceeds of the burglary for his "travel expenses."[139] Amongst all this dissipation and escapism, it is Fāṭimah who seems to display the resolution. She begins to challenge her husband's hallowed statements as "great words, but just words; you were good at dealing with words, but that's all. These words need action." And, in order to confirm her changing attitude, she asks herself the all-important question at the end of her section, "I wonder what would happen if you came back now! I think I'd welcome you with the words: 'How are you? Your son's grown up but he'll reject you too!' "[140]

Before considering the qualities of the quartet of novels as a whole, some comments should be made about this fourth work as an attempt to pick up some threads from the first three and to follow a single narrative line with them. It is my opinion that the experiment is less than successful. In each of the first three novels the reader is aware that a strong political undercurrent pervades the work. The concentration on one major character and the author's rare ability to fuse elements of past, present and future into a single frame of consciousness both serve to produce a concentrated, if open-ended, ex-

139. Ibid., 274.
140. Ibid., 282–83.

perience; each novel merits a separate existence of its own. The fourth novel avoids repetition by concentrating (apart from Kāẓim) on ancillary characters from the earlier works, but unfortunately the author seems to allow his political agenda to insert itself too obtrusively into the narrative. After the subtle investigations of the inner thoughts and aspirations of the characters in the first three works, the way in which opportunist and escapist are disposed of at the end of the last novel seems too neat and tidy. Indeed, their motivations, which lead to the eventual conclusion, are not a little predictable and obvious. And, by making use, in this last novel with so many "voices," of the same narrative technique as in the other three, the author has not allowed himself to penetrate deeply into the mental processes of each character; even in a work which is twice as long as any of the others, there is simply not enough opportunity to do so. The overall result seems unfocused and contrived.

The above comments are concerned with the fourth novel both as a separate work and as a "capstone" for the entire quartet. I now turn to a considertion of the merits of the earlier works and of those techniques which Ismāʿīl Fahd Ismāʿīl has used in this complex undertaking.

A significant place in any assessment of the impact of these works must be given to Ismāʿīl's use of language. Rare indeed are any excursions into a prolix narrative style in these novels; the emphasis is on short utterances, often in the form of exclamations or, on a more inward mental level, the terse cerebrations of the stream of consciousness. This technique is particularly obvious at the beginning of each novel where the reader is often left in a suspense of anonymity and mystery until the scattered segments of narrative begin gradually to provide a background against which to view the mental ramblings of the major character. From the stylistic point of view, it seems to be no accident that the comments on the back cover of the first novel come from three poets, ʿAbd al-wahhāb al-Bayyātī, Ṣalāḥ ʿAbd al-ṣabūr, and—already quoted—ʿAbd al-raḥmān al-Abnūdī. The language throughout remains a fully grammatical, standard, written Arabic; on the rare occasions where he uses a colloquial word, it is placed within quotation marks and given a specific footnote.[141] The style which emerges, however, is no ordinary narrative prose. The extreme economy of diction which Ismāʿīl chooses as the best means of transmitting his multilayered projection

141. Ismāʿīl, *Al-Ḥabl,* 13, 79.

of the inner mind of his characters forces him to use his words with all the artistry of a prose poet or craftsman of the shortest of short stories.

It is this great talent of Ismāʿīl to use words to convey mood as accurately and effectively as reality, and indeed to fuse the two together, which makes this series of novels a fascinating contribution to the Arabic novel. Nor should this literary estimate of their value leave unstated the fact that they provide from within a vivid portrait of Iraq during the 1960s. That is the stated goal of the author, and he achieves it with distinction.

Al-Zaynī Barakāt, Jamāl al-Ghīṭānī

The excellent English translation of this novel preserves the Arabic title almost exactly: *Zayni Barakat.*[142] The impact of the original and translated titles on the reader is thus much the same: one that provokes a sense of curiosity, of estrangement. For the modern Arab reader, the name "Barakāt" is certainly not unusual; it is, after all, the family name of one of the novelists discussed in this chapter. Once the text has revealed to readers that the full name of the personage represented by the title is Barakāt ibn Mūsā, they will, no doubt, sense in the name a certain archaic quality, but will otherwise not feel unduly defamiliarized. "Al-Zaynī," however, is another matter. The word is connected with the sense of "finery, decoration," and thus might be rendered as "the illustrious one." We are not long into the narrative before we encounter the text of an official decree issued by the Sulṭān from the Citadel in Cairo on 8 Shawwāl, 912 A.H. (equivalent to 21 February 1507) stipulating that "we have bestowed [on Barakāt ibn Mūsā] the title of 'al-Zaynī,' the which is to be appended to his name for the remainder of his days."[143]

The reader of this novel is to be taken back in time to a turbu-

142. Jamāl al-Ghīṭānī, *al-Zaynī Barakāt* (Cairo: Dār Ma'mūn li-al-ṭibāʿah, 1975), originally published in Damascus in 1971; English trans. by Farouk Abdel Wahab (London: Penguin and New York: Viking, 1988). One can make a contrast here between the decision to retain the title of this work unchanged and the questionable consequences of the opposite choice in the case of the English and French translations of Maḥfūẓ's *Trilogy.* I have discussed the issues of cultural attitude involved at length in "The Impact of the Translated Text: The Case of Najīb Maḥfūẓ's Novels," *Edebiyat,* n.s., 4, no. 1 (1993): 87–117.

143. Al-Ghīṭānī, *Al-Zaynī Barakāt,* 28; trans., 24. The translations included here are my own.

lent period in Egyptian history. The temporal focus of the work is the year 1516–17, when Ottoman armies defeated the forces of the Egyptian Mamlūk Sulṭān, Al-Ghūrī, at the battle of Marj Dābiq. In the novel the means by which the Egyptian people are made aware of the impact of this defeat is, as is the case with much other information, by public proclamations, this time in the name of a new and unfamiliar title of authority, the *khunkār,* an Ottoman Turkish term that gives direct verbal illustration to the brutal realities of a new source of military and political control over their city and homeland. *Al-Zaynī Barakāt* is thus a novel about history, a work of fiction that makes use of historical documents, but it clearly belongs to a different category of writing than those historical novels that were analyzed in earlier chapters of this work. Al-Ghīṭānī, it must be remembered, belongs to a younger generation of Arab novelists, one born after the Second World War (he was, in fact, born in 1945). He is a member of what we might term "the children of the Egyptian Revolution," and his writings reflect a variety of fictive reactions to the course of its history, recent though it may be, and especially to the status of the novelist within the societal framework that it has created. *Al-Zaynī Barakāt,* in particular, is written in the tense and recriminatory period that followed the defeat of 1967, a time when, as we have already noted, there was a profound reexamination of the very bases of Arab culture and the contemporary societies constructed on their alleged principles. Al-Ghīṭānī, himself a self-educated and passionately committed student of Egypt's history and the local culture of Cairo's older quarters, gives us some clues concerning his motivations: "The artist records things that are not mentioned in the writings of historians, the pages of newspapers, and the records of almanacs. . . . In my view he is a very particular kind of historian, since his task it to preserve the essence of a particular temporal period from oblivion, from the relentless process of eradication within that fearsome cosmic void called time."[144]

The reader of *al-Zaynī Barakāt* is drawn into a vivid recreation of a troubled historical era three and a half centuries earlier, but the techniques of the narrative and the atmosphere that they create provide abundant clues to the author's contemporary purpose. We alluded above to the initial impact of the title itself. However, even in steering the reader back in time to the sixteenth century, the author

144. Jamāl al-Ghīṭānī, "Ba'ḍ mukawwināt 'ālamī al-riwā'ī," *Al-Ādāb* 2–3 (Feb.–Mar. 1980): 113.

has already initiated his ironic play. The historical chronicles that are so wonderfully imitated within the text of the novel are based on that inexorable logic of time to which al-Ghīṭānī refers in the above quotation; their organizing principles and their titling devices are, as illustrated in the text of the novel, those of time, of years, of events in sequential order. The very mention of a single name in such a prominent way is thus a modern interpolation into a pastiche of medieval historiography. Even then, having given the character of al-Zaynī Barakāt such prominence, the author continues with his narrative games by making al-Zaynī Barakāt the focus of the work without ever permitting him to speak. The aura surrounding this figure is created by the wealth of other types of textual source, both oral and written, which convey the impact of his authority and the mystery that surrounds it. The picture that we receive is created by the way in which these various accounts interact with each other, all crafted through a virtuoso patchwork of "sources" of varying reliability.[145] We will now examine the brilliant artifice of the novel itself before considering its contemporary significances.

The novel begins with a conscious gesture of structurization; in the words of Kermode's book title, with the "sense of an ending." The text is prefaced with the quotation: "Every last must have its first; for every beginning there will be an ending." As if to emphasize this process of setting limits, the opening section of the novel introduces a first-person narrator, the only example of such a mode in a novel with a variety of narrative modes: a Venetian traveler named Visconti Gianti.[146] Turning to the end of the narrative, the

145. The use of the word "patchwork" is intended to evoke al-Ghīṭānī's initial profession as a carpet designer. Samia Mehrez draws attention to this fact in her excellent study of this novel, "Al-Zaynī Barakāt: Narrative Strategy," *ASQ* 8, no. 2 (Spr. 1986): 120–42 (based on her dissertation, "Bricolage as Hypertextuality: A Study of Narrative," Ph.D. diss., Univ. of California, Los Angeles, 1985). Among other studies of this novel, I would cite: Sāmiyah As'ad, "Yaktub al-riwā'ī al-tārīkh," *Fuṣūl* 2, no. 2 (Jan.–Feb. 1982): 67–73; Fayṣāl Darrāj, "Al-Intāj al-riwā'ī wa-al-ṭalī'ah al-adabiyyah," *Al-Karmal* 1 (Winter 1981): 134–37; C. K. Draz, "In Quest of New Narrative Forms: Irony in the Works of Four Egyptian Writers (1967–1979): al-Ghīṭānī, Yaḥyā T. 'Abdallah, Ṭubyā, Ṣun'allāh Ibrāhīm," *JAL* 12 (1981): 137–44; Walīd Hamarneh, "Some Narrators and Narrative Modes in the Contemporary Arabic Novel," in *The Arabic Novel Since 1950* [*Mundus Arabicus* 5: 205–36] (Cambridge, Mass.: Dār Mahjar, 1992); Sa'īd Yaqṭīn, *Taḥlīl al-khiṭāb al-riwā'ī,* 136–42; 252–61, 358–67; idem, *Infitāḥ al-naṣṣ al-riwā'ī* (Beirut: Al-Markaz al-thaqāfī al-'Arabī, 1989), esp. 48–51, 60–68.

146. Al-Ghīṭānī, *Al-Zaynī Barakāt,* 5; trans., xxiv. Critics who have discussed this

reader discovers that the ending is also entrusted to this narrator, and furthermore that the initial quotation is not merely a convenient platitude, but an indication that the beginning of the novel—its first section—is in fact the beginning of the end (the year 1516) and not the chronological beginning.[147] The internal events of the narrative, recounted under the narrative umbrella of its six sections (termed "canopies"), are thus framed by the vision of an outsider, an occasional visitor to Cairo; this external function is underlined when al-Ghīṭānī entitles the final section of the book, "Khārij al-surdāqāt" (Outside the canopies). This Venetian traveler communicates to his readers his fears at being a foreigner, a Christian, while he listens to conversations among the inhabitants of Cairo. But, while the passages narrated by the Venetian give the reader a valuable sense of the atmosphere in the city, the primary function of the passages of his travel narrative that are interspersed throughout the novel is to indicate the process of change as seen from the outside. As we have just noted, the opening of the novel, Gianti's first section, describes the city just before the defeat at the hands of the Ottoman army. The picture is grim, but its main characteristic is the emphasis on change:

> These days the whole of Egypt is in an uproar. This is a Cairo I don't recognize, not like the one I got to know earlier. People's way of talking has changed too; I thought I knew the language and its patois pretty well. The city looks like an invalid on the point of bursting into tears, a woman scared of being raped late at night. . . . Cairo, as I see it now, is like a blindfolded man on his back waiting for some hidden fate to strike him.[148]

His account of the following year makes up the final section of the novel. It too records a transformed scenario: "I have traveled far and wide, but I have never seen a city as crushed as Cairo is today. I plucked up the courage to venture outside. A deathly pall hangs

---

novel in English have transcribed this Italian name in a variety of ways, but, bearing in mind the Arabic transliteration, "Gianti" seems closest. On the subject of first-person narration, it is true that the character of Sa'īd al-Juhaynī also indulges in a one-line, first-person outburst, but I would suggest that it can hardly be considered a narrative; see *Al-Zaynī Barakāt,* 238; trans., 235.

147. These different aspects of narrative time are explored by Yaqṭīn in both his studies of the Arabic novel (and al-Ghīṭānī's novel in particular): *Taḥlīl al-khiṭāb al-riwā'ī,* 89–147, and *Infitāḥ al-naṣṣ al-riwā'ī,* 48–51.

148. Al-Ghīṭānī, *Al-Zaynī Barakāt,* 9, 16; trans., 1, 9.

over everything, cold and irresistible. Ottoman soldiers are roaming everywhere, attacking people's homes. In these times walls have lost all value; the concept of a door is non-existent."[149]

As is usually the case with such frame structures, there is a linkage between the outer narrative and the wide variety of texttypes within it. This visitor to Cairo, whose first-person narratives convey to the reader the only directly personal impressions in the narrative, informs us of a personal acquaintance he has, a friend, Shaykh Muḥammad Aḥmad ibn Iyās, who permits him to quote from his own account of events in Egypt the narrative of Sulṭān al-Ghūrī's departure from Cairo to confront the Ottoman armies in Syria.[150] While Gianti appears to be a fictional invention of al-Ghīṭānī, Ibn Iyās (1448–1522) was an Egyptian historian of this period, and his historical account, with its florid title, *Badā'i' al-zuhūr fī waqā'i' al-duhūr* (The choicest blooms concerning the events of fate, or, if we wish to replicate the original rhyme, concerning the incidence of dooms) so characteristic of the period, is cited in *al-Zaynī Barakāt* not only in the Venetian traveler's impressions of the year 922 A.H. [1516] but also in the account of the battle at Marj Dābiq and of al-Zaynī Barakāt's beating at the hands of his Ṣūfī master.[151] The way in which authentic historical texts are included, with masterful pastiches of their particular discourse and that of other types of communication, is one aspect of the brilliance of al-Ghīṭānī's intertextual play to which we now turn as we investigate the inner core of the narrative.

While events of enormous moment are taking place on the broader strategic level, the access that the Egyptian populace has to information is completely controlled and indeed manipulated. Pieces of information about the pending disaster are available: al-Zaynī Barakāt is well aware that the Ottomans are planning an attack on Egypt, and the inevitability of war is obvious even to a young student at al-Azhar.[152] However, to the majority of people, the potential impact of such a major confrontation and conflict remains an unknown quantity. Everyone is bound up with the sheer process of survival, and officialdom is preoccupied with the serious business of survival and self-interest within an environment where power is everything

149. Ibid., 239; trans., 239.
150. Ibid., 187–88; trans., 185–86.
151. Ibid., 211–12, 213–15; trans., 208–9, 210–12.
152. Ibid., 127, 182; trans., 125, 179.

and authority is maintained through terror and a network of spies. This is a society which prepares manuals instructing spies on the methods of maintaining surveillance on each other.[153] How telling it is that Ibn Iyās's accounts of the disastrous battle at Marj Dābiq and of al-Zaynī Barakāt's beating are juxtaposed in the narrative.

Al-Zaynī Barakāt is the *muḥtasib* of Egypt, a position of enormous power involving the supervision of monopolies, marketing standards, coinage, weights and measures, and the preservation of public morality in the name of Islam and the state.[154] The holder of this office wields enormous power and, according to the way in which he chooses to manipulate the patterns of authority at his disposal, can make the life of the Egyptian populace tolerable or the reverse. At the chronological beginning of *al-Zaynī Barakāt* [912 A.H./ 1507] a decree is promulgated by the Sulṭān announcing that ʿAlī ibn Abī al-Jūd is to be removed from the post of *muḥtasib;* he has treated the populace badly and robbed them of their property. The post is to be entrusted to one Barakāt ibn Mūsā, henceforth to be known by the title al-Zaynī. The advent of al-Zaynī causes considerable anxiety to at least one other authority figure, Zakariyyā ibn Rāḍī, the Chief Spy of Cairo. Zakariyyā is appalled to find how little his elaborate network of spies has uncovered about al-Zaynī. They maintain an ongoing process of collecting data on anybody and everybody, and yet the file on al-Zaynī is extremely thin. Al-Zaynī's appointment as *muḥtasib* places him right in the middle of the manipulative space between the Sulṭān, the ultimate authority in the land, and the huge espionage apparatus controlled by Zakariyyā that observes the minutest aspect of the life of every single Egyptian.[155] Zakariyyā immediately determines to find out as much as possible about the new appointee and, upon reflection, determines that his best interests lie in cooperating with him. However, if the Sulṭān represents one kind of authority in the life of the mysterious figure

153. Ibid., 205; trans., 203.

154. A previous holder of this post in Egypt was the great historian al-Maqrīzī (1346–1442). He wrote an interesting work in economic history, *al-Ighāthah,* and a detailed study of the topography of Egypt entitled *Mawāʿiẓ al-iʿtibār fī dhikr al-khiṭaṭ wa-al-āthār* (which served as a model for a nineteenth-century work of the same type by ʿAlī Mubārak [1823–93] and for yet another fictional pastiche by al-Ghīṭānī, *Khiṭaṭ al-Ghīṭānī* (Al-Ghīṭānī's city guide) (Beirut: Dār al-Maṣīrah, 1981).

155. The report that Zakariyyā sends to al-Zaynī Barakāt by carrier pigeon provides a good illustration of the amount of intimate personal detail that the system of spies is shown to be able to produce. See al-Ghīṭānī, *Al-Zaynī Barakāt,* 147–54; trans., 143–50.

of al-Zaynī Barakāt, then Shaykh Abū al-Suʿūd symbolizes another, that of Ṣūfī master over a follower. His presence in the narrative is indicated by chapters that bear the name of the village from which he exerts control over a large group of his followers: Kūm al-Jāriḥ. Al-Zaynī Barakāt obeys the Shaykh's summons and accompanies one of these followers, a young Azhar student from upper Egypt named Saʿīd al-Juwaynī, to the Shaykh's home for vetting as soon as al-Zaynī's appointment is known. It is Shaykh Abū al-Suʿūd's name that is invoked by al-Zaynī Barakāt as "his master" when he is compelling the people of upper Egypt to pay their taxes in advance. As already noted, it is the Shaykh who has the authority to call al-Zaynī Barakāt a dog and then order that he be beaten and detained for "doing wrong to Muslims by grabbing their property."[156] Saʿīd, the young student who escorts al-Zaynī Barakāt to see the Shaykh, is himself allotted a central role in the narrative. Being from upper Egypt, Cairo is a strange place to him, and his accounts provide the reader with vivid impressions of the life of the populace, but, apart from providing such detail, his principal role is to reflect the development in attitudes towards the "régime" of al-Zaynī Barakāt. Initially, it is Zakariyyā ibn Rāḍī who employs yet another Azhar student, ʿAmr ibn al-ʿAdawī, to spy on Saʿīd (as well as others); it is, in fact, a carefully dated report from ʿAmr that conveys the news of al-Zaynī's visit with Saʿīd to the house of the Shaykh. However, as the cooperation between Chief Spy Zakariyyā and the *muḥtasib* al-Zaynī Barakāt increases, it is the latter who engineers Saʿīd's downfall by arranging for his beloved, Samāḥ, the daughter of Shaykh Rīḥān, to be married off. The narrative threads thus work down and up the chains of authority: from the Sulṭān to Zakariyyā, from the Shaykh to Saʿīd; and across them, from ʿAmr to Saʿīd. And somewhere in the midst of this maze, the mysterious figure of al-Zaynī Barakāt manipulates all possible angles and avenues.

As the narrative proceeds, it becomes clear that al-Zaynī Barakāt is a master at what would today be recognized as public relations. His term of office opens with a flood of proclamations, all delivered by criers in new uniforms: market regulations are to be enforced, commodities are to be available at a fixed price, certain Mamlūk emirs who have been oppressing the populace are to be arrested. In a move so radical that it alarms certain centers of authority, al-Zaynī even orders that, as a safety measure, lanterns are to be hung on the

156. Ibid., 45, 209, 211; trans., 43, 206, 208.

streets of Cairo at night. The proclamation provokes a legal dispute, with the majority of scholars opposing the measure, spurred on, no doubt, by the fact that a large band of Mamlūk emirs goes to the Citadel and expresses their vigorous opposition to the Sulṭān. The measure is supported at the official level by the chief judge of the Ḥanafī rite and in more private and less exalted circles by Saʿīd al-Juwaynī (in the hearing of ʿAmr, of course). However, two terse decrees from the Sulṭān announce the dismissal of the Ḥanafī judge and the cancellation of al-Zaynī's orders. In political terms, of course, the defeat of this measure does no harm whatsoever to al-Zaynī Barakāt's popular appeal.

As the "unholy alliance" between al-Zaynī Barakāt and Zakariyyā develops and expands, the ambivalence of Saʿīd—the popular conscience of the novel—towards al-Zaynī becomes more marked, as he explains to the Shaykh. While some monopoly holders are punished, others are allowed to continue earning huge profits at the people's expense.[157] Saʿīd is perplexed as to why al-Zaynī should need to co-operate with a sinister figure such as Zakariyyā, the Chief Spy. His fears and questions are well-founded as it turns out. When Saʿīd's student colleague, ʿAmr ibn al-ʿAdawī, tells Zakariyyā about Saʿīd's utter infatuation with the beautiful Samāḥ, Zakariyyā proceeds to inform al-Zaynī of the fact. The plan to crush Saʿīd is put into effect: Samāḥ, his beloved, is married off, and Zakariyyā's spies are instructed to harass Saʿīd wherever he goes. In a transformation fraught with symbolic meaning, the latter's ambivalence now changes to opposition. While al-Zaynī is at al-Azhar mosque, delivering a highly publicized and histrionic sermon in the colloquial dialect (a departure from normal practice carefully noted by the narrator, in this case the Venetian traveler), a voice from the crowd calls him a liar.[158] In the section that soon follows, Saʿīd agonizes over the way in which his own life and that of the Egyptian populace is being manipulated, and makes his fatal shout. He knows that arrest and torture are inevitable; the narrative spares us the details, but one of Saʿīd's jailers notes that entry into one of Zakariyyā's cells marks a dividing line in anyone's life. Saʿīd does indeed emerge from the experience a changed and broken man. His anguished cry, "Oh, how they have destroyed me and leveled my strongholds!" singled out in the narrative, is clearly a moment of great symbolic significance.

157. Ibid., 106–7; trans., 105–6.
158. Ibid., 172, 175; trans., 169, 172.

As the news of the disastrous military defeat reaches Cairo, Saʿīd has been crushed and ʿAmr has been dismissed by Zakariyyā for his poor performance as a spy; his future status is to be examined. Al-Zaynī Barakāt is under detention in the home of Shaykh Abū al-Suʿūd, whose followers are being pursued by Ottoman forces.[159] It is left to the Venetian traveler to narrate the outcome. As things begin to settle down under the new regime, al-Zaynī Barakāt is rumored to be meeting people, including the traitorous Mamlūk, Khayrbey. Rumor is then confirmed by sight: Gianti sees al-Zaynī Barakāt riding a horse and accompanied by all the trapping of the office of *muḥtasib.* Ottoman currency has replaced that of the Mamlūks, but al-Zaynī Barakāt, master politician and manipulator, is restored to office.

This exploration of events and characters has already revealed a good deal concerning the richness of this narrative, but we should now examine its structuring in more detail. The two narratives in which the Venetian traveler, Gianti, gives his impressions of Cairo during the year 922–23 A.H. (1516–17) provide a framing structure, as we noted above, one that contains within it six numbered sections, termed *surādiqāt,* which I choose to translate as "canopies."[160] The sixth of these units, set at Kūm al-Jāriḥ, the home of Shaykh Abū al-Suʿūd, is devoted entirely to the narration of Saʿīd al-Juwaynī, culminating in the anguished cry of despair that has already been quoted. The very brevity of this section, its concentration on the anguished thoughts of a single individual, and its place immediately before Gianti's final depiction of a devastated city, all these factors afford the sixth *surādiq* a strong symbolic function as an act of closure relative to the other five similarly titled sections. Each of the other five "canopies" contains within it a variety of texts, presented in different ways. Beyond the numerical assignation itself (First Canopy, Second Canopy, etc.), the first three provide a short description of the principal events or themes contained within the section; the second, for example reads, "The Second Canopy: al-Zaynī Barakāt's star dawns bright, his position is confirmed; fortunes in the ascendant, destiny ever expanding."[161] The fourth and fifth canopies, on

159. Ibid., 231; trans., 228.

160. According to the Arabic dictionary of Lane (4:1348), a *surādiq* is an awning or canopy, something that overhangs an area in order to provide cover or shelter. Farouk Abdel Wahab uses "pavilions," certainly an attractive alternative, although, to me at least, it suggests a more permanent structure reaching to the ground.

161. Al-Ghīṭānī, *Al-Zaynī Barakāt,* 63; trans., 61.

the other hand, provide no details, thereby providing a tacit acknowledgment of the fact that much of their content is concerned with the espionage activities of Zakariyyā and his cooperation with al-Zaynī Barakāt. These two sections include "secret documents" concerning the preparations for and presentations at a convention of Chief Spies from the entire Arab world region that Zakariyyā brings together in Cairo.

Within each of these larger sections are a number of designated subdivisions, labeled in a variety of ways. The first such method is that of providing the name of the person who narrates the segment; there are three such: Zakariyyā ibn Rāḍī, Saʿīd al-Juhaynī, and ʿAmr ibn al-ʿAdawī. These narratives contrast directly with those of the Venetian traveler in that they consist of personal accounts and reflections conveyed through the third person. An omniscient narrator takes the reader inside the mind of the character involved to reveal emotions, motivations, and reactions. Thus, when Zakariyyā decides to visit the house of al-Zaynī Barakāt following the defeat of the Egyptian army in 1516,

> Who knows? It could well be that Zakariyyā would be in a similar fix and only al-Zaynī could get him out of it. Troubled times indeed! No one can feel safe for himself or his family, particularly anyone in a situation like Zakariyyā's. . . . He would never have thought he'd witness such destruction: minarets like frozen letters sticking up into the sky; his son, Yāsīn, and his harem sent away to Upper Egypt. . . . At last, al-Zaynī's house! In a little while, he'll be listening, the second time they've talked since al-Zaynī was allowed to leave the Shaykh's house. How stupid he was, thinking thousands of times of eliminating him! A wry smile forms on his lips. Did he really have such an idea? Really?[162]

When ʿAmr is summoned to appear at the Spies office to be reprimanded for his inefficiency, the feelings he expresses are a wonderful summary of the circumstances and values that have motivated his actions:

> His tongue wouldn't function. What was the man going to do to him? When the emissary tracked him down in Fusṭāṭ, he prepared a big speech: the only thing he needed was some kind of shelter, a

162. Ibid., 228–29; trans., 227.

> place where he could work as a servant, cleaning and washing . . . he'd done his utmost to serve Zakariyyā well. . . . Had a single report of his ever failed to be accurate? Hadn't he managed to expose dozens of provocateurs? But at the crucial moment he couldn't think of anything else to say.[163]

Thus, between the outermost frame of the narrative, that of Gianti, which makes use of the personalizing "I" to convey the impressions of a visitor who knows the least about the details of the local situation, and the central focus of the novel, al-Zaynī Barakāt, who is given no narrative voice whatsoever, a powerfully ironic narrative situation is created in which the reactions of these three narrators, the Chief Spy and the two Azhar students, serve to fill in parts of the cognitive space between the foreigner, to whom everything is strange, and the insider, who gives the appearance of knowing everything and using such knowledge to his own advantage. Each of these narrators has a role to play in the central drama of the novel, but each is also given a more personal touch through family detail. With Zakariyyā it takes the form of his desire to spend more time with his infant son; ʿAmr is acutely conscious of his own poverty and anxious about his mother; and Saʿīd, as we have already seen, is hopelessly in love with Samāḥ (and, with ʿAmr, Zakariyyā, and al-Zaynī Barakāt cooperating to engineer his downfall, it is indeed hopeless).

A different method of labeling, that of place, is used to represent another key character, Shaykh Abū al-Suʿūd. Kūm al-Jāriḥ comes to symbolize not only the Shaykh himself, but also the influence that he commands over his followers. It will be recalled that the sixth of the "canopies" carries the subtitle "Kūm al-Jāriḥ" and is entirely devoted to the narrative of Saʿīd. It is to this place that al-Zaynī Barakāt has to go to obtain initial approval for assuming his post and later to be castigated for abusing its powers. While these sections also focus on the role of one particularly significant player in the narrative drama, the discourse used is different. For, while the first of these sections may serve to describe in a focused fashion the general environment of the Shaykh's entourage, the later passages employ a much less direct mode of discourse, one that is very redolent of Ṣūfī writings, which, in the form of the works of the Spanish mystic Ibn

163. Ibid., 217; trans., 215.

ʿArabī (1165–1240), al-Ghīṭānī was to exploit with such complex mastery in his *Kitāb al-tajalliyyāt* (Book of illuminations). When Saʿīd is crushed by the marriage of Samāḥ to someone else, the Shaykh's musings are captured in a remarkable piece of writing that begins:

> Spaces with neither beginning nor end in the eyes of the striver, the foot-traveler; his nourishment comes from love of the Higher Entity, a passion that binds him to the uttermost parts of the earth. These he traverses, reflecting on the lessons learned and bewailing both beginning and end. What agony for the heart in wrecked homes, in a populous land where people have forgotten both first and last! How sweet it is for a sailor to stand at the helm of his boat with the sails unfurled. The universe is a sea; it is all a huge sea. The boat leans over to change course and changes course to lean over.[164]

At a remove from these more personalized sections there are also a number of "reports" that are dispatched both up and across the chain of authority. The primary recipient and dispatcher of this textual genre is, needless to say, Zakariyyā, as, for example, when he sends al-Zaynī a request to notify him concerning the proclamations he is making, and at the same time send the Sulṭān a complaint about al-Zaynī doing precisely that. While these passages may not provide as direct an insight into the motivations of the characters as do the passages we have just discussed, they do serve to provide valuable pieces of information and opinion that interact in both positive and negative ways with the more personalized sections; as, for example, when Zakariyyā's first letter to al-Zaynī Barakāt politely reminds him of the existence of his elaborate spy system and goes on to request "that you avail yourself of the heralds under our control so that we can review what it is they are announcing and the things about which they are informing the populace. While this may seem like a trifling matter to you, it may have the very direst consequences."[165]

These narratives, quotations (authentic and simulated), and reports are interspersed with other texts: quotations from the Qur'ān, cover pages of secret documents, memoranda, and many public proclamations, the efficacy and impact of which are well appreciated by Zakariyyā, as the previous quotation illustrates. These serve not

164. Ibid., 157; trans., 151.
165. Ibid., 59–60; trans., 58.

only to reflect the information that the populace receives and the modes by which they do so, but also the myriad ways through which the operatives of the state succeed in manipulating the system, mostly to their own advantage and the disadvantage of the people at large. There is a constant interplay between the discussions among people who know, and the announcements to the Egyptian people of part or all of what it is that they know, manipulated by both occasion and the selection of both material and language to meet the needs of authority and power. The reader thus participates in the entire process, as a wide variety of people do their utmost to survive in the kind of atmosphere that such a regime creates. Saʿīd and ʿAmr are both crushed, but for entirely different reasons. Al-Zaynī Barakāt is castigated and then released, only to emerge, the supreme political opportunist, in the same post under a complete new regime.

What makes this novel such a fascinating essay in narrative is that there is, in fact, no one who "knows" everything. On the most practical level, one might observe that the process of dividing up information into segments has long been a device used by those organizations who wish to maintain secrecy and that the presence of such a situation in al-Ghīṭānī's novel serves to enhance the atmosphere of oppressive surveillance that pervades the work. Within a more literary-critical framework, we can observe that each of the contributors to the novel's narrative knows a certain amount and places the information at his disposal into the collective assemblage of documents. Through that process of collection the image of al-Zaynī Barakāt is built up, but well before the conclusion of the novel, Zakariyyā has come to an important realization:

> For months now he had realized that al-Zaynī had not created a special information-gathering apparatus. He didn't employ a single spy; they were all regular employees of the *muḥtasib*. . . . Zakariyyā now realized that he'd been utterly and completely fooled. His dearest wish would have been to discover that al-Zaynī actually did have a network of spies working for him, but the truth was that it was just a rumor put around by al-Zaynī himself. The whole system was put together in the air; created, yet not.[166]

The organizing narrator of *al-Zaynī Barakāt* uses the interstices created by these gaps of information provided by the various texttypes to provide a startling picture of a figure who becomes a master ma-

166. Ibid., 225–26; trans., 225.

nipulator of the system, who uses all the devices of public relations to develop and foster a particular image, and who is able to use this combination of popularity and terror to survive a disastrous defeat and emerge relatively unscathed, at least on the political level; and of a society so intent on watching itself that it ignores its own larger needs and interests.

"Those who ignore history are condemned to repeat it" is a famous quote of George Santayana. In the wake of a defeat as total as that of June 1967, it is not surprising that Arab intellectuals should reexamine their history in a search for lessons and examples. Al-Ghīṭānī, student of Egyptian history, creative writer imprisoned during the regime of ʿAbd al-nāṣir, returned to the sixteenth century and discovered a set of circumstances that bear an uncanny resemblance to those of his own time. Like al-Zaynī Barakāt, President ʿAbd al-nāṣir made full use of the media at his disposal. As revelations of the early 1970s showed, the country was in the grip of a vast security apparatus; Zakariyyā's dreams of a futuristic spy system—a sardonic narrative touch indeed!—sound only too familiar.[167] The news of the 1516 defeat of the Egyptian army is kept from the people, just as the events of June 1967 were, and ʿAbd al-nāṣir was to emerge as President in the wake of the defeat, as al-Zaynī Barakāt is reappointed to his position of *muḥtasib.* The utterly callous way in which Saʿīd al-Juhaynī, the young Azhar student, is emotionally demolished may be seen as one writer's response to the way in which the Egyptian revolution chose to deal with issues of intellectual and cultural significance.

Al-Ghīṭānī's novel, however, should not be pigeonholed as merely a reflection of a particular historical moment or period. It is a major contribution to the development of a modern Arabic novelistic discourse, one that makes use of history and texttypes to indulge in a rich exercise in irony, one that constantly draws readers' attention to its transtextual connections and invites them to participate in the process of unraveling the mystery that is the novel's title. Hilary Mantel well summarizes the work's value in both original form and translation when she comments: "This is a most distinguished book, by turns elegant and terrifying . . . it will be a mark of our insularity if it does not now become widely known."[168]

167. Ibid., 201–2; trans., 210.

168. Gamal al-Ghitani, *Zayni Barakat,* London: Penguin, 1988, back cover.

Al-Waqā'i' al-gharībah fī-ikhtifā' Sa'īd Abī al-naḥs al-mutashā'il, Emile Ḥabībī

Novel titles are usually quite short; three or four words tend to suffice. Perhaps it is the relative length of the genre itself and the desired structural complexity of its contents (when compared, say, with the short story) that may account for the writer's urge to move readers quickly beyond the title itself. One might add that, in these contemporary times, publishers and librarians are among those who clearly find shorter titles preferable. During the medieval period of Arabic writing quite the opposite was the case. The norm developed whereby book titles were to be elaborate, more often than not consisting of two parts: a first which consisted of an attractive image of some kind, and a second which described the work's topic(s). The two segments were to rhyme with each other. The works of al-Maqrīzī and Ibn Iyās cited in connection with al-Ghīṭānī's novel (discussed above) are good examples of this trend. On all these counts therefore, the title of Emile Ḥabībī's novel, which will be discussed in this section, draws conspicuous attention to itself. Translated as literally as possible, it reads: "The strange occurrences concerning the disappearance of Sa'īd, father of ill-fortune, the pessoptimist."[169] As such, it is a conscious evocation of earlier genres in both its length and structure, and contains a good deal of information and allusion. Through its coinage of a nonexistent word *mutashā'il,* it also suggests to its readers that they will be confronting a narrator who enjoys playing with language. They are forewarned to be on the lookout for the unusual ("strange occurrences"); a character called Sa'īd is to disappear; and Arabic readers who know that the name *Sa'īd* literally means "happy" or "lucky" notice that they are faced with a double oxymoron, the one involving "pessoptimist," the other between *sa'īd* (happy) and *naḥs* (ill-fortune).

If the title of this work uses word play to invite the reader into its fictional world, the structuring of the text itself picks up on the promise. The work is divided into three sections. They first appeared at intervals in *al-Ittiḥād,* the Arabic newspaper of the Israeli Communist Party of which Ḥabībī was editor; he has also served as a

169. It will be seen that the title of the English trans. of the novel, *The Secret Life of Saeed, Ill-fated Pessoptimist: A Palestinian Who Became a Citizen of Israel,* while preserving the complexity of the original, is an act of considerable interpretation.

Communist Party member of the Israeli Knesset. The whole work was published in book form in Haifa in 1974, then in Beirut in the same year, and in a third edition in Jerusalem in 1977.[170] Each section is prefaced with a poem, the poignancy of whose message underscores the overarching seriousness of a work which at the surface carries sardonic humor and self-deprecation to levels unprecedented in Arabic fiction. The work opens, for example, with a defiant message from the well-known Palestinian resistance poet, Samīḥ al-Qāsim:

> You men!
> You women!
> You shaykhs, rabbis, and cardinals!
> You nurses and weaving women!
> Long have you waited,
> and yet the postmen have never knocked on your doors
> bringing you across desiccated fences
> those letters you so yearn. . . .
> Wait no more, you men and women!
> Take off your night-clothes
> and write yourselves
> those letters you so yearn![171]

This preface talks of initiative and action. The one which introduces the second book brings in an entirely different, yet equally forceful sentiment, in an extract from a poem by Sālim Jubrān, like Ḥabībī himself a Communist and contributor to *al-Ittiḥād:*

> Just as a mother loves her disfigured child, so do I love
> my own beloved, my country.[172]

The creative oxymoron implicit in the "Saʿīd, father of ill-fortune" of the title has already drawn attention to the role which names are to play in this work, and the seriousness of overall purpose reflected in these poetic preludes is also carried over into the titles given to the three books. Each is the name of a woman. The first is Yuʿād, a word that implies "to be returned." The second is Bāqiyah (she who

170. I am using here the third (1977) edition of Ḥabībī, *Al-Waqāʾiʿ al-gharībah.*
171. Ibid., 9; trans., 1. The translations included here are my own.
172. Ibid., 89 trans., 67.

stays behind), and the third Yuʿād the second.[173] In the context of the work of a Palestinian writer living in Israel, the symbolic resonance of these names hardly needs to be emphasized. However, within our discussion here of the structural logic of the novel, one can also observe that the circular movement implicit in this sequence of title names—the enforced journey into exile (with the "yearning" to return) juxtaposed with the act of remaining—serves to encapsulate the history and the agony of the Palestinian people since 1948 and further underlines the themes contained within the poetic prefaces to each book. The structure may even be regarded as a traditional three-stage quest narrative—departure, time away, return—but with the organizational logic inverted by the initial starting point of exile, internal and external. While the text of *al-Waqāʾiʿ al-gharībah* represents a constant process of ironic interplay between the serious and the sardonic, the patent and the symbolic, a return to the frame level which occurs at the beginning of each "book" acts as a continuing reminder to the reader that this is a work of fiction devoted to the Palestinian experience in all its tragic dimensions.[174] This is underlined by the way in which the text comes to an end. A penultimate section (which announces itself to be "The crowning touch") has Saʿīd describing to the recipient of his letters the arrival of the chief of "the men from outer space," who sweeps him up into the sky, to the great delight of Saʿīd's acquaintances who are watching below. This, however, is not the end; the final segment reverts to the recipient of Saʿīd's letters and his concern about the fate and whereabouts of their sender. Switching to a third-person narrative in present time, a narrator has this "gentleman" speak to a general audience in the second-person plural ("you as a group"), and all "for the sake of truth and history":

> Whereupon the gentleman who had received these remarkable letters left. He still nurses the hope that you will all help him search for this Saʿīd person.
>
> "But where do you plan to look?" . . .

173. Each book also conspicuously carries its date of publication on its title page: Bk. 1, 1972; bk. 2, late 1972; bk. 3, mid-1974.

174. For studies of the use of irony in this work, see Akram F. Khater, "Emile Ḥabībī: The Mirror of Irony in Palestinian Literature," *JAL* 24, no. 1 (Mar. 1993): 75–94; and Samia Mehrez, "Al-Mufāraqah ʿinda James Joyce wa-Emile Ḥabībī," *Alif* 4 (Spring 1984): 33–54.

> My dear Sirs, how do you ever plan to find him if you don't bump into him somehow?![175]

As noted above, the three sections of this work were published separately; in the case of the third book, after a period of some two years. Internal evidence suggests that, as was the case with Dickens, readers' reaction and comments on earlier sections may have made their way into later ones. Ḥabībī, for example, seems to make wonderful use of comments that were apparently made concerning the similarity between his work and Voltaire's *Candide:* "I remember some friends of your friend discussing the contents of your first letter to him. What they said was that you'd made preparations for a great leap ahead, but landed up going backwards some two hundred years and still falling short of *Candide.*"[176] The narrator's reaction is to call the bluff of these "friends of his friend" by using a complete chapter to explore the "unusual similarity" between the two works, providing all necessary footnotes to the French text and even supplying the details concerning the work's translation into Arabic. Whatever the connection here between the narrator's incorporation of this section into his text and the author's own reactions to comment, the result is to incorporate an interesting metafictional dimension into the narrative, providing yet another instance to illustrate the veracity of Kermode's comment noted earlier, that "the use of fiction as an instrument of research into the nature of fiction, though certainly not new, is much more widely recognized." Within the framework of Ḥabībī's own text, one is left to wonder whether it is the narrator or author who, in the context of this particular chapter, contributes to the metafictional debate by protesting that the friend to whom Saʿīd's letters are being given is merely the conveyor of the message; his only task is just that—transmission.[177]

As the above quotation notes, the narrative situation in this work involves sets of letters sent to a narrator with the request that he tell the story. The first book begins by detailing this arrangement, thus providing a verbal link to the "letters" mentioned in the initial poem of Samīḥ al-Qāsim. The actual Arabic phrase with which the first

175. Ḥabībī, *Al-Waqāʾiʿ al-gharībah,* 206–8; trans., 161–63.

176. Ibid., 94–99; trans., 72–75.

177. Kermode, *The Art of Telling,* 53. The same effect occurs when "for the first time Saʿīd resorts to footnotes," a section that itself includes its own footnotes: Ḥabībī, *Al-Waqāʾiʿ al-gharībah,* 58–60; trans., 44–45. For the metafictional protest, see ibid., 94; trans., 72.

chapter opens is: "Saʿīd, the father of ill-fortune, the pessoptimist, wrote to me and said. . . ." This desire on the narrator's part to establish from the outset the source of his story serves in the Arabic context as a direct evocation of the tradition of classical Arabic narrative, a tradition in which the authenticity of the message being transmitted was of crucial importance for the verification of *ḥadīth*, the accounts of the actions of Muḥammad, the Prophet of Islam, upon which the behavior of Muslims was to be based in those circumstances where the Qur'ān itself did not provide instruction. The chain of transmission *(isnād)* thus became a necessary prelude to any narrative that was to aspire to authenticity. This structural feature, deeply rooted in traditional Arabic narrative, was later imitated in the belles-lettrist genre of the *maqāmah*. The *maqāmāt* of Badīʿ al-zamān al-Hamadhānī (d. 1008), almost certainly the originator of the genre, begin thus: "ʿĪsā ibn Hishām [the name of the narrator] narrated and said." The word for "to narrate" used in this context is *ḥaddatha*, a verb associated with the technical term *ḥadīth* noted above.[178] Like the opening of the *maqāmah*, Ḥabībī's first sentence establishes the name of the source and recipient of the narrative, but, as is the case in the classical *maqāmah* genre, the antics of the person so named call into question the "authenticity" of his message. From the outset, then, Ḥabībī is to lead his readers into an intertextual maze, one involving not only the great cultural heritage of the classical past but a variety of transcultural references. Saʿīd's request to the narrator is as follows: "Pass on my story, the most incredible thing to happen to a human being since Moses' staff, Jesus's resurrection, and the election of the Lady-bird's husband as president of the United States." Saʿīd continues his narration by saying that he has disappeared. He has met some creatures from outer space and is soaring high above everyone, as noted in our reference above to the text's closure. In response to a question as to why they chose a person like him, he replies that in fact he chose them; he has been searching for them all his life.[179] Being now fully aware of the uses to which Ḥabībī puts his verbal virtuosity and of its ancestry in the classical tradition, we need to pause once again in order to point out another pun of signficance in the interpretation of this narra-

178. In a most useful and suggestive study, James T. Monroe has explored the ironic dimensions implicit in the *maqāmah* genre, its structure and societal contexts: *The Art of Badīʿ az-zamān al-Hamadhānī as Picaresque Narrative* (Beirut: American Univ. of Beirut, 1983).

179. Ḥabībī, *Al-Waqāʾiʿ al-gharībah*, 15; trans., 5.

tive. The Arabic word for space is *fiḍā'* and for people from space *fiḍā'iyyīn.* A single change, from the emphatic consonant *ḍaad* to the unemphatic *daal,* provides the word *fidā'iyyīn* (those who sacrifice themselves), the name adopted by the Palestinian guerrilla movement that emerged following the 1967 defeat. Saʿīd, the pessoptimist who during the course of this novel works as an Israeli collaborator, begins his account by telling us that, by joining the "people in space," he has discovered his life's dream. As is often the case in modern fiction, the beginning proves to be the end.

Having established the structural parameters in this way, the narrator is led by Saʿīd's "letters" back to the beginning, to the earliest stages of his life and to the chronological framework for the first book, the period after 1948.[180] The farcical element immediately makes its way into the narrative, as Saʿīd informs the reader through the title of the second section that he owes his life in Israel to "the kind offices of a donkey." We learn that his father was killed during the 1948 fighting and that Saʿīd would have suffered the same fate if a donkey had not crossed the line of fire and died after being hit by the bullet that was heading in Saʿīd's direction. This concentration on the role of the donkey and the lack of any further comment from Saʿīd on either the death of his father or his own close brush with death, needless to say, enhances the reader's awareness of the posture that he is adopting in recounting his life story: he may act the fool and describe his antics in a humorous way, but beyond the farce there lies a message of the most intense seriousness, one that, as we have already noted, is clearly expressed within the outer frame of the narrative but which is not only visible at certain points within the story but also implicit in the ironic gaps within his wise fool's story that Saʿīd's letters leave for the reader to fill.

The first book focuses on the period following the Palestinian defeat in 1948, "that fiendish year, the date of which I can never forget since the events before and after it have come to serve as a historical watershed for my entire life."[181] The Palestinian people have been scattered in all directions; families have been split in the panic of rapid departure, homes are now occupied by strangers from the West, and whole villages have been demolished.[182] Within

180. The second section opens with the sentences: "Let us begin at the beginning," 16; trans., 6.

181. Ibid., 69; trans., 53.

182. Ibid., 32–33; trans., 21– 22.

the context of this chaotic tragedy Saʿīd reenters Israel from Lebanon in search of an acquaintance of his father called Adon Safsarcheck, a name with the literal meaning of "broker" but also conveying all the significances of the word "operator." Saʿīd soon discovers that the quickest road to safety is to play the fool, replicating the antics of the admirable animal that has saved his life. He is co-opted to work as a member of the Union of Palestinian Workers, informing on Communists in the process, and becomes an assistant to Yaʿqūb, a junior official of Sephardic origin in the Department of Arab Affairs, both of them being under the command of "the Big Man of short stature," an Ashkenazi Jew from Europe who is quite as prepared to insult the Oriental origins of his Jewish subordinate as he is the Arabs.[183]

The above description of the "scenario" and events of the first book is deceptive, in that it does not reflect the way in which the narrative technique randomizes the presentation. The effect is achieved in the main through two techniques. The first is best described as a modern adaptation of the classical trope of *istiṭrād* (digression). These passages may take the form of entire chapters devoted to "research" or "footnotes," or segments within a single chapter, often in the form of anecdotes and jokes ("did you hear the one about. . . .").[184] Then there are the narrative "prolepses" and "analepses" (to use Genette's terminology) in which Saʿīd looks back to events earlier in his life and forwards to the further "disasters" of 1956 and 1967. In one of these retrospectives we learn of Saʿīd's love for a girl he meets at school, Yuʿād. They have a series of clandestine meetings until her family finds out, at which point they try to terminate the relationship. However, she and her family are among those who disappear during the events of 1948; the link is severed, but the memory lingers in Saʿīd's mind. In all these cases the narrator is at pains to make clear to the reader that he is fully conscious of his own role as director of the narrative. Following the digression on the origins of the concept of "pessoptimism," the narrator invites his readers to "return" to the point at which the story was suspended (and the verb used, *li-naʿud* once more recalls the title of the book, "Yuʿād"). True to the traditions of narratives serialized in the press, the tenth chapter begins with a summary of the main events of the tale thus far. And into this rich and subversive mixture of event,

183. Ibid., 135; trans., 106.
184. E.g., ibid., 13–14; trans., 3–4.

description, and anecdote is inserted a veritable feast of intercultural allusion: from Napoleon to Tamerlaine, from Saladin to Richard the Lionheart, from Jules Verne to Ibn ʿArabī, from Newton to al-Bīrūnī, to which are added several telling quotations from Palestinian poets such as Maḥmūd Darwīsh and Tawfīq Zayyād.

The second principle whereby the narrative sequence is randomized is through another device which finds a parallel in classical texts, that of listing of number of "firsts." No less than seven chapters in this first book (which comprises almost half the entire work) are concerned with origins and first occasions. We may perhaps replicate Ḥabībī's own delight in the juxtaposition of the classical and modern, the Middle Eastern and Western, by pointing out that the famous classical anthologizer, al-Thaʿālibī (961–1038), makes use of the same organizing principle in his collection of anecdotal information, *Laṭāʾif al-maʿārif,* and that Gerard Genette, within his famous study on narrative devoted to Proust, points to the narrative usefulness of descriptions of "firsts," namely that they serve to imply a series of further occurrences of the same event.[185]

There is one chapter in this book in which the narrative mood is quite different: the highly symbolic, dreamlike depiction of Saʿīd's meeting with the man from outer space in the catacombs of ʿAkkah.[186] Here Saʿīd acknowledges to his mythically depicted interlocutor that he is on a quest, to which the man from outer space responds that he is always available when needed, and most especially when Saʿīd's energy level flags. And with that, the man vanishes, leaving Saʿīd to wake up in what is significantly described as "the real dawn."

Towards the end of the first book, Yuʿād and her sister "infiltrate" back into their home town of Haifa, but she is discovered by the security forces in Saʿīd's house and is carried off screaming: "This is my country, my home; he's my husband." As Saʿīd continues his work for Yaʿqūb in the Department of Arab Affairs, Yuʿād, true to her name, vows to return.

The second book, entitled "Bāqiyah" (she who remains), focuses on the life of the Arab community during the early stages of the Israeli state; Sālim Jubrān's prefatory poem talks about mother and child, and that finds a reflection in the contents of the book. How-

185. Al-Thaʿālibī, *Laṭāʾif al-maʿārif* (Cairo: ʿĪsā al-Bābī al-Ḥalabī, 1960), 5–23; English trans.: *The Book of Curious and Entertaining Information,* trans. C. Edmund Bosworth (Edinburgh: Edinburgh Univ. Press, 1968), 38–51; Genette, 72.

186. Ḥabībī, *Al-Waqāʾiʿ al-gharībah,* 48–54; trans., 35–40.

ever, it is not until the fourth chapter of this book that Saʿīd is instructed by the man from outer space to continue with the innermost narrative of the former's "secret." Before that, the two men both frame and introduce the second book by exploring the various dimensions of the new situation in Israel, using both *Candide* in the West and the philosophy of the Brethren of Purity in the East as vehicles for analogies for life in Israel. A new and more acid tone characterizes these segments, and it is repeated in another major interpolation into the text, a further piece of "research," this one on the "Oriental imagination." In a searing indictment of Israeli policies towards its Arab population, the distorted Western view of the Middle East and its people is filtered through the tales of *A Thousand and One Nights* (the "City of Brass," for example) in order to illustrate the way in which "justice" is meted out by the Israeli authorities.[187]

Saʿīd's quisling status is now emphasized by the fact that he is married to Bāqiyah, the girl from Ṭanṭūrah—the one who remains—upon the recommendation of "the Big Man" and his henchman, Yaʿqūb, so that Saʿīd can carry on his supposed surveillance and subversion of the Communist Party in that particular region. With Bāqiyah, Saʿīd acquires two precious entities: her family treasure, which is buried in a sea cave, and a son. In a work in which, as we have already seen, names assume a substantial symbolic function, the fact that Bāqiyah wants to call their son Fatḥī (victorious) after her father, that the "Big Man" disapproves, and that they therefore settle on the name Walāʾ (fidelity) is clearly of major importance, particularly in view of the way in which the narrative now develops. Walāʾ is taciturn child, although he does go to the seashore with his father to watch the latter's futile attempts to recover Bāqiyah's family treasure.

The primary issues, narrated to represent this phase of the confrontation between the Palestinian people and the Israeli state, take the form of the continuing saga of the disappearance of villages, the process of finding work in Israel (with Saʿīd serving as representative of the Union of Palestinian Workers), and the vexed question of land ownership and property rights. A notable instance of the last category looks forward to the aftermath of Black September 1970 (a time period that is sardonically described as being B.H. [*baʿd Ḥuzayrān*—after June 1967]), when Jordanian forces launched a fierce attack on Palestinians. Thurayyā, a seventy-year-old woman

187. Ibid., 129–32; trans., 100–104.

from Lyddah, makes use of the "open bridge" policy to return to her old home. After a search of the house under the watchful eye of the Israeli police, she finds the box of heirlooms that she had hidden away and left behind in 1948, but they are immediately expropriated by "the man in charge of Israeli territories." She returns to Jordan across the bridge empty-handed.[188] Saʿīd is in danger of suffering the same fate when "Evil personified" (a wonderful intertextual reference to the pre-Islamic vagabond poet of that name, Ta'abbaṭa Sharran) arrives and claims his furniture as "enemy property." The problem is only resolved when Saʿīd and his immediate "boss," Yaʿqūb, point out to these authorities that, since all Arabs are state property, anything that they own must also constitute state property as well.[189]

Saʿīd and his wife are so involved in protecting the existence of their treasure under the sea that they neglect their taciturn child, a decision which comes home to roost when, on a fateful day in the fall of 1966, the "Big Man" bursts in on Saʿīd to announce that Walā' has joined the *fidā'iyyīn.* He has "found the treasure-chest" and used it to purchase weapons and explosives. Bāqiyah and Saʿīd are ordered to go to the vault in Ṭanṭūrah where Walā' is known to be hiding, and persuade him to give himself up. It goes without saying that the discussion between parents and child that ensues constitutes the fiercest possible condemnation of those who would collaborate rather than confront. Saʿīd becomes a double loser when his wife joins her son; they both dive into the sea and disappear. He is left to wonder whether they will return or not, but then comes 5 June 1967.

The third and final book of *al-Waqā'iʿ al-gharībah* is entitled "Yuʿād the second," implying a repeat of the return. The period depicted is now the aftermath of the June War of 1967, the *naksah* (setback). The frame of the narrative opens with Saʿīd announcing the advent of the end, finding himself perched on the top of a stake, unable to move. He assumes that the whole thing is a dream—a nightmare, in fact. But then he wonders to himself how dreadful it would be to wake up and discover that this nightmare was in fact reality. Faced with such a choice he opts to stay on top of the stake, until, that is, the return of Yuʿād restores his confidence. This book continues the narrator's description of Arab life within Israel: the

188. Ibid., 121; trans., 95.
189. Ibid., 122; trans., 96.

cordoning off of villages, the blowing up of houses, claims and counterclaims regarding agricultural expertise, and the greening of the land. Saʿīd notes that he met this second Yuʿād for the first time where such meetings between Palestinians often occur, namely in or near prisons. He has been arrested for showing his loyalty and following instructions once too often: when he hears on the radio that Arabs are to raise the white flag of surrender, he does so too, failing to understand that he is considered a citizen of Israel and that the instruction is intended for Arabs in the occupied territories. This leads into the most harrowing chapter in the entire work, a description of prison life and torture. Reflecting Ḥabībī's sardonic tone, the chapter in which Saʿīd is beaten and kicked into unconsciousness is entitled "how Saʿīd finds himself in the midst of a pre-Islamic–Shakespearean poetry circle"; Saʿīd has unfortunately quoted Shakespeare to the effect "what's in a name," and the "circle" of guards proceed to taunt him with his erudition with each successive blow they administer.[190] It is in this infamous Shaṭṭah prison that Saʿīd meets another person named Saʿīd who is a *fidāʾī*. Our narrator, Saʿīd, is eventually released and, getting a ride in a private car from Nablus, he discovers that the occupants, the driver and a woman passenger, have been inquiring without success for the woman's brother, a man in Shaṭṭah prison named Saʿīd. Saʿīd yells that he is Saʿīd, but the girl angrily says that the Saʿīd she is searching for is her brother. Even so, the girl's name is Yuʿād; she is the daughter of the first Yuʿād, and the Saʿīd in prison is her son. This happiness of rediscovery after twenty years is short-lived, however.[191] When Saʿīd, our "pessoptimist," and Yuʿād return to their old home, the very same scenario is reenacted: the house is raided by Israeli soldiers, and Yuʿād is carried away, screaming the same defiant phrase her mother had used twenty years earlier.[192]

Ḥabībī's black humor continues to the end. The final chapter, "Happy ending—clinging to the stake," finds all the principal characters in the work coming to see Saʿīd on top of his stake. Here the stake assumes a polyvalent symbolic force, with each of the characters viewing it in a different way: to the big man of little stature, it is not a stake at all, but rather a television antenna; Yaʿqūb suggests

190. Ibid., 167–69; trans., 128–33.

191. Saʿīd even plays on the meaning of his name, "happy": see ibid., 181; trans., 138.

192. Ibid., 201; trans., 155.

that everyone has their own stake; and a member of the younger generation informs Saʿīd that his only choice is to join them "on the streets." Saʿīd refuses to come down, and, just as a young man is to the point of chopping it down, the chief of "the men from outer space" (the *fiḍāʾiyyīn*) appears to rescue Saʿīd from his predicament. The words that he addresses to Saʿīd could hardly carry more symbolic resonance: "You can no longer stand your miserable reality, and yet you refuse to pay the price needed to change it. And now you come crying to me."[193] And, to cries of rejoicing from the Palestinians below, Saʿīd flies away in a kind of apotheosis. The second Yuʿād looks to the future: "when this cloud passes over, then the sun will shine." The frame of the outer narrative is closed when the gentleman who has been the recipient of Saʿīd's letters reports that all attempts to discover the identity of this Saʿīd have failed.

This description of the book's sequencing serves to illustrate the way in which the inexorable course of time—1948, 1956, 1967—is reflected in the different books, all this within the larger framework of the outer narrative. We noted above that the first of the books covers almost half the entire work, but we can go beyond that to suggest that its overall tone is also different. As the work proceeds and the full dimensions of the Palestinian tragedy are exposed, the tone becomes more acid and recriminatory, often attaining heights of rancor the force of which is very redolent of Swift. The references to journalism, to the Knesset, and to the role of the Communists lend the story a direct linkage to the author that seems less present in the earlier part of the book. But, as we have also noted above, one of the principal features of this wonderful narrative is its apparent randomness, the brilliantly wayward evocation, indeed invocation, of earlier narratives and other genres of writing in an intercultural admixture that yet remains quintessentially modern and Palestinian in mode and mood. This is an aspect of Ḥabībī's work that, needless to say, conceals beneath it the height of artistry. One of the principal features of that very artistry is, of course, the style in which the work is couched. Not only are the chapters brief in the extreme, engendering an almost breathless narrative pace, but within them sentences are also short, an acknowledged characteristic of anecdotes and jokes and indeed of the rhyming prose *(sajʿ)* that has been the predominant discourse of the *maqāmah* genre. There is no place here for the lingering, lovingly painted descriptions of the

193. Ibid., 205; trans., 159.

"realistic" novel of earlier times. The situation to be depicted is too urgent, narrative time is too valuable and indeed fractured, and the focus must therefore be that of epic—on narrative, incidents, and the actions and sufferings of a nation.

The exploitation of irony in this work, the way in which the narrative demands of the readers that they interpret what they are reading in ways utterly at variance with the initially apparent, makes of it a truly unique exercise in modern Arabic fiction. The humor and sarcasm range all the way from the subtle and rib-tickling to a bitter and withering tone behind which lies a scarcely concealed sense of anger and frustration. As Northrop Frye, among many others, has reminded us, comedy is a deadly serious business, the mode through which society addresses itself critically to the problems of its present. And, as several studies (better left unnamed) have proved convincingly, the detailed analysis of the processes of humor is the surest way of destroying it. Suffice it to say, then, that humor expressed through the use of heavy irony may serve as a useful means of achieving emotional separation from topics whose dimensions demand the strongest possible repudiation. Thus when, as Saʿīd suggests in the third book, a nightmare proves to be not merely an ephemeral dream but a continuing disaster, irony presents itself as a thoroughly useful means of expressing the inexpressible.[194] Ḥabībī has addressed himself to this very topic in noting that his resort to sarcasm of this kind has two causes: "Firstly sarcasm is a weapon to protect oneself from one's own weaknesses; and secondly, it allows for the expression of a tragedy that is too great for this human conscience of mine to endure."[195]

With *al-Waqāʾiʿ al-gharībah,* Emile Ḥabībī has made an enduring and truly individualistic addition to modern Arabic fiction. His message concerns not only the way in which the confrontation of Israel with its Arab citizens has distorted so many of the ideals of early Zionists, but also the need for those very Palestinian Arabs living as citizens in Israel to find the means to assert themselves as contributing members of society. The book's engaging spontaneity of mood can perhaps be at least partially explained by reference to Ḥabībī's own thoughts on the subject: "When I wrote *The Pessoptimist,* I felt an internal explosion going on inside me. I had not intended to write a

194. See Mehrez, "Al-mufāraqah ʿinda James Joyce wa-Emile Ḥabībī," 35.

195. Maḥmūd Darwīsh and Ilyās Khūrī, "Emile Ḥabībī—anā huwa al-ṭifl al-qatīl," *Al-Karmal* 1 (Winter 1981): 190.

novel. A particular moment arrived, it seems, and I started writing without the slightest idea of where I was going. It was an experiment, one that allowed the interior mind to take off on its own."[196] That experiment has bequeathed to us a moving, tragicomic commentary on the Palestinian condition, all the more forceful and challenging in its continuing impact for being written by a genuine insider, a Palestinian Arab citizen of Israel who in 1992 was awarded Israel's highest literary prize.

Al-Nihāyāt, ʿAbd al-raḥmān Munīf

Structural analyses of a number of poems from the pre-Islamic period have shown with great clarity that the traditional notion that the *qaṣīdah* possesses no unity of purpose can no longer be justified; these studies show clearly that the unifying thread which runs through these poems is based on a series of oppositions involving lack and the elimination of lack, of "plerosis" and "kenosis" (as used by Hamori in quoting Gaster). To continue with Adnan Haydar, another student of this early Arabic poetry,

> The harshness of the desert, the constant movement of the tribe from place to place in search of herbage, the anxiety experienced as a result of this unstable life, the necessary severing of love and friendship ties, the belief in the relativity of all values, the strong indulgence in life, the bitter consciousness of the imminence of death, the heroic attempts to relive the happy moments of the past, and the necessary striving for the immortalization of those moments: all these are components of the pre-Islamic vision.[197]

These interpretations and others like them inevitably come to mind upon a first reading of ʿAbd al-raḥmān Munīf's novel *al-Nihāyāt* (1978; *Endings,* 1988).[198] Consider the opening: "Drought. Drought

196. Ibid., 194.

197. See Andras Hamori, *On the Art of Medieval Arabic Literature* (Princeton: Princeton Univ. Press, 1974), 12; Adnan Haydar, "The *muʿallaqa* of Imru' al-Qays: Its Structure and Meaning," part 1, *Edebiyat* 2, no. 2 (1977): 227–78.

198. ʿAbd al-raḥman Munīf, *Al-Nihāyāt* (Beirut: Dār al-Ādāb, 1978); English trans.: *Endings,* trans. Roger Allen (London: Quartet, 1988). Munif holds a Ph.D. in oil economics from the Univ. of Belgrade, has edited the Iraqi journal *Al-Nafṭ wa-al-Tanmiyah* (oil and development), and after a period of living in France, now resides in

again! When drought seasons come, things begin to change, Life and objects change. Humans change too, and no more so than in their moods! Deep down, melancholy feelings take root. They may seem fairly unobtrusive at first. But people will often get angry. When that happens, these feelings burst out into the open, assertive and unruly."[199] The emphasis on the desert, intense heat, the dangers of travel, the search for food, all these features and others set this novel apart from others written in Arabic. Novels written by Arab authors have tended to a large degree to take as their subjects the city and its inhabitants, and particularly the bourgeoisie, thus emulating at least the initial stages in the development of most of the Western novel traditions. There have, of course, also been novels which deal with life in the countryside, from the very early *Zaynab* of Haykal to ʿAbd al-ḥakīm Qāsim's *Ayyām al-insān al-sabʿah* which we have just analyzed. There have also been novels, parts of which have been set in the desert, for example Ghassān Kanafānī's *Rijāl fī al-shams* and *Mā tabaqqā la-kum.* However, Munīf's attention to a depiction of this particular segment of contemporary Arab society takes the Arabic novel to previously unexplored venues.

The setting of the novel is a village called al-Ṭībah, which is situated right on the edge of the desert. The way in which the narrative of this novel approaches this tiny and tight-knit community resembles nothing so much as a camera shot from above, first taking in the general surroundings and gradually zeroing in on more particular details. This approach applies as much to the dimension of time as it does to space: the opening segments (there are no numbered chapters) are concerned with habitual time: customs, attitudes, and general problems, the climate and environment being chief among them, as the above quotation clearly illustrates. It is only after readers have been presented with a thoroughly detailed background that they begin to encounter specific people, at a particular time. The omniscient narrator has a particular eye for detail; one might almost say that it is the eye of a social scientist, concerned with characteristics and models of usual behavior (noting, of course, variations from the norms as they have been described). From such an approach readers inevitably find themselves drawn into the world cre-

---

Damascus. He expresses a number of opinions about Arabic novels in general and his own in particular in *al-Maʿrifah* 204 (Feb. 1979): 188–99. See also Jabrā, *Yanābīʿ al-ruʾyā*, 36–40.

199. Munīf, *Al-Nihāyāt,* 5; trans., 1.

ated by a narrator who shares with them an immense concern with nature and the environment. The very devotion with which each phenomenon is described and inserted into its context recalls the opinion of Roman Jakobson: "'He is fond of dwelling on unessential details' is the classic judgment passed on the innovators by conservative critics of every era."[200]

The narrative's principal focus is to depict the hardships implicit in the rugged life that this community faces on a continuing basis. Such a way of life serves to create strong bonds between the inhabitants of the village and also, in times of crisis, to bring back home those sons of the community who have decided to seek their fortunes elsewhere, and particularly in the "big city." In this unusual work, that favorite venue for the spatial dimension of the novel genre (the "burgher's epic" in Hegel's well-known phrase) becomes a distant, uncaring, and inimical place. It is in this particular example of the modern metropolis that bureaucrats have been debating for some time whether or not to build a large earth dam near the site of the village in order to alleviate the more gruesome aspects of life during the hot season.

The major means by which the community survives is by hunting, although the more sensible members of the community realize that indiscriminate slaughter of birds and animals will work to their disadvantage. It is with this in mind that the villagers view with suspicion and resentment the groups of guests from the city who come out to the village in order to hunt for sport.

The narrative mode that we have discussed above is at some pains to make it clear that, if there is to be a principal "character" in this work, it is surely the community as a whole. The actions of individuals are portrayed, but their import is seen within the framework of the larger picture, namely the village as a unit. Whatever characterization they receive emerges from the description of their actions and the effect that they have on the village (or subsets of it), and not from any attempt at analysis of individual motivations, and still less from dialogue, of which there is comparatively little. In fact, the reader is supplied with only four named characters in a work which covers one hundred eighty-seven pages. Instead, we hear a good deal more about "al-Ṭībah," "the old folk," "young people," and the like.

This then is very much a novel that focuses on community and

200. See Jakobson, 22.

environment, but readers are gradually—very gradually—led towards a specific series of events that underline the work's environmental message. In fact, the manner in which a series of flashbacks recalling previous momentous occasions in the history of the village are recounted serves to lend the narrative certain elements of a folktale, something that is clearly entirely appropriate to the situation of the novel. The novel does, in fact, have a hero, but he must surely be among the most unusual figures in Arabic fiction to occupy such a function; and no more so than in the way in which he is described by the narrator. His name is ʿAssāf, and he is a taciturn loner; above all, he is known to be a fanatical fighter for the preservation of the fragile environment in which he lives. The fact that he is also generally recognized to be the best hunter in the region and the one person able to survive the worst caprices of the weather makes his relationship with the village an acutely uneasy one. In some ways, his position in this novel and his demeanor towards the people of the village (and theirs towards him) replicates the status of the *ṣaʿālīk,* the vagabond poets of the pre-Islamic period. He has often warned the villagers and their visitors about over-hunting the area, but his words have gone unheard. It is ironic therefore that, when four guests *(ḍuyūf)* arrive by car one day to hunt in the wake of a turbulent village meeting at which the ever-diminishing supply of game has been discussed, ʿAssāf reluctantly agrees to take them far into the desert to a place that only he knows where these men stand a chance of finding some game to hunt. When they start hunting, the men shoot from a car while ʿAssāf walks in the morning sun with his ever-faithful hunting dog. His prowess as a hunter is proved when he manages to bag over twenty birds during the morning while the four men in the car can only catch five. As the sun rises higher in the sky, they all stop for lunch. In an insane gesture, the city sportsmen decide to resume hunting even though it is midday. For some inexplicable reason—perhaps an act of sheer resignation—ʿAssāf agrees. Once again, he sets out on foot while the men ride in the car. A gigantic sandstorm comes up; its portrayal, in both natural and human terms, is one of the most vivid pictures in a work that is full of almost tactile descriptions. The entire group is marooned. Next day, a rescue party arrives to find the men in the car almost dead, but they soon recover when given food and drink. Not so ʿAssāf. After a prolonged search he is found almost buried by sand with his dog covering him to protect him from the vultures circling overhead. Both are dead. When the sorrowful procession returns to the village, the whole community erupts into an expression of grief and anger. ʿAssāf's body is carried into the house of the Mukhtār, and a large number of the men of the village conduct a wake over the body, telling a remarkable series of fourteen tales of varying lengths. Two of them are actually taken from the *Kitāb al-ḥayawān* (Book of animals) by al-Jāḥiẓ (a renowned polymath and model of classical prose style), but the context is completely appropriate since all the tales concern episodes involving animals, birds, dogs, goats, cats, and gazelles. In the morning, the village builder, Abū Zakū—who, as we are told sardonically, also digs graves—goes out to prepare for the burial ceremony. The final pages of the novel are devoted to a description of the funeral procession to the cemetery, which involves not only the entire village and other villagers who have returned from the city for the occasion, but people from the entire surrounding area. As people split up to return to their homes following the burial, a group of men set off for the city to try once more to get the earth dam built, the measure which may help to ward off some of the more capricious attacks by nature on the village of al-Ṭībah.

Let us now examine Munīf's narrative method in greater detail. The individuals and groups just described do indeed participate in this series of events, which is presented in chronological order. However, we have suggested above that the primary focus of this work is not on individuals, but rather on a community involved in a constant and apparently hopeless struggle with the forces of nature. That this is the case becomes clearer when we consider the format of the work. Fully the first third of the book is taken up with a description of the village, its environs, its people, and their perennial problems of sheer survival. Al-Ṭībah, the major focus of the story, is mentioned in the first section,[201] and its people are given a general characterization in the second; in this latter regard, we learn a fact which is to be of some importance to the later stages of the work. "The people in al-Ṭībah know how to turn a story in that incredible way which makes everything seem to be of primary importance. This talent is passed on from father to son. As a result, in other people's eyes they come to seem special and even manage to persuade and exert some influence."[202] In other words, the villagers are masters at telling tales in a particular way, a very prevalent traditional craft in the Arab world, that of the *ḥakawātī*, a figure that has become a

201. Munīf, *Al-Nihāyāt,* 11; trans., 7.
202. Ibid., 13; trans., 8.

favorite narrative device with experimental dramatists.[203] In such a context the narrator finds himself challenged to replicate the villagers' narrative techniques and skills in fulfilling his own function in the novel. As the resort to a series of separate narratives during the wake makes clear, this is a narrative that is very conscious of the power of storytelling.

The third section brings us to the description of the physical environment: "Al-Ṭībah is where the desert starts . . . to the south, the ground gradually loses color and limestone rocks can be seen. It changes by stages until you come close to the horizon, and then there are sand-dunes at first followed by the desert itself."

This emphasis on the impersonal aspects of the village and its surroundings continues for several chapters; we learn *en passant* that the events which are to follow must occur "following the War,"[204] but for the purposes of this novel any further specificity of time is regarded as irrelevant. The unchanged and perhaps unchanging nature of the community's way of life is thus given even greater emphasis. And then, following the description of a particularly crazed year of hunting, comes the first mention of any individual, namely ʿAssāf, at whose door the blame is laid for all this madness: "'That great maniac, ʿAssāf, he's the one who's to blame for all this misery!'"[205] The name and the figure come straight out of the blue, and the narrator follows his normal practice by crafting the story so that it is through the eyes of the village that readers of the novel first encounter this remarkable character. The following section proceeds to give the villagers' version of ʿAssāf's demeanor and role, along with some stories about his relationship with his one-eyed dog.[206]

In the next section time becomes more specific: "There has never been a year like this one before."[207] We are not told what year it is, but the situation has moved from a description that is almost removed from the dictates of time into a particular sequence of events which brings the novel to its climax. The portents for a severe drought are all bad, and, to make things worse, the spring rains

203. Quite apart from the Ḥakawātī troupe that performs among the Palestinian community in Israel and elsewhere, there is the figure of the *ḥakawātī* in Saʿdallāh Wannūs's play, *Mughāmarat ra's al-Mamlūk Jābir* (The adventure of Mamlūk Jābir's head): *al-Maʿrifah* 105 (Nov. 1970); 187–284.

204. Munīf, *Al-Nihāyāt,* 25; trans., 17.

205. Ibid., 27; trans., 19.

206. Ibid., 31; trans., 22–25.

207. Ibid., 35; trans., 25.

come very early and are of little use. As the situation gets worse, the villagers who have moved to the city send provisions of all kinds and eventually return themselves:

> As their feet touched the soil of al-Ṭībah and their eyes fell on the houses, they were filled with a profound sense of sorrow and chided themselves inwardly for waiting so long. The comparison between their life in the city and that of the people in al-Ṭībah gave them a guilty conscience. However, these initial feelings of sadness and regret soon gave way to a powerful desire to do something. Perhaps this time al-Ṭībah would be saved; then it might survive until the dam was built.[208]

It is into this situation of transition from the general to the specific in time and situation that the guests from the city come: "That very afternoon towards the end of summer, four guests arrived in two cars, along with friends of theirs from al-Ṭībah." The stage is set for the series of events that take up the rest of the novel. When the hunting expedition returns to the village with the dead body of ʿAssāf and the men gather at the Mukhtār's house, the narrative mode changes again. Time is now frozen as the series of stories unfolds. These tales, however, are not outside the general framework of the narrative, in that they all concern animals and thus contribute to the general portrait of the villagers and their interests. In fact, several of them have a particular reference to the moral that is to be drawn from ʿAssāf's warnings when he was alive and from his unnecessary death. There is, for example, the story of a man who is frustrated one day when he fails to shoot a mountain goat. On the next day, he finds it again. He cannot understand why the animal is standing absolutely and uncharacteristically still. He shoots, and immediately hears the animal scream. The sight that greets him however is unforgettable:

> One more step, and he was there. His gleaming eyes were riveted on the goat's horns. There was the tiny kid with its head and a small part of its body already out. He watched the mother staggering over to the left but still doing her best to thrust the newborn creature out into the light of the world; she wanted to be rid of it before she died. As the goat looked at her offspring, her eyes were filled with tears![209]

208. Ibid., 50; trans., 39.
209. Ibid., 117; trans., 89.

A similarly repugnant picture of wanton and needless destruction is provided by a story of the local Bey. "Even when he laughed, his eyes had a cruel expression. When he decided to scold or be sarcastic, you felt really scared, but. more than that, your basic instinct was to run away."[210] He brings to the village an open-backed truck with a swivel chair mounted on it, and proceeds to use it to indulge in an orgy of killing. "No words on earth can possibly describe the scene that ensued. As bullets flew all over the place, the whining sound created a terrifying extravaganza of noise in the open desert spaces. The gazelles charged hither and thither in every direction in a state of total panic; and that made the scene all the more horrifying. The Bey was shouting his head off at every salvo; he seemed almost drunk or crazy."[211]

Following this succession of stories, which display man's affection and admiration for animals, the traits which they show towards each other and even mankind, and his disgust at those who abuse and interfere with nature, it is hardly surprising that the death of ʿAssāf, who has all along warned them about such things and their consequences, now assumes proportions which turn his funeral into a collective purging of the community. Such is the emotion created by the all-night vigil, the return of so many of the village children from elsewhere, and the arrival of people from the neighboring regions, that the village women, of whom absolutely nothing is heard throughout the work, appear at the grave site and begin a mournful chanting and dancing; as the narrator informs us, "none of the men objected or interfered while this was going on."[212] As everyone returns to the village, a new resolve is in the air. The departure of some of the men of the village for the city is clearly intended as a sign of a change in resolve. In the Mukhtār's words: "If they agree to have the dam built, I'll come back on top of a bulldozer and begin the job myself. Then al-Ṭībah will begin to appreciate the real meaning of life, instead of having to endure this living death it leads every single day."[213] The men of the village have, of course, been to the city on this mission before. But, as *al-Nihāyāt* (Endings) concludes, we are left with the strong impression that the effects of ʿAssāf's death are too powerful to allow the same thing to happen this time as has

210. Ibid., 160; trans., 122.
211. Ibid., 164; trans., 126.
212. Ibid., 180; trans., 138.
213. Ibid., 183; trans., 140.

happened all the other times. Perhaps his death and its moral will at last bring some relief to the village and its struggling people. This ending may perhaps be the end of a process of beginning.

We have noted above the unusual nature of the environment and community into which Munīf introduces his readers through this remarkably original work of fiction. Beyond that, however, we should observe that this novel introduces into the tradition of contemporary Arabic fiction a feature of considerable originality, one that may, from many points of view, be seen as a reversion to previous narrative types. The narrator of this work is not concerned with the presentation of a single version of events, nor is he particularly bothered by the possibility that his story takes some time to unfold. Like the storytellers of the popular tradition of Arabic culture, the environment into which the act of narrating his tale is placed affords him as much time as he needs. Economy is not a factor, and elaboration and variation are elements to relish. There is no perceived need here to meet any of the pressures and demands of contemporary life that have, in so many societies, made the short story the preferred fictional genre; such demands belong to the life of the city, a milieu far removed from the scenario of this work and from the storytelling world of its narrator. Here the tale is allowed to unfold at its own natural pace. If there are different versions of the details and sequence of particular events in the village community that need to be recorded, then the narrator is at some pains to make sure that each is given its due weight.

In our first chapter, we noted John Updike's discomfort with the narrative technique that Munīf uses in the first volume of his quintet of novels, *Mudun al-milḥ*.[214] Stating that Munīf does not appear to understand the conventions of the novel, he proceeds to compare Munīf's narrative technique with that of a traditional campfire storyteller. One can only express regret that, having so clearly identified the most predominant feature of Munīf's narrative mode in this and other works, Updike allows his own cultural expectations to predominate, and claims some implicit prerogative to prescribe the nature and parameters of the novel within a different culture and process of generic development. Within a historical perspective of trends in the Arabic novel, it seems more reasonable to suggest that it is precisely the introduction of elements from the indigenous narrative tradition, by Munīf and others, that constitutes one of the principal features of innovation in the Arabic novel in recent years.

214. See Updike's review in the *New Yorker*, 17 Oct. 1988; 117.

Ḥikāyat Zahrah, Ḥanān al-Shaykh

The title *Ḥikāyat Zahrah* (Zahrah's tale), whether in Arabic or English, contains within it a creative ambiguity.[215] Is this a story about Zahrah, a girl from the Shiʿite community of southern Lebanon, now living with her family in Beirut as the male members of the Lebanese "nation" proceed to rip it apart during the protracted civil war that begins in 1975? Or is it a tale that has Zahrah as its narrator, one that reveals her own world view to us through the items of narrative that she chooses to include and exclude? In fact, Ḥanān al-Shaykh chooses to combine these possibilities, thereby providing us with not only a most effective fictional account of Lebanese society at a time of extreme crisis, but also an important addition to the still relatively small library of fiction in Arabic written by women. This combination invites—indeed requires—us to look at not only the story being narrated, but also the story of the narration itself. For each of these facets—topic and mode of presentation—presents the reader with a degree of ambiguity and complexity that contributes in no small way to the success of this novel as a reflection of a woman's view of a truly fractured society.

Zahrah is the principal narrator of this tale. It is through the filter of her consciousness that the present time of the narrative is seen. She describes incidents; through conversations, she relays opinions, her own and those of others; and through the linkage of her observations and feelings to flashbacks to earlier times and events, she gives us much insight into her emotional state. In the first part of the narrative, the time frame is an elongated one. Not only is Zahrah the narrative voice in three of the five sections, but narrative detail is used to illustrate her progression from child to adult. The later narrator is well aware of the reason for her mother's trysts, but the younger girl only notes that the two adults have "some obscure dealings" going on.[216] Zahrah depicts the terrible dysfunc-

215. Ḥanān al-Shaykh, *Ḥikāyat Zahrah* (Beirut: Dār al-Nahār, 1980). The title of the English trans., *The Story of Zahra,* trans. Peter Ford (London: Quartet, 1986) does not seem to me fully to capture the creative ambiguities of the original. Indeed, this translation, undertaken "with the author's cooperation," must be considered a heavily abridged version of the original text. It differs from the original in quite significant (and unfortunate) ways, some of which will be discussed during the analysis of the novel.

216. Al-Shaykh, 18; trans., 10. This young narrator also hates the pink rubber doll she has to play with, has a whole series of childish questions to ask about bat droppings, and is thoroughly embarrassed when the pair of lovers laugh at her. See ibid., 10, 16; trans., 2–3, 8.

tions of the Lebanese state through the story of her broken family with its complex web of hopeless relationships. Through the grotesque symbol of her pimples she mutilates her own body and finds satisfaction in doing so. That same body is the playground for a series of men: her cousin Qāsim; Mālik, a friend of her brother and her seducer; her mother's brother Hāshim; and her husband, Mājid, each of whom uses her within the framework of his own set of complexes vis-à-vis this society in the process of total breakdown. Zahrah's narrative in the first part of this book is a narrative of silence. The work opens with silence of the most literal kind: her mother has her hand clasped firmly over her mouth. As we will note below, that very act may serve as a symbol for the first part of the book, a symbol of suppression and oppression, of a quest for refuge—the resort to the bathroom as a place of safety. In the case of Zahrah, the consequence of all this is a descent into madness. That madness is also narrated by Zahrah as narrator. We read it through the language of the narration itself; the repeated act of "seeing with closed eyes" indicates in fact a catatonic state. "As I open my eyes I feel like closing them again. It feels as though salty water is swimming in space. With my eyes closed, all I can see is my father's watch between his fingers as he adjusts the time; and my mother with zucchini tops covering her face and using a sugar dipilatory on her feet."[217] Zahrah can also depict her descent into this state, as when she is able to characterize the sound of her own voice as that of an ostrich. At the outermost level she is also able to reflect on the very nature of the self-image that the narrative is creating.[218]

It is immediately after she has described her "ostrich voice," and declared to her Uncle Hāshim that he is at fault, that Zahrah allows two other narratives to impinge upon her own, those of Hāshim and Mājid. Not only is she telling her own narrative, but, like her narrative forebear, Shahrazād, she is orchestrating those of others as well.[219]

217. Ibid., 98; trans., 78.

218. "The fear that my image might be subverted, the image of which I had made hundreds of copies for distribution to everyone who had known me since childhood." See ibid., 41, 42; trans., 32, 33.

219. It is in this context that the translated version of this novel really transforms the narrative impact in a most unfortunate way. In the original text the two male narrators tell their narratives in the first person without any indication as to identity, thus demanding of the readers that they glean the identity of the narrator from a reading of Uncle Hāshim's attempts at justifying his actions and emotions toward his niece (replicated in Mājid's chapter, although his motivations seem less

These two chapters not only provide interesting commentaries on the motivations of the two men, but also present a different picture of Zahrah herself; here we find ourselves with the rich narrative situation of a female participant narrator allowing two male characters to present, in narrative form, their views on the female character, who also serves as the story's primary orchestrator. The two men also provide a valuable spatial dimension, in that both of them reside in Africa, that "place of transit," of exile and impermanence; Lebanon, by contrast, is entirely Zahrah's narrative domain. Above all, these two chapters in the first part of the work present different views of the same situation, within which readers are challenged to make judgments concerning motivations. This applies most particularly, of course, to the wildly contrasting views of Zahrah and her uncle concerning his behavior towards her while she is staying with him in Africa.

If part one of this novel traces Lebanon's descent into the abyss of civil war through a portrait of a particular family, then the second part places the reader centrally into the conflict and the completely fractured society that is its natural consequence. Time here is of necessity foreshortened, particularly by contrast with the first part. The narrative is transformed accordingly, and the reader is made aware of the fact from the very outset. Whereas in the first part we are concerned with Zahrah's disjointed and often bemused memories of life in Lebanon, the brutality of war has now done its task on the narrator's consciousness as well as on society at large.[220] The first

subtle). In the translated text the inserted titles, "Uncle" and "Husband," remove that process of discovery. This criticism of the translation can, in fact, be applied to all the "headings" that are supplied for the English text. An unanswered question remains as to why such additions to the original text were thought to be necessary.

220. In this connection, the following quotation is of considerable interest and relevance:

> Dr. Antranik Manoukian, the manager of Lebanon's only mental-health clinic, the Asfourieh Hospital for Mental and Nervous Disorders, told a symposium held in Beirut after the summer of 1982 that his patients who were caught in the middle of some of the worst Israeli shelling and bombing actually got better mentally and required less medication and treatment during the fighting than when it was over. This was largely due to the fact that the patients focused all their limited mental faculties on trying to survive the chaos and so actually became healthier. That could be said of most Lebanese to some degree or another, which is why the real mental-health crisis for Lebanon will come when the civil war ends and peace and quiet

voice we encounter is that of the radio announcer, a constant connection with "reality," but Zahrah's voice is also at hand to inform us that she has put on so much weight that she seems like a totally different person; only the pimples on her face provide a clue. While the first part of the novel is a narrative of silence and suppression, the second part portrays an environment of noise; all the demons have been released, and the resulting din is all-pervasive. Zahrah and her mother both scream as they seek refuge in the basement from the continuous stream of bomb attacks; and Zahrah herself screams in ecstasy as the sniper makes love to her, and she invokes the name of her father as she does so.[221] As the conflicts within the society in the first part of the novel become open warfare in the second, so does the pent-up tension inside Zahrah find some release in a relationship with a figure who personifies the war, Sami the sniper. As she herself notes in her narrative, the pimples that have marred her face—the primary visual symbol of the tensions of the first part—begin to disappear: "I still wore no make-up; the explosions of war had successfully obliterated the ones on my face."[222]

The situation in which the narrator of a work of fiction is also a participant in the action of the narrative is one where the games of irony can be pursued with particular relish. Such is certainly the case in *Ḥikāyat Zahrah.* Beyond the issues that we have just explored, there are two other aspects that render the role of the narrator in this tale that much more complex and therefore interesting. In the context of the "reliability" of the narrator, Zahrah the participant's madness, as conveyed by Zahrah the narrator, is clearly an interesting dimension to the story. Following the second abortion that results from her affair with Mālik, she is taken to a mental hospital where she is given ECT, electro-convulsive therapy, a treatment about which there is still considerable controversy within the psychiatric community. What is especially interesting in the context of Zahrah's tale is that "a vast medical literature provides strong evidence that ECT causes permanent brain damage, including loss of

---

> return. Only then, when people let down their guard and take stock of all they have lost, will they truly become crazy. Until then, many Lebanese won't simply survive, they may even thrive.

See Thomas L. Friedman, *From Beirut to Jerusalem* (New York: Anchor, 1989), 45.

221. Al-Shaykh, 147, 176; trans., 116, 137.

222. Ibid., 174; trans., 137.

memory and catastrophic deterioration of personality."[223] While it is clear that Zahrah is not alone among her relatives in having been treated for mental illness, the real issue raised by the novel is that madness is a condition defined by society. The very question "What is madness?" is one that was a central concern in the writings of Michel Foucault and that has been posed in the works of several modern Arab littérateurs, Adūnīs and Najīb Maḥfūẓ among them.[224] In a search for terminology that will be both more accurate and less socially prejudicial (analogous with "hearing-impaired" for "deaf") the term mentally ill or mentally disturbed is now often preferred. The narrative makes it clear that Zahrah is indeed ill and disturbed, but it also suggests strongly that the disturbing agent is not merely a chemical process inside the brain. Zahrah's narrative makes a direct connection between her ECT treatment and Mālik's duplicity.[225] Beyond that, there is, of course, the larger question of exactly who it is in this story who is mad or disturbed. As noted above, the novel strongly implies that the narrator's account of her own mental illness, the product of a sick society and family situation, is replaced in the second part by a more lucid account of the entire society going mad. Varieties of "disturbance," in other words, serve a crucial function in the narrative contract of this novel.

A second issue involving irony and the narrator concerns the ending of the novel, always an interesting topic of discussion. Of all possible endings, death is, as Frank Kermode notes in *The Sense of an Ending,* the most terminal. On reading the concluding page of *Ḥikāyat Zahrah* we have the strong impression that Zahrah has been killed, but it is Zahrah the narrator who describes the scene. "He has killed me," she says, in itself an unusual sentence for a narrator to utter, and then goes on to describe how "I see rainbows in the white heavens coming towards me in terrifying profusion."[226] That same

223. See "Week in Review," *New York Times,* 1 Aug. 1993, 17. In this context Zahrah's self-analysis ("From that point I began to appreciate that I was a difficult person to talk to, as though I had some kind of unmoving substance inside me") is especially interesting. See Al-Shaykh, 133; trans., 108.

224. For example, Michel Foucault, *Madness and Civilization* (New York: Pantheon, 1965). For Adūnīs's use of the concept, see Kamāl Abū Deeb, "The Perplexity of the All-knowing: A study of Adonis," *Mundus Artium* 10, no. 1 (1977): 163–81; for Najīb Maḥfūẓ, see "Hams al-junūn," in *Hams al-junūn* (Cairo: Maktabat Miṣr, 1938 [?]), 4; English trans.: "The Whisper of Madness," trans. Akef Abadir and Roger Allen in *God's World* (Minneapolis: Bibliotheca Islamica, 1973), 47.

225. Al-Shaykh, 40; trans., 32.

226. Ibid., 227; trans., 184.

narrator who oversees Zahrah's narration of her own madness (and, incidentally, who can enter her brother, Aḥmad's, mind to describe his attitude towards her)[227] presumably enables her to indulge in the ultimate narrative act, the description of her own death. The creative ambiguities of the situation can perhaps be best illustrated by the fact that, as Zahrah dies, she describes herself as closing her eyes, which may never have been open before; when she is describing her mental disturbance at its height, she can say: "No sooner do I open my eyes than I want to close them again."[228]

This complex narrative framework is used to portray a Lebanese Shiʿite family from the south. Zahrah the narrator makes use of the nexus of familial relationships to provide the reader with a picture that is a reflection of the ills of the larger society. Of those relationships the most significant by far is that with her mother. It hardly needs mentioning that the mother-daughter relationship has been the object of much discussion within the realms of psychology and that recent trends in feminist thought have emphasized the problematic nature of the young woman's attempts to "escape" the bonds that link her to her mother and find her own individuality within a societal framework that has been dominated by male values.[229] When we consider the nature of the relationship between Zahrah and her mother—quite apart from her relationships with her male relatives—the role of the mother-daughter relationship in this narrative becomes especially significant. The linkage is expressed through the image of the orange and the navel, one that reflects not only a close proximity in general but also the particular fetal bond that connects mother and child. In view of the narrator's effective portrayal of Zahrah's mental states, it is thus especially significant that she makes frequent reference in her narrative to her desire to assume the fetal position. In spite of continuous references to this orange-navel image throughout the novel, its implications are subverted at every turn. It is perhaps almost natural for the youthful narrator at the beginning of the novel to express a temporary "hatred" of her mother for a particular incident. But this mother takes her daughter on her trysts, a sequence of events symbolized by the repulsive pink

227. Ibid., 183; trans., 143.

228. Ibid., 227, 98; trans., 184, 78.

229. I must express here my gratitude to Sabah al-Ghandour and Mary Tahan (Univ. of Pennsylvania) whose detailed (and as yet unpublished) studies of this and other fictional works by Arab women authors has contributed greatly to my appreciation of this aspect of *Ḥikāyat Zahrah*.

rubber doll she is given by her mother's lover. The true extent of her feelings finds much more vivid expression much later in the novel when the reader learns that, in spite of the fact that Zahrah is the best student in her school, she turns in a blank page when asked to write a composition on the topic of "And paradise lies under the mother's feet."[230] While it is the name of her mother (along with her brother, Aḥmad) that Zahrah invokes when she is shot at the end of the narrative, it is the same mother whose trysts are the direct cause of a potentially catastrophic episode in Zahrah's childhood. She is savagely beaten by her father, who wants to find out the truth about her mother's love affair; as the child Zahrah expresses her wish to be as close to her mother as the orange and navel, she hears her mother lie and learns a lesson that she will use frequently herself, namely to "escape" to the bathroom.[231] When a young girl growing up in a thoroughly traditional, male-dominated society is presented with a model of maternal love that is so fraught with conflicting ideals and emotions, it is hardly surprising that she should be somewhat "disturbed," the more so if there is a family history of mental illness. When Zahrah has discovered that she is pregnant, one can only gauge the extent of her anger when her mother—whose love affair has provided her with a very early education on matters sexual—offers her hints on how to make herself more attractive. As Zahrah herself notes, living with such a person in Lebanon itself would be intolerable; in such a context, Africa becomes, like the bathroom, a place of escape and refuge.[232] In summary then, the fluctuating and unstable nature of this most elemental of relationships—mother and daughter—becomes in this narrative the most powerful indication of the societal catastrophe into which it is placed.[233]

There is one emotion that finds even these two female charac-

230. Al-Shaykh, 211; trans., 168. The quotation is from the *ḥadīth* (traditions) recording the statements and actions of the Prophet Muḥammad.

231. Ibid., 226, 18–20; trans., 183, 11–12.

232. Ibid., 216; trans., 173. Note too that, as Zahrah is about to shout for help through the window, she has to clear away some orange peels—the vestiges of the fruit.

233. The power of this relationship, once again in the Lebanese context, is captured in a more positive light by the statement of Munā Saʿūdī: "For months now I have been feeling a tremendous longing for death, or rather to put an end to this continuity, but the lucid presence of the great woman that is my mother forbids me to do anything about it, her love is the only authority to judge my action." Munā Saʿūdī, quoted in *Women of the Fertile Crescent,* ed. Kamal Boullata (Washington, D.C.: Three Continents, 1978), 25.

ters in complete unanimity: a visceral hatred of Ibrāhīm, the father-figure to the family. I use the phrase "father-figure" because the personage that emerges from the portrait provided by Zahrah the narrator is, perhaps not unnaturally, a caricature. The aspect presented by Zahrah's father to the outside world is of a hopeless pedant totally enslaved by time. The picture she paints of his appearance and behavior—the uniform, the Hitler-like moustache, and the way he rings a bell upon entering the house—is withering. Inside the family home he is both tyrant and cuckold. He beats and disparages his wife and daughter, showing the clearest favoritism towards his son, Aḥmad:

> He would always insist on ringing the bell before entering the house.
>
> "How are you, Daddy?"
>
> "Where's Aḥmad?"[234]

His wife repays this treatment by refusing to bear him any more children, to the extent of aborting a fetus and leaving it in a dish on public display. With similar defiance Zahrah chooses to invoke the image of her father while she is experiencing orgasm with the sniper, hoping that he would hear her screams of pleasure and see her sprawled on the floor. As she notes in a powerful paragraph, the war and its societal consequences have rendered his voice and his belt impotent. And yet, once Zahrah has come to accept the doctor's verdict that she is pregnant, all the old concerns come rushing back in a passage of genuine verbal savagery in which Zahrah the narrator records her father's indictment of the effect of her mother's earlier antics with her lover on her own daughter's behavior.[235] How truly ironic, then, that it is the very father-figure who, while condemning his own son's activities during the war, launches into a ringing defense of Lebanon as it has been.[236]

The other offspring of these parents is the son, Aḥmad. In spite of the fact that both parents show him preferences of all kinds—in food, in concern about success at school, in anxiety about his activ-

234. Al-Shaykh, 15, 27. It should be noted that the English trans. completely misinterprets this important exchange between Zahrah and her father by omitting the reference to "Daddy" and thus making it seem as though it is the father who says "How are you?" See trans., 7, and for the other passage, 19.

235. Al-Shaykh, 176, 187, 211; trans., 137, 147–48, 169.

236. Ibid., 138; trans., 112.

ities during the war, Zahrah clearly feels a sisterly love and affection towards him. Aḥmad's behavior during the war tests that affection severely. Utterly spoiled, listless, and without aspirations, Aḥmad is everyone's nightmare of the person who gets sucked into the vortex of conflict because for him life has no real purpose; there is nothing better to do. Indeed, such is his delight in the killing, stealing, and drug-dealing that are an inevitable part of the sectarian strife that he actually wants the war to continue.[237] The debauching effects of this and other similar conflicts are graphically illustrated as Zahrah upbraids her brother for masturbating openly in her presence while attempting to justify his heroic participation in the fighting through a hopelessly jumbled understanding of the political dimensions involved.[238] As a young man completely out of control during the Lebanese civil war, and relishing the sordid opportunities that it provides, he comes to symbolize the petulant and domineering attitudes within the society that, having helped engender the war, now sustain it.[239] In that attribute Aḥmad can be linked fairly directly to his mother's brother, Uncle Hāshim, whose own political escapades have led him into exile in Africa.[240]

For Zahrah, Africa presents itself as a means of escape from the family atmosphere that has driven her to madness and most especially from the tortuous relationship with her mother. She travels to an unnamed country with a substantial Lebanese community, one where political exiles become part of a society that replicates the commercial and societal ethic of the homeland to a large degree.[241] The African segment of the narrative is presented from three perspectives, those of Zahrah herself, her uncle, and her husband. Her

237. Ibid., 183; trans., 144.

238. Ibid., 180; trans., 140–41.

239. Those attitudes are explored in detail in two significant studies of women's writings about war: Accad, *Sexuality and War,* and Cooke, *War's Other Voices.* Both works contain lengthy analyses of *Ḥikāyat Zahrah.*

240. Compare, e.g., Zahrah's account of her Aunt Wafā''s description of her uncle as a youth: Al-Shaykh, 22–23; trans., 13–14.

241. Several West African nations house very large Lebanese communities. In the Ivory Coast, e.g., "80 per cent of the buildings belong to Lebanese, as well as more than 70 per cent of the wholesale and 50 per cent of the retail trade." What is even more significant in the context of this novel, "since large-scale fighting broke out in Lebanon in 1975, 'other' Lebanese have arrived here. . . . Some of them give the impression of coming here for a rest between spells of fighting in Beirut. They're terribly arrogant." See "The Ivory Coast's Lebanese scapegoats face hostility," *Manchester Guardian Weekly,* 25 Mar. 1990.

relationship with Mājid, her husband, is the less complex of the two relationships, clearly representing class distinctions within Lebanese society. His reasons for marrying Zahrah are disarmingly straightforward and are candidly expressed from the outset. His chapter opens with the statement that he married her without even knowing her. To the son of a shoeshine, she represents a higher class; and she is a female body available to him whenever he wishes.[242] While Zahrah's bizarre conduct is a complete mystery to him, his attitudes and conduct are completely predictable, and his account of the relationship—such as it is—is the direct obverse of Zahrah's. Far more complex is the relationship between Zahrah and her uncle, one in which an attempt to reconcile the past of both nation and family with the chaotic complexities of the present are reflected into two conflicting visions. While Uncle Hāshim's attitude toward Africa, its people, and its Lebanese residents, is clearly ambivalent, to put it mildly, his continuing love for his homeland is of a frightening intensity. Before his attentions to Zahrah begin to go beyond those of uncle to niece, she can describe his political attitudes as being "idealistic": "At first I didn't bother arguing with him or paying attention, but he kept talking about politics all the time. I came to realize how desperate he was to go back home. Here he was in Africa, thinking all the time about a symbolic homeland, imagining that it was the real thing."[243] That this relationship is doomed to be problematic is emphasized when Zahrah indicates that her uncle's behavior is as bad as her father's, whereupon she heads for the bathroom.[244]

Uncle Hāshim's narrative of Zahrah's stay in Africa is in some ways an inverse reflection of hers, but in others, it differs significantly. It accurately duplicates her own reading of his motivations by illustrating both his nostalgia for his homeland and his political fanaticism. His is a narrative of memories, of a fondly recalled past that has been demolished, a past that may have provided some of his life's most notable moments but that has since turned into a nightmare present—the one that Zahrah's arrival brings into his isolated existence. Small wonder then that the relationship of uncle and niece should be confused and ambiguous. For her, Hāshim's attentions go far beyond normal avuncular affection into the realm of sexual abuse, pure and simple. For him, Zahrah's lengthy letters

242. Al-Shaykh, 89; trans., 69.
243. Ibid., 23; trans., 15.
244. Ibid., 29; trans., 21.

have always represented a crucial linkage to the country and society for which he continually longs; her arrival in the country of his exile represents direct contact with that which he misses the most, and from the outset he clings to it with all his being.[245] As the chapter that he narrates draws to a close, he proceeds to pour out his feelings towards Zahrah, whose physiognomy so resembles his sister's and his own. Sending her a ticket to travel to Africa, he declares, was the only genuinely successful activity he has ever undertaken; the time he has spent in her company represents the only real relationship he has ever had. Perhaps the closest he comes to anything resembling an admission that his attentions have transcended the bounds of acceptable conduct is when he confides that, were she not his niece, he would have wanted to marry her. As Zahrah withdraws into silence and then retreats to the bathroom, his inability to comprehend her pleas seems inexplicable and inexcusable. Hāshim and Zahrah, male and female, uncle and niece, Lebanon's past and present, have encountered each other, and the result has been misunderstanding and abuse. The chapter and its functions on the symbolic level have no closure.[246]

The second part of this novel finds Zahrah recovering some of her mental equilibrium as the civil war rages around her. Her mode of confrontation with the realities of the conflict takes the form of an attempt to interrupt the fighting on a purely local level and with a strictly personal gesture. She begins a relationship with Sāmī, the sniper, "the god of death," hoping to put a stop to his activities. She permits him to use, indeed to abuse, her body; in fact, their first encounter constitutes a rape. But through her meetings with this personification of death, who is fully prepared to exploit her body for his own sexual gratification, Zahrah herself finds a release from all the tensions that have built up inside her, most notably those resulting from her familial situation. Her ascent to the roof in order to meet the sniper is depicted as something akin to a personal liberation. Zahrah the narrator gives us an account of her first real experience of sexual pleasure, tellingly linked to the past: "In the sound of my screams of pleasure there was all the agony and illness of days gone by when I would huddle in some corner or other or else in the

245. Large segments of Hāshim's reflections about his homeland (and its songs) and about his political views are omitted from the English trans.; see, e.g., Al-Shaykh, 72–75.

246. Ibid., 75–78 ; trans., 55–60.

bathroom, clutching myself, desiring all the while to go back into the womb like a fetus. I found it exhausting because I no longer felt in charge of my own body. . . . Now my entire body was shivering in ecstasy for the first time in thirty years."[247] However, that link to the past is too strong to be so easily severed. The return of Zahrah's mother to Beirut, from the comparative security of the south, coincides with her own discovery that she is four months pregnant. Zahrah learns the news at a clinic specializing in male circumcision; in this narrative of Lebanese society even this most feminine of mysteries is exposed in the context of a masculine rite of passage. Abortion is out of the question, something that the sniper finds hard to believe. He talks to Zahrah about marriage, but it is a bluff. As a sniper with a civil war to fight, families and children cannot be part of the agenda. By shooting Zahrah he aborts her fetus in his own particular way. As she sees rainbows in a sky of white clouds rushing towards her, the tale of her life, of abuse and abortion, comes to a close. Meanwhile the war continues. . . .

That this novel is rich in symbols is already clear from this brief account of some of its narrative features. The orange and navel, the pimples on Zahrah's face, and the pink doll, all assume larger functions in the context of Zahrah's account of her attempts to face a reality with no logic. Geography also plays a large symbolic role: Africa as exile and escape, and "the South" as haven of Lebanese Shiʿite values and customs. Other spatial features have an equally significant function. The most obvious, of course, is the bathroom, which, for both mother and daughter, serves as a refuge "from time and place," a place where one can curl up and replicate the comforting warmth of the mother's womb. Similarly psychological in its symbolic potential is the frequent reference in this narrative to looking at things through windows. At one point, Zahrah expresses the desire to become a window herself, "a window like this one or any other, through which people can look and find everything outside to be in motion, while the window itself stays silent and in place"; later, she notes that she has become obsessed with looking out of the window.[248] But one of the most important, as well as one of the most culturally specific, symbols is that of the *qarīnah,* a kind of guardian spirit that impinges upon Zahrah's unconscious self in interesting ways. The first mention of this figure occurs when Zahrah has

247. Ibid., 166–67; trans., 131.
248. Ibid., 121, 169; trans., 99, 134.

locked herself in the bathroom in her uncle's apartment in Africa. Recalling her affair with Mālik and her mother's skill at stripping before men, she returns in a flashback to her childhood in Lebanon. At this stage, the *qarīnah* is a frightening, nightmarish entity, connected with life in the south of Lebanon and its personification, her grandfather. As Zahrah recounts her growing up and the changes she undergoes in the process, this figure becomes more explicit, assuming a directly sexual function in her decision to go to the sniper.[249]

Beyond the skill with which Ḥanān al-Shaykh has constructed this narrative and its symbolic richness, we must also make mention of the language that she has adopted and, in particular, the skillful interweaving of different levels of discourse. As noted in previous chapters, the issue of language use is one that has concerned (or perhaps, beset) the novelist writing in Arabic from the outset. In this novel Ḥanān al-Shaykh provides a completely authentic mingling of the standard written language for descriptions with a Lebanese colloquial dialect for conversations and introspection, and the blend of the two affords the narrative an authenticity that binds it closely to its topic and location. It hardly needs to be pointed out that the profusion of references in the text to Lebanese culture—its songs, its folkloric images, and its political history (large segments of which are regrettably excluded from the English version of the text)—adds a valuable further dimension to the atmosphere engendered by the language itself. In addition to these modes of linking language with the world that the author wishes to create, we can also point to the way in which particular words and phrases are used to illustrate the narrator's mental state. The "triggers" which lead into flashbacks are particularly successfully handled, but perhaps most remarkable of all is the use of repeated verbs (such as "seeing" and "fearing") to reflect the obsessive nature of Zahrah's consciousness at certain points.[250]

Like Ḥalīm Barakāt's novel *ʿAwdat al-ṭāʾir ilā al-baḥr,* analyzed above, Ḥanān al-Shaykh's *Ḥikāyat Zahrah,* is linked to a period in history—the Lebanese civil war—that appears, at least thus far (1993), to have been transcended. However, beyond the specificities of place and time that it manages to depict with such authenticity and artistry, the novel incorporates other themes within its narrative framework. Of those the most obvious is the status of women in society in general and in the Middle East in particular. This novel

249. Ibid., 155–56, 173; trans., 122–23, 137.

250. Ibid., 37, 98, 159; trans., 29, 78, 126.

represents an important step in the developing process whereby Arab women are using fictional genres to portray their status, their emotions, and their aspirations in ways that are increasingly frank and experimental. Beyond these particular concerns, however, it needs to be said that the overarching subjects of this novel: mankind's violence towards his fellow creatures, the complexities of sexuality, the agonies of exile, are not confined to Lebanon. Ḥanān al-Shaykh's novel thus carries a message that is both continuing and universal.

Nazīf al-ḥajar, by Ibrāhīm al-Kūnī [Kawnī]

As the contemporary novel has continued its search for modes of discourse through which to reflect and advocate the continuing processes of change, writers have resorted to a variety of technical options: manipulation of point of view and even attempts to eliminate it altogether; different styles and structures, including poetry; and the fracturing of chronological sequences—these are just a few examples. Many Arab authors have made use of these techniques in creating their novels, and, as such, their works have joined the repertoire of world fiction, albeit at a certain chronological distance from trends in Western literary traditions. As we have suggested above, the fact that Najīb Maḥfūẓ can be dubbed the Dickens or Balzac of Cairo in 1988 may be considered a somewhat crass assertion by Western writers of such patterns of influence. Arab writers who would look within their own culture for modes of expression that are authentic and original, for ways of contributing to the development of the novel genre on a broader scale, have clearly faced a difficult task, most particularly when it comes to transporting their work across the boundaries of their own culture.

Different patterns of history and of geographical space and intertextual plays on traditional modes of narration have served as successful vehicles for new and original voices such as those of Jamāl al-Ghīṭānī and ʿAbd al-raḥmān Munīf, whose novels we have analyzed above. The figure of ʿAssāf in Munīf's *al-Nihāyāt* assumes mythic proportions in his struggle and self-sacrifice on behalf of the community; the village of al-Ṭībah becomes symbolic of every community fighting a continuing battle with the encroaching desert. There are no such villages, however, in Ibrāhīm al-Kūnī's *Nazīf al-ḥajar* (When rocks bleed, 1990). The geographical environment into which he places his readers is one where villages and settlements of any kind are as remote as they can possibly be. Indeed the proliferation of place-names in the novel—the massifs of Messak Settafet and Messak Mellet, the regions of Tassīlī, Tamanrasset, and Fezzān, and towns such as Tombuktu, Ghāt, Agadez, and Kano—serves as a realistic evocation of a region and landscape that are as unfamiliar to most Arab readers as they are to those of other languages: the desert wastes of southwestern Libya and the regions in all directions with which the nomads who inhabit this harshest of habitats maintain intermittent contact.[251] This is to be a novel of solitude, of isolation. The environment is cruel, capricious, and uncompromising. Human beings can only survive its hardships by establishing and maintaining the subtlest of balances between themselves and the animal species that have adapted themselves to its exigencies: camels, gazelles, and goats. Needless to say, this process, and the trials that it involves, engender bonds between humans and animals that become the subject of poems and tales; depictions of human and animal virtues often fuse the two species into a unified vision through descriptions and narratives that assume mythic proportions, as continual repetition and renewal turn them into the deepest possible reflection of their people's mores, fears, and aspirations. In such tales humans and animals often share attributes and even exchange them. In the particular case of al-Kūnī's work, the story engendered through a contemporary novelistic exemplar of such an environment manages to evoke all kinds of intertextual references to the cultural heritage of the Arab people. What is of particular interest in the context of the Arabic novel in general is the unique way in which this story manages to reflect the interweaving of the Arab and African cultural traditions through contacts within the region represented by the modern nation-states of Libya, Algeria, Mali, Niger, and Nigeria; as the area is described in the novel itself, "in the great Sahara itself . . . from Ghadames to Tombuktu and from Jabal Nafūsah to Agadez."[252]

The narrative of this novel is concerned with the consequences of a rupture in this delicate balance of forces between human beings

251. For these and other place-names found in the text, see the *Times Atlas of the World* (Boston: Houghton Mifflin, 1967), map 85, squares A4–7.

252. Ibrāhīm al-Kūnī, *Nazīf al-ḥajar* (When the stone bleeds) (London: Riad El-Rayyes, 1990), 51. Al-Kūnī (b. 1948) is a Libyan journalist who has studied at the Gorky Institute in Moscow. He is now devoting himself full time to writing and has produced three collections of short stories and four novels. The final page of this novel notes that it was completed in Moscow in May 1989.

and nature. It is the detailing of the events surrounding this rupture that provides the central sequential story of the novel, but the need to explore the background and causations involved requires a whole series of flashbacks ("analepses" in Genette's terminology) which break up the narrative, most particularly in the first half of the book, and represent by far the largest segment of the work as a whole. The reader is thus provided with clear indications as to the nature of the balance favored by the narrator of the story. As if to underscore such lines of interpretation, the events that occur at those points in time which serve as triggers for the variety of analepses (and, in some cases, prolepses as well)—in other words, the most recent chronologically—are told in the past tense. It is at the points where the novel's discourse is at its most gnomic and mythical—where the narrator records a sense of what is normal, expected, and in accord with the laws of nature—that the present tense is consistently invoked:

> In the desert noises are deceptive and illusory; at dawn and twilight the very silence can make a distant sound seem so close that it sounds just like a loud yell.
>
> There are no secrets in the desert, however isolated you are.
>
> The key factors are endurance and patience. Endurance, that's the secret to it all.
>
> In the desert human beings die from one of two opposites: thirst or flood.
>
> Of all desert creatures gazelles are the most sensitive and alert. They can smell the scent of a human being at a considerable distance. The only time they can be spotted is at dawn or on days when the wind drops to nothing and the air is completely still. . . . Gazelles can show enormous endurance in adversity. Their mode of running is different from that of all other animals. Unlike the wild sheep, for example, which takes to the rocky hillsides when chased, the gazelle doesn't zigzag but moves over the desert wastes in a straight line. It believes that any infringement of the rules of the chase constitutes an offense against decency, something that invites censure. Rather than using crafty stratagems the gazelle opts for sheer heroism. Tricks and deceit are eschewed as it chooses to adhere to the rules of chivalry.[253]

253. Al-Kūnī, *Nazīf al-ḥajar,* 15–16, 36, 69, 85, 103–4. The animal that is the principal focus of this novel is called in Arabic *wadān.* Most Arabic dictionaries do not

As the above quotations make clear, the narrator of this novel is thoroughly familiar with the desert and its species. Quite apart from the set of inherited values that emerges clearly from these segments of the story he has to tell, the descriptions of the scenery—the mountains and valleys, the floods and flora they produce, the different lights according to the time of day—suggest that we are reading the text of a storyteller who is anxious to present the contemporary reader with images and descriptions that will afford a clear link to the mythic ideals created by the corpus of pre-Islamic poetry in Arabic.[254]

While the narrator provides the story with a structure through a skillful weaving between these modes of discourse and their different time frames, the novel also possesses an "outer" structuring mechanism in the form of a series of quotations culled from a wide variety of sources: the Qur'ān and the Bible, Sophocles and Ovid, the mystical writings of al-Niffarī (d. 965), and the observations of Herodotus and Henri Lhote. Those that preface the work as a whole are taken from the Qur'ān: "There is no creature on the earth, nor any bird flying in the sky, but that they are nations like yourselves" [Sūrah 6, v. 38] and, from the Old Testament of the Bible, the story of Cain's murder of his brother Abel and God's curse upon Cain: "And now you are cursed from the ground, which has opened its mouth to receive your brother's blood from your hand. When you till the ground, it will no longer yield to you its strength; you will be a fugitive and a wanderer on the earth" [Genesis, Chapter 4, vv. 11–12].

Title and prefatory quotations thus provide a particularly gloomy impression with which to broach the text itself. With relatively few words, the opening paragraphs manage to cluster together many of the narrative features that we have been describing:

---

list it, but R. Dozy's *Supplement aux dictionnaires arabes,* vol. 2 (Leiden: E. J. Brill, 1927), W-D-N, provides the answer. The word is of Berber origin and designates the wild sheep known in both English and French as the mouflon. Henri Lhote, whose name is cited by Al-Kūnī in the text has the following to say about this animal: "The mouflon, especially, seems to have played an important role in the beliefs of the ancient Saharan populations. Pictures of this beast are to be seen in profusion on the painted walls of the Tassili." See Henri Lhote, *The Search for the Tassili Frescoes,* trans. Alan Houghton Brodrick (London: Hutchinson, 1959), 120–21. Perhaps the animal depicted in the illustration between pages 112 and 113 (along with a god) is a "wadān."

254. I would refer interested readers to the translations of a selection of these poems (and an excellent introduction to their use of imagery) in *Desert Tracings,* ed. Michael Sells (Middletown, Conn.: Wesleyan Univ. Press, 1989).

> It is only when he starts praying that the billy-goats feel like butting each other in front of him. As evening falls and the blazing disk high up in the sky begins its daily farewell, threatening all the while to return the next day and complete the task of burning to a cinder everything it hasn't managed to burn today, Asūf digs his hands into the valley's sands and starts to do the sunset prayer.
>
> He heard the sound of the engine in the distance and decided to give God his due quickly so that he'd be finished before the Christians arrived. In recent years, he'd got used to welcoming them to the valley to look at the wall-carvings.

The burning sun is a constant, the animals have their habits, and a solitary human being fulfills his obligations as a Muslim. However, the balance represented by these "constants" is about to be disturbed: a car is approaching (an event couched in the past time noted above), and Asūf assumes that tourists are coming. According to his world view, people are not differentiated by nationality or even by their status as foreigners; the entire "other" is designated by the term "Christians." In fact, Asūf is mistaken in his assumption, and the error will cost him his life. The car contains two men who are initially described but not named. They are not interested in the wall-carvings, but in hunting animals for meat. They have heard stories concerning Asūf's prowess as a hunter, and in particular as a hunter of wild sheep; they want him to help them find some. Eventually we learn that the name of the avid hunter (and meat-eater) is Qābīl Ādam (Qābīl is Arabic for Cain), and the import of the prefatory quotation cited above becomes clearer, particularly when Asūf detects "a strange gleam" in Qābīl's eye.[255] Asūf informs the two men that wild sheep are exceedingly difficult to track down, but they are not to be deterred. Taking Asūf with them, they venture far into the desert. As Asūf becomes more and more despondent and stubborn, Qābīl's satanic nature comes to the fore. Faced with his own unnatural craving for flesh and the continuing obduracy of Asūf, Qābīl crucifies the bedouin on a rock and, in a final act of lunatic frenzy, slits his throat.

This sequence of events has taken us to the conclusion of the novel on one level. Bearing in mind the link between the figure of Qābīl in the story and the initial quotation, it is clearly an important one. Yet the richness of the narrative comes to a far greater degree from the process of providing the background to the motivations of

255. Al-Kūnī, *Nazīf al- ḥajar,* 21.

these two men, whose tragic confrontation constitutes such a powerful allegory of the clash between tradition and modernity and, in more environmental terms, of the terrifying ability of technology to disturb the delicate balance in the ecological system. The clash of values acted out in the conflict between Asūf and Qābīl is explored in great detail through the flashbacks that make up the core of this novel. The time frame for these retrospectives is the entire life of Asūf, a gauge that is linked both to events within the narrative itself ("several years after his father's death," and "four years of drought") and to external factors, the dragooning of Libyan youth by the Italians to fight in Ethiopia, for example, and the advent of Western companies to drill for oil.[256]

The first flashback is linked to the issue of foreign tourists mentioned in the opening paragraphs. While grazing his goats in the desert valleys, Asūf has discovered a large carving engraved into the walls of a valley: it depicts a veiled human figure, "the gigantic lord of the valley, with his sacred wild sheep standing erect by his side contemplating the distant horizon."[257] Here, of course, is a perfect symbol of a pre-Islamic monument, showing man and animal in a state of harmony. An Italian archeologist has come to inspect the site and has instructed Asūf to serve as its custodian (*ʿassās,* a word that also implies bodyguard). Tourists who now come intermittently to stare at the carving in wonder are met by a bemused Asūf, who also faces towards the monument as he prays not towards Mecca, but in the direction of this rock-carved idol, a gesture which—in his eyes, at least—is seen by the pagan god and his animal companion as a pleasing gesture. This utterly heterodox blend of the pagan and the Islamic is one of many themes explored in the next series of flashbacks, which constitute the central portion of the novel. It begins immediately after the arrival of the two men, who remain unnamed at this point, and explores Asūf's childhood, his relationship to his father, and his education (the last two being essentially one and the same thing). His father teaches him to recite the Qur'ān, but also makes sure that he knows about the power of the *jinn* and the efficacy of the amulets provided by the fortune-tellers in Kano and Tombuktu. He also shows his son how to deal with animals and how to hunt each species. As he tells his son on one occasion, "Do you think animals don't understand just because they can't talk like you?

256. Ibid., 57, 86; 89, 103.
257. Ibid., 18.

They're much more intelligent than you or me!" When accompanying his father on these educational journeys into the desert, he hears his father recite traditional *mawwāl* poems that extol the virtues of the solitary life:

> The desert is a treasure. a reward for those who would
> escape a life of slavery, the agony of servitude;
> There one finds contentment, oblivion, and the heart's
> desire.[258]

One particular story that the father tells has clearly affected his entire outlook on life. The wild sheep, as he has taught his son, is a particularly difficult animal to hunt; it is "the spirit of the mountains."[259] One day, having tracked one of these creatures to a spot from which it cannot escape, he aims his antique rifle, but watches in disbelief as the animal throws itself off a high rock rather than be shot. If this story appears remarkable, Asūf's mother has an even more amazing tale about his father to impart to her son, the one she is forced to reveal in the face of her son's continuing questions as to why his father refuses to train him to hunt wild sheep. Before Asūf was born, we learn, the father was hunting a wild sheep high up in the mountains, lost his footing, and found himself hanging from a precipice with no hope of rescue. It was the very same wild sheep he was hunting that lowered its horns and rescued him. Since that time, Asūf's father has kept a solemn pledge not to hunt that particular animal.[260] The linkage of this animal species, the one depicted on the rock carving, to this family is thus a particularly close one.

Solitude and bare survival are the needs of Asūf's father and the values that he passes on to his son. They are not, however, the values of Asūf's mother, who constantly complains about the very solitude that her husband so relishes and the lack of human contact that will condemn her son to a similar existence. It is this solitude and the father's fear of being captured by the marauding Italians that keep the family far out in the desert and leads eventually to the father's death. The narrator's structuring of his tale has already provided the reader with several premonitions: that, in spite of his solemn pledge, the father will go out hunting wild sheep, that he will not

258. Ibid., 59, 28.
259. Ibid., 30.
260. Ibid., 53.

return to his family, and that his death will be unpleasant.[261] His father not only breaks his pledge but, if Asūf's tracking instincts are correct, has gone against every lesson he ever taught his son by grabbing the animal by the horns. The son finds his father's corpse high in the mountains where the animal has dragged him, and the linking of this death to a previous one, and of human to animal, cannot be clearer: "This crazed animal had broken the old man's neck, just as earlier on he himself had broken that other wild sheep's neck when it committed suicide."[262] It is now the task of the son to take charge of keeping the family alive. As his mother forces him to learn how to barter with passing caravans and to talk to strangers—something he has never done—and calls him a "little girl" for being so utterly shy and inept, he allows himself to express a feeling of rancor towards his dead father "who had brought him up to be so afraid of people."[263]

It is against this carefully constructed cultural backdrop and in the particular context of Asūf's almost paralyzing fear of human contact that the next interpolation of the Qābīl narrative—with its conversation between Asūf and the two men, now given the names Qābīl Ādam and Masʿūd Masʿūd al-Dabbāsh—begins the process of setting up the inevitable clash of values that is to follow. Asūf's life has clearly witnessed some changes, not least in his ability to conduct a minimal conversation, but there are many other ways in which his life is an uncanny mirror of his father's. The most direct link is the pledge: "It was the pledge that had prevented the son from inheriting his father's profession. The father would never have died if he had not broken the pledge. Pledges are no joke. The wild sheep knows that. However could it be otherwise when the animal is the spirit of the mountains; spirits emanate from the spirit of God; they are aware of everything."[264] Like his father, Asūf forgets about the pledge, hunts a wild sheep to a spot high in the mountains, and finds himself hanging helplessly from a precipice. As was the case in the description of his father's plight before him, this precipice is given the name *hāwiyah* in Arabic, which (as a footnote on page 57 of the text explains) is believed by Ṣūfīs to be the seventh and lowest level of purgatory. As he hangs there suspended by his arms for hours on end, his entire life appears before him: his mother and

261. Ibid., 11, 35, 37.
262. Ibid., 38.
263. Ibid., 43.
264. Ibid., 61.

father and their disagreements, the values his father taught him, and the unique blend of beliefs that he has tried to uphold. As he is about to lose consciousness and fall to his death, "the creature kept moving and pulled him back from the mouth of the abyss . . . the *jinnī* that just had saved his life was still moving across the stony desert, slowly, silently, calmly . . . he could just make out its features. O Lord! It's the wild sheep, the very same one. His victim, his executioner. But then, who's the victim here and who's the executioner? Which one's the human, and which the animal?" It is at this precise moment that he sees in his animal rescuer's eyes the sad yet friendly gaze of his own father, wondering why he, too, is torturing his fellow creatures.[265]

The father's spirit has completed the link between humans and animals. Asūf himself is accorded a similar mythic status in the lore of his fellow men when he is transformed into a wild sheep and escapes from the Italian soldiers who have drafted him into the army. Ṣūfī sages declare him to be a saint, but, as far as Asūf is concerned, what this episode represents is his last contact with settled people.[266] He returns to the desert wastes his father has taught him to love and respect, and quits eating meat. When his mother, who had consistently complained about a lack of contact with other humans, is swept away in a flash flood, the final link is severed. It is Asūf's gruesome task to search the valleys for as much of her body as he can recover. In a clear intertextual reference to the conclusion of the renowned *Muʿallaqah* of Imru' al-Qays—where a flash flood and drowned animals become a symbol of renewal and growth—the narrator comments that "water brings life to the desert, just as it brought death to his aged mother."[267]

Now that the narrator has managed to pull together the various strands of Asūf's life from different sources and through skillful interweaving of time periods to link them to the present crisis of the novel, he now turns his attention to the other major participant in

265. Ibid., 74.

266. Ibid., 89–90.

267. Ibid., 86. It is worth noting that, perhaps as a reflection of the very harshness of the environment he is depicting, al-Kūnī "pulls no punches" when it comes to descriptions of cruel killings and death. The discovery of the father's body and Asūf's own death provide two instances from this novel (38, 104). In *Al-Tibr* (The ore) (London: Riad El-Rayyes, 1990), the novel ends with the hero being torn apart between two camels and then beheaded.

the conflict: Qābīl Ādam. Qābīl has been ill-starred from birth. Orphaned while a baby, he is handed over to an aunt. Seeking a charm that will protect him against what appears to be a family curse, she accepts the advice of a sage to give him some gazelle's blood to drink. However, both she and her husband die soon after, and the foundling baby is picked up by Ādam, the leader of a passing caravan. Beginnings such as this do not augur well for later life. From childhood onward he has a voracious appetite for meat, and in order to satisfy his craving he becomes an avid hunter. None of the measures that he or his companion, Masʿūd, take to quench his desires are successful, and his urge to hunt animals reaches demonic proportions. Whereas for Asūf's world the incursions of "the West" constitute an infringement, for Qābīl's it presents a golden opportunity. Following the advent of oil companies and the American navy (in the personage of John Barker, a former student of Eastern mysticism in California), Qābīl is able to make use of modern technology to help him in his maniacal quest for meat. Thanks to John Barker, he is able to substitute a repeating rifle for his old Ottoman model, allowing him indiscriminately to cut down whole herds at a time; and he now has access to a Landrover which makes it possible for him to extend his hunting terrain and to pursue the gazelles to exhaustion. "Qābīl didn't give much thought to infringing the laws of nature. All he was worried about was hunting the maximum number of gazelles so that he could extinguish the flame that burned in his very teeth, quench his hunger, and sell whatever was left over to the American officer."[268]

Under this type of onslaught, the gazelles instinctively begin to move out into the more inaccessible regions of the desert, precisely those areas where Asūf and his father have preferred to eke out their living. As the lines in the life stories of Asūf and Qābīl move inexorably closer together, the narrator returns us once again to the current crisis point in the novel, the futile quest that Qābīl and Masʿūd have undertaken with Asūf to hunt wild sheep. As the narrator notes, the final conflict between Qābīl and Asūf erupts suddenly, and it is surely significant that the trigger takes the form of Asūf quoting a phrase of his father: "Only the earth of the grave will ever be enough to sate mankind." It is this phrase that drives Qābīl ber-

268. Al-Kūnī, 104.

serk and leads him to crucify Asūf on the rock.[269] For a third time in this novel, a human being is suspended over the *hāwiyah,* the abyss between life and death.

The gazelles within the range of Qābīl and his modern hunting methods have been decimated and seek refuge in the realm of nature to which Asūf has adapted. The narrative is interrupted once more. This time, however, the reader is not taken to another time frame or venue within the world of human consciousness, but into the animal world itself. Asūf's father has become a wild sheep in his son's eyes; Asūf himself has become a wild sheep in his companion's eyes. Now the linkage of humans and animals is carried a stage further as the reader is presented with an animal narrative which, as is often the case, carries with it a very high level of allegorical significance. The chapter is entitled "The Covenant." The gazelle-narrator uses the slaughter of the species at the hands of man and his modern weapons as a context for the recounting of a piece of gazelle lore. God has imprisoned his spirit within three confinements: time, place, and body. To leave any one of them implies an infringement of the Creator's scheme for his creatures. That they should be forced to abandon their natural environment for the wastes of the desert is the result of man's temperament. The gazelle elder suggests that what is needed in order to appease mankind is a gesture of sacrifice. Objections are raised, pointing out the futility of any attempt to reform man's basic destructive instincts. However, the elder points out that the sacrifice is actually to the Creator and not to mankind; she volunteers to be the sacrificial victim herself, but it is the narrator's mother who takes on the role. In the only first-person narrative to be found in the novel, the young gazelle rues the fact that the pact between gazelles and humans was purchased at a heavy price, with his own mother's blood.[270]

For Qābīl no such pacts exist; nature is there for him to enjoy, to exploit, to eradicate. Even John Barker, the American who has provided him with the wherewithal to hunt gazelles to extinction for miles around, now turns against him: "You, Qābīl, must have your cake and eat it. You have no love for the desert, and so it has never managed to purify you."[271] It is, however, the same John who now agrees to carry the insane craving one stage further by hunting from

269. Ibid., 111. Asūf's father's phrase provides the title for the relevant chapter.
270. Ibid., 117–22.
271. Ibid., 129.

a helicopter. As they search far and wide with minimal success, the gazelles cease to be the only target; even the notoriously inaccessible wild sheep joins the list. The linkage of Qābīl's insatiable needs to the rock carvings and to the life experiences of Asūf and his father is now complete. In the final chapter, which gives the novel its title (literally, "the bleeding of rocks/stones") the mysterious powers of the wild sheep catch up with Qābīl, who has had a frightening dream about Asūf and this perverse and mysterious creature that has brought him, along with Asūf and his father, to the brink of the *hāwiyah.* That linkage between Asūf (and his father) and the wild sheep that others have detected earlier in the narrative now becomes clear to Qābīl too, but only at that climactic moment when the madness towards which his entire life has been leading reaches its acme: "I have my victim. Look. Can't you see the wild sheep hanging over there? He's a wild sheep. How come I didn't realize it earlier? What a stupid fool I am!"[272] As Masʿūd tries in vain to restrain his companion, Qābīl kills what his crazed mind believes is the long-sought wild sheep and cuts off its head. The blood pours down a tablet on which the following is inscribed in the Twareg alphabet:

> I am Matkhandūsh, the mighty seer. I forewarn generations to come that salvation will come when the sacred wild sheep bleeds and blood pours from the rocks. Then the miracle will occur that will wash away the curse, purify the earth, and cover the desert in floodwaters.[273]

In Munīf's novel, *al-Nihāyāt,* which was analyzed above, the desert was a permanent presence in the lives of the people of the village of al-Ṭībah, and yet the focus of the village was on the community and, in particular, on its most eccentric member. For most of the villagers the city was a remote and generally alien entity, but the village itself operated as a self-contained social unit; in particular, people were gathered into clusters in order that their views should be made known to others. Within the harsh and capricious environment created by al-Kūnī's novel, on the other hand, a community such as Munīf's al-Ṭībah, isolated though it may be and permanently threatened by the impinging desert, represents something akin to "civilization," in that survival depends on the concepts of community and cooperation; people know, talk to, and help each other. Al-

272. Ibid., 153–54.
273. Ibid., 155.

Kūnī, on the other hand, has taken the Arabic novel far into the desert wastes, and the "hero" he places into that environment has been raised by his father in such a way that, at least initially, he is completely incapable of any verbal communication with other human beings.

Al-Kūnī has created here a unique and innovative combination of the most traditional and modern. The "liminal" world of solitude and endurance, of respect for animals and the likelihood of sudden death, into which the reader is introduced is an intrinsic and indivisible part of the literary heritage of the Arabs, adopting all the functions and significance of a myth. The resort at several points in the novel to the metafictional device of narrating the storytelling act—most noticeably, the one involving an animal narrator—further underlines these linkages through time. I would also suggest that the very way in which the novel makes use of flashback is very similar to earlier exploitation of this narrative device rather than more contemporary ones. The narrators of al-Shaykh's *Ḥikāyat Zahrah,* for example, provide very clear psychological triggers which serve as links between their own conscious present and the various incidents from the past that it invokes. In al-Kūnī's novel, on the other hand, the retrospects (which consume the bulk of the novel's text) are not intended to provide the reader with further insights into any character's psychological motivations. The narrative present—told in past time—becomes the vehicle on to which can be loaded two separate life stories. The way in which these two strands are drawn together presents a means of exploring the implications of the folkloric heritage and the values it endeavors to inculcate for the generation of Arabs who have witnessed the incursions of Italian and other colonialists, and the often destructive impact of Western-produced technology on not only the environment itself but also on the mores of humans. A modern fantasy in which the possibility of animals and humans not only living in harmony and balance but also assuming each other's traits is terminated in a scene of surpassing viciousness, and emerges as a thoroughly appropriate reflection of the contemporary Arab intellectual's questioning of the current priorities and directions of his people. Al-Kūnī's novel, its techniques and its conclusion, places it firmly into that realm of contemporary fiction which Edwār al-Kharrāṭ describes as "the contemporary-mythical current, which resorts to legend, fantasy, [and] folk-tale . . . whether in a contemporary or in a historical setting." Al-Kharrāṭ describes this trend as being "the most complex . . . richest in promise and achievement" and goes on to note that "the blending of myth and contemporary theme, if not done in lucid and at least competent terms, can create a permanent fissure in both structure and vision."[274] The above analysis of al-Kūnī's contribution, with its focus on structure and linkages, is intended to suggest that he has provided another notable addition to this particular trend whereby the invocation of the heritage of the past becomes a genuinely innovative gesture.

In the context of drama in Arabic, it has often been noted that the use of the standard written language of Arabic in dialogue will often assist in the creation of worlds and atmospheres that are intended to be fantastic or surreal. Such is also the case with al- Kūnī's novel, where all the features of the standard language are used in the process of creating the desert landscape in which Asūf and his family live. The earlier quotation from the start of the novel gives some idea of al-Kūnī's familiarity with the scenery involved and his masterful use of imagery, but a further example may help to underline the impression:

> He stood there watching as the stubborn goats stretched their front legs to get at the green branches on the acacia trees . . . while on the other side of the valley a large billy-goat with two huge curved horns was busy flirting with a beautiful silver-flecked she-goat. Right alongside another really scruffy goat stood angrily watching the two of them flirting. The she-goat was responding to the billy-goat's gestures by turning her neck and rubbing her nostrils against his with a series of rapid kisses.[275]

This same level of language carries over into the relatively small amount of dialogue. But here too, the anticipated "awkwardness" in the use of the written medium for oral expression serves to reinforce rather than obstruct the impact of the conversation. Whether the participants in the dialogue are Asūf, Qābīl, and Masʿūd with one scenario, or Qābīl and John Barker in another, the stilted nature of the communication adds an element of authenticity to the situation, in that in the former case Asūf has already been portrayed as anything but an accomplished conversationalist, while in the latter the use of two separate languages—Arabic and English—is being reflected on the printed page.

274. See Edwār al-Kharrāṭ, "The Mashriq," in Ostle, 191.
275. Al-Kūnī, *Nazīf al-ḥajar,* 57–58.

Nazīf al-ḥajar presents a unique vision within the context of the contemporary novel in Arabic. Its concentration on such an uncompromising venue and its minimal concern with many of the usual narrative comforts of fictional writing make it an unusual reading experience for the majority of its potential audience who live predominantly in the cities of the Arab world. The direction that he has chosen to take in his fictional writing and the "implied reader" that his works demand bring to mind a contrast recently made by Edna O'Brien in a comment on the readership of Western fiction: "Each of us looks for something different in a work of fiction. Some like the ordinary so as to feel reaffirmed and 'at home,' and some seek the extraordinary, those daring distortions of realism that, by stunning verbal feats, hurtle the reader to fantastic latitudes."[276] Al-Kūnī's other novels display a similar interest in the use of the remote in both time and place as a means of commenting in fictional form on the intolerable imminences of contemporary existence; indeed, with this concentration in method he seems almost to be flaunting his lack of concern for the more frequently traveled paths of modern Arabic fiction. My choice of *al-Nihāyāt* by the then little-known Munīf as the final novel in the 1982 version of this chapter seemed something of a risk at the time, one that appears to have been worthwhile in light of his now wide reputation in the Middle East and, via translations, in the West as well. It will be for future decades to determine whether Ibrāhīm al-Kūnī's similarly prolific initial output is the signal of the arrival of another new and original fictional voice in Arabic as the genre continues its quest for ways of expressing change and difference.

276. Edna O'Brien in the *New York Times Book Review,* 14 Feb. 1993: 1.

5

Conclusion

In Yūsuf Idrīs's contemporary miniparable, "al-Martabah al-muqa‘‘arah" (The concave mattress), a newlywed husband lying on the marriage bed keeps asking his wife whether the world has changed. As long as he remains alive, her consistent reply is that it has not changed; whereupon he resumes his slumber.[1] Among the many possible interpretations of this nihilistic vision, one is clearly that it is important to ask the right questions; in computer jargon, "garbage in, garbage out." The world is indeed in a constant process of change, and so is the perception and knowledge that we bring to the task of living and surviving in it. As we noted in the initial chapter of this work, the novel still appears to present itself to the creative writer as the literary genre that best reflects this *Weltanschauung*. While the topics that the novel treats will most often address themselves to the process of change itself, the many ways in which it continues to develop as a genre mirror the changes in our own modes of analysis that attempt to help us deal with its complications. As Frank Kermode has recently expressed it: "And yet it can be argued that even in the present state of things the novel may be the best available instrument of ethical enquiry; that its own extraordinary variety of means equips it as our best recorder of human variety, even at a time when biography is challenging that position; and that its capacity for wit and humour and poetry continues to exist and even to expand."[2]

Many critics have commented on the fact that, faced with our awareness of a world of ever-increasing complexity, fiction is chal-

1. Yūsuf Idrīs, "Al-Martabah al-muqa‘‘arah," in *Al-Naddāhah* (Cairo: Dār al-Hilāl, 1969), 70–71; English trans.: "The Concave Mattress," in *In the Eye of the Beholder*, trans. Roger Allen (Chicago: Bibliotheca Islamica, 1978), 119–20.

2. See *London Review of Books* 14, no. 19 (8 Oct. 1992): 14.

lenged to find new topics and modes of expression. As Kermode noted above, biography is enjoying a particular vogue at the moment (1993). In a world in which "realism" has come to be seen as just as much a creation of artifice as any other mode of vision, the resort to biography as a preferred mode of expression may reflect not only the television age's aspiration for documentary "accuracy" and "the public's right to know," but also a desire to utilize a genre that advertizes itself as an objective recording of "facts," even though it is palpably obvious, of course, that the biographical genre (and especially the autobiographical) shares far more with fiction than general perceptions might lead one to believe. In such an environment, fiction becomes an attractive genre of resort for many writers:

> Samuel Beckett was one of the first to realise that in a predominantly agnostic and sceptical age, nothing could be more irrelevant than the novel whose plot continued to imitate the workings of a benign deity; the writer's new task, on the contrary, consisted in finding "a form that accommodates the mess." Half a century has gone by since then, and still, both in and out of the mainstream, novelists are struggling to adapt their narrative strategies to the demands of a reality which, as any glance at the newspaper will remind us, grows daily more grotesque and unmanageable. In particular the threat of terrorism begins to look forever closer and more insistent when passed through the media's magnifying lens, and any writer seeking to address this subject must face up to the possibility that tidy endings are not to be relied upon; that our lives (our narratives, in other words) run the perpetual risk of truncation by sudden, unexpected acts of violence which are dauntingly inexplicable in terms of cause and effect.[3]

The first version of this work on the novel in Arabic was written some fifteen years ago. Since that time, the world, the novel, and its exemplars in Arabic have all undergone significant transformations, processes that I have tried to reflect—to the extent that space has allowed—in the preceding chapters. As we approach the middle of

3. Jonathan Coe, "Wheezes," review of *Cleopatra's Sister*, by Penelope Lively, *London Review of Books* 15, no. 9 (13 May 1993): 21. Compare this with Richard Gott's comment: "This uncontrolled enthusiasm for writing fiction ought perhaps to be considered, not as the self-advertisement of a few inflated egos, but rather as an indictment of our late 20th-century English society. The reality is so unattractive, the politics so banal, the general level of culture so poor, that people desperately seek something different in the only other world available, the world of the imagination." *Manchester Guardian Weekly*, 6 Feb. 1992.

the final decade of the twentieth century, "the present state of things" presents an equivocal picture, to put it mildly. Cultures continue to misunderstand each other with alarming regularity. Agencies such as Amnesty International and publications such as *The Index on Censorship* make abundantly clear that the deprivation of human rights and torture remain popular options for many governments in order to control or suppress the will of their populace—including their authors. As the developed world becomes richer and exploits more of the world's resources (which we realize now more than ever to be limited), so the poorer nations sink further into an abyss of disease, overpopulation, and starvation. Meanwhile, local conflicts between different communities living alongside each other continue to filter into and out of the world's consciousness: for example, in Cambodia, in Chad, in the Sudan, in Northern Ireland, and in the area to the south of Morocco. With the dismantling of the Soviet-style Communist system that assumed such political prominence in the decades following the Second World War, the peoples of certain areas within the former Union of Soviet Socialist Republics (USSR)—be it the Balkans or Central Asia—have made use of the aftermath of the collapse to turn the clock back and refight the battles of previous centuries. Here notions of change as a forward-moving force working in the cause of something called "progress" seem wide of the mark; the old adage, *plus ça change, plus c'est la même chose* seems to capture the mood of cynicism and despondency far more accurately. In a world that is becoming ever more closely linked in the political and economic spheres on a global level, all these situations and events must inevitably impinge upon the peoples of the Middle East and upon the consciousness of writers who strive to deal with the political and social consequences within their own national communities.

Faced with a "grotesque and unmanageable reality" of such proportions: a Western culture of seemingly enduring economic superiority that manages to impose its strategic priorities, economic agenda, and cultural values without impediment, and crushing social problems of overpopulation, illiteracy, and starvation, it is hardly surprising that people in many countries of the Middle East have expressed their frustrations at this hegemonic balance in a reactive fashion. The most prominent societal phenomenon (and certainly the one most closely watched in the West) has led people to search within their own cultural milieu for alternative systems upon which to base their personal and societal beliefs and practices; for many the activities of popular Islamic groups and preachers, conveniently but misleadingly grouped together by Western commentators under the name of "fundamentalists," have seemed to fulfill such needs. The support systems provided by such religious movements have afforded many people from all walks of life an increasingly popular political and social mechanism through which to strive to "accommodate the mess," primarily through the advocacy of an entirely different set of moral parameters and sociopolitical expectations. However, novelists in the Arab world have in general failed to find either consolation or inspiration within such contexts; instead they have had to embark on their own quest for an alternative discourse through which to address this same set of circumstances. As the above quotations make clear, this quest for new modes of expression clearly replicates the motivations of their peers in other world literary traditions.

One of the novelists whose views I cited in the conclusion to the first edition of this work was the Egyptian, Edwār al-Kharrāṭ. In recent years he himself has obviously found in the novel a medium for expressing his own visions in fictional form, but he has also written eloquently about the process of writing itself, closely echoing the comments of Beckett cited above and many other commentators on the contemporary novel: "If modernist creative writing in Arabic literature is in continuity with an old valid legacy, it is at the same time certainly a break-away from the conformism of the realist mode, a constant questioning with no pretence to ready answers, a leap into the dark by neither a complacent nor a complaisant literary enterprise."[4]

In spite of—or perhaps one should say, because of—such a view of life, of present realities and future possibilities, Arab authors continue to feel themselves impelled to produce novels that will attempt to reflect on the complexities of their contemporary world.[5] Indeed, during the lifespan of the first edition of this work, the field has increased and expanded in interesting ways, involving the process of creative writing itself, and, equally significant, the activities of publication outlets that make the novels available to their potential readership. Several factors serve to impede any accurate numerical measure of the increase in novel writing. In some regions it is feasi-

4. Al-Kharrāṭ, "The Mashriq," in Ostle, 187.

5. These developments in novel writing in Arabic are well explored by Ṣabrī Ḥāfiẓ in "Al-Riwāyah wa-al-wāqiʿ," *Al-Nāqid* 34, no. 26 (Aug. 1990): 34–39.

ble for resident scholars with close contacts to the publication process (such as Jean Fontaine in Tunisia) to provide precise information, but for countries like Egypt and Lebanon the sheer bulk of works published and the variety of outlets from which they appear make any precise reckoning implausible. In spite of such realities, however, it is possible to indicate certain trends. There are countries—Saudi Arabia, and the Gulf States, for example—where the amount of publication currently underway in the realm of fiction represents a clear increase over previous minimal levels. Furthermore, while the volume of publication to emerge from Lebanon (traditionally the least trammeled of the publication markets in the Arab world) has not diminished in any notable way throughout the period of the civil war, the difficulties of finding channels through which to distribute such books to other Arab countries, when coupled with the political isolation of Egypt for part of the same period (in the wake of the Camp David accords of 1979 and the subsequent transfer of the Arab League headquarters to Tunis), have served to emphasize the increased availability of fictional works and criticism of them published in other Arab countries such as Morocco and Iraq. It needs to be emphasized that this set of impressions—and that is what in essence they are—reflects the view of a Western scholar surveying the situation from the outside, but, as we have noted earlier, such is the situation in much of the Arab world regarding both censorship and book distribution that it may be only from such an "external" perspective that a somewhat accurate assessment of the situation may be obtained.

Beyond these circumstances occasioned by differing patterns and paces of cultural development and the complexities of Arab international contacts, we can draw attention to another interesting and important change in the patterns of creativity and publication within the realm of the novel in Arabic, namely the palpable increase in the publication of novels written by women writers. One can, of course, point to various developments in the societies concerned as obvious factors in these changes: the wider availability of women's education, for example, and a concomitant (albeit gradual) shift in attitudes in several countries where women have begun to enter the professional workforce. Research into the earlier periods in the modern Arabic literary renaissance, however, has shown clearly that within their own societal environment women writers have been sharing their creative output with each other from the outset. With the completion of more studies in this area (and on a broader scale), the role of female writers in the development of modern Arabic fictional genres will need to be reconsidered.

In the introduction to this edition I laid even more stress than in the first edition on its introductory nature and purpose. If the 1982 publication was an attempt to sample an already rich tradition, recent decades have seen that corpus grow in both sheer numerical terms and variety; for the author of a work such as this it presents a genuine *embarras de richesses*. The very proliferation of Arabic novels and critical studies of them shows with abundant clarity that the genre continues to fulfill its function as a mirror of the society within which it is created and a powerful advocate of the need for understanding and change. However, in any attempt at assessing the degree to which the present work has been able to represent this larger generic tradition, one of the more obvious conclusions to be drawn from the wealth of material that is now available, and the variety of political and social contexts across the region into which it has been introduced, is that the sample presented here must be acknowledged as constituting an even smaller percentage of both the fiction and criticism currently available than was the case with the first edition. Arab novelists and critics continue to provide us with an ever-increasing body of materials for research, and scholars in the West who specialize in Arabic literature studies are making use of a variety of theoretical approaches in preparing more detailed studies of the work of individual writers and national traditions. Many of these are listed in the bibliography, but once again the increased size of that section of this volume can be only a partial reflection of the wealth of current activity in both the Arab world and the West. Finally—and, in the context of an introductory work written in English, most significantly—attention must be drawn to the large increase in the availability of Arabic novels in translation, a reality also reflected in the bibliography. However, with the notable exception of Najīb Maḥfūẓ, the list of translated novels continues to mirror the particular interests of the translators involved rather than any systematic attempt to represent the geographic and thematic variety of the tradition as a whole; there continues, for example, to be heavy emphasis on Egyptian, Palestinian, and Lebanese writers. Even so, the increased availability of Arabic novels in translation is gradually but inevitably coming to be more representative of the tradition as a whole than was the case a decade ago.

Within the cross-cultural context implicit in the composition of a book written in English about the novel in Arabic, the year 1988 and the award of the Nobel Prize in Literature to Maḥfūẓ is clearly a significant historical event, and for at least two reasons. Most obviously, the announcement brought the very existence of the novel tradition in Arabic and its most notable exponent to the attention of a vastly broader readership than before. Translators of the works of other Arab novelists are now more able and willing to test the apparent receptivity of this public to further examples of fiction from a region and culture that has for centuries been regarded (perhaps, stereotyped) as quintessentially exotic, alien, and—all too often—inimical. Compilers of anthologies of world literature are now beginning the process of incorporating examples of contemporary Arabic fiction into their works, aimed not only at the general reading public but at school-age children. It is too early to assess the long-term impact of these developments on the reception of Arabic fiction and its placement within the environment of "world literature," but one must presume that any shift from a virtual zero position will represent some kind of improvement in cross-cultural understanding. The initial reception of Maḥfūẓ's works (and, to a lesser extent, those of Munīf as well) suggests that the formerly prevalent claims of many book publishers regarding a "lack of market" for Arabic novels were, as many of us have suspected for some time, a convenient inaccuracy. Secondly, the Nobel Award provided confirmation, albeit delayed by several decades, of the fact that Maḥfūẓ's novels of the late 1940s, 1950s, and 1960s can be seen in retrospect as marking the end of the Arabic novel's beginnings and the establishment of a firm platform on which new generations of writers could proceed to build the accomplished tradition that we enjoy today. With improvements in communication and publication, involving contacts not only between Arab novelists and critics themselves but also between them and colleagues in the Western (and Eastern) world, the student of the novel in Arabic is today confronted with a genre of truly stimulating variety in both theme and technique.

I began this second edition by appending a new introduction to that of the first edition. Let me bring the work to a necessarily open-ended closure, first by reproducing the words of Edwār al-Kharrāṭ with which I concluded the first edition, not least because they are as valid today as they were in 1982:

> Why do I write then? I write because I don't know why I write. Does the impulse come from some powerful force? I know that I use it as a weapon to bring about change, change both in the self

> and others . . . for something better, more beautiful perhaps . . . something warmer to ward off the bitter chill of barbarity and loneliness . . . something soothing in the oppressive heat of violence and suffocation. . . . I write because I want there to be something in what I write—in everything I write—which will make even a single reader lift his head proudly and feel with me that in the end the world is not a desolate, meaningless landscape. . . . I write because the world's a riddle, woman is a riddle and so is my fellow man. All creation is a riddle . . . that is what I want to write about, and that is why I write[6]

and then by allowing Ilyās Khūrī, another accomplished novelist and critic whose writings we have discussed in the pages above, to comment on the writing process in an era in which we become ever more aware of the complexities of our existence and of our consciousness of it:

> Writing in times of transition takes the form of a journey towards what we do not know and towards the shock of writing what we know, which will lead us to discover how writing changes things and does not only reflect them.
>
> Astonishment is the main seduction of writing, and the parallel mirrors of the words create the impossibilities of this journey towards the discovery of our changing world.
>
> To write becomes a synonym of adventure. It is the adventure of the text when it is assimilated by time and the anonymous reader. The text cannot exist without its second writer. The reader who rewrites while reading, which conversely obliges the writer to reread while writing.[7]

6. Edwār al-Kharrāṭ, *Al-Ādāb* (Feb.–Mar. 1980): 110.

7. Elias Khoury, "The Unfolding of Modern Fiction and Arab Memory." *Journal of the Midwest Modern Language Association* 23, no. 1 (Spring 1990): 8.

Glossary

Bibliography

Index

Glossary

ʿaraq: a strong, colorless liquor often diluted with water; akin to the Greek ouzo.

aṣālah: cultural authenticity.

ʿashāʾiriyyah: tribalism.

Burdah: literally "mantle," the name given to two famous poems in Arabic; the first by Kaʿb ibn Zuhayr (d. 645), the second by al-Būṣīrī (d. 1294).

dhikr: literally the mention of God's name, and thus the word used to designate Sufi ritual.

farrāsh: doorman, cleaner.

fidāʾī, fidāʾīyyin: freedom fighter (prepared for self-sacrifice).

ḥadīth: a tradition, story regarding the Prophet Muḥammad.

ḥakawātī: a popular storyteller.

iltizām: commitment.

imām: prayer leader, religious leader.

infitāḥ: Sādāt's policy of economic "opening up" of markets.

isnād: chain of authority for a *ḥadīth.*

jinnī, jinn: demon, sprite.

kaffiyyah: the headdress worn in many Arab countries, often used as protection against the sun and/or sand.

The Maghrib: northwest Africa.

mahjar: the name given to the school of littérateurs who settled in the Americas during the late nineteenth and early twentieth centuries; their acknowledged leader was Jubrān Khalīl Jubrān.

maqāmah, maqāmāt: a prose genre in Arabic literature combining verbal virtuosity with a picaresque portrayal of society. It was almost certainly used for the first time by Badīʿ al-zamān al-Hamadhānī (d. 1008).

mawwāl: popular form of poem/song.

muftī: someone who delivers fatwas or legal opinions.

muḥtasib: person responsible for weights and measures (and morality).

mukhtār: head of a village or small town.

Muʿallaqah: a famous collection of pre-Islamic odes.

al-nahḍah: the modern cultural renaissance.

al-nakbah: the disaster; the 1948 war.

al-naksah: the setback; the 1967 war.

qarīnah: "daemon," guardian spirit.

qaṣīdah: usually translated as "ode," the Arabic word used to describe the polythematic poem in classical Arabic literature, the earliest examples of which date from no later than the sixth century A.D.

qiṣṣah: "story," normally used with the adjective *qaṣīrah* (short) to describe the short story genre.

riwāyah: literally "narrative," but now used by the majority of Arabic critics as "novel."

saj': a style of prose exploiting the potentialities of Arabic morphology to produce rhyming patterns, often with great lexical virtuosity. Found in much Arabic prose from an early age (including the Qur'ān itself), it is particularly associated with the *maqāmah* genre (see above).

shaykh: religious authority (also "old man").

sīrah sha'biyyah: popular folk tale (e.g. those of 'Antar, Baybars, the Banī Hilāl, etc.).

thawrat al-taṣḥīḥ: Sādāt's "correctional revolution" of 1971–72.

turāth: heritage.

'umdah: the head of the village community in Egypt, selected from among the local influential families. The position was used by Egyptian littérateurs as a butt for jokes concerning both corruption and rustic naïveté.

waqf: a religious endowment property.

Bibliography

A Listing of Novels Cited

Please note that what follows is a listing of novels that are cited in the text of this book; it is not intended to be a complete listing of the works of any author. English translations of complete novels (not extracts) are listed when available; translations into other Western languages are only included when no English translation exists. The country of birth of the author is provided in brackets after each name.

ʿAbdallāh, Yaḥyā al-Ṭāhir. [Eg.] *Al-Ṭawq wa-al-aswirah* (The necklet and bracelets). Cairo, 1975.

Abū Jadrah, Rashīd. [Alg.] *Al-Marth* (Maceration). Algiers, 1984; French translation: *La macération.* Translated by Rashīd Abū Jadrah and Moussali. N.p., 1985.

———. *al-Tafakkuk* (Dissipation). Beirut: Dār ibn Rushd, 1981; French translation: *Le démantelement.* Translated by Rashīd Abū Jadrah. Paris: N.p., 1982.

Anṭūn, Faraḥ. [Leb.] *Al-Ḥubb ḥattā al-mawt* (Love till death). Alexandria, 1898.

———. *Al-ʿIlm wa-al-dīn wa-al-māl* (Science, religion and money). Alexandria, 1905.

———. *Urīshalīm al-jadīdah aw fatḥ al-ʿArab bayt al-maqdis* (New Jerusalem or the conquest of the holy city). Alexandria, 1904.

———. *Al-Waḥsh, al-waḥsh, al-waḥsh aw al-siyāḥah fī arz Lubnān* (Tourism at the cedars of Lebanon). Alexandria, 1903.

al-ʿAqqād, ʿAbbas Mahmud. [Eg.] *Sārah.* Cairo, 1938; English translation: *Sara.* Translated by M. M. Badawi. Cairo: General Egyptian Book Organization, 1978.

al-ʿArwī, ʿAbdallāh. [Mor.] *Al-Ghurbah* (Exile). Rabāṭ: Dār al-nashr al-Maghribiyyah, 1971.

ʿAwwād, Tawfīq Yūsuf. [Leb.] *Al-Raghīf* (The loaf). Beirut: Dār al-Makshūf, 1939.

———. *Ṭawāḥīn Bayrūt.* Beirut, 1972; English translation: *Death in Beirut.* Translated by Leslie McLoughlin. London: Heinemann, 1976.

Ayyūb, Dhū al-nūn. [Irq.] *Al-Duktūr Ibrāhīm* (Dr. Ibrahim). Baghdad, 1939.

———. *Al-Yād wa-al-arḍ wa-al-mā'* (Hand, earth, and water). Baghdad 1948.

Ba'albakkī, Laylā. [Leb.] *Al-Ālihah al-mamsūkhah* (Deformed deities). Beirut, 1960.

———. *Anā aḥyā* (I am alive). Beirut: Dār Majallat Shi'r, 1963.

Badr, Liyānah. [Pal.] *'Ayn al-mir'āt* (The eye of the mirror). Casablanca: Dār Tūbqāl li-al-nashr, 1991.

———. *Būṣlah min ajl 'abbād al-shams.* Beirut: Dār Ibn Rushd 1979; English translation: *A Compass for the Sunflower.* Translated by Catherine Cobham. London: Women's, 1989.

Barakāt, Ḥalīm. [Syr.] *'Awdat al-ṭā'ir ilā al-baḥr* (The return of the flying Dutchman to the sea), 1969; English translation: *Days of Dust.* Translated by Trevor Le Gassick. Wilmette, Ill.: Medina, 1974.

———. *Sittat ayyām.* Beirut: Dār Majallat Shi'r, 1961; English translation: *Six Days.* Translated by Bassam Franjieh and Scott McGhee. Washington, D.C.: Three Continents, 1990.

Barrādah, Muḥammad. [Mor.] *La'bat al-nisyān* (The forgetting game). Rabat: Dār al-Amān, 1987.

Baydas, Khalīl. [Pal.] *Al-Wārith* (The heir). Maṭba'at Dār al-Aytām al-Islāmiyyah, 1920.

al-Bustānī, Sa'īd. [Leb.] *Dhāt al-khidr* (Lady of the boudoir). Serialized in *Al-Ahrām,* 1884.

al-Bustānī, Salīm. [Leb.] *Al-Huyām fī jinān al-Shām* (Passion in Syrian gardens), 1870.

al-Dabbāgh, Ghānim. [Irq.] *Ḍajjāh fī al-zuqāq* (Din in the alley). Baghdad, 1975.

Farmān, Ghā'ib Ṭu'mah. [Irq.] *Khamsat aṣwāt* (Five voices). Beirut: Dār al-Ādāb, 1967.

Fayyāḍ, Tawfīq. [Pal.] *Majmū'ah 778* (778 group). 1974.

Ghallāb. 'Abd al-karīm. [Mor.] *Dafannā al-māḍī* (We have buried the past). Beirut: Al-Maktab al-tijārī, 1966.

———. *Sab'at abwāb* (Seven doors). Cairo: Dār al-Ma'ārif, 1965)

Ghānim, Fatḥī. [Eg.] *Al-Jabal* (The mountain). Cairo: Dār al-Hilāl, 1959.

al-Ghīṭānī, Jamāl. *Khiṭaṭ al-Ghīṭānī* (Al-Ghīṭānī's city-guide). Beirut: Dār al-Maṣīrah, 1981.

———. [Eg.] *Kitāb al-tajalliyyāt* (Book of illumination). Cairo: Dār al-Mustaqbal al-'Arabī, 1983–87.

———. *Al-Zaynī Barakāt.* Cairo: Dār Ma'mūn li-al-ṭibā'ah, 1975. Originally published: Damascus: Wizārat al-Thaqāfah, 1971; English translation: *Zayni Barakat.* Translated by Farouk Abdel Wahab. London: Penguin and New York: Viking, 1988.

Ḥabībī, Emile. [Pal.] *Ikhṭiyyeh.* (What a shame). Nicosia: Mu'assasat Bisān Brīs, 1985.

———. *Sudāsiyyat al-ayyām al-sittah* (Sextet on the six days). Beirut: Munaẓẓamat al-Taḥrīr al-Filasṭīnī, 1980; Italian translation: *Sestina dei sei giorni in Palestina: Tre racconti.* Translated by Isabella Camera d'Afflitto. Rome: Edizioni Ripostes, 1984.

———. *Al-Waqā'iʿ al-gharībah fi-ikhtifā' Saʿīd Abī al-naḥs al-mutashā'il* (Jerusalem: Manshūrāt Ṣalāḥ al-dīn, 1974, 1977); English translation: *The Secret Life of Saeed, the Ill-fated Pessoptimist: A Palestinian Who Became a Citizen of Israel.* Translated by Salma Khadra' al-Jayyusi and Trevor Le Gassick. New York: Vantage, 1982. Reprint. London: Zed, 1985.

Ḥaddād, Nīqūlā. [Eg.] *Asīrat al-ḥubb* (Prisoner of love). Cairo, n.d.

———. *Fātinat al-Imperator* (Enchantress of the emperor). Cairo, 1922.

———. *Ḥawwā' al-jadīdah* (Modern Eve). Cairo, 1906.

al-Hādī, Muḥammad ibn Ṣāliḥ. *Fi bayt al-ʿankabūt.* Tunis: Al-Dār al-ʿArabiyyah li-al-kitāb. 1976.

al-Ḥakīm, Tawfīq. [Eg.] *ʿAwdat al-rūḥ.* Cairo: Maṭbaʿat al-raghā'ib, 1933; English translation: *Return of the Spirit.* Translated by Williams M. Hutchins. Washington, D.C.: Three Continents, 1990.

———. *ʿUṣfūr min al-sharq.* Cairo: Maṭbaʿat lajnat al-ta'līf, 1938; English translation: *A bird from the east.* Translated by R. Bayly Winder. Beirut: Khayat, 1966.

———. *Yawmiyyāt nā'ib fī al-aryāf* (Diary of a public prosecutor in the provinces). Cairo: Maṭbaʿat lajnat al-ta'līf, 1937; English translation: *The Maze of Justice.* Translated by Aubrey S. Eban. London: Harvill, 1947.

Ḥaqqī, Maḥmūd Ṭāhir. [Eg.] *ʿAdhrā' Dinshaway.* Cairo, 1907; English translation: *The Virgin of Dinshaway.* Translated by Saad el-Gabalawy. In *Three Pioneering Egyptian Novels,* 17–48. Fredericton, N.B.: York, 1986.

Ḥatātah, Sharīf. [Eg.] *Al-ʿAyn dhāt al-jifn al-maʿdanī.* Cairo: Dār al-Thaqāfah al-jadīdah, 1981; English translation: *The Eye with an Iron Lid.* London: Onyx, 1982.

Haykal, Muḥammad Ḥusayn. [Eg.] *Zaynab.* Cairo: Maktabat Nahḍat Miṣr, 1963. English translation: *Zainab.* Translated by John Mohammed Grinsted. London: Darf, 1989.

Ḥijāzī, ʿAbd al-Nabī. [Syr.] *Al-Sindyānah* (The oak tree). Damascus, 1971.

Ḥusayn, Ṭāhā. [Eg.] *Adīb.* Cairo: Maṭbaʿat al-Iʿtimād, 1935; French translation: *Adib ou l'aventure occidentale.* Translated by Amina and Moenis Taha-Hussein. Cairo: Dār al-Maʿaref, 1960.

———. *Al-Ayyām.* Vol. 1: Cairo: Dār al-Maʿarif, 1944; English translation: *An Egyptian Childhood.* Translated by E. H. Paxton. London: Routledge, 1932; Washington, D.C: Three Continents, 1981; Vol. 2: Cairo: Matbaʿat al-Maʿārif, 1940; English translation: *A Stream of Days.* Translated by Hilary Wayment. Cairo: Anglo-Egyptian Bookshop, 1943; Vol. 3: Cairo, 1972; English translation: *A Passage to France.* Translated by Kenneth Cragg. Leiden: E. J. Brill, 1976.

———. *Duʿā' al-karawān.* Cairo: Maṭbaʿat al-Maʿārif, 1942; English translation: *The Call of the Curlew.* Translated by A. B. as-Safi. Leiden: E. J. Brill, 1980.

———. *Shajarat al-bu's* (Tree of misery). Cairo: Maṭba'at al-Ma'ārif, 1944; French translation: *L'arbre de la misère.* Translated by Gaston Wiet. Cairo: Dār al-Ma'aref, 1964.

Hūhū, Aḥmad Riḍā. [Alg.] *Ghādat Umm al-Qurā* (The maid of the city). Tunis: Maṭba'at al-Tulaylī, 1947.

Ibn Hadūqah, 'Abd al-ḥamīd. [Alg.] *Rīḥ al-janūb* (South wind). Algiers, 1971.

Ibn Jallūn, 'Abd al-majīd. [Mor.] *Fī al-ṭufūlah* (In childhood). N.p.: Maṭba'at al-Atlās, 1957.

Ibn Ṣāliḥ, Muḥammad al-Hādī. [Tun.] *Fī bayt al-'ankabūt* (In the spider's house). Tunis: Al-Dār al-'Arabiyyah li-al-kitāb, 1976.

Ibrāhīm, Ṣun'allāh. [Eg.] *Najmat Aghusṭus* (August star). Cairo, 1974; French translation: *Etoile d'août.* Paris: Sindbad, 1987.

———. *Tilka al-rā'iḥah.* Cairo, 1966; English translation: *The Smell of It.* Translated by Denys Johnson-Davies. London: Heinemann, 1971.

Idrīs, Suhayl. [Leb.] *Aṣābi'unā allatī taḥtariq* (Our burning fingers). Beirut: Dār al-Ādāb, 1962.

———. *Al-Ḥayy al-Lātīnī* (The latin quarter). Beirut: Dār al-'Ilm li-al-Malāyīn, 1953.

———. *Al-Khandaq al-ghamīq* (The deep trench). Beirut: Dār al-Ādāb, 1958.

Idrīs, Yūsuf. [Eg.] *Al-'Ayb* (The shame). Cairo: Mu'assasat Rūz al-Yūsuf, 1962.

———. *Al-Ḥarām.* Cairo: Al-Sharikah al-'Arabiyyah li-al-ṭibā'ah, 1959; English translation: *The Sinners.* Translated by Kristen Peterson-Ishaq. Washington, D.C.: Three Continents, 1984.

Ikhlāṣī, Walīd. [Syr.] *Shitā' al-baḥr al-yābis* (Winter of the dry sea). Beirut: Manshūrāt 'Uwaydāt, 1965.

Ismā'īl, Ismā'īl Fahd. [Kuw.] *Al-Ḍifāf al-ukkhrā* (Other shores). Beirut: Dār al-'Awdah, 1973.

———. *Al-Ḥabl* (The rope). Beirut: Dār al-'Awdah, 1972.

———. *Kānat al-samā' zarqā'* (The sky was blue). Beirut: Dār al-'Awdah, n.d.

———. *Al-Mustanqa'āt al-ḍaw'iyyah* (The light-swamps). Beirut: Dār al-'Awdah, 1971.

Ismā'īl, Ṣidqī. [Syr.] *Al-'Uṣāt* (The rebels). Beirut: Dār al-Ṭalī'ah, 1964.

al-Jābirī, Muḥammad al-Ṣaliḥ. [Tun.] *Yawm min ayyām Zamrā* (One day in Zamra). Tunis: Al-Dār al-Tūnisiyyah li-al-nashr, 1968.

al-Jābirī, Shakīb. [Syr.] *Naham* (Greed). Aleppo: Al-Maṭba'ah al-'ilmiyyah, 1937.

Jabrā, Jabrā Ibrāhīm. [Pal.] *Al-Baḥth 'an Walīd Mas'ūd* (The search for Walid Mas'ud). Beirut: Dār al-Ādāb, 1978.

———. *Al-Ghuraf al-ukhrā* (The other rooms). Beirut: Maktabat al-Sharq al-Awsaṭ, 1987.

———. *Al-Safīnah.* Beirut: Dār al-Nahār, 1970; English translation: *The Ship.* Translated by Adnan Haydar and Roger Allen. Washington, D.C.: Three Continents, 1985.

———, and ʿAbd al-raḥmān Munīf. *ʿĀlam bi-lā kharāʾiṭ.* (A world with no maps). Beirut: Al-Muʾassasah al-ʿArabiyyah li-al-dirāsāt wa-al-nashr, 1983.

Jannat, Muḥammad al-Mukhtār. [Tun.] *Nawāfidh al-zamān* (Windows of time). Tunis: Al-Sharikah al-Tūnisiyyah li-al-tawzīʿ, 1974.

Jubrān, Jubrān Khalīl. [Leb.] *Al-Ajniḥah al-mutakassirah.* Beirut, 1908; English translation: *Broken Wings.* Translated by Antony R. Ferris. New York: Citadel, 1957.

———. *Al-Arwāḥ al-mutamarridah.* Beirut, 1908; English translation: *Spirits Rebellious.* Translated by Antony R. Ferris. New York: Philosophical Library, 1947.

Kāmil, ʿĀdil. [Eg.] *Mallīm al-Akbar* (Mallim the great). Cairo: Lajnat al-nashr li-al-jāmiʿiyyīn, 1944.

Kanafānī, Ghassān. [Pal.] *Mā tabaqqā la-kum.* In *Al-Āthār al-kāmilah.* Vol. 1, *Al-Riwāyāt.* Beirut: Dār al-Ṭalīʿah, 1972. English translation: *All That's Left to You.* Translated by May Jayyusi and Jeremy Reed. Austin: Univ. of Texas Press, 1990.

———. *Rijāl fī al-shams.* In *Al-Āthār al-kāmilah.* Vol. 1, *Al-Riwāyāt.* Beirut: Dār al-Ṭalīʿah, 1972; English translation: *Men in the Sun.* Translated by Hilary Kilpatrick. London: Heinemann, 1978; Washington, D.C.: Three Continents, 1978.

Khalīfah, Saḥar. [Pal.] *ʿAbbād al-shams* (The sunflower). Beirut: Al-Farabī, 1980.

———. *Lam naʿud jawārī la-kum* (No longer your handmaids). Beirut: Dār al-Ādāb, 1974.

———. *Mudhakkirāt imraʾah ghayr wāqiʿiyyah* (Memoirs of an unrealistic woman). Beirut: Dār al-Ādāb, 1986.

———. *Al-Ṣubbar.* Jerusalem: Manshūrāt Galileo, 1976; English translation: *Wild Thorns.* Translated by Trevor Le Gassick and Elizabeth Fernea. London: Saqi, 1985.

Khalīl, Badawī ʿAbd al-qādir. [Sud.] *Hāʾim ʿalā al-arḍ aw rasāʾil al-ḥirmān.* (Roaming the earth, or letters of deprivation), 1954.

al-Kharrāṭ, Edwār [Eg.] *Rāmah wa-al-tinnīn* (Rāmah and the dragon). Beirut: Al-Muʾassasah al-ʿArabiyyah li-al-dirāsāt wa-al-nashr, 1979.

Khurayyif, Al-Bashīr. [Tun.] *Barq al-layl* (Night lightning). Tunis: Al-Sharikah al-qawmiyyah li-al-nashr wa-al-tawzīʿ, 1961.

———. *Al-Daqlah fī ʿarājīninā* (Dates in the palm trees). Tunis: Al-Dār al-Tūnisī li-al-nashr, 1969.

Khūrī, Colette. [Syr.] *Ayyām maʿahu* (Days with him). Beirut: Al-Maktab al-tijārī, 1959.

———. *Laylah wāḥidah* (A single night). Beirut: Manshūrāt Ẓuhayr Baʿalbakkī, 1961.

Khūrī, Ilyās. [Leb.] *Abwāb al-madīnah* (City gates). Beirut: Dār Ibn Rushd, 1981. English translation: *Gates of the City.* Translated by Paula Haydar. Minneapolis: Univ. of Minnesota Press, 1992.

———. *Al-Jabal al-ṣaghīr.* Beirut: Dār al-Ādāb, 1977; English translation: *Little Mountain.* Translated by Maia Tabet. Minneapolis: Univ. of Minnesota Press, 1989.

———. *Riḥlat Ghāndī al-ṣaghīr* (Little Ghandi's journey). Beirut: Dār al-Ādāb, 1989. English translation: *The Journey of Little Ghandi.* Translated by Paula Haydar. Minneapolis: Univ. of Minnesota Press, 1994.

al-Kūnī [Kawnī], Ibrāhīm. [Lib.] *Al-Majūs* (The magi). Benghazi: Dār al-kutub al-waṭaniyyah, 1991.

———. *Nazīf al-ḥajar* (When the stone bleeds). London: Riad El-Rayyes, 1990.

———. *Al-Tibr* (The ore). London: Riad El-Rayyes, 1990.

Lāshīn, Maḥmūd Ṭāhir. [Eg.] *Ḥawwā' bi-lā Ādam.* Cairo, 1934; English translation: *Eve Without Adam.* Translated by Saad el-Gabalawy. In *Three Pioneering Egyptian Novels,* 49–94. Fredericton, N.B.: York, 1986.

al-Madanī, ʿIzz al-dīn. [Tun.] *Al-ʿUdwān* (The assault). Tunis: Al-Dār al-Tūnisī, 1969.

al-Madīnī, Aḥmad. [Mor.] *Zaman bayna al-wilādah wa-al-ḥulm* (Time between birth and dream). Rabat: Dār al-nashr al-Maghribiyyah, 1976.

Maḥfūẓ, Najīb. [Eg.] *ʿAbath al-aqdār* (Fates' mockery). Cairo: Al-Majallah al-jadīdah, 1939.

———. *Awlād ḥāratinā* [1959]. Beirut: Dār al-Ādāb, 1967; English translation: *Children of Gebelawi.* Translated by Philip Stewart. London: Heinemann, and Washington, D.C.: Three Continents, 1981.

———. *Bayn al-qaṣrayn.* Cairo: Maktabat Miṣr, 1956; English translation: *Palace Walk.* Translated by William M. Hutchins and Olive Kenny. New York: Doubleday, 1990.

———. *Bidāyah wa-nihāyah.* Cairo: Maktabat Miṣr, 1951; English translation: *The Beginning and the End.* Translated by Ramses Awad. Cairo: American Univ. in Cairo Press, 1985.

———. *Hams al-junūn.* Cairo: Maktabat Miṣr, 1938 [?].

———. *Al-Ḥubb taḥta al-maṭar* (Love in the rain). Cairo: Maktabat Miṣr, 1973.

———. *Al-Ḥubb fawq haḍbat al-haram* (Love on the pyramid plateau). Cairo: Maktabat Miṣr, 1979.

———. *Al-Karnak* (Al-Karnak café). Cairo: Maktabat Miṣr, 1974; English translation: *Al-Karnak.* Translated by Saad el-Gabalawi. In *Three Egyptian Novels.* Fredericton, N.B.: York, 1988.

———. *Khān al-Khalīlī.* Cairo: Maktabat Miṣr, 1945 [?].

———. *Layālī alf laylah* (Nights at a thousand nights). Cairo: Maktabat Miṣr, 1982.

———. *Al-Liṣṣ wa-al-kilāb.* Cairo: Maktabat Miṣr, 1962; English translation: *The Thief and the Dogs.* Translated by M. M. Badawi and Trevor Le Gassick. Cairo: American Univ. in Cairo Press, 1984.

———. *Al-Marāyā.* Cairo: Maktabat Miṣr, 1972; English translation: *Mirrors.* Translated by Roger Allen. Chicago: Bibliotheca Islamica, 1977.

———. *Mīrāmār.* Cairo: Maktabat Miṣr, 1967; English translation: *Miramar.* Translated by Fatma Moussa-Mahmoud. Cairo: American Univ. in Cairo Press, 1978.

———. *Al-Qāhirah al-jadīdah* (Modern Cairo). Cairo: Maktabat Miṣr, 1946.

———. *Qaṣr al-shawq.* Cairo: Maktabat Miṣr, 1957; English translation: *Palace of Desire.* Translated by William M. Hutchins, Lorne Kenny, and Olive Kenny. New York: Doubleday, 1991.

———. *Qushtumur.* Cairo: Maktabat Miṣr, 1989.

———. *Riḥlat ibn Faṭṭūmah.* Cairo: Maktabat Miṣr, 1983; English translation: *The Journey of Ibn Fattouma.* Translated by Denys Johnson-Davies. New York: Doubleday, 1992.

———. *Al-Shaḥḥādh.* Cairo: Maktabat Miṣr, 1965; English translation: *The Beggar.* Translated by Kristin Walker Henry and Narriman Warraki. Cairo: American Univ. in Cairo Press, 1986.

———. *Al-Sukkariyyah.* Cairo: Maktabat Miṣr, 1957; English translation: *Sugar Street.* Translated by William M. Hutchins and Angele Botros Samaan. New York: Doubleday, 1992.

———. *Al-Summān wa-al-kharīf.* Cairo: Maktabat Miṣr, 1962; English translation: *Autumn Quail.* Translated by Roger Allen. Cairo: American Univ. in Cairo Press, 1985.

———. *Thartharah fawq al-Nīl.* Cairo: Maktabat Miṣr, 1966; English translation: *Adrift on the Nile.* Translated by Frances Liardet. New York: Doubleday, 1993.

———. *Yawm qutila al-zaʿīm.* Cairo: Maktabat Miṣr, 1985; English translation: *The Day the Leader Was Killed.* Translated by Malak Hasem. Cairo: General Egyptian Book Organization, 1989.

———. *Zuqāq al-midaqq.* Cairo: Maktabat Miṣr, 1947; English translation: *Midaq Alley.* Translated by Trevor Le Gassick. London: Heinemann, and Washington, D.C.: Three Continents, 1974.

Marrāsh, Faransīs. [Leb.] *Ghābat al-ḥaqq* (The forest of truth). Aleppo: Al-Maṭbaʿah al-Mārūniyyah, 1865.

———. *Durr al-ṣadaf fī gharāʾib al-ṣudaf* (Quirks of fate). Beirut, 1872.

al-Masʿadī, Maḥmūd. [Tun.] *Al-Sudd* (The dam). Tunis: Sharikat al-nashr li-shamāl Ifrīqiyyah, 1955.

al-Māzinī, Ibrāhīm. [Eg.] *Ibrāhīm al-Kātib.* Cairo: Maṭbaʿat Dār al-Taraqqī, 1931; English translation: *Ibrahim the Writer.* Translated by Magdi Wahba. Cairo: General Egyptian Book Organization, 1976.

Midfaʿī, Walīd. [Syr.] *Ghurabāʾ fī awṭāninā* (Strangers in our own domains). Beirut: Dār al-Nahār, 1974.

Mīnah, Ḥannā. [Syr.] *Baqāyā ṣuwar* (Picture fragments). Damascus: Manshūrāt wizārat al-thaqāfah, 1974.

———. *Al-Maṣābīḥ al-zurq* (Blue lamps). Beirut: Dār al-fikr al-jadīd, 1954.

———. *Al-Shams fī yawm ghāʾim* (Sun on a cloudy day). Damascus: Manshūrāt wizārat al-thaqāfah, 1973.

———. *Al-Shirā' wa-al-'āṣifah* (The sail and the storm). Beirut: Maktabat Raymond al-jadīdah, 1966.

———. *Al-Thalj ya'tī min al-nāfidhah* (Snow comes in through the window). Damascus: Manshūrāt wizārat al-thaqāfah, 1969.

Munīf, 'Abd al-raḥmān. [Sau.] *Al-Ashjār wa-ghtiyāl Marzūq* (The trees and Marzuq's assassination). Beirut: Dār al-'Awdah, 1973.

———. *Mudun al-milḥ* (*Cities of salt*). Beirut: Al-Mu'assassah al-'Arabiyyah li-al-dirāsāt wa-al-nashr. (1) *Al-Tīh,* 1984; English translation: *Cities of Salt,* 1987; (2) *Al-Ukhdūd,* 1985; English translation: *The Trench,* 1991; (3) *Taqāsīm al-layl wa-al-nahār,* 1988; English translation: *Variations on Night and Day,* 1993; (4) *Al-Munbatt* (Stranded), 1988; and (5) *Bādiyat al-ẓulumāt* (Desert of darkness), 1988.

———. *Al-Nihāyāt.* Beirut: Dār al-Ādāb, 1978; English translation: *Endings.* Translated by Roger Allen. London: Quartet, 1988.

———. *Sharq al-Mutawassiṭ* (East of the Mediterranean). Beirut: Dār al-Ṭalī'ah, 1975; French translation: *A l'est de la Méditerranée.* Translated by Kadhem Jihad and Marie-Ange Bertapelle. Paris: Sindbad, 1985.

———. *Sibāq al-masāfāt al-ṭawīlah* (Long-distance race). Beirut: Al-Mu'assasah al-'Arabiyyah li-al-dirāsāt wa-al-nashr, 1979.

Muṣṭafā,Shākir. [Sud.] *Ḥattā ta'ūd* (Till she returns). N.p., 1959.

Naṣrallah, Emily. [Leb.] *Iqlā' 'aks al-zaman.* Beirut: Mu'assasat Nawfal, 1981; English translation: *Flight Against Time.* Translated by Issa J. Boullata. Charlottetown, N.B.: Ragweed, 1987.

———. *Al-Rahīnah* (The pawn). Beirut: Mu'assasat Nawfal, 1973.

———. *Shajarat al-diflah* (The oleander tree). Beirut: Mu'assasat Nawfal, 1968.

———. *Tilka al-dhikrayāt* (Those memories). Beirut: Mu'assasat Nawfal, 1980.

———. Ṭuyūr Aylūl (September birds). Beirut: Al-Mu'assasah al-ahliyyah li-al-ṭibā'ah wa-al-nashr, 1962; German translation: *Septembervogel.* Translated by Veronika Theis. Basel: Lenos Verlag, 1988.

Naṣrallāh, Ibrāhīm, [Pal.] *Barārī al-ḥummā.* Beirut: Mu'assasat al-abḥāth al-'Arabiyyah, 1985; English translation: *Prairies of Fever,* 1993.

Nu'aymah, Mīkhā'il. [Leb.] *Mudhakkirāt al-arqash.* Beirut: Maktabat Ṣādir, 1949; English translation: *Memoirs of a Vagrant Soul, or the Pitted Face.* New York: Philosophical Library, 1952.

al-Qa'īd [also al-Qu'ayyid], Yūsuf. [Eg.] *Akhbār 'izbat al-Minaysī.* Cairo: n.p., 1971; English translation: *News from the Meneisi Farm.* Translated by Marie-Therese F. Abdel-Messih. Cairo: General Egyptian Book Organization, 1987.

———. *Al-Ḥarb fī barr Miṣr.* Beirut: Dār Ibn Rushd, 1978; English translation: *War in the Land of Egypt.* Translated by Olive and Lorne Kenny and Christopher Tingley. London: Saqi, 1986.

———. *Shakāwā al-Miṣrī al-faṣīḥ* (Gripes of the eloquent Egyptian). Cairo: Dār al-maṣīrah, 1981–85.

———. *Yaḥduth fī Miṣr al-ān* (It's happening in Egypt now). Cairo: Maṭbaʿat Dār Usāmah li-al-ṭabʿ wa-al-nashr, 1977.

Qāsim, ʿAbd al-ḥakīm. [Eg.] *Ayyām al-insān al-sabʿah.* Cairo: Dār al-Kātib al-ʿArabī li-al-ṭibāʿah wa-al-nashr, n.d. [1969?]; English translation: *The Seven Days of Man.* Translated by Joseph N. Bell. Cairo: General Egyptian Book Organization, 1989.

———. *Qadar al-ghuraf al-muqbiḍah* (Fate of the oppressive rooms). Cairo: Matbūʿāt al-Qāhirah, 1982.

al-Rubayʿī, ʿAbd al-raḥmān Majīd. [Irq.] *Al-Washm* (The tattoo). Beirut: Dār al-ʿAwdah, 1972.

al-Saʿdāwī, Nawāl. [Eg.] *Imraʾah ʿinda nuqṭat ṣifr.* [1975] Beirut: Dār al-Ādāb, 1979; English translation: *Woman at Point Zero.* Translated by Sherif Hetata. London: Zed, 1983.

———. *Suqūṭ al-Imām.* Cairo: Dār al-Mustaqbal al-ʿArabī, 1987; English translation: *Fall of the Imam.* Translated by Sherif Hetata. London: Methuen, 1988.

Ṣāliḥ, al-Ṭayyib. [Sud.] *Mawsim al-hijrah ilā al-shamāl.* Beirut: Dār al-ʿAwdah, 1967; English translation: *Season of Migration to the North.* Translated by Denys Johnson-Davies. London: Heinemann, 1969.

Sālim, Jūrj. [Leb.] *Fī al-manfā* (In exile). Beirut: Manshūrāt ʿUwaydāt, 1962.

al-Sammān, Ghādah. [Syr.] *Kawābīs Bayrūt* (Beirut nightmares). Beirut: Dār al-Ādāb, 1976.

Ṣarrūf, Yaʿqūb. [Leb.] *Amīr Lubnān* (Prince of Lebanon). Cairo: Maṭbaʿat al-Muqtaṭaf, 1907.

———. *Fatāt al-Fayyūm* (Girl of Fayyum). Cairo: Maṭbaʿat al-Muqtaṭaf, 1908.

———. *Fatāt Miṣr* (Girl of Egypt). Cairo: Mulḥaq al-Muqtaṭaf, 1905.

al-Sayyid, Maḥmūd Aḥmad. [Irq.] *Fī sabīl al-zawāj* (On the marriage path). In *Āʿmāl kāmilah li-Aḥmad Maḥmūd al-Sayyid.* Baghdad: Dār al-ḥurriyyah, 1978.

———. *Jalāl Khālid.* In *Āʿmāl kāmilah li-Aḥmad Maḥmūd al-Sayyid.* Baghdad: Dār al-ḥurriyyah, 1978.

al-Sharqāwī, ʿAbd al-rahmān. [Eg.] *Al-Arḍ.* Cairo, 1954; English translation: *Egyptian Earth.* Translated by Desmond Stewart. London: Heinemann, 1962; Austin: Univ. of Texas Press, 1990.

al-Shaykh, Ḥanān. [Leb.] *Ḥikāyat Zahrah.* Beirut: Dār al-Nahār, 1980; English translation: *The Story of Zahra.* Translated by Peter Ford. London: Quartet, 1986.

al-Sibāʿī, Fāḍil. [Syr.] *Thumma azhara al-ḥuzn* (Then sadness bloomed). Beirut: Maktabat al-Ḥayāh, 1963.

Sulaymān, Nabīl. [Syr.] *Al-Sijn* (Prison). N.p., 1972.

al-Tābiʿī, ʿAlyāʾ. [Tun.] *Zahrat al-ṣubbar.* Tunis: Dār al-janūb li-al-nashr, 1991.

Ṭāhir, Bahāʾ. [Eg.]. *Qālat Ḍuḥā* (Duhā said). Cairo: Dār al-Hilāl, 1985.

———. *Sharq al-nakhīl* (East of the palm trees). Cairo: Dār al-mustaqbal al-ʿArabī, 1985.

Taymūr, Maḥmūd. [Eg.] *Salwā fī mahabb al-rīḥ* (Salwā blowing in the wind). Cairo: Maktabat al-Ādāb, 1947.

al-Tikirlī, Fu'ād. [Irq.] *Al-Raj' al-ba'īd* (Distant return). Beirut: Dār Ibn Rushd, 1980.

'Ubayd, 'Īsā. [Leb.] *Thurayyā*. Cairo, 1922.

'Usayrān, Laylā. [Leb.] *'Asāfīr al-fajr* (Dawn birds). Beirut: Dār al-'Awdah, 1968.

Waṭṭār, al-Ṭāhir. [Alg.] *Al-Lāz*. Algiers: Al-Sharikah al-waṭaniyyah, 1974; French translation: *L'as*. Paris: Temps actuelles, 1983[?].

———. *Al-Lāz, al-'ishq wa-al-mawt fī al-zaman al- ḥarāshī* (Al-Laz: Love and death in the Ḥarāshī times). Beirut: Dār Ibn Rushd, 1982.

———. *Al-Zilzāl* (The earthquake). Beirut: Dār al-'ilm li-al-malāyīn, 1974.

Zarzūr, Fāris. [Syr.] *Ḥasan Jabal*. Damascus: Wizārat al-Thaqāfah, 1969.

———. *Al-Ḥufāt* (Without shoes). Damascus, 1971.

———. *Lan tasquṭ al-madīnah* (The city will not fall). Damascus: Dār al-I'tidāl, 1969.

———. *Al-Mudhnibūn* (Sinners). Damascus, 1974.

Zaydān, Jūrjī. [Leb.] *Armānūsah al-Misriyyah,* Cairo: Manshūrāt Majallat al-Hilāl, 1896.

———. *Al-Ḥajjāj ibn Yūsuf*. Cairo: Manshūrāt Majallat al-Hilāl, 1902.

———. *Istibdād al-Mamālīk* (Mamlūk tyranny). Cairo: Manshūrāt Majallat al-Hilāl, 1893.

———. *Shajarat al-Durr*. Cairo: Manshūrāt Majallat al-Hilāl, 1914.

al-Zayyāt, Laṭīfah. [Eg.] *Al-Bāb al-maftūḥ* (The open door). Cairo: Al-Maktabah al-Anglo-Misriyyah, 1960.

Zifzāf, Muḥammad. [Mor.] *Al-Mar'ah wa-al-wardah* (The woman and the rose). Beirut: Manshūrāt Ghalūrī, 1972.

Secondary Sources

In Arabic

'Abdallāh, Muḥammad Ḥasan. *Al-Rīf fī al-riwāyah al-'Arabiyyah*. Kuwait: Al-Majlis al-waṭanī li-al-thaqāfah wa-al-funūn wa-al-adab, 1989.

———. *Al-Wāqi'iyyah fī al-riwāyah al-'Arabiyyah*. Cairo, 1971.

'Abd al-Qādir, Fārūq. *Izdihār wa-suqūṭ al-masraḥ al-Miṣrī*. Cairo: Dār al-fikr al-mu'āṣir, 1979.

Abū Iṣba', Ṣāliḥ. *Filasṭīn fī al-riwāyah al-'Arabiyyah*. Beirut: Markaz al-abḥāth al-Filasṭīniyyah, 1975.

Abū Maṭar, Aḥmad. *Al-Riwāyah fī al-ādab al-Filasṭīnī 1950–75*. Beirut: Al-Mu'assasah al-'Arabiyyah li-al-dirāsāt wa-al-nashr, 1980.

Abū Nāḍir, Maurice. *Al-Alsuniyyah wa-al-naqd al-adabī fī al-naẓariyyah wa-al-mumārasah*. Beirut: Dār al-Nahār, 1979.

Abū Niḍāl, Nazīh. *Adab al-sujūn*. Beirut: Dār al-Ḥadāthah, 1981.

Adūnīs [ʿAlī Aḥmad Saʿīd]. *Zaman al-shiʿr* (The time of poetry). Beirut: Dār al-ʿAwdah, 1972.

al-ʿAdwān, Amīnah. *Maqālāt fī al-riwāyah al-ʿArabiyyah al-muʿāṣirah.* Amman: al-Muʾassasah al-ṣuḥufiyyah al-Urdunniyyah, 1976.

ʿAfīfī, Muḥammad. *Al-Fann al-qaṣaṣī wa-al-masraḥī fī al-Maghrib al-ʿArabī 1900–1965.* N.p.: Dār al-Fikr, 1971.

———. *Al-Qiṣṣah al-Maghribiyyah al-ḥadīthah.* Casablanca: Maktabat al-Waḥdah al-ʿArabiyyah, 1961.

al-ʿAlī, Ṣāliḥ et al. *Al-Adab al-ʿArabi fī āthār al-dārisīn.* Beirut: Dār al-ʿIlm li-al-Malāyīn, 1971.

al-ʿĀlim, Maḥmūd Amīn. *Al-Riwāyah al-ʿArabiyyah bayna al-wāqiʿ wa-al-īdyūlūjiyyah.* Latikia: Dār al-Ḥiwār, 1986.

al-ʿĀnī, Shujāʿ Muslim. *Al-Riwāyah al-ʿArabiyyah wa-al-ḥaḍārah al-Ūrūbiyyah.* Baghdad: Manshūrāt Wizārat al-thaqāfah wa-al-funūn, 1979.

al-ʿAqqād, ʿAbbās Maḥmūd. *Ibn al-Rūmī: ḥayātuhu min shiʿrihi.* Cairo: Maṭbaʿat Ḥijāzī, 1938.

———, and Ibrāhīm al-Māzinī. *Al-Dīwān.* Cairo: N.p., 1921.

Aʿraj, Wāsinī. *Al-Nuzūʿ al-wāqiʿī al-iqtiṣādī fī al-riwāyah al-Jazāʾiriyyah.* Damascus: Ittiḥād Kuttāb al-ʿArab, 1985.

———. *Al-Uṣūl al-tārīkhiyyah li-al-wāqiʿiyyah al-ishtirākiyyah fī al-adab al-riwāʾī al-Jazāʾirī.* Beirut: Muʾassasat Dār al-kitāb al-ḥadīth, 1986.

Asʿad, Sāmiyah. "Yaktub al-riwāʾī al-tārīkh," *Fuṣūl* 2, no. 2 (Jan.–Feb. 1982): 67–73.

al-Ashtar, ʿAbd al-karīm. *Dirāsāt fī adab al-nakbah.* N.p.: Dār al-Fikr, 1975.

ʿAṭiyyah, Aḥmad Muḥammad. *Al-Baṭal al-thawrī fī al-riwāyah al-ʿArabiyyah.* Damascus: Wizārat al-thaqāfah, 1977.

ʿAṭwī, ʿAlī Najīb. *Taṭawwur fann al-qiṣṣah al-Lubnāniyyah al-ʿArabiyyah baʿd al-ḥarb al-ʿālamiyyah al-thāniyah.* Beirut: Dār al-āfāq al-jadīdah, 1982.

al-ʿAwf, Najīb. *Darajat al-waʿy fī al-kitābah.* Casablanca: Dār al-nashrah al-Maghribiyyah, 1980.

ʿAyyād, Shukrī. "Al-Riwāyah al-ʿArabiyyah al-muʿāṣirah wa-azmat al-ḍamīr al-ʿArabī." *ʿĀlam al-fikr* 3, no. 3 (Oct.–Dec. 1972): 619–48.

Badr, ʿAbd al-muḥsin Ṭāhā. *Najīb Maḥfūẓ: al-ruʾyā wa-al-adāt.* Cairo: Dār al-thaqāfah li-al-ṭibāʿah wa-al-nashr, 1978.

———. *Al-Riwāʾī wa-al-arḍ.* Cairo: Al-Hayʾah al-Miṣriyyah al-ʿāmmah li-al-kitāb, 1971.

———. *Taṭawwur al-riwāyah al-ʿArabiyyah al-ḥadīthah fī Miṣr.* Cairo: Dār al-Maʿārif, 1963.

Bahrāwī, Ḥasan. *Bunyat al-shakl al-riwāʾī.* Casablanca: Al-Markaz al-thaqāfī al-ʿArabī, 1990.

Barrādah, Muḥammad. *Al-Riwāyah al-ʿArabiyyah.* Beirut: Dār Ibn Rushd, 1981.

———. "Al-Taʿaddud al-lughawī fī al-riwāyah al-ʿArabiyyah," *Mawāqif* 69 (Autumn 1992): 162–78.

Darrāj, Fayṣal. "Dirāsah fī riwāyah Saḥar Khalīfah: Qawl al-riwāyah wa-aqwāl al-wāqiʿ." *Shuʾūn Filasṭīniyyah* 112 (1981): 108–29.

———. "Al-Intāj al-riwā'ī wa-al-ṭalī'ah al-adabiyyah." *Al-Karmal* 1 (Winter 1981): 118–43.

Darwīsh, Maḥmūd, and Ilyās Khūrī. "Emile Ḥabībī—anā huwa al-ṭifl al-qatīl." *Al-Karmal* 1 (Winter 1981): 190.

Duwārah, Fu'ād. *'Asharah udabā' yataḥaddathūna.* Cairo: Dār al-Hilāl, 1965.

———. *Fī al-riwāyah al-Miṣrīyyah.* Cairo: Dār al-Kātib al-'Arabī, 1968.

Faranjiyyah, Bassām. *Al-Ightirāb fī al-riwāyah al-Filasṭīniyyah.* Beirut: Mu'assasat al-abḥāth al-'Arabiyyah, n.d. [1990?].

al-Fayṣal, Samar Rūḥī. *Malāmiḥ fī al-riwāyah al-Sūriyyah.* Damascus: Manshūrāt ittiḥād al-kuttāb al-'Arab, 1979.

———. *Al-Sijn al-siyāsī fī al-riwāyah al-'Arabiyyah.* Damascus: Manshūrāt ittiḥād al-kuttab al-'Arab, 1983.

———. *Tajribat al-riwāyah al-Sūriyyah.* Damascus: Ittiḥad al-kuttāb al-'Arab, 1985.

al-Fayyūmī, Ibrāhīm Ḥusayn 'Abd al-hādī. *Al-Wāqi'iyyah fī al-riwāyah al-'Arabiyyah al-ḥadīthah fī bilād al-Shām.* 'Amman: Dār al-Fikr, 1983.

Ghanāyim, Maḥmūd. *Tayyār al-wa'y fī al-riwāyah al-'Arabiyyah al-ḥadīthah: Dirāsah uslūbiyyah.* Beirut: Dār al-Jīl, 1992.

al-Ghīṭānī, Jamāl. "Ba'ḍ mukawwināt 'ālamī al-riwā'ī." *Al-Ādāb* 2–3 (Feb.–Mar. 1980): 113.

Hādī, Fāḍil 'Abbās. "Qaḍiyyat Filasṭīn wa-al-riwāyah al-'Arabiyyah al-mu'āṣirah." *Shu'ūn Filasṭīniyyah* 11 (July 1972).

Ḥāfiẓ, Ṣabrī. "Azmat al-ḥurriyyah fī al-riwāyah al-mu'āṣirah." *Ḥiwār* 11, no. 4 (May–June, 1964): 52–62.

———. "Bibliogrāfīyā al-riwāyah al-Miṣriyyah 1876–1969." *Majallat al-Kitāb al-'Arabī* 1 (July 1970).

———. "Ittijāhāt al-riwāyah al-Miṣriyyah ba'd al-thawrah." *Al-Majallah* 9 (July 1965): 102–11.

———. "Maḥmūd Ṭāhir Lāshīn wa-mīlād al-uqṣūṣah al-Miṣriyyah." *Al-Majallah* (Feb.–Mar. 1968).

———. "Ma'sāt Filasṭīn fī al-riwāyah al-'Arabiyyah al-mu'āṣirah." *Al-Ādāb* 4 (1964).

———. "Al-Riwāyah wa-al-wāqi'." *Al-Nāqid,* 34, no. 26 (Aug. 1990): 34–39.

Ḥamīd, Laḥmadānī. *Al-Riwāyah al-Maghribiyyah wa-ru'yā al-wāqi' al-ijtimā'ī.* Casablanca: Dār al-Thaqāfah, 1985.

———. *Fī al-tanẓīr wa-al-mumārasah: Dirāsāt fī al-riwāyah al-Maghribiyyah.* Casablanca: Manshūrāt 'Uyūn, 1986.

Ḥaqqī, Yaḥyā. *Fajr al-qiṣṣah al-Miṣriyyah.* Cairo: Al-Hay'ah al-Miṣriyyah al-'āmmah li-al-kitāb, 1975.

Ḥarb, Ṭalāl. "Fusḥat al-ikhtiyār: Dirāsah bunyawiyyah." *Al-Ādāb* (July–Aug. 1980): 24–31.

Ḥasan, Muḥammad Rushdī. *Athar al-maqāmah fī nash'at al-qiṣṣah al-Miṣriyyah al-ḥadīthah.* Cairo: Al-Hay'ah al-Miṣriyyah al-'āmmah li-al-kitāb, 1974.

al-Hawārī, Ibrāhīm. *Naqd al-mujtama' fī Ḥadīth 'Īsā ibn Hishām.* Cairo: Dār al-Ma'ārif, 1981.

Haykal, Aḥmad. *Al-Adab al-qaṣaṣī wa-al-masraḥī: min aʿqāb thawrat 1919 ilā qiyām al-ḥarb al-kubrā al-thāniyah*. Cairo: Dār al-Maʿārif, 1971.

Hilāl, Muḥammad Ghunaymī. "Al-mu'aththirāt al-gharbiyyah fī al-riwāyah al-ʿArabiyyah." *Al-Ādāb* (Mar. 1963): 17–25.

Ḥusayn, Ṭāhā. *Min adabinā al-muʿāṣir*. Beirut: Dār al-Ādāb, 1958.

———. *Mustaqbal al-thaqāfah fī Miṣr*. Cairo: Maṭbaʿat al-Maʿārif, 1938.

Ibn Dhurayl, ʿAdnān. *Adab al-qiṣṣah fī Sūriyyā*. Damascus: Manshūrāt Dār al-Fann al-ḥadīth al-ʿalamī, n.d.

———. *Al-Riwāyah al-ʿArabiyyah al-Sūriyyah*. Damascus: N.p., 1973.

Ibrāhīm, Nabīlah. "Al-Mufāraqah," *Fuṣūl* 7, nos. 3–4 (Aug.–Sept. 1987): 131–41.

al-ʿĪd, Yumnā. *Al-Rāwī: al-mawqiʿ wa-al-shakl*. Beirut: Mu'assasat al-abḥāth al-ʿArabiyyah, 1986.

Idrīs, Yūsuf. *Al-Naddāhah*. Cairo: Dār al-Hilāl, 1969.

ʿIzz al-dīn, Yūsuf. *Al-Riwāyah fī al-ʿIrāq: Taṭawwuruhā wa-athar al-fikr fīhā*. Cairo: Maʿhad al-buḥūth wa-al-dirāsāt al-ʿArabiyyah, 1973.

Jābirī, Muḥammad al-Ṣāliḥ. *Al-Qiṣṣah al-Tūnisiyyah*. Tunis: Mu'assasat ʿAbd al-karīm ʿAbdallāh, 1975.

Jabrā, Jabrā Ibrāhīm. *Al-Ḥurriyyah wa-al-ṭūfān*. Beirut: Dār Majallat Shiʿr, 1960.

———. *Yanābīʿ al-ru'yā*. Beirut: al-Mu'assasah al-ʿArabiyyah li-al-dirāsāt wa-al-nashr, 1979.

———. *Al-Riḥlah al-thāminah*. Sidon: Al-Maktabah al-ʿaṣriyyah, 1967.

Kannūn, ʿAbdallāh. *Aḥādīth ʿan al-adab al-Maghribī al-ḥadīth*. Casablanca: Dār al-Thaqāfah, 1981.

Khashabah, Sāmī. "Al-Wāqiʿiyyah fī al-riwāyah al-ʿArabiyyah al-muʿāṣirah." *Al-Ādāb* (May 1970): 11–12.

Khaṭīb, ʿAbd al-karīm. *Al-Riwāyah al-Maghribiyyah*. Rabat: Al-Markaz al-jāmiʿī, 1971.

al-Khaṭīb, Ḥusām. *Al-Riwāyah al-Sūriyyah fī marḥalat al-nuhūḍ*. Cairo: Al-Munaẓẓamah al-'Arabiyyah li-al-tarbiyah wa-al-thaqāfah wa-al-ʿulum, 1975.

———. *Riwāyāt taḥta al-mijhar*. Damascus: Manshūrāt ittiḥād al-kuttāb al-ʿArab, 1983.

al-Khaṭīb, Muhammad Kāmil. *Al-Mughāmarah al-muʿaqqadah*. Damascus: Manshūrāt wizārat al-thaqāfah, 1976.

Khiḍr, ʿAbbās. "Al-Munūlūg al-dākhilī fī *Alf laylah wa-laylah*." *Al-ʿArabī* (Aug. 1980): 120–22.

———. *Al-qiṣṣah al-qaṣīrah fī Miṣr mundhu nash'atihā ḥattā sanat 1930*. Cairo: Al-Dār al-Qawmiyyah li-al-ṭibāʿah wa-al-nashr, 1966.

Khiḍr, Suʿād. *Al-Adab al-Jazā'irī al-muʿāṣir*. Beirut: Al-Maktabah al-ʿaṣriyyah, 1967.

Khūrī, Ilyās. *Tajribat al-baḥth ʿan ufq*. Beirut: P.L.O. Research Centre, 1974.

Kurd ʿAlī Muḥammad. *Mudhakkirāt*. Damascus, 1948–51; English translation: *The Memoirs of Muhammad Kurd Ali: A Selection*. Translated by

Khalil Totah. Washington: American Council of Learned Societies, 1954.

al-Maʿaddāwī, Anwar. *Kalimāt fī al-adab.* Sidon: Al-Maktabah al-ʿaṣriyyah, 1966.

Māḍī, Shukrī ʿAzīz. *Inʿikās hazīmat Ḥuzayran ʿalā al-riwāyah al-ʿArabiyyah.* Beirut: Al-Muʾassasah al-ʿArabiyyah li-al-dirāsāt wa-al-nashr, 1978.

Maḥfūz, ʿIṣām. *Al-Riwāyah al-ʿArabiyyah al-ṭalīʿiyyah.* Beirut: Dār Ibn Khaldūn, 1982.

al-Malāʾikah, Nāzik. *Qarārat al-mawj* (Bottom of the wave). Beirut, 1957.

Malti-Douglas, Fedwa. "Al-Waḥdah al-naṣṣiyyah fī ʿLayālī Saṭīḥʾ." *Fuṣūl* 3, no. 2 (Jan.–Mar. 1983): 109–17.

Maṣāyif, Muḥammad. *Al-Riwāyah al-ʿArabiyyah al-Jazāʾiriyyah al-ḥadīthah bayna al-wāqiʿiyyah wa-al-iltizām.* Algiers: Al-Dār al-ʿArabiyyah li-al-kitāb, 1983.

Mehrez, Samia. "Al-Mufāraqah ʿinda James Joyce wa-Emile Ḥabībī," *Alif* 4 (Spring 1984): 33–54.

Mīnah, Ḥannā. "Wajhan li-wajh." *Al-ʿArabī* (October 1987): 97–104.

Muḥammadiyyah, Aḥmad Saʿīd et al., eds., *Al-Ṭayyib Ṣāliḥ: ʿabqarī al-riwāyah al-ʿArabiyyah.* Beirut: Dār al-ʿAwdah, 1976.

Muraydan, ʿAzīzah. *Al-Qiṣṣah wa-al-riwāyah.* Damascus: Dār al-Fikr, 1980.

al-Mūsawī, Muḥsin Jāsim. "Ḥawla mafhūmay al-shakhṣiyyah wa-al-buṭūlah fī al-riwāyah al-ʿArabiyyah al-muʿāṣirah." *Al-Mawqif al-adabī* (Dec. 1979–Jan. 1980): 168–87.

———. *Al-Mawqif al-thawrī fī al-riwāyah al-ʿArabiyyah al-muʿāṣirah.* Baghdad: Manshūrāt Wizārat al-Iʿlām, 1975.

———. *Al-Riwāyah al-ʿArabiyyah: al-nashaʾah wa-al-taḥawwul.* Beirut: Dār al-Ādāb, 1988.

Muṣṭafa, Shākir. *Al-Qiṣṣah fī Sūriyā ḥattā al-ḥarb al-ʿālamiyyah al-thāniyah.* Cairo: Maʿhad al-buḥūth wa-al-dirāsat al-ʿArabiyyah, 1957.

al-Naḥḥās, Hāshim. *Najīb Maḥfūẓ ʿalā al-shāshah.* Cairo: Al-Hayʾah al-Miṣriyyah al-ʿāmmah li-al-kitāb, 1975.

Najm, Muḥammad Yūsuf. *Al-qiṣṣah fī al-adab al-ʿArabī al-ḥadīth fī Lubnān.* Beirut: Dār al-thaqāfah, 1966.

al-Nāqūrī, Idrīs. "Al-Shakl al-fannī fī al-riwāyah al-maghribiyyah." *Al-Mawqif al-adabī* (Dec. 1979–Jan. 1980): 40–63.

al-Nassāj, Sayyid Ḥāmid. *Panorāmā al-riwāyah al-ʿArabiyyah.* Beirut: Al-Markaz al-ʿArabī li-al-thaqāfah wa-al-ʿulūm, 1982.

Peled, Mattityahu. *Al-Uqṣuṣah al-Taymūriyyah fī marḥalatayn.* Tel Aviv: Tel Aviv Univ., 1977.

al-Qadrī, Īmān, "Al-Ishām al-niswī fī al-riwāyah al-ʿArabiyyah," *Al-Maʿrifah* (Sept.–Oct. 1990): 76–123.

al-Qalamāwī, Suhayr. *Alf Laylah wa-Laylah.* [Cairo, 1939] Cairo: Dār al-Maʿārif, 1966.

Qāsim, Qāsim ʿAbduh and Ḥāmid Ibrāhīm al-Hawārī. *Al-Riwayah al-tārīkhiyyah fī al-adab al-ʿArabī al-ḥadīth.* Cairo: Maṭbaʿat Dār al-taʾlīf, 1977.

Qāsim, Sīzā. *Bināʾ al-riwāyah.* Cairo: Al-Hayʾah al-Miṣriyyah al-ʿāmmah, 1984.

———. "Al-mufāraqah fī al-qaṣṣ al-ʿArabī al-muʿāṣir," *Fuṣūl* 2 no. 2 (Jan.–Mar. 1982): 143–51.

al-Qiṭṭ, ʿAbd al-ḥamīd ʿAbd al-ʿazīm. *Bināʾ al-riwāyah fī al-adab al-Miṣrī al-ḥadīth.* Cairo: Dār al-Maʿārif, 1982.

al-Rabīʿī, Maḥmūd. *Qirāʾat al-riwāyah.* Cairo; Dār al-Maʿārif, 1974.

Rāghib, Nabīl. *Qaḍiyyat al-shakl al-fannī ʿinda Najīb Maḥfūẓ.* Cairo: Al-Hayʾah al-Miṣriyyah al-ʿāmmah li-al-kitāb, 1975.

al-Rāʿī, ʿAlī. *Dirāsāt fī al-riwāyah al-Miṣriyyah.* Cairo: Al-Muʾassasah al-Miṣriyyah al-ʿāmmah li-al-taʾlīf wa-al-tarjamah wa-al-ṭibāʿah wa-al-nashr, n.d. [1964].

Ramitch, Aḥmad Yūsuf. *Usrat al-Muwayliḥī wa-atharuhā fī al-adab al-ʿArabī al-ḥadīth.* Cairo: Dār al-Maʿārif, 1980.

Razzāqī, ʿAbd al-ʿAlī. "Al-Taʿrīb fī al-Jazāʾir," *Al-Ādāb* (June 1980): 70–74.

Al-Riwāyah al-ʿArabiyyah: Wāqiʿ wa-āfāq. N.p.: Dār Ibn Rushd, 1981.

al-Rubayʿī. ʿAbd al-raḥmān Majīd, *Al-Shāṭiʾ al-jadīd: Qirāʾah fī kuttāb al-qiṣṣah al-ʿArabiyyah.* Tunis: Al-Dār al-ʿArabiyyah li-al-kitāb, 1983.

al-Saʿāfīn, Ibrāhīm. *Taṭawwur al-riwāyah al-ʿArabiyyah al-ḥadīthah fī bilād al-Shām 1870–1967.* Baghdad: Manshūrāt Wizārat al-thaqāfah wa-al-iʿlām, 1980.

al-Saʿdāwī, Nawāl. *Mudhakkirātī fi sijn al-nisāʾ.* Cairo: Dār al-Mustaqbal al-ʿArabi, 1984; English translation: *Memoirs from the Women's Prison.* Translated by Marilyn Booth. London: Women's, 1986.

Saʿīd, Jamīl. *Naẓarāt fī al-tayyārāt al-adabiyyah al-ḥadīthah fī al-ʿIrāq.* Cairo: Maʿhad al-dirāsāt al-ʿArabiyyah al-ʿāliyah, 1954.

Saʿīd, Khālidah. "Al-Riwāyah al-ʿArabiyyah bayna 1920–1972." *Mawāqif* 28 (Summer 1974): 82.

Ṣāliḥ, Fakhrī. *Fī al-riwāyah al-Filasṭīniyyah.* Beirut: Dār al-kitāb al-ḥadīth, 1985.

Sālim, Jūrj. *Al-Mughāmarah al-riwāʾiyyah.* Damascus: Manshūrāt ittiḥād al-kuttāb al-ʿArab, 1973.

Samʿān, Injīl Buṭrus. *Dirāsāt fī al-riwāyah al-ʿArabiyyah.* Cairo: al-Hayʾah al-Miṣriyyah al-ʿāmmah li-al-kitāb, 1987.

al-Sayyab. *Diwan.* Beirut: Dar al-ʿAwdah, 1971.

al-Sharqāwī, Ḍiyāʾ. "Al-Miʿmar al-fannī fī riwāyat *al-Safīnah.*" *Al-Maʿrifah* 193–94 (Mar.–Apr. 1978): 7–57.

al-Shārūnī, Yūsuf. *Dirāsāt fī al-riwāyah wa-al-qiṣṣah al-qaṣīrah.* Cairo: Al-Maktabah al-Anglo-Misriyyah, 1967.

———, ed. *Al-Laylah al-thāniyyah baʿd al-alf.* Cairo: Al-Hayʾah al-Miṣriyyah al-ʿāmmah li-al-kitāb, 1975.

Shawkat, Maḥmūd. *Al-Fann al-qaṣaṣī fī al-adab al-ʿArabī al-ḥadīth.* Cairo: Dār al-Fikr, 1963.

al-Shidyāq, Aḥmad Fāris. *Al-Sāq ʿalā al-sāq fīmā huwa al-Fāryāq.* Paris, 1855.

al-Shīṭī, Sulaymān. *Al-Ramz wa-al-ramziyyah fī adab Najīb Maḥfūẓ.* Kuwait: Al-Maṭbaʿah al-ʿaṣriyyah, 1976.

Shukrī, Ghālī. *Azmat al-jins fī al-qiṣṣah al-ʿArabiyyah.* Beirut: Dār al-Āfāq al-jadīdah, 1978.

———. *Al-Muntamī, dirāsah fī adab Najīb Mahfūẓ.* Cairo: Dār al-Maʿārif, 1969.

———. *Al-Riwāyah al-ʿArabiyyah fī riḥlat ʿadhāb.* Cairo: ʿĀlam al-Kutub, 1971.

Ṣubḥī, Muḥyī al-dīn. *Al-Baṭal fī maʾziq.* Damascus: Manshūrāt ittiḥād al-kuttab al-ʿArab, 1979.

Sulaymān, Nabīl. "Naḥwa adab al-sujūn." *Al-Mawqif al-adabī* 3, nos. 1 and 2 (May–June 1973): 137–41.

Suwaydan, Sāmī. *Abḥāth fī al-naṣṣ al-riwāʾī al-ʿArabī.* Beirut: Muʾassasat al-abḥāth al-ʿArabiyyah, 1986.

al-Ṭālib, ʿUmar. *Al-Fann al-qāṣaṣī fī al-adab al-Irāqī al-ḥadīth.* Najaf, Iraq: Matbaʿat Nuʿmān, 1971.

———. *Al-Ittijāh al-wāqiʿī fī al-riwāyah al-ʿIrāqiyyah.* Beirut: Dār al-ʿAwdah, 1971.

Tāmir, Zakariyyā. "Al-Aʿdāʾ." In *Numūr fī al-yawm al-ʿāshir,* 3ff. Beirut: Dār al-Ādāb, 1978. English translation: "The enemies." Translated by Roger Allen. *Nimrod* 24, no. 2 (Spring-Summer 1981): 61–70.

Ṭarābīshī, Jūrj. *Ramziyyat al-marʾah fī al-riwāyah al-ʿArabiyyah.* Beirut: Dār al-Ṭalīʿah, 1981.

———. *Al-Rujūlah wa-īdīyūlūjiyyat al-rujūlah fī al-riwāyah al-ʿArabiyyah.* Beirut: Dār al-Ṭalīʿah, 1981.

———. *Sharq wa-gharb: rujūlah wa-unūthah.* Beirut: Dār al-Ṭalīʿah, 1977.

———. *Unthā ḍidd al-unūthah.* Beirut: Dār al-Ṭalīʿah, 1984.

Tarāzī, Philip de. *Tārīkh al-ṣaḥāfah al-ʿArabiyyah.* Vols. 1–3. Beirut: Al-Maṭbaʿah al-adabiyyah, 1913; Vol. 4, Beirut: Al-Maṭbaʿah al-Amrīkiyyah, 1933

al-Thaʿālibī. *Laṭāʾif al-maʿārif.* Cairo: ʿĪsā al-Bābī al-Ḥalabī, 1960. English translation: *The Book of Curious and Entertaining Information.* Translated by C. Edmund Bosworth. Edinburgh: Edinburgh Univ. Press, 1968.

ʿUmar, Muṣṭafā ʿAlī. *Al-Qiṣṣah fī al-adab al-Miṣrī al-muʿāṣir.* Cairo: Dār al-Maʿārif, 1982.

Wādī, Fārūq. *Thalāth ʿallāmāt fī al-riwāyah al-Filasṭīniyyah: Ghassān Kanafānī, Emile Ḥabībī, Jabrā Ibrāhīm Jabrā.* Acre: Dār al-Aswār, 1981.

Wādī, Ṭāhā. *Dirāsạt fī naqd al-riwāyah.* Cairo: Al-Hayʾah al-Miṣriyyah al-ʿāmmah li-al-kitāb, 1989.

———. *Ṣūrat al-marʾah fī al-riwāyah al-muʿāṣirah.* Cairo: Markaz kutub al-Sharq al-Awsaṭ, 1973.

al-Yāghī, ʿAbd al-raḥmān. *Al-Juhūd al-riwāʾiyyah.* Beirut: Dār al-ʿAwdah, 1972.

Yaqṭīn, Saʿīd. *Infitāḥ al-naṣṣ al-riwāʾī.* Beirut: Al-Markaz al-thaqāfī al-ʿArabī, 1989.

———. *Taḥlīl al-khiṭāb al-riwāʾī.* Beirut: Al-Markaz al-thaqāfī al-ʿArabī, 1989.

Yāsīn, Bū ʿAlī, and Nabīl Sulaymān. *Al-Adab wa-al-īdīyūlūjiyyah fī Sūriyyā 1967–1973.* Beirut: Dār Ibn Khaldūn, 1974.

In Western Languages

Abrams, M.J. *A Glossary of Literary Terms,* New York: Holt, Rinehart and Winston, 1971.

Abu Deeb, Kamāl. "The Perplexity of the All-Knowing: A Study of Adonis." *Mundus Artium* 10, no. 1 (1977), 163–81.

Abū Haidar, Farida. "The Bipolarity of Rachid Boujedra," *JAL* 20, no. 1 (1989): 40–56.

Abu Lughod, Ibrahim. *Arab Rediscovery of Europe*. Princeton: Princeton University Press, 1963.

Abou-Saif, L. "Najīb al-Rīḥānī: From Buffoonery to Social Comedy." *JAL* 4 (1973): 1–17.

Accad, Evelyn. *Sexuality and War: Literary Masks of the Middle East*. New York: New York University Press, 1990.

Allen, Roger. "The Arabic Novel and the Quest for Freedom." JAL (forthcoming).

———. "The Beginnings of the Arabic Novel," and "The Mature Arabic Novel Outside Egypt," In *Modern Arabic Literature*. The Cambridge History of Arabic Literature Series, 180–92, 193–222. Cambridge: Cambridge Univ. Press, 1992.

———. "Egyptian Drama and Fiction in the 1970s." *Edebiyat* (1976): 219–33.

———. "Ḥadīth ʿĪsā ibn Hishām by Muḥammad al-Muwailiḥī: A Reconsideration." *JAL* (1970): 88–108.

———. "The Impact of the Translated Text: The Case of Najīb Maḥfūẓ's Novels." *Edebiyat* n.s. 4, no. 1: 87–117).

———. "Najīb Maḥfūẓ in World Literature." In *The Arabic Novel Since 1950* [*Mundus Arabicus* 5: 121–42]. Cambridge, Mass.: Dār Mahjar, 1992.

———. "Narrative Genres and Nomenclature: A Comparative Study." *JAL* 23, no. 3 (Nov. 1992): 208–14.

———. "The Novella in Arabic: A Study in Fictional Genres." *IJMES* 18, no. 4 (Nov.1986): 473–84.

———. *A Period of Time*. Reading, England: Garnet, 1993.

———. "Poetry and Poetic Criticism at the Turn of the Century." In *Studies in Modern Arabic Literature*, edited by R. C. Ostle, 1–17. Warminster, England: Aris and Phillips, 1975.

———. "Some New al-Muwailihi Materials." *Humaniora Islamica* 2 (1974): 139–80.

———. "Writings of Members of 'the Nāzlī Circle'." *JARCE* 8 (1969–70): 79–85.

———. "Some Recent Works of Najīb Maḥfūẓ." *JARCE* 14 (1977): 101–10.

———. ed. *Critical Perspectives on Yusuf Idris*. Colorado Springs: Three Continents, 1994.

———. ed. *Modern Arabic Literature*. Library of Literary Criticism Series. New York: Ungar, 1987.

Amin, Samir. *The Maghreb in the Modern World*. London: Penguin, 1970.

The Arabic Novel Since 1950: Critical Essays, Interviews, and Bibliography. [*Mundus Arabicus* 5] Cambridge, Mass.: Dār Mahjar, 1992.

Auerbach, Erich. *Mimesis: The Representation of Reality in Western Literature*. Princeton: Princeton University Press, 1971.

ʿAwwād, Ḥanān. *Arab Causes in the Fiction of Ghādah al-Sammān 1961–1975*. Sherbrooke, Canada: Editions Naaman, 1983.

Badawi, M. M. "Commitment in Contemporary Arabic Literature." *Journal of World History* 14, no. 4 (1972): 858–79.

———. *A Critical Introduction to Modern Arabic Poetry*. Cambridge: Cambridge Univ. Press, 1975.

———. "*The Lamp of Umm Hāshim*: The Egyptian Intellectual Between East and West." *JAL* 1 (1970): 145–161.

———. "Al-Māzinī: the novelist." *JAL* 4 (1973): 112–45.

———. *Modern Arabic Literature and the West*. London: Ithaca, 1985.

———. "Two Novelists from Iraq: Jabrā and Munīf." *JAL* 23, no. 2 (July 1992): 140–54.

Badran, Margot, and Miriam Cooke, eds. *Opening the Gates: A Century of Arab Feminist Writing*. Bloomington: Indiana Univ. Press, 1990.

Baker, Raymond William. *Egypt's Uncertain Revolution under Nasser and Sadat*. Cambridge, Mass.: Harvard Univ. Press, 1978.

Baldissera, Eros. "La narrativa feminile in Siria." *Quaderni di studi arabi* 2 (1984): 87–106.

———. "Shakīb al-Jābirī, pionere del romanzo siriano." *Quaderni di studi arabi*. Vol. 4 (1986): 117–128.

Bamia, Aida. "The North African Novel: Achievements and Prospects." In *The Arabic Novel Since 1950*. [*Mundus Arabicus* 5: 61–88.] Cambridge, Mass.: Dār Mahjar, 1992.

Barakat, Halim. "Arabic Novels and Social Transformation." In *Studies in Modern Arabic Literature*, edited by R. C. Ostle, 126–39. Warminster, England: Aris and Phillips, 1975.

———. *Visions of Social Reality in the Contemporary Arab Novel*. Washington, D.C: Center for Contempoary Arab Studies, Georgetown Univ., 1977.

Barthes, Roland. *Writing Degree Zero*. Boston: Beacon Press, 1967.

Bates, H. E. *The Modern Short Story 1809–1953*. London: Robert Hale, 1988.

Beard, Michael, and Adnan Haydar, eds. *Naguib Mahfouz: From Regional Fame to Global Recognition*. Syracuse: Syracuse Univ. Press, 1993.

Beaton, Roderick, ed. *The Greek Novel*. London: Croom Helm, 1988.

Berque, Jacques. *Cultural Expression in Arab Society Today*. Austin: Univ. of Texas Press, 1978.

Binder, Leonard, ed. *The Study of the Middle East: Research in the Humanities and Social Sciences*. New York: Wiley, 1976.

Booth, Wayne. *The Rhetoric of Fiction*. Chicago, Univ. of Chicago Press, 1961.

Boukous, Ahmed. "La situation linguistique au Maroc." *Europe* (June–July 1979): 18.

Boullata, Issa J. "Encounters Between East and West: A Theme in Contemporary Arabic Novels." *MEJ* 30, no. 1 (Winter 1976): 44–62.

———. *Trends and Issues in Contemporary Arab Thought*. Albany, New York: State Univ. of New York Press, 1990.

———. ed. *Critical Perspectives on Modern Arabic Literature*. Washington, D.C.: Three Continents, 1980.

———. ed. *Modern Arab Poets 1950–1975*. Washington, D.C.: Three Continents, 1976.

Boullata, Kamal, ed. *Women of the Fertile Crescent: Modern Poetry by Arab Women*. Washington, D.C.: Three Continents, 1978.

Brugman, J. *An Introduction to the History of Modern Arabic Literature in Egypt*. Leiden: E.J. Brill, 1984.

Cachia, Pierre. *An Overview of Modern Arabic Literature*. Edinburgh, Edinburgh Univ. Press, 1990.

———. *Ṭāhā Ḥusayn: His Place in the Egyptian Literary Renaissance*. London: Luzac, 1956.

Caton, Steven C. *Peaks of Yemen I Summon*. Berkeley: Univ. of California Press, 1990.

Connelly, Bridget. "The Structure of Four Bani Hilal Tales." *JAL* 4 (1973): 18–47.

Cooke, Miriam. *War's Other Voices*. Cambridge: Cambridge Univ. Press, 1988.

———. "Women Write War: The Feminization of Lebanese Society in the War Literature of Emily Naṣrallāh." *Bulletin of the British Society for Middle Eastern Studies* 14, no. 1 (1988): 52–67

Cox, R. G. *The Pelican Guide to English Literature*. Vol. 6, *From Dickens to Hardy*. London: Pelican, 1958, 1960, 1963.

Culler, Jonathan. *Structuralist Poetics*. Ithaca, N.Y.: Cornell Univ. Press, 1975.

D'Afflitto, Isabella Camera. "Sulla Narrativa dei territori occupati (*al-ḍiffah wa-al-qiṭaʿ*)." *Oriente Moderno* 5, nos. 7–9 (Luglio–Settembre 1986): 145–53.

Darwīsh, Maḥmūd. *Aḥmad al-Zaʿtar*. Translated by Rana Kabbani. Washington, D.C.: Free Palestine, 1976.

Draz, C. K. "In Quest of New narrative Forms: Irony in the Works of Four Egyptian Writers (1967–1979): Al-Ghīṭānī, Yaḥyā T. ʿAbdallah, Ṭūbyā, Sunʿallāh Ibrāhīm," *JAL* 12 (1981): 137–44.

Elkhadem, Saad. *History of the Egyptian Novel: Its Rise and Early Beginnings*. Fredericton, N.B.: York, 1985.

Ende, Werner. "Europabild und kulturelles Selbstbewusstsein . . . ." D. Phil. diss. Hamburg Universitat, 1965.

Europe: revue littéraire mensuelle. "Littérature marocaine." June–July 1979.

Evin, Ahmet. *Origins and Development of the Turkish Novel*. Minneapolis: Bibliotheca Islamica, 1983.

Ferguson, Suzanne. "The Rise of the Short Story as a Highbrow, or Prestige Genre." In *Short Story Theory at a Crossroads*, edited by Susan Lohafer and Jo Ellyn Clarey, 179. Baton Rouge: Louisiana State Univ. Press, 1989.

Fernea, Elizabeth Warnock, and Bassima Qattan Bezirgan. *Middle Eastern Muslim Women Speak*. Austin: Univ. of Texas Press, 1977.

Fernea, Robert. *Nubians in Egypt*. Austin: Univ. of Texas Press, 1973.

Fish, Stanley. *Is There a Text in This Class?* Cambridge, Mass. Harvard Univ. Press, 1980.

Fontaine, Jean. *Romans arabes modernes.* Tunis: Institut des belles lettres arabes, 1992.

———. *20 Ans de littérature tunisienne.* Tunis: Maison Tunisienne de l'édition, 1977.

Forster, E. M. *Aspects of the Novel.* London: Penguin, 1966.

Foucault, Michel. *Madness and Civilization.* New York: Pantheon, 1965.

Friedman, Thomas L. *From Beirut to Jerusalem.* New York: Anchor, 1989.

Genette, Gérard. *Narrative Discourse: An Essay in Method.* Translated by Jane E. Lewin. Ithaca, N.Y.: Cornell Univ. Press, 1980.

Ghazi, Ferid. *Le roman et la nouvelle en Tunisie.* Tunis: Maison Tunisienne de l'édition, 1970.

Ghazoul, Feryal. *The Arabian Nights: A Structural Analysis.* Cairo: Cairo Associated Institution for the Study and Presentation of Arab Cultural Values, 1980.

Gibb, H. A. R. *Studies on the Civilization of Islam.* Edited by Stanford J. Shaw and William Polk. London: Routledge, 1962. Originally in *Bulletin of the School of Oriental Studies* 4 (1926–28): 745–60; 5 (1928–30): 311–22, 445–66; 7 (1933–35): 1–22.

Gohlman Susan. "Women as Cultural Symbols in Yaḥyā Ḥaqqī's *The Saint's Lamp.*" *JAL* 10 (1979): 117–27.

Gouryh, Admer. "The Fictional World of Walīd Ikhlāṣī." *World Literature Today* (Winter 1984): 23–27.

Gran, Peter. *Islamic Roots of Capitalism.* Austin: Univ. of Texas Press, 1979.

Guth, Stephan. *Zeugen einer Endzeit.* Berlin: Klaus Schwarz Verlag, 1992.

Hafez, Sabri. "The Egyptian Novel in the Sixties." *JAL* 7 (1976): 68–84.

———. *The Genesis of Arabic Narrative Discourse: A Study in the Sociology of Modern Arabic Literature.* London: Saqi, 1993.

———. "The State of the Contemporary Arabic Novel: Some Reflections." *The Literary Review Supplement.* The Arab Cultural Scene. London: Namara, 1982.

Hagg, Tomas. *The Novel in Antiquity.* Berkeley: Univ. of California Press, 1983.

al-Ḥakīm, Tawfīq. *The Return of Consciousness.* Translated by R. Bayly Winder. New York: New York Univ. Press, 1985.

Hamarneh, Walid. "Some Narrators and Narrative Modes in the Contemporary Arabic Novel." In *The Arabic Novel Since 1950* [*Mundus Arabicus* 5:205–36]. Cambridge, Mass.: Dār Mahjar, 1992

Hamori, Andras. *On the Art of Medieval Arabic Literature.* Princeton: Princeton Univ. Press, 1974.

Harlow, Barbara. "Readings of National Identity in the Palestinian Novel." In *The Arabic Novel Since 1950* [*Mundus Arabicus* 5:89–108]. Cambridge, Mass.: Dār Mahjar, 1992

Hartmann, M. P. W. *The Arabic Press in Egypt.* London: Luzac, 1899.

Hawi, Khalil. *Kahlil Gibran: His Background, Character and Works.* Beirut: American Univ. of Beirut Oriental Series no. 41 (1963).

Haydar, Adnan. "The *mu'allaqa* of Imru' al-Qays: Its Structure and Meaning. Part 1. *Edebiyat* 2, no. 2 (1977): 227–78.

Heiserman, A. R. *The Novel Before the Novel: Essays and Discourses about the Beginnings of Prose Fiction in the West.* Chicago: Univ. of Chicago Press, 1977.

Hourani, Albert. *Arabic Thought in the Liberal Age.* London: Oxford Univ. Press, 1962.

Hunter, J. Paul. *Before Novels: The Cultural Context of 18th-Century English Fiction.* New York: Norton, 1990.

Husayn, Taha. *The Future of Culture in Egypt.* Translated by Sidney Glazer. Washington, D.C.: American Council of Learned Societies, 1954.

Idris, Yusuf. *In the Eye of the Beholder.* Edited by Roger Allen. Chicago: Bibliotheca Islamica, 1978.

Iser, Wolfgang. *The Implied Reader: Patterns of Communication in Prose Fiction from Bunyan to Beckett.* Baltimore: Johns Hopkins Univ. Press, 1974.

Jabra, Jabra Ibrahim. "Modern Arabic Literature and the West." *JAL* 2 (1971): 76–91.

Jad, 'Ali B. "'Abd al-raḥmān al-Sharqāwī's *Al-Arḍ*." *JAL* 7 (1976): 88–100.

———. *Form and Technique in the Egyptian Novel.* London: Ithaca, 1983.

Jakobson, Roman. "Problems in the Study of Language and Literature." In *Language in Literature,* edited by Krystyna Pomorska and Stephen Rudy, 47–49. Cambridge, Mass.: Belknap Press of Harvard Univ., 1987.

Jayyusi, Salma. *Trends and Movements in Modern Arabic Poetry.* Leiden: E. J. Brill, 1977.

———. "Two Types of Hero in Contemporary Arabic Literature." *Mundus Artium* 10, no. 1 (1977): 35–49.

———. ed. *An Anthology of Modern Palestinian Literature.* New York: Columbia Univ. Press, 1992.

———. ed. *Modern Arabic Poetry: An Anthology.* New York: Columbia Univ. Press, 1987.

Johnson-Davies, Denys, trans. *Modern Arabic Short Stories.* London: Heinmann, and Washington, D.C.: Three Continents, 1976.

Jomier, J. "La vie d'une famille au Caire d'après trois romans de M. Naguib Mahfuz." *Mélanges de l'institut dominicain des études orientales* 4 (1957).

Kermode, Frank. *The Art of Telling: Essays on Fiction.* Cambridge, Mass.: Harvard Univ. Press, 1983.

———. *The Sense of an Ending: Studies in the Theory of Fiction.* New York: Oxford Univ. Press, 1967.

Khater, Akram F. "Emile Habībī: The Mirror of Irony in Palestinian Literature." *JAL* 24, no. 1 (Mar. 1993): 75–94.

al-Khatībī, 'Abd al-kabīr. *Le roman maghrebin,* 2d ed. Rabat: Société Marocaine des Editeurs Reunies, 1979.

Khoury, Elias, "The Unfolding of Modern Fiction and Arab Memory." *Journal of the Midwest Modern Language Association* 23, no. 1 (Spring 1990): 1–8.

Khulusi, Safa'. "Modern Arabic Fiction with Special Reference to Iraq." *IC* 30 (1956): 199ff.

Kilpatrick, Hilary. "The Arabic Novel—a single tradition?" *JAL* 5 (1974): 93–107.

———. "The Egyptian Novel from *Zaynab* to 1980." In *Modern Arabic Literature.* The Cambridge History of Arabic Literature, 223–69 Cambridge: Cambridge Univ. Press, 1992.

———. "Ḥawwā' bilā Ādam: An Egyptian Novel of the 1930s," *JAL* 4 (1973): 48–56.

———. *The Modern Egyptian Novel.* London: Ithaca, 1974.

———. "Tradition and Innovation in the Fiction of Ghassān Kanafānī." *JAL* 7 (1976): 53–64.

Knipp, C. "The *Arabian Nights* in England: Galland's Translation and Its Successors." *JAL* 5 (1974): 44–54.

Kurd ʿAli, Muhammad. *Memoirs.* Translated by Khalil Totah. Washington, D.C: American Council of Learned Societies, 1954.

Lane, Edward. *An Account of the Manners and Customs of the Modern Egyptians.* London: Everyman, 1954.

Laroui, Abdallah. *The Crisis of the Arab Intellectual.* Berkeley: Univ. of California Press, 1976.

Leavis, Q. D. *Fiction and the Reading Public.* London: Chatto and Windus, 1932.

Le Gassick, Trevor. "The Arabic Novel in Translation." In *The Arabic Novel Since 1950* [*Mundus Arabicus* 5:47–60]. Cambridge, Mass.: Dār Mahjar, 1992.

———. "The Literature of Modern Egypt." *Books Abroad* 46, no. 2 (Spring 1972): 232 ff.

———. "The Luckless Palestinian." *MEJ* 34, no. 2 (Spring 1980): 215–23.

———. "A Malaise in Cairo: Three Contemporary Egyptian Authors." *MEJ* 21, no. 4 (Sept. 1967): 145–56.

———. "Some Recent War-related Fiction." *MEJ* 25, no. 4 (Sept. 1971): 491 ff.

———. ed. *Critical Perspectives on Naguib Mahfouz.* Washington, D.C.: Three Continents, 1991.

Levin, Harry. *Contexts of Criticism.* New York: Atheneum, 1963.

Lukacs, Georg. *The Theory of the Novel.* Translated by Anna Bostock. Cambridge, Mass.: MIT Press, 1971.

Maḥfūz, Najīb. *God's World.* Translated by Akef Abadir and Roger Allen. Minneapolis: Bibliotheca Islamica, 1973.

Makarious, Raoul, and Laura Makarious, eds. *Anthologie de la littérature arabe contemporaine: le roman et la nouvelle.* Paris: Editions du Seuil, 1964.

Malti-Douglas, Fedwa. *Blindness and Autobiography: Al-Ayyām of Ṭāhā Ḥusayn.* Princeton: Princeton Univ. Press, 1988.

———. *Structures of Avarice.* Leiden: E. J. Brill, 1985.

Medvedev, P. N. and Mikhail Bakhtin. *The Formal Method in Literary Scholarship: A Cultural Introduction to Sociological Poetics.* Baltimore: The Johns Hopkins Univ. Press, 1978.

Mehrez, Samia. "Al-Zaynī Barakāt: Narrative Strategy," *ASQ* 8, no. 2 (Spring 1986): 120–42.

———. "Re-writing the City: The Case of *Khiṭaṭ al-Ghīṭānī*." in *The Arabic Novel Since 1950* [*Mundus Arabicus* 5:143–68]. Cambridge, Mass.: Dār Mahjar, 1992.

Mikhail, Mona. "Man and the Sea: Intertextual Perspectives in Edwār al-Kharrāṭ's Turābhā zaʿfarān." In *The Arabic Novel Since 1950* [*Mundus Arabicus* 5:191–204]. Cambridge, Mass.: Dār Mahjar, 1992.

Milson, Menahim. "Najīb Maḥfūẓ and the Quest for Meaning." *Arabica* 17 (June 1970): 155–86.

———. "Some Aspects of the Modern Egyptian Novel." *Muslim World* 11, no. 2 (July 1970): 237–46.

Miquel, André. "La technique du roman chez Neguib Mahfouz." *Arabica* 10 (1963): 74–89.

Molan, Peter. "Sinbad the Sailor, a Commentary on the Ethics of Violence." *JAOS* 98, no. 3 (July–Sept. 1978): 237–47.

Monroe, James T. *The Art of Badīʿ az-zamān al-Hamadhānī as Picaresque Narrative.* Beirut: American Univ. of Beirut, 1983.

Moosa, Matti. "Naqqāsh and the Rise of the Native Arab Theatre in Syria." *JAL* 3 (1972): 105–17.

———. *The Origins of Modern Arabic Fiction.* Washington, D.C.: Three Continents, 1983.

Moosa-Mahmoud, Fatma. *The Arabic Novel in Egypt.* Cairo: General Egyptian Book Organization, 1973.

al-Mousa, Nedal M. "The Arabic *Bildungsroman:* A Generic Appraisal." *International Journal of Middle East Studies* 25, no. 2 (May 1993): 223–40.

al-Musawi, Muhsin Jāsim, "Metafiction as a Theoretic Discourse in Contemporary Arabic Writing." *Gilgamesh* 2 (1988): 51–59.

My Grandmother's Cactus. Selected and translated by Marilyn Booth. London: Quartet, 1991.

Naimy, Nadim. "The Mind and Thought of Khalīl Gibrān." *JAL* 5 (1974): 55–71.

Nasr, Ahmad A. "Popular Islam in al-Ṭayyib Ṣāliḥ." *JAL* 11 (1980): 88–104.

Nijland, C. *Mīkhā'īl Nu'aymah: Promotor of the Arabic Literary Revival.* Istanbul: Nederlands Historisch-Archaeologisch Instituut, 1975.

Ostle, Robin, ed. *Modern Literature in the Near and Middle East 1850–1970.* London: Routledge, 1991.

———. ed. *Studies in Modern Arabic Literature.* Warminster, England: Aris and Phillips, 1975.

Pantucek, Svetozar. *La littérature algérienne moderne.* Prague: Oriental Institute in Academia, 1969.

Peled, Mattityahu. *Religion My Own: The Literary Works of Najīb Maḥfūẓ.* New Brunswick, N.J.: Transaction, 1984.

Pérès, Henri. "Editions successives de Ḥadīth ʿĪsā ibn Hishām." *Mélanges Louis Massignon* 3 (1957): 233–58.

———. "Le roman, le conte et la nouvelle dans la littérature arabe moderne." *Annales de l'institut des études orientales* 3 (1937): 266 ff.; 5 (1939–41): 137 ff.

———. "Le roman historique dans la littérature arabe." *Annales de l'institut des études orientales* 15 (1957): 5 ff.

Philipp, Thomas. *Gurgi Zaidan, His Life and Thought.* Beirut: Orient-Institut der Deutschen Morgenlandishen Gesellschaft–Franz Steiner, 1979.

Pinault, David. *Story-Telling Techniques in the* Arabian Nights. Leiden: E. J. Brill, 1992.

Reid, Donald M. *The Odyssey of Farah Antun.* Minneapolis: Bibliotheca Islamica, 1975.

Rizzitano, Umberto. "Il 'racconto' *(qiṣṣah)* nella narrativa araba contemporanea del Marocco." In *Atti del terzo congresso di studi arabi e islamici.* Ravello: Istituto Universitario Orientale di Napoli, 1967.

Said, Edward. "On Repetition." In *The World, the Text, and the Critic.* Cambridge, Mass.: Harvard Univ. Press, 1983.

Sakkut, Hamdi. *The Egyptian Novel and Its Main Trends 1913–1952.* Cairo: American Univ. in Cairo Press, 1971.

Samoeil, Simon. "Arabic Novels Since 1950: A Selected Bibliography of Critical Studies." In *The Arabic Novel Since 1950* [*Mundus Arabicus* 5:237–54] Cambridge, Mass.: Dār Mahjar, 1992.

Scholes, Robert. *Structuralism in Literature.* New Haven: Yale Univ. Press, 1974.

———, and Robert Kellogg. *The Nature of Narrative.* London: Oxford Univ. Press, 1966.

Sells, Michael, trans. *Desert Tracings.* Middletown, Conn.: Wesleyan Univ. Press, 1989.

Semah, David. *Four Egyptian Literary Critics.* Leiden: E. J. Brill, 1974.

Sharabi, Hisham. *Nationalism and Revolution in the Arab World.* Princeton: Van Nostrand, 1966.

Ṣiddīq, Muḥammad. "The Contemporary Arabic Novel in Perspective." *World Literature Today* (Spring 1986): 206–11.

———. "The Fiction of Saḥar Khalīfah: Between Defiance and Deliverance." *ASQ* 8, no. 2 (1986): 143–60

———. "Jabrā Ibrāhīm Jabrā and the Novel of Subjective Aesthetics." In *The Arabic Novel Since 1950* [*Mundus Arabicus* 5:169–90]. Cambridge, Mass.: Dār Mahjar, 1992.

———. *Man Is a Cause: Political Consciousness and the Fiction of Ghassān Kanafānī.* Seattle: Univ. of Washington Press, 1984.

———. "Mikhail N'aimy as Novelist." *Al-ʿArabiyya* 15, nos. 1 and 2 (Spring and Autumn 1982): 27.

———. "The Process of Individuation in al-Tayyib Salih's novel *Season of Migration to the North.*" *JAL* 9 (1978): 67–104.

Smith, Charles. "Love, Passion and Class in the Fiction of Muḥammad Ḥusayn Haykal." *JAOS* 99, no. 2 (1979): 249–61.

Somekh, Sasson. *The Changing Rhythm.* Leiden: E. J. Brill, 1973.

Sowayan, Saad Abdullah. *Nabati Poetry.* Berkeley: Univ. of California Press, 1985.

Starkey, Paul. "From the City of the Dead to Liberation Square: The Novels of Yūsuf al-Qaʿīd," *JAL* 24, no. 1 (Mar. 1993): 62–74.

Ṭarābīshī, George. *Woman Against Her Sex: A Critique of Nawāl el-Saadawi.* Translated by Basil Hatim and Elisabeth Orsini. London: Saqi, 1988.

Tomiche, Nada. *Histoire de la littérature romanesque de l'Egypte moderne.* Paris: Maisonneuve et Larose, 1981.

———. "L'héritage culturel: source d'information dans la littérature romanesque de l'Egypte et du monde arabe." In *The Arabic Novel Since 1950* [*Mundus Arabicus* 5:109–20]. Cambridge, Mass.: Dār Mahjar, 1992.

Toorawa, Shawkat. "Movement in Maḥfūẓ's *Tharthara Fawq al-Nīl,*" *JAL* 22, pt. 1 (Mar. 1991): 53–65.

Trilling, Lionel. *The Liberal Imagination.* New York: Scribners, 1940 and 1950.

———. *Sincerity and Authenticity.* Cambridge, Mass.: Harvard Univ. Press, 1971.

Vial, Charles. "Ḳiṣṣa." In *EI*^{2}. Leiden: E. J. Brill, 1954– , in progress.

———. *Le personnage de la femme dans le roman et la nouvelle en Egypte de 1914 à 1960.* Damascus, 1979.

Walsh, P. G. *The Roman Novel.* Cambridge: Cambridge Univ. Press, 1970.

Watt, Ian. *The Rise of the Novel.* London: Penguin, 1963.

Waugh, Patricia. *Metafiction: The Theory and Practice of Self-conscious Fiction.* London: Methuen, 1984.

Wellek, René, and Austin Warren. *Theory of Literature.* New York: Harcourt, 1956.

Wieland, Rotraud. *Das Bild der Europaer in der modernen arabischen Erzähl- und Theaterliteratur.* Beiruter Texte und Studien 23, Beirut: Orient-Institut der Deutschen Morgenlandischen Gesellschaft, 1980.

———. *Das erzählerische Frühwerk Maḥmūd Taymūrs: Beitrag zu einem Archiv der modernen arabischen Literatur.* Beirut: Orient-Institut der DMG, 1983.

Index